Ann Rule is a former Seattle policewoman and the author of eight best-selling books, including two previous Crime Files volumes, *A Rose for Her Grave* and *You Belong to Me*. Her other books are *If You Really Loved Me*, a chilling chronicle of a millionaire's murderous secret life; *Everything She Ever Wanted*, the terrifying story of a sociopathic Georgia belle and her fatal allure; *Small Sacrifices*, the horrific account of a woman's homicidal assault on her three young children; *The Stranger Beside Me*, the fascinating tale of Rule's dawning horror as she realised her friend and co-worker, Ted Bundy, was a serial killer; *Possession*, a searing novel of mind control and sexual enslavement on a lonely mountain-top; and *Dead by Sunset*, the nightmare story of a charismatic man and the women who always gave him what he wanted – sex, money, even their very lives. Many of these are available in paperback from Warner Books.

When she is not attending trials and researching new books, Ann Rule lives near Seattle, Washington.

ANN RULE

A Fever in the Heart
and Other True Cases

Ann Rule's Crime Files: Vol. 3

WARNER BOOKS

A *Warner* Book

First published in the United States in 1996
by Pocket Books, a division of Simon & Schuster, Inc.
First published in Great Britain in 1996 by Warner Books
Reprinted 1997, 2001

Copyright © 1996 by Ann Rule

The moral right of the author has been asserted.

A CIP catalogue record for this book
is available from the British Library.

ISBN: 0 7515 1573 6

Printed and bound in Great Britain
by Clays Ltd, St Ives plc

Warner Books
A Division of
Little, Brown and Company (UK)
Brettenham House
Lancaster Place
London WC2E 7EN

www.littlebrown.co.uk

For my friend
Olive Morgan Blankenbaker, born 1910,
and
for my mother,
Sophie Hansen Stackhouse, 1906–1995,
two brave women who lost their only sons
much too soon.

They taught me how to survive tragedy and loss
and how to grow old with grace and dignity.

Acknowledgments

This book has been more than twenty years in the making. Down through those years, so many people have helped me research, understand, and find documentation for *A Fever in the Heart* and the other five cases included. No one ever forgets murder cases where tragedy and betrayal are linked so closely, and time does little to dull the pain. Because of that, I particularly appreciate the many people who talked to me during the trial, and later searched their memories to help me.

And so I thank: Olive Blankenbaker, Vernon Henderson, Yakima County Prosecuting Attorney Jeff Sullivan and his staff, Mike McGuigan, the Yakima Police Department, Robert Brimmer, Mike Meyers, Marion Baugher, the late Mike Brown, Lonna K. Vachon, "Pleas" Green, the *Yakima Herald-Republic* (especially Librarian Donean Sinsel and Reporter James Wallace), the Yakima Valley Regional Library (especially Janna Davis and Jacob Warren), Mike Blankenbaker, and John Sandifer.

Chuck Wright, Joyce Johnson, the Seattle Police Department's Homicide Unit, Bernie Miller, Roy Moran, Benny DePalmo, the late Dick Reed and George Cuthill, the Pierce County, Washington, Sheriff's Office, Walt Stout, Mark French, the Oregon State Police, the Marion County, Oregon, Sheriff's office, Jim Byrnes, Dave Kominek, Mel Gibson, the King County Police Department, Ted Forrester, Roger Dunn, Columbia County, Oregon, District Attorney Marty Sells, Phil Jackson, Herb McDonnell, the Bellevue,

Acknowledgments

Washington, Police Department, Gary Trent, Mark Ericks, and scores more detectives, patrolmen, deputy prosecutors, and corrections officers whose dedication helped to apprehend, convict, and supervise the "antiheroes" in these cases from my crime files.

I would also like to commend the many winesses who had the courage to come forward and testify in court.

Although it often seems as though I never see *anyone* but my two dogs and two cats and my computer screen, I am always aware of my own private cheering section out there, and that helps! My gratitude goes to my editors: Bill Grose (who conceived the idea of Ann Rule's True Crime Files); my constant and caring editor, Julie Rubenstein; Molly Allen, my quick-thinking and sharp-eyed line editor; and Leslie Stern, who helps organize our creative chaos. Also, Paolo Pepe, who works with me so graciously to create our book covers, and Gina Centrello, our president and publisher.

Despite the fact that I seldom come up for air, I find I still have friends, and I appreciate them doubly because they *do* understand deadlines. To: Donna Anders, Gerry Brittingham, Tina Abeel, Lisa and Bryan Pearce—and Taryn and Ashlyn, Ruth and Greg Aeschliman—and Kirsten, Peter and Brad, Anne and Haleigh Jaeger, Sue and Joe Beckner, Maureen and Bill Woodcock, Martin and Lisa Woodcock, Lola Cunningham, Mary Lynn Lyke, Susan Paynter, Bill and Shirley Hickman, Ione and Jack Kniskern, Austin and Charlotte Seth, Clarene and Jan Shelley, Millie Yoacham and Eilene Schultz, Peter Modde, Bill Hoppe, Jennie and Harley Everson, Hank Gruber, Nils and Judy Seth, Erik Seth, Bill and Joyce Johnson, Verne and Ruth Cornelius, Barbara Easton, Jeanne Hermens and Jack Livengood, Mike Shinn and Kari Morando, Kalen Thomas and Amy Lowin, Dan "The-Sausage-Man" House, Verne Shangle, Betty May and Phil Settecase, Sue and Bob Morrison, Jennifer and Siebrand Heimstra, Bill and Ginger Clinton, Hope Yenko, Lois Duncan, Joe and Jeannie Okimoto, Carol and Don McQuinn, John Saul, Edna Buchanan, Anne Combs, Michael Sack, Judine and Terry Brooks, and Margaret Chittenden.

Acknowledgments

With the age of being "on-line," I have made a host of new friends whom I may never see in person. Still, they have been wonderful to "talk" to. So thank you to the Time-Warner True Crime Forum, the Author's Forum, and the CNN Forums. Thank you, Darlah and Nathan Potechin, Madeleine Kopp, Karen Ellis, Deanie Mills, Pat Moses-Caudel, Emily Johnston, Joseph Carey, William Diehl, Lowell Cauffiel, Joe Bob Briggs and Clark Howard.

To my family: Laura, Leslie, Andy, Mike, and Bruce. Rebecca and Matthew, Ugo, Nancy, and Lucas Saverio Fiorante. To all of Chris Hansen's descendants who have scattered to the four winds: Michigan, Wisconsin, Nevada, California, Florida, and the Northwest, and to the Stackhouse Clan that began in Nankin, Ohio. I love you all.

If it had not been for Joan and Joe Foley, my literary agents, and Mary Alice Kier and Anna Cottle, I would still be writing in my flooded basement in Washington State. Thanks for the dry feet and the roof over my head!

And now I thank all of you who read my books. You cannot know how much it means to hear, "I stayed up all night reading." That is music to an author's ears. If you are not already on the mailing list for my quarterly newsletter, and you would like to be, please write to me at: P.O. Box 98846, Seattle, Washington 98198.

In tragic life, God wot
No villain need be! Passions win the plot;
We are betrayed by what is false within.

—George Meredith, *Modern Love*

Contents

Author's Note

It has been said that there are no new stories under the sun. Even those dramas and tragedies that are true are only a reprise of something that has happened before. I suspect that is an accurate analysis.

In this third volume of my true crime files, I note that I have either subconsciously or inadvertently chosen four cases that share a common theme: personal betrayal. Since I am a great believer in the premise that we do nothing *accidentally,* it must be the right time to contemplate homicides that occur because the victim or victims have been betrayed by someone they have come to trust. In most of the following cases, the victims have believed in their killers over a long time; in one case, the victims have put their faith too quickly in the wrong men. There is something especially heartbreaking about love and friendships betrayed. The thought that some of the victims in this book must have recognized that betrayal at the very last moments of their lives may be difficult to cope with.

In the final two cases, the system trusted a criminal's rehabilitation—and innocent people paid for this mistake.

All serve to remind us that things are seldom what they seem. And to be wary.

The title case in *A Fever in the Heart* occurred very early in my career as a true crime writer, so early, in fact, that I felt I had neither the courage nor the technical skill to undertake a book. To be truthful, I admit that I was afraid to attempt a book; I could not even imagine myself turning out three or four hundred pages.

Even so, I attended the entire trial that resulted from an intensive police investigation in Yakima, Washington. Because of a change in venue, the trial took place during one uncharacteristically hot summer in Seattle. I was there in the courtroom every day, utterly fascinated by the havoc wrought by one man's "love" for a beautiful woman. But this was not the kind of tender, romantic love we usually think of. This was obsessive love, a consuming passion that ate at a theretofore well-adjusted man as surely as acid eats into metal, until all the values he had believed in eroded.

I saw all the "characters" in this modern-day classic tragedy in person, and became friends with some of them. This was not simply a case of multiple murder; it involved the bonding and later disintegration of many families. Anyone who wrote about it would have to go back decades to even begin to explain the extent of the loss. I knew that the story needed to be told, and close family members asked me to delve deeper, but after some agonizing debates with myself, I let it pass. I didn't think I could do it justice.

I would be years before I undertook my first book, *The Stranger Beside Me*. After my view of the Ted Bundy story was published, I wrote a dozen more books but I kept coming back to "A Fever in the Heart." During all that time, I kept my notes, the pictures my daughter took in the courtroom, and those given to me by relatives of the victims. I think I knew that someday I *would* write the whole story, because I moved all the paraphernalia of "A Fever in the Heart" with me every time I changed residences.

Two decades later, I still find this chillingly ironic story of murder in Yakima, Washington, full of the most compelling series of circumstances I have ever encountered. Everyone involved was a winner—intelligent, physically attractive, charismatic, athletically gifted, and surrounded by love.

What on earth went wrong? It will take a whole book to try to sort it out, and I am finally ready to do that.

* * *

Author's Note

In addition to "A Fever in the Heart," you will find five other cases that I have never forgotten: "Mirror Image," "Black Leather," "I'll Love You Forever," "Murder Without a Body," and "The Highway Accident."

I hope you enjoy them all!

Ann Rule
Seattle, 1996

A Fever in the Heart

The day after a holiday is always something of a letdown—even if the celebrations were successful and families and friends have managed to get together without allowing half-forgotten slights and old wounds to bubble to the surface. In New York City and in Yakima, Washington, and in every city and hamlet in between, families who coexist all year tend to become dysfunctional with the pressure of holiday emotions. Perhaps humans expect more out of life during the festive season. Those over the age of ten are usually disappointed.

1

In 1975 the Friday after Thanksgiving in Yakima was icy and bleak. In the spring, Yakima, and all of Yakima County, is scented by what seems like a continuous froth of apple and peach blossoms from a thousand orchards; in the summer, it is rich with growing things, and in the autumn, the tree branches are pregnant with fruit. However, in the last dark week of November 1975, Yakima was bitterly cold with lowering clouds that promised snow all day but never quite delivered by the time night fell.

Saturday would mark the twelfth anniversary of one of America's most stunning catastrophes. November 22, 1963. The day President John F. Kennedy was assassinated in Dallas while he was at the peak of his powers, dead-shot to the brain before he had time to sense the presence of danger. The date was the first in a series of grim similarities, albeit on a smaller stage.

Even though newly hung Christmas decorations were up on the light poles, it was hard to feel festive in Yakima. On that night of November 21, 1975, the sun set far too soon. For those people whose memories made their hearts heavy with sorrow and loss, there was a sense of "One down, and one to go." Thanksgiving was gone, and Christmas would be there before anyone realized it.

It was so cold.

* * *

Gerda Lenberg lived in a duplex at 506 East Lincoln in Yakima. Many streets in town were named after numbers or letters or names of presidents, and most of them had alleys that ran behind backyards, slicing the blocks in two, and allowing residents to park off the main streets. Gerda always described where she lived precisely: "On the right-hand side on the corner of Sixth or Lincoln—or of Lincoln and the alley."

The latter was more accurate. Gerda lived in a semibasement level apartment; her bedroom window was set in a well, and located smack-dab on the alley.

Most evenings, Gerda sipped a bourbon and water, ate dinner, and then watched television until ten when she went to bed. She followed her pattern that dark Friday night of November 21, 1975. She turned out her lights, and then raised the bedroom window to get some fresh air. She wasn't afraid of burglars; it was a good neighborhood with lots of apartments, private homes, and churches nearby. In the daytime, there were dozens of older people who walked south down the alley to church activities.

Gerda could never be absolutely sure of the order of events that happened later that night. Either she woke up from a disturbing dream in the middle of the night or something she heard outside awakened her. She lay there trying to decide whether to get up. Later, she was fairly certain that she was already wide-awake when she heard footsteps running in the alley. "And I thought," she said, "well, that's kind of odd this time of night, because it was so quiet so I knew it was past midnight. And then it sounded like somebody bumped a garbage can or something . . . kind of a 'metal' sound."

Gerda Lenberg lay there, not disoriented but curious and a little apprehensive, as she heard "firecrackers" popping beyond her window. "It was three or four, like you light them right in succession."

It might have been a few minutes or a little longer before she heard running footsteps again, this time heading in the opposite direction—north—and coming from a short distance away, thudding directly above her window, and then fading. She was positive the person was running. She was

4

used to hearing the faltering steps of elderly people walking through the alley to church. This was nothing like that.

"It was kind of a hollow sound like they might have had heavy soles or clogs," she remembered.

That wouldn't mean much later in helping to identify the person running. In the midseventies, practically everyone under thirty wore shoes with improbably built-up soles and Cuban heels—just as they wore polyester leisure suits with stitching on the lapels, plaid sports coats, bell-bottom pants, and "poor boy" sweaters.

Gerda Lenberg didn't believe she had heard anything that unusual or frightening. Only firecrackers and someone running in the chilly night. She glanced instinctively at the clock on the wall next to her bed. It was a decorative clock with Roman numerals, fancy rather than functional. She was never really sure exactly what time it was, but she could see it was somewhere between five or ten minutes after two in the morning. She turned over and was asleep in a short time.

"The next morning," Gerda recalled, "I remarked they were sure starting the Fourth of July early because somebody was shooting off firecrackers."

Dale Soost lived several buildings down the alley from Gerda's duplex. They had never met; he didn't know many people in the neighborhood of his apartment house at 208 North Sixth. He was employed by the State of Washington as a systems analysis programmer and was working on a project to automate the Superior Courts in the state. This phase of his contract had brought him to Yakima County.

Soost retired about midnight that Friday after Thanksgiving. He knew he wasn't going to get much sleep because he had to be up at four to go deer hunting. As it was, he got even less sleep than he expected; he was awakened suddenly in the hours before dawn by the sound of shots. As a hunter he was familiar with both rifles and pistols and he knew a gunshot when he heard one. "It was one shot," he would say later. "One shot, followed by two in rapid succession . . . bang . . . bang-bang."

Soost looked out his window to see if he could see

anything. The shots sounded as if they had come from the other end of his apartment house. His unit was on the alley, and the noise seemed to have come more from the street side. He thought they had been fired closer to Sixth Street. It was long before the era of "drive-by shootings," and Soost wasn't particularly concerned. He put it down to somebody shooting in the air.

He crawled back into bed and caught another few hours of sleep. By five A.M., Soost was on the sidewalk in front of the brick-facaded apartment house where he lived, dressed in hunting gear, and waiting for his companions to pick him up. It was still that impenetrable black of a winter's pre-dawn and he jumped a little when a man walked toward him on the sidewalk. Then he saw it was another resident of his apartment complex, a man he often nodded to, but who he didn't really know. It turned out that the man, Rowland Seal, was going hunting too—duck hunting. He was also waiting for his ride.

Seal was a body and fender mechanic by trade, but his avocations kept him so busy he didn't normally have time to chat with his neighbors. He was filled up every hour of every day, and although he recognized people who lived in his apartment house and knew where most of them worked, Seal didn't socialize, considering idle conversation a waste of valuable time.

While they looked up Sixth Street for approaching head-lights and paced back and forth to keep warm, Rowland Seal and Dale Soost made small talk about the noises they'd both heard in the night. Seal said he too had been awakened by the sound of shots. He was a most precise man and he knew the exact time. His digital watch and the digital clock next to his bed had both read 2:05 A.M.

Eventually they agreed that while it was true they lived in town, Yakima wasn't that big and it *was* hunting season. Somebody must have gotten a little anxious to get started. There were a lot of would-be Nimrods out there.

Since it was so early and so cold, both men immediately noticed the woman who emerged from the big frame house next to the apartment house. At first, they figured she was coming out in her robe to get the morning *Yakima Herald-*

Republic. But she crossed the frosty porch and then walked slowly down the front steps and onto the lawn dusted half-white from a desultory snowfall. Almost as if she were walking in her sleep, she disappeared around the side yard toward the alley.

Suddenly, the silent icy air was shattered by screams. The woman was calling out the name of the man Rowland Seal knew she lived with. "Morris! Morris!" she cried over and over.

Soost and Seal were caught off-guard. For a long moment, they stared at each other. A few seconds later, the young woman ran back into view and disappeared into her house.

Seal murmured, "Morris's dog must have got shot last night."

Soost didn't know the neighbors, but he figured Morris was the woman's husband or maybe her boyfriend. If someone had shot his dog, he was going to be upset. The woman had certainly seemed shaken. While the two hunters stood awkwardly, hesitant about what they should do, the woman next door ran out of her house again. She was still screaming and she seemed on the verge of complete hysteria, "Oh, my God! He's *dead.* Oh, my God!"

Rowland Seal was the kind of man who stepped up when he saw an emergency, and he was sure he was seeing one now. While Dale Soost hung back, Seal hurried over to her and said, "We'll call an ambulance." It seemed the right thing to say, but he didn't even know if you *could* call an ambulance for a dog.

The woman didn't seem to understand what he was saying to her. Seal had no choice but to bring her back to reality with firm words. "I wasn't too gentle or too courteous," he recalled, "but I said, 'Get in there and call an ambulance,' and so she did."

While the young woman was in the house, Rowland Seal walked along the side of the thin wire fence separating the apartment house property from the lawn next door. The fence was more of a psychological barrier than a physical one, not much more than chicken wire. Seal felt the hairs prickle at the back of his neck. It was still dark but he could see that it was not a dog at all—but a man—who lay on his

7

back in an open gate between the area where the people next door parked their cars and the side yard of their house. The man lay in the shadows and it was so dark near the gate that at first Seal could see only a white shirt and a white face. But there was more. He *could* make out scarlet stains—*blood?*—on the man's face. He couldn't be sure who it was, but it was a big man. That and the blood were all he could see for certain. Peering from his side of the fence, Seal was unable to get any closer than five or six feet from the body.

He forced himself to conquer his shock and headed back to the sidewalk. The young woman had emerged from her house again and this time two small children and a large dog trailed after her.

Leaving the children and dog on the porch, she ran back to the body crying, "Oh, my God, he's dead. He's been shot. My God. He's shot. He's dead. . . ."

Rowland Seal saw that the woman was getting more and more frantic, and he didn't want the kids to catch her hysteria. He instructed her very carefully to take the children into the house and to call the police.

For a moment the scene on the porch seemed eternal, a frozen tableau, until the slender, dark-haired woman turned and headed into the house. "And then," Seal remembered, "a police officer came and then another one and then another one. When the third one came, I thought everything was under control, and I gave my name and address and told him I was going duck hunting and he could find me at my address."

Rowland Seal was nothing if not pragmatic; he went ahead with the day he had planned. He could do nothing to help the man who lay in the snow. Nor could he help the woman. The police would take care of it.

A shaken Dale Soost went ahead with his day too.

And so did Gerda Lenberg. She had no idea at all that anything earthshaking had occurred in the dark hours between Friday night and Saturday morning. It wasn't until Sunday morning when she read the paper that she looked up and said slowly, "Oh, my lord, that wasn't firecrackers at all. . . ."

8

2

It **never** should have ended the way it did. There are some people whom destiny smiles upon, human beings blessed with wonderfully classic good looks, intelligence, and talents and skills that far surpass the average—people who grow up surrounded by love and high hopes. In Yakima, Washington, in that window of time in the 1970s, there were four people like that, an oddly assembled quartet of players whose lives would grow so intertwined and hopelessly entangled that they could never seem to pull apart. The very "oxygen" of their freedom to live and breathe was soon compromised by their closeness. The obsessive desire of one player damned the happiness of the other three forever.

Possibly the end of the game had been fated decades before; certain choices each of them made had brought them to this place.

Olive Morgan Blankenbaker was one of four daughters born to Esther and Ray Morgan, who named all their girls somewhat whimsically (and horticulturally): Hazel, Fern, Olive, and Iris. Their maternal grandfather, Ernst Skarstedt, was a writer of some note in his native Sweden and his intelligence and sensitivity came through undiluted to his descendants.

Olive was born in 1910 near Wapato in Yakima County. She would spend all of her working years in the court systems of Washington. She began as a court secretary, but her true goal was to be a court reporter. This was long before the era of stenotype machines or computer disks. Court reporters wrote in beautifully executed script.

It was also long before television was anything more than a scientific phenomenon demonstrated at world's fairs. Radios were the home entertainment in vogue when Olive was a young woman in her twenties. Huge console radios with shiny mahogany cabinets and ornately carved facades were the status symbols of the thirties. Franklin D. Roosevelt had his "fireside chats" over the radio, kids listened to "Jack Armstrong, the All-American Boy," and "The Lone Ranger," and dance bands from a ballroom "high atop" some hotel far away enchanted late-night listeners.

Olive Morgan met Ned Blankenbaker in Yakima where he worked as a radio salesman in a radio and musical instrument store. She was a slender, beautiful young woman with marcelled curls and a sweet smile. Ned always seemed to be standing outside the store to catch a little sun just when Olive came walking downtown on her way to lunch. He was a short, stocky man with thick wavy hair and interesting eyes. Those eyes followed Olive as she passed by, and she knew it. He would stand on his tiptoes to make himself look taller when Olive walked by.

"Some other girls I knew knew him and they introduced us," Olive says. "I liked him the moment I met him."

It wasn't long before Ned and Olive began to talk, and then he asked her to go dancing. That's what all the young people did then. There were dance halls with lanterns swaying in the wind, and everyone tried to emulate Fred Astaire and Ginger Rogers. "Ned was a great dancer," Olive remembers. "We'd go out to Bock's Café where you could dance. It was just up the street from the music store. We knew everyone."

Songs like "Blue Moon" and "Anything Goes" were popular. FDR was in his first term in office and Social Security had just been voted in. The night before Olive Morgan married Ned Blankenbaker on September 25, 1935, Joe Louis took away Max Baer's heavyweight crown. Huey Long had been assassinated in Louisiana two weeks before, and war clouds were lowering in Europe. But all that was so far away. Yakima, in the center of Washington State, was seemingly insulated from the world outside. Olive was twenty-five years old when she married Ned, and she expected her marriage would last forever.

Ned and Olive Blankenbaker were married seven years before they had their only child. Morris Ray Blankenbaker was born on December 16, 1942. Thirty-two-year-old Olive was transfixed with love for this sturdy baby boy who made her holiday season the best she had ever had. As it almost always is, it was a "White Christmas" in Yakima. Although the world was at war and everything was rationed, everything in Olive's life at that moment was perfect.

A half-century later, looking back she would ask, "Why should it be that way? When people are so happy, why does it all have to disappear?"

For Olive's wonderful world did disappear. Somehow, the Blankenbaker marriage didn't work very well after Morris was born. In all, Olive and Ned were married nine years; Morris was barely two when Olive was left to raise him alone. Over the years, his father would remain a part of Morris's life and pay regular child support, but Ned fathered two more sons—Morris's half brothers, Mike and Charles. It was Olive who was always there for Morris Blankenbaker. Her love for him was so unselfish that she encouraged him to spend time with his father and his younger brothers. They would become an important part of his life.

Olive could easily have smothered Morris and made him a mama's boy, but she didn't. Morris was a natural athlete, a kid who was always running and leaping and playing ball. He had plenty of scrapes, bruises, and sprains, but Olive just sighed and bound up his wounds. She bit her lip when she felt she was about to ask him to give up the sports he adored. She knew it wouldn't do any good, anyway.

Olive signed up for a correspondence course to learn how to use the stenotype machine. She and Morris were living with her family in Wapato, and she managed to combine her studying with camping trips with her son. "I'd fix a big pot of stew and put it over the campfire, while Morris and his two friends—Indian boys from the Wapato Reserva-

11

tion—would go exploring in the forest. They could take the dog and have fun and I could study."

In the meantime, Olive was working as a court reporter, using Gregg shorthand. She sat through everything from divorces to murder trials, taking down all the proceedings in her fine hand. She worked in the Yakima County Superior Court, and then transferred over to Federal Court in Seattle, where Federal Judge Bowen, an elderly man who disliked change, was delighted to discover that there was still one court reporter in the Seattle area who could transcribe courtroom proceedings with a pen. "When he saw me writing with a pen on a notebook, he set up a whole bunch of proceedings for me to cover. He hated those little black machines," Olive remembered. "I never told him that I *could* write with one of those little black machines. We went all up and down the Washington coast from Bellingham to Vancouver hearing cases."

Judge Bowen was ninety-three and still on the bench when he asked Olive if she would consider working in Yakima, and of course she agreed readily. That was home. She and Morris moved back into her mother's house just outside town, and Olive worked days and evenings to keep up with the punishing schedule of cases that were filed into Judge Bowen's court.

Morris always came home for lunch to his Grandmother Morgan's house. "You could see him coming a block away—running," Olive said. "And he took her picket fence with a high jump every day. My mother loved to see that boy eat."

Morris Blankenbaker was a handsome child with tight blond curls and brown eyes. When he was five, he posed proudly for his mother's Brownie camera in his cowboy shirt, tooled belt with the silver buckle, and western boots. He was a Cub Scout, and into more athletic events with every year. He went out for tumbling and scrambled up to the top of the pyramid of bodies. "He broke his arm, of course," Olive recalled. "That was Morris."

One summer, when Morris was seven, Olive took him for an automobile trip all across Canada. "We stopped wherever there was a swimming pool," she said. "Even at seven, he swam like a fish, and he could dive off the high board, doing somersaults in the air. People used to gather around to watch him."

Olive was running her own kind of marathon in the Yakima Superior Court. "I kept up for a long time, but I finally had to quit," she said. "I was just about breaking down, because I was working for the most effective judge, and everyone was filing their cases in his court."

As common as it is in the 1990s, a single mother raising a son was a rarity in the 1940s. There were fathers who were away during the war certainly, but divorced mothers were far from the norm and it wasn't easy for Olive. She kept trying to find a job that would give her more time with Morris. She moved to Vancouver, Washington, where Morris went to Fort Vancouver High School.

Later, they moved to Spokane, ". . . to a big court with a lot of cases."

Back in Yakima again, Morris went to Washington Junior High and then Davis High School. He was the golden boy who could do anything. He was on the "A" squad of the track, baseball, football, and wrestling teams. He played the trombone and the French horn, marching in the Davis High band, carrying the huge horn as lightly as a feather. His mother remembers the band triumphantly playing "Bonaparte's Retreat" as they marched down the field.

It hardly seemed possible that one kid could participate in so many activities—but Morris did. He played baseball, ran track, and wrestled, and he was the star fullback on the football squad. The crowd shouted his name again and again as he made touchdowns. *"MOR-RIS BLANK-EN-BAKER! MOR-RIS BLANK-EN-BAKER!"*

In the summertime, Morris worked as a lifeguard in Yakima parks. From his teens well into his twenties, he always had an audience of adoring girls who carefully spread their towels out so they would be directly in his line of vision. He appreciated the view, but Morris didn't date much. He scarcely had time. In the end, there was only one girl he ever went steady with. Only one girl he ever really loved.

Jerilee. *Jerilee Karlberg.**

One of Morris's coaches at Davis High School during his senior year in 1961 was Talmadge Glynn Moore. Of course, nobody called Moore by his full name, and very few people called him "Glynn"; everyone knew him by "Gabby." Morris had known Gabby since he and Olive came back to Yakima in the midfifties—ever since junior high. He figured Gabby had coached him in about every sport there was at one time or another: wrestling, football, track. Gabby was almost exactly nine years Morris's senior. Morris's birthday was on December 16, and Gabby's was on the twenty-first. But when Morris was a schoolboy, Gabby was a grown man, married with a family, and their worlds were completely different. Morris always called Gabby "Coach"; he always would, even after he too was an adult.

When Morris graduated from Davis High in 1961, he took home just about every athletic honor. He received the Traub Blocking and Tackling trophy, and he was voted "Best Athlete of the Year." Best of all, Morris was offered a four-year football scholarship to Washington State University in Pullman. All he had to do was keep his grades up and do what came naturally as an athlete.

Olive was living and working in Spokane then, and Morris visited on holidays and weekends when he didn't have a game. Morris was playing right halfback for the Washington State Cougars. His mother didn't have the time or money to get to his games, but she did manage to get to Spokane to watch him play once.

"That was when Washington State played the University of Washington," Olive said. "They played in Spokane at

---

*The names of some individuals in the book have been changed. Such names are indicated by an asterisk (*) the first time each appears in the narrative.

night under the lights. I got to go to that game. It was so terribly cold. We were wrapped up in blankets with long underwear and everything. I even remember the date—it was November twenty-fourth, 1962. It was a real good game, and he played all the way through. I was so proud of him," Olive remembered. "He was so handsome and they kept shouting 'Morris Blankenbaker! Morris Blankenbaker!'"

Even so, for the first time in his athletic career, there were other halfbacks at Washington State University who made the starting lineup more often than Morris did. He was 5'11", tall and 175 pounds. That was plenty big enough in high school; in college, there were players who dwarfed him. Dennis McCurdy, Herman McKee, and Clarence Williams were playing halfback for the Cougars too and they were 6'1", 6'3", and 6'2" respectively, and they all weighed over 190. Morris's dreams of becoming a professional football player before he started a coaching career seemed less realistic than they once had.

Besides that, there was Jerilee. Jerilee Karlberg was three years behind Morris in school, and she attended the other public high school in Yakima: Eisenhower High. Morris barely knew her when he was in high school but he got to know her well when he went back to Yakima to visit his hometown. He had always been a guy who dated casually. As far as any of his friends remember, Morris was never serious about any girl in high school.

Jerilee Karlberg was another story. Outwardly, she seemed to be what every teenage girl in the sixties yearned to be. She had a perfect figure: slender, but full-breasted. She had clouds of dark hair and blue eyes and she wasn't just pretty; she was beautiful. Her skin was flawless and her features were enchanting. She was petite and entirely feminine. And of course she was a cheerleader for Eisenhower High.

"Jerilee was everything we wanted to be," one of her peers remembered. "She was pretty and slender and popular—so popular with boys. Her father was Henry Karlberg* and he had his own real estate company. He let

Jerilee drive his new Cadillac whenever she wanted. While we all *yearned* after the 'jocks,' Jerilee *married* Morris Blankenbaker, the super athlete of them all. We envied her . . . I suppose some of us hated her. Or at least *resented* her. It's hard to put into words. Maybe you had to have lived in Yakima in the sixties to really understand."

Jerilee Karlberg may have appeared to have had everything, but her life was far from perfect. She had her insecurities in high school and often smiled to hide private heartbreak. True, she came from an affluent family and she was gorgeous, but the world she knew was falling apart. Henry and Marge,* Jerilee's parents, had divorced and her father had remarried and begun a new family. The world she had always known blew away like dandelion fluff in the wind. No one can ever really know for sure, but Jerilee's attitude toward males may well have changed radically then.

She was devastated for a long time when her parents divorced. Morris was something solid for her to hold on to, and she loved him for that more than for his prowess on the football field. She wasn't really that interested in sports. She could see that everyone liked Morris, and he seemed to have scores of friends. Morris was handsome and built like a young Greek god with bulging biceps and a "washboard" stomach that rippled with muscles. He was a college man and he made the boys at Eisenhower High look like wimpy kids. There was no question that Jerilee was completely in love with Morris.

Jerilee was still in high school when she started dating Morris, and she begged him to come to Yakima to take her to her proms. She didn't want to miss the most memorable social events of any teenage girl's school years, yet she refused to go with anyone else. For Morris, it was almost a four hundred-mile round-trip, but he made it willingly. He posed with Jerilee who wore lovely formal gowns with the corsages he'd given her. Sometimes, the long trips back to Yakima cut into his study time and his grades suffered, but it didn't matter. Morris Blankenbaker was in love for the first time in his life.

Jerilee certainly had the intelligence to go to college, but she didn't want that; she wanted her own family. On August 28, 1965, three months after she graduated from Eisenhower High School, Jerilee and Morris were married. She was just eighteen. He was twenty-two.

"They had a big church wedding in the Presbyterian church," Olive remembered. "With a huge reception at the Chinook Hotel in Yakima. They served food and had liquor and everything . . ."

Henry Karlberg had put on a wonderful wedding for his daughter. Had it been up to her, Olive would have chosen not to serve liquor at the reception. It was just one of the things that carved a chasm between Olive and Jerilee's family, one that they all crossed tentatively for years to come. Olive and Morris had not exactly lived a hardscrabble existence, but nothing had ever come easy. No big houses and certainly no fancy cars.

For decades after that wedding in 1965, Olive and Jerilee Blankenbaker would have an ambivalent relationship. It was to be expected. They both loved Morris. He was Olive's only child, the son she had struggled so hard to raise, and he could do no wrong in her eyes. She had wanted so much for him to graduate from college before he got married, and Jerilee had detoured him from that goal. For her part, Jerilee at eighteen was perhaps a little spoiled. She was not nearly as expert at either housework or a career as Olive was. Eventually, however, the two women would come to have a kind of grudging respect for one another.

The newly married Mr. and Mrs. Morris Ray Blankenbaker moved to Tacoma, Washington, where Morris planned to obtain his bachelor's degree at Pacific Lutheran University. He hadn't given up on his ambition to get his degree and become a coach. It would just take a little longer.

Morris had dropped out of Washington State and joined the Marine Corps Reserves before the draft could scoop him up. This meant that he had to train in the desert outside Coronado, California, for a few weeks each year, and risk being called to active duty in Vietnam. He was lucky; he didn't have to go to war and eventually he made lance corporal. Four years later, in February of 1969, he was honorably discharged from the Reserves.

3

Talmadge Glynn "Gabby" Moore had coached at Davis High School in Yakima since the 1960–61 school year. Like Morris, he was a Yakima boy, although he wasn't a native. Gabby was born in the depths of the Depression in Missouri—four days before Christmas, 1931. His family moved to Yakima when he was a child and Gabby attended school there, graduating from North Yakima High School in 1950. He too was a sports hero. He received North Yakima High's football inspirational trophy. But Gabby Moore, like so many teenagers graduating in the early fifties, went off to the Korean War instead of to college. He served in the Air Force from 1951 to 1955.

When he was discharged, Gabby came back to Yakima. He was a very handsome young man then with straight blond hair and heavy-lidded dark eyes. Gabby Moore, who looked like the jock that he was, clean-cut and in great shape, wanted to be a high school coach. He went to college on the GI Bill—first to Yakima Valley Community College, and then to Central Washington State College (now Central Washington University) in Ellensburg where he got his BA in 1958. Two years later, he received his master's degree at the same college.

Gabby's education wasn't easy; he taught and coached while he was going to college. He had married by then, to Gay Myers, and during the time Gabby was getting his education and beginning his career as a teacher they had three babies: Sherry,* Kate,* and Derek.* Gay, who was

18

startlingly attractive with smoky blond hair and a lithe figure, eventually became a physical education teacher herself.

As they are in most small towns in America, sports were king in Yakima, and the Moores were so much a part of the fabric of the town, of its educational system and its sports circle. Gabby Moore had taught in tiny Union Gap first, and then at Washington Junior High in Yakima. He moved steadily up the career ladder. In 1960 he was hired to teach and coach at Davis High School where he stayed to become a much-admired fixture. Gabby taught math and driver training and was the track coach and the assistant football coach. One year he was the head football coach.

But the gridiron wasn't his forte; it was at wrestling that he excelled as a mentor. He became, arguably, one of the most outstanding wrestling coaches in America. He could have moved on up to college coaching—he was certainly skilled enough—but he had sunk deep roots in Yakima.

Gabby Moore was the impetus behind bringing "kid wrestling" to Yakima. The town's boosters were pleased, and the Yakima Junior Chamber of Commerce honored him for that program by giving him the trophy for "Outstanding Physical Education Educator" for 1969. Moore's wrestling team took the Washington State Championship in 1972. He was a member of the selection committee in the Washington Cultural Exchange with Japan, where wrestling is a major sport. Gabby found a way to travel to the Orient with his star athletes so that they could wrestle with the best.

Athletes from many graduating classes had passed through Gabby's wrestling programs and they never forgot him. He could take a boy with no particular aptitude for sports and turn him into a champion. He could, and he *did,* not once but many times. His athletes loved Gabby, and he cared deeply for his boys.

Beyond his solid place at Davis High, Gabby Moore had other compelling reasons to prefer Yakima to one of the college towns on the "coast" near Seattle or to the east: Pullman or Moscow, Idaho, where Washington State and

19

the University of Idaho were located. He and Gay had an extended family in Yakima with a closeness that anyone would envy, a tight circle of love and emotional support.

Gabby's father-in-law, Dr. A. J. Myers, was an osteopathic physician and surgeon who owned and operated the Valley Osteopathic Hospital on Tieton Drive in Yakima. "Doc" Myers had practiced medicine in Yakima for more than thirty years and in 1952 he built Valley Hospital.

"Doc" and Gabby met for the first time shortly before Gabby married Gay, and they soon became fast friends. Myers was Gabby's doctor and his friend, a relationship that existed outside of Gabby's marriage.

In those days Gabby Moore was a family man and a revered coach. He was twenty-seven when Morris Blankenbaker graduated from high school, and they kept in touch, although only sporadically. There was no reason to think that their lives would touch again in much more than a tangential way.

While Morris Blankenbaker was an Adonis of a young man who was everyone's friend, Gabby Moore's popularity came from his compelling, persuasive personality. As he aged, his appearance changed from that of a good-looking young coach to one of an average-looking man who seemed older than he really was. All coaches at every level are under pressure to win. Gabby didn't handle stress well. The pressure to win—much of it self-driven—got to him and he developed primary hypertension in his early thirties. Gabby's high blood pressure was serious enough to concern his father-in-law. A. J. Myers did his best to convince Gabby that elevated blood pressure was nothing to ignore, but his warnings usually fell on deaf ears. Gabby Moore continued to demand too much of himself and of his athletes. When he concentrated on something, it was with every fiber of his being; he did nothing halfway.

With the years, Gabby's hair thinned and he was beginning to resort to "comb-overs" and deliberately careless bangs over his forehead. By the time he was in his late thirties, despite his sports activities, Gabby had a burgeoning paunch that his wrestlers teased him about. He wasn't the handsome young coach he had been in his twenties;

Gabby had come to look like a thousand other high school teacher-coaches in America.

But that hardly mattered. It was his personality that shone through. An alumna remembered that, as a teacher of driver's training, Gabby was so calm—so patient.

"I had Gabby for driver's training," recalled the woman, who worked in the Yakima County District Attorney's Office, twenty years after graduation. "I *liked* him. We all did. I remember he always told us to 'Look for a way out'— to expect trouble, and be ready to get out of the way. He wasn't temperamental. He wasn't mean. He was a great guy . . . I still can't understand what happened. . . ."

For most of his years of teaching and coaching, Gabby Moore was a dynamic, charismatic man who could make anyone believe anything. And if *he* believed, his listeners believed. If he said a kid from Yakima could make it to the Olympics and bring home a gold medal, then, by golly, the kid would go for it. He would not listen to excuses. "If you got a problem," Gabby would say, "you eliminate the problem—and you win." While Gabby was known to have a short fuse on occasion, it didn't affect his job or his status at Davis High School.

Gay Myers Moore was a beautiful woman and, unlike Gabby, she grew more attractive as she approached middle age. Gay was teaching girls' physical ed at Lewis & Clark Junior High. Both Moores were busy with their teaching schedules and raising three youngsters, but they made a great couple. Their marriage seemed as solid as Gibraltar.

No one really *knows* how things are in a marriage, though, not from the outside looking in. Maybe Gabby focused too much on his wrestling squads and forgot that his family needed him too. He not only had after-school practice, he usually brought some of his wrestlers home for practice-after-practice. There weren't enough hours in the day for him to have had much time to spend with his wife— at least during wrestling season.

In 1965, just after Morris and Jerilee got married, he and Gabby Moore had no closer a relationship than Gabby did with any of his ex-athletes from Davis. They sometimes saw one another in Yakima when Morris and Jerilee came home to visit their relatives on holidays or during the summer, but that was about it.

Morris had precious little free time. The curriculum at Pacific Lutheran University was far more demanding than the classes he had taken at Washington State. PLU attracted students with the highest academic records. And Pacific Lutheran is a private university where the tuition is a lot higher than a state school. This time, Morris had no football scholarship—he didn't have time to play football. Both he and Jerilee had to work so that they could make it financially.

Jerilee might have *looked* like a fragile, dependent girl who needed a man to look after her, and, yes, maybe she had played that role a time or two because boys seemed to like it. Inside, though, she was strong and smart; she just wasn't used to letting it show. She was the kind of woman who combined a kittenish quality with profound sensuality—a Brigitte Bardot or a Claudine Longet kind of woman. Physically, Jerilee resembled Longet a great deal.

Jerilee Blankenbaker was highly intelligent. She and Morris needed the money she could bring in, and she was determined to get a job. She applied at a bank in Tacoma even though they hadn't advertised for new employees. She simply strode in and said, "I want a job."

The bank manager drew up a chair and asked her to sit down.

"The bank had a test they gave to everyone," Olive Blankenbaker recalled. "They handed Jerilee this great big stack of checks, and they said, 'There's one forgery in there. See if you can find it.' And do you know, *she* found it—and nobody ever had before. She is really bright. You've got to give her credit."

Jerilee was hired at once. Not only was her appearance an asset to the bank, but she was obviously smart. They hadn't guessed wrong on her. Although she had no training and was fresh out of high school, she was a quick study and she proved to be a very valuable employee. She began as a clerk, but she rose rapidly to a position of trust officer.

Morris found a job at Western State Hospital in Steilacoom, Washington's state institution for people who are profoundly psychotic. He worked the late shift from three to eleven P.M. It was a demanding job. He was at work for the evening meal and then he helped medical personnel get patients settled down for the night with a variety of medications. He always had to be ready for trouble. The most placid patients sometimes had psychotic breaks with no warning at all. Morris knew that one of the reasons he had been hired was his muscular build. But Morris's innate kindness and his calm manner seemed to soothe the more disturbed patients at Western State.

No matter how difficult the night's work had been, Morris still had to study when he got home close to midnight. While he worked nights, Jerilee worked days. Her "banker's hours" ended just as his job began. In the little time they had together, they got along well. If they argued at all, their discussions were about money or in-laws. Jerilee had assumed that Olive would continue to send money to Morris until he got out of college, while Olive figured that he was a grown man now, and a married man as well. She had looked forward to cutting back on the heavy workload she had carried since he was a baby.

Jerilee was upset about that, Olive remembered, but it wasn't a big problem. Mostly, Jerilee was homesick for Yakima and for her own mother and sister. She didn't know anyone in Tacoma, and she spent most evenings alone because Morris was working. She was uneasy too; sometimes people escaped from Western State Hospital. PLU's campus had a lovely sweeping greensward and scores of huge trees, but the streets nearby quickly disintegrated into high-crime areas. When Morris was gone, it seemed to Jerilee that every sound was magnified.

Morris had hoped to finish college at Pacific Lutheran, but Jerilee was so miserable and homesick that he finally agreed to move back to Yakima, find a job there, and attend Central Washington State College in Ellensburg on a part-time basis. A move would mean that his degree would take a year or two longer than he had hoped. In truth, it would be six years before Morris Blankenbaker graduated from college.

23

Back in Yakima, Morris took a "temporary" job with the phone company as a telephone lineman. It wasn't his ultimate goal, but he liked scampering up poles with spiked boots and the camaraderie of the crews he worked with. And he was happy being back in the county where he was raised, back with his good friends. He had grown up in the big old house where his grandparents lived and he often stopped in for his coffee break, bringing his whole crew with him. His grandmother Esther looked forward to fussing over Morris and his fellow linemen, and she usually had something baking in the oven just in case.

All the while, Morris plugged away at his college degree at Central Washington College. It was only thirty-five miles to Ellensburg, but it was a rough thirty-five miles before the freeway was built: across the Twin Bridges, and then along the riverbanks outside of Yakima and across great stretches of barren land and winding roads through hills that were more like mountains, past squared-off buttes. Eastern Washington is not at all like the rainy and mild western half of the state. In winter, blizzards often made State Road 821 virtually impassable while, in summer, sand storms full of tumbleweeds blinded drivers who headed north out of Yakima toward Ellensburg. It was a great road for sightseers, as it curved along the Yakima River, but it was a student commuter's nightmare.

Gabby Moore, Morris's old track coach, was taking classes at Central Washington too, and he and Morris often car-pooled. They renewed their friendship, but it was a different kind of friendship now; they were both adults. In the spring of 1969, Gabby's and Gay's three kids were growing up and Jerilee was pregnant with her first baby.

Sometimes, Gabby and Morris went hunting or spear fishing together on weekends. They often went whitewater rafting and boating on the Yakima River. Theirs was a male friendship; the Moores and the Blankenbakers didn't socialize. Jerilee scarcely knew Gabby.

Rick* Blankenbaker was born on May 5, 1969, and Jerilee was swept up in first-time motherhood. Amanda* was born a little over a year later on September 1, 1970. The young

Blankenbakers had it all: a happy marriage, a little boy, and a little girl. Old photographs show Jerilee and Morris posing happily with their babies: Morris hoisting his chunky young son high with one muscular arm; Jerilee riding on Morris's shoulders on a whirligig as the family plays in the park; Jerilee and the kids proudly presenting Morris with a birthday cake. Looking at the photos, it seems impossible that it could not have gone on that way forever.

The young Blankenbakers had every reason to believe that they would grow old together and watch their children and grandchildren live out their lives in Yakima too.

Olive Blankenbaker was in her midfifties when Morris married Jerilee. It seemed to her that it was too late then to find anyone marriageable who appealed to her. More out of habit than anything else, Olive kept up much the same heavy work pace she had set for herself so long before. She did, however, stop court reporting and accepted an offer to go to work for J. P. "Pete" Tonkoff of the Yakima firm of Tonkoff and Holst. It proved to be the best job she had ever had, a steady—if intense—schedule, with more benefits than any of her other positions.

Pete Tonkoff, a native of Bulgaria, was a "great attorney," dynamic and dramatic in the courtroom. He was not in the least impressed with city lawyers. He once subpoenaed Eleanor Roosevelt as a witness in a case he was bringing against Fulton Lewis. Olive would work for Pete Tonkoff for ten years, driving in from her family's old homestead near the Yakima River in an "old jalopy." She loved the challenge of working for Tonkoff. She admired his brilliance, even his occasional bombasity.

The years passed. Olive was in her sixties, but she was as efficient as ever and indispensable to Tonkoff and Holst. At some point, Pete Tonkoff took one look at the car she drove through blizzards and summer heat alike and bought her a new one, gruffly saying he didn't want her missing work because her old car had broken down.

Olive's ideal job ended suddenly on July 18, 1973, when Pete Tonkoff was lost and presumed dead after the Beechcraft he owned and was piloting disappeared over Lake

Pontchartrain in Louisiana. Tonkoff had been flying in to handle a New Orleans case. He had been coming in for a landing when the tower ordered him to make another go-round because the runway was occupied. He never came back. Later, his plane was found deep in the lake. His death was only the first blow that Olive Blankenbaker would suffer in the mid-1970s.

"Up until then," she said, "everything was good. I thought it would last forever."

4

All too often the falling-down of lives is like dominoes tumbling. When one falls, it knocks over the next, and the next, and on and on until everything is flattened. In the early 1970s, Gabby Moore was at the very peak of his profession, with his athletes winning more honors every year. His own son, Derek, made the football team at Davis, and another generation of Moores played for the Pirates. His daughters, Sherry and Kate, were pretty girls and good students.

Who can say what detours human beings from a smooth road ahead? The "midlife crazies," maybe. Unfulfilled dreams? On occasion, it is a near-tragedy that serves as a wake-up call that life doesn't go on forever.

Gabby Moore came so close to dying one summer day that he may well have reevaluated his life and realized that he had slid into middle age without ever seeing it looming on the horizon. Had it not been for Morris Blankenbaker, Gabby Moore never would have made it much past forty.

It happened on one of the river trips that Morris and Gabby often took. The day began like any other. The two men had parked one of their cars near Olive's place close by the Yakima River and driven the other up to Ellensburg. There, they pushed off in a boat and headed downriver toward Yakima. They had made this trip dozens of times before. But this time something went wrong, and their boat capsized in a powerful undercurrent, scattering its occupants and their gear alike.

Both Morris and Gabby were plunged beneath the surface of the river, sucked deeper and deeper, down where the sunlight was swallowed up and they had to dodge floating debris and sunken logs in an underwater obstacle course. Morris was the strong swimmer and he quickly fought his way to the surface. Somehow Gabby ended up beneath the bank along the river's edge, his feet entangled in the clutch of vines and roots that flourished in the deep water. There was no way he could ever have gotten out of their death grip by himself and he was virtually invisible from the surface of the river.

Morris wasn't worried about himself; he was like an otter in the water. As a younger man, he had tormented his friends and his mother by swimming underwater so long they were sure he had drowned. But he was only "counting" until he was confident he had broken his own record for holding his breath. Satisfied, he then would burst up triumphantly just as they were all running for a lifeguard to pull him out.

Now, in the whitewater that overturned their drift-boat, Morris dove again and again, looking for Gabby. Finally he saw him flailing his arms helplessly, his feet held in the vise of the underwater vegetation. Morris wrenched Gabby free and took him to the top. Gabby flopped on the bank like a dying fish, throwing up. But he was breathing and he was alive.

"I wish he'd never made it," Olive Blankenbaker would say with quiet bitterness many years later. "I wish Morris had left him there in the river."

Olive would remember that she had felt an aversion to Gabby Moore from the first time she met him out there at her river place. She never said anything to Morris, because she couldn't put her finger on what it was about Gabby that set her teeth on edge.

Morris was unaware that his mother didn't like Gabby. The two men remained fast friends. They hunted and fished and sometimes worked out at the YMCA together. Morris was flattered when Gabby sought his advice on football plays. Morris attended a number of Gabby's teams's wrestling matches and he sometimes helped coach the heavyweight wrestlers. The two men talked often, almost every day.

In December of 1973, Gabby confided to Morris the shocking news that he and Gay were getting a divorce. He said he would be moving out of his family home after Christmas. Morris was stunned. Gabby and Gay had been married almost two decades, and Morris had had no idea they were having problems. From what Gabby told him, it was Gay who wanted out of the marriage, and Gabby who was fighting to keep it together.

Gabby asked Morris if he might move in with him and Jerilee for a few weeks, just until he and Gay tried to settle their problems. Morris was all for it if it would help Gabby salvage his marriage. A "time-out" might be just what Gabby's marriage needed.

Jerilee Blankenbaker was definitely not enthusiastic when Morris approached her with the suggestion that they invite Gabby to stay with them until he pulled himself together. His divorce was hurting him bad and he wasn't taking it well, Morris explained. Gabby was lonesome and lost outside the family he had been used to.

Jerilee didn't really know Gabby Moore. At twenty-seven she had two little children to take care of, not to mention her full-time job at a Yakima bank; she had more than enough to do without helping Morris baby-sit his old coach. It wasn't that she was selfish or uncaring, it was simply that she and Morris were just getting their own lives on track. Morris had his college degree, and he was teaching at last. She couldn't envision bringing Gabby into their home without incurring problems. She didn't have time to cook and clean up after another man, to do his laundry, and she didn't feel like giving up her privacy.

Morris argued that it wouldn't be for very long. Gabby was probably going to be getting back with Gay; if he didn't, he would soon be looking for his own place. Morris said he just couldn't turn the guy away in good conscience. And that was typical of Morris. He *had* a conscience, and he cared a lot about Gabby.

A future prosecuting attorney named Jeff Sullivan was Gay Moore's divorce attorney. Much later, Sullivan would scarcely recall the divorce proceedings, which led him to believe that the dissolution of the Moore marriage was uncomplicated. "No-fault" divorces had just come into effect in Washington State at that time and Sullivan cannot remember if Gabby was any more reluctant than the average man to get a divorce. In fact, it was Sullivan's impression that Gabby *wanted* the divorce. In any case, the proceedings were calm enough that they did not stand out in his mind.

That was not the way Gabby described it to Morris, however. Bereft, Gabby confided in his athletes and in his friends. He seemed lost, frightened of the future, and angry at the same time. Of all of Gabby's friends, Morris Blankenbaker was the one who worried the most about what would happen to Gabby when he didn't have Gay any longer. At first, it didn't occur to Morris that he was hearing only one side of the story: a side that showed Gabby in the best light.

Morris had saved Gabby's life once, and he was ready to do it again. It was almost as if he were living out the Chinese proverb that says that once you save someone's life, it belongs to you forever after and you remain responsible for that person. Gabby was in bad shape and Morris was not a man to ever walk away from any of his friends when they were as down as Gabby seemed.

Gabby had other friends, and his about-to-be ex-father-in-law was still close to him, but that didn't make the long nights alone any easier. He needed to be around people. Morris saw Gabby as a victim, and Gabby did nothing to dissuade him. There were many things that Gabby did not confide in Morris. Certainly, Morris had no idea how much Gabby was drinking or how insanely jealous he was of Gay.

Had Morris known, he might have rethought his offer to Gabby to move in. But he didn't know, and he worked hard to convince Jerilee that Gabby needed a place to stay where people cared about him. Finally, she gave in, and Gabby Moore moved in with the family in January of 1974.

Whatever Gabby was doing to effect a reconciliation, it wasn't working. Gay Moore went ahead with her divorce action. She wasn't divorcing Gabby because there was another man; she just wanted a different kind of life. Gabby's moods were too unpredictable and he was almost paranoid, believing that she *was* interested in someone else. With a teaching job and three teenagers to raise, Gay had no time to think about a new relationship.

Although Jerilee Blankenbaker had been against Gabby Moore's moving into her home, she soon changed her mind. She could see why Morris and he were such good friends. He was a nice guy, and he was fun to have around. More than that, though, Gabby's old charisma that had always drawn people to him was still working. When he wanted to be, he was the most charming man in the room, full of anecdotes and jokes, confident and bristling with goodwill. He was compelling, a man who seemed taller, handsomer, and more successful than he really was. He brought that force of energy to the Blankenbaker house, and when his eyes met Jerilee's, she found it almost impossible to look away.

No one could ever say when Jerilee began to view Gabby in a new light. Sharing a house with someone is an intimate experience—sometimes pleasant, sometimes uncomfortable. Gabby was there in the morning with his eyes sleepy and his hair tousled, and he was usually there as they all went to bed. In truth, Jerilee was living with two men, one her husband and one an interloper. But he was a disturbingly fascinating interloper. She knew that he drank a little, but she had no idea how much. Gabby was careful to be his most charming when he was with Jerilee. If there was an early hint that she found him special, perhaps it was the way she called him "Glynn" instead of Gabby, as everyone else did. She didn't like his nickname.

It was *Morris* who began to see his best friend with more critical eyes. He saw traits in Gabby he had never noticed before. "Morris said he could just see a change in Glynn," Jerilee said much later. "And Glynn would drink for two or three days without sleeping and do things that were unlike his character. He took a gun up to his ex-wife's house and he made threats toward her, and Morris could just . . . well, he lost his respect for him."

But Morris didn't immediately confide in Jerilee about the negative things he was seeing in Gabby. Since she hadn't known him at all well before he moved in with them, she couldn't see the alarming change.

"I didn't know Glynn Moore that well previous to that," she admitted. Morris didn't tell Jerilee how much Gabby was drinking, or how bizarre his behavior became when he *did* drink. He didn't tell her about the obsessive, almost psychotic jealousy Gabby was exhibiting toward Gay.

Later, Jerilee would see the other side of Gabby, the one that made Morris pull back from the friendship. But by the time Morris distanced himself from his old coach, it was far too late to stop what was happening in his own home.

Someone who wasn't there cannot possibly say when things began to go awry in the Blankenbaker marriage. One can only conjecture.

Jerilee and Morris had been married eight years, and they had long since grown accustomed to each other. Gabby Moore was a new element in the equation. He clearly found Jerilee enchanting. He listened to what she had to say, and he was quick to jump up to help her clear the dinner table. It soon began to seem natural to have him there; he was like part of the family. And then it was more than that—he *was* part of the family.

Gabby Moore needed to talk about his feelings, and Jerilee listened. Gabby was, as a song popular in that era said, "a giant of a man brought down by love"—a condition that is ultimately appealing to most women. At first, Jerilee probably felt sorry for him as she listened to him talk about his lost marriage. The only side to Gabby she had ever seen—and that was at a distance—was the macho coach, the sportsman, her husband's friend. Now, as he poured his heart out to her, she must have sensed that he had emotional depths she had never realized. Jerilee was undoubtedly touched when she saw how the end of his marriage had diminished his joy in life and in his successes. He would have made it seem that he was telling her secrets that no one else knew, that he trusted her enough to reveal weakness that he would show only to her.

Jerilee must have realized why Morris had felt so sorry for him. His heart was broken, his children were lost to him, and every day was a challenge. Yet, somehow he gathered the strength to go on, to paste a smile on his face and go off to school to teach and to coach.

The stage was set for disaster. Before he was aware of all the circumstances and the many-faceted sides to Gabby's personality, Morris had invited a predator into his home. He had thought nothing of leaving Gabby alone with Jerilee. He was disgusted when he realized how much Gabby was drinking—disgusted and disappointed in the man he had once idolized, but Morris wasn't worried and he wasn't wary.

He should have been. At some point Jerilee's relationship with Gabby had metamorphosed. Gabby no longer grieved for his lost wife and family; he was in love with his best friend's wife. Although he didn't tell her right away, watching Jerilee may have made Gabby glad he was free. His wholehearted pursuit to win her love suggests that he didn't even reflect on the fact that *she* was not.

At first glance, it seemed highly unlikely that Gabby would be attractive to Jerilee. He was forty-two years old, and nowhere near as handsome as Morris. Morris had put on some weight but, underneath, he was still solid muscle. Gabby was soft and out of shape. He was not in good health, although the Blankenbakers didn't know how precarious Gabby's physical condition was. But Gabby had one big advantage: He was an unknown quantity to Jerilee. She had been with Morris since she was seventeen, and at twenty-seven she was no longer an immature teenage beauty queen. She was a lovely woman who had made a place for herself in the business world.

To Morris, Jerilee was still Jerilee. They had achieved the comfortable familiarity of a long-term marriage. Morris loved his wife devotedly but he was used to having her around. The exhilarating, breathtaking romance of a new relationship just wasn't there any longer. How could it be?

Gabby played on that; he pushed back any thoughts he had about the ethics of what he was doing to Morris. He had moved into his friend's life and he felt comfortable there. He wanted it all for himself. Gabby had always gone against the odds in sports. He was now prepared to beat the odds when it came to love. He wanted Jerilee Blankenbaker and he was ready to be whoever he had to be to win her away from Morris.

Morris and Jerilee's home now housed a three-adult family. If Morris noticed that Jerilee no longer complained about the nuisance of having Gabby live with them, he didn't mention it. He just hoped that Gabby would make other living arrangements as soon as possible. He wanted his old life back.

Morris may even have been relieved that Jerilee didn't complain any longer about the loss of their privacy or about the extra work it was to have Gabby live with them. Gabby seemed to enjoy being around five-year-old Rick and four-year-old Amanda too.

Apparently, Gabby never tired of looking at Jerilee. His eyes followed her appreciatively as she moved around her kitchen fixing supper and when she got her toddlers ready for bed. Although she was very intelligent, she was not an aggressive woman. She bent with seeming ease to the needs and requests of the men in her life. Jerilee had looked for so long to Morris for protection and approval. Now, subtly, it appears that she began to lean on Gabby. Although she had good female friends, she was a man's woman, soft and pretty and sweet.

No one but the participants knew just when the balance finally shifted in the Blankenbaker household. The change was cataclysmic, but it occurred so silently that it was as if a deep fissure in the earth had crunched one seismic plate against another and cracked every wall in the house. The marriage *looked* sound, but a gypsy wind blowing across the land could have flattened the whole thing. Obviously, Jerilee began to feel as if she were sleeping with the wrong man when she went to bed with her husband. She must have thought of the man in the guest bedroom, who was unquestionably thinking of *her* and seething at the situation.

No one who knew them or who encountered them later believes that Jerilee had planned to fall in love with Gabby, and it would probably be fair to say that he had not expected to fall in love with her. He had simply switched his obsession with Gay to Jerilee, with barely a pause in between. Even Gabby—who was quite used to having his own way—must have seen the shame of stealing the woman who belonged to the man who had literally saved his life, who had rescued him from drowning. Undoubtedly, Gabby recognized what he was about to do, but it didn't deter him.

It was Jerilee he wanted now and he was going to have her.

Gabby led Jerilee to believe that his financial picture was far brighter than it really was. He promised her that once they were married, he would buy her a wonderful brick house and that she could furnish it however she liked without ever worrying about the cost. The lifestyle he painted for her sounded secure and happy and without any problems at all. Gabby seemed to love her with a passion and a fervor that the more taciturn Morris had never demonstrated. Morris made commitments and kept them—that was the way he showed his love. Gabby was all fire and promises.

The very fact that Gabby was fifteen years older than Jerilee may have drawn her to him. She had felt so forlorn when her father divorced her mother, even though he remained a part of her life. Indeed, her father had been about Gabby's age when he left her mother. Gabby had the confidence of a mature man. He seemed a dependable rock:

half lover/half father. He was such a hero at Davis High School, and in Yakima itself. Morris had a teaching job too, of course, but he hadn't yet begun to achieve the status that Gabby had.

Whatever it was—chemistry, pragmatism, true love— Jerilee had become completely mesmerized by Gabby Moore. When he asked her to leave Morris and marry him, she accepted. It could not help but seem that she threw away her marriage with scarcely a backward glance.

Gabby had nothing to throw away; he was already figuratively on the street with a suitcase when Jerilee and Morris took him in. It wasn't that he was destitute—he had money—but he was not a man who could live by himself. He never had been.

Once they had admitted the obvious, there was apparently no going back for Jerilee and Gabby. It was spring in Yakima and the apple trees were blossoming. They were in love and they were not going to turn away from the overpowering emotion that swept over them. It had all happened in less than three months. . . .

When Jerilee told Morris that she was leaving him for Gabby, he was poleaxed. She was the only woman he had ever loved. But like many powerfully built men, Morris was gentle and not the kind to rage and threaten. He was too hurt. If Jerilee wanted a divorce, he would give it to her. There was nothing else for him to do. He let her walk away from him with one proviso, though. He made it clear that he still loved her. If she ever needed him, if she ever came to her senses, he would take her back.

Morris wasn't in a position to ask for custody of his children. Rick and Amanda were preschoolers. How would he take care of them? Olive couldn't be expected to take on the daily care of two little kids, and, besides, she was still working full-time. He knew that Jerilee would let him see them whenever he could, and so he didn't fight her for them. In his heart, he believed that she and the children would be coming back to him.

It happened with such swiftness. When 1974 began, Morris Blankenbaker had considered himself married for life. By March, only a little over two months later, Jerilee had filed for divorce. Since uncontested divorces in Washington State take ninety days, she was a free woman by June. She and Morris would have been married for nine years on August 28, but, of course, they never made it that far.

Coincidentally, Morris's marriage had lasted almost exactly as long as his parents' marriage.

Jerilee came back to Morris once, but only for a very brief time. She was pulled in two directions. Her conscience and the familiar warmth and dependability of the man she had left drew her back. But when she was living with Morris again, Gabby wouldn't let her alone. He was the most persuasive person she had ever encountered. He kept reminding her that *he* was the one she loved, and that he could not go on living without her. He played "their" song, and her resolve melted.

> Lay your head upon my pillow,
> Hold your warm and tender body close to mine.
> Hear the whisper of the raindrops falling soft
>   against the window,
> And make believe you love me one more time. . . .

Unlike most men in his situation, Morris was remarkably civilized. Although he was crushed by the betrayal of both his wife and his best friend, he actually allowed Gabby back in his house to discuss their dilemma. The three of them, each side of the hopeless triangle, had stilted, awkward discussions. Sometimes, Gabby would show up at suppertime and they all sat together at the table again, unspoken thoughts heavy in the air. It was as if there were some solution to be found, some ending where all three of them could be happy, and yet they all knew there was none. Whatever happened, one of them was going to lose.

Of them all, Morris was the strongest, heartbroken as he was. Gabby was full of bluster and persuasive arguments but he held on to Jerilee like the drowning man he had once been, and Jerilee was torn, caught in a situation she could never have imagined a few months earlier.

Olive Blankenbaker, still troubled by the tableau she encountered two decades ago, recalled an evening when she inadvertently walked in on one of those meetings. "I took two steaks over to Morris and Jerilee . . . and Moore was there. I said, 'I guess I should have brought *three* steaks. I didn't know you had company.' Gabby just hung his head and looked away. I even felt kind of sorry for him, but that was before I realized what he had done to Morris."

Years after it had all been played out, Olive could not speak of Gabby as anyone other than "Moore," and she could not keep the disgust and rage from her voice. For all of her life, she had worked to make her son happy and there had finally come a time when she had no power whatsoever to ease the searing pain he was suffering.

Hammering away at Jerilee with skewed logic and raw emotion and relentless pleas, it wasn't long before Gabby Moore had convinced her to leave Morris once again and come back to live with him.

This time, Morris realized his marriage was truly over.

When his life disintegrated, Morris Blankenbaker could not bear to be in Yakima any longer, despite the fact that his mother, his brothers, his children, and his friends were all there. Everywhere he went there were reminders of Jerilee. Worse, there was every likelihood that he would actually run into his wife with her new husband. Yakima wasn't big enough to avoid that.

Gabby Moore *was* Jerilee's new husband; he married her almost before the ink on her divorce papers was dry. He couldn't risk the possibility that she would change her mind.

On September 14, 1974, Jerilee Blankenbaker became Jerilee Moore. Along with Amanda and Rick and Gabby's sixteen-year-old son, Derek, she and Gabby formed a new family. As he had promised, Gabby bought a house for them all to live in. It wasn't quite as lavish as he had promised, but it was a nice house.

Morris's and Jerilee's children were very young. They must have been confused to find themselves in a different house, without their daddy, and to see their mother living with the man who had come to stay with them after Christmas.

The swiftness with which Morris's marriage had vaporized stunned everyone who knew him. In a big city, the exchange of marital partners might have gone relatively unnoticed, but in Yakima, Washington, everyone seemed to be talking about the scandal.

Morris moved to Hawaii, a long, long way from his memories of the year just past, from a dozen years of memories of Jerilee. The weather was tropical, the vegetation lush and exotic; nothing looked or smelled or felt the least bit like Yakima, Washington. He figured that maybe there he could forget Jerilee. But this geographical solution to a shattered world didn't work. Morris was still alone. His pain had followed him every mile of the way.

Knowing how lonesome Morris was, and missing him, a bunch of his friends withdrew their savings and booked passage to Hawaii to visit him. They had barely arrived when Olive was rushed to the hospital back in Yakima. She warned Morris's half brothers and her own sisters not to tell Morris she was sick and they promised that they wouldn't. But Olive's ex-husband, Ned, came to visit her and he misunderstood the doctors' assessment of her condition. Ned thought they had said that her condition was terminal.

"He got on the phone to Morris, and said, 'Come right home. Your mother is dying.' I was disgusted," Olive recalled. "The whole lot of them got on a plane with Morris and came back to see if I was okay. They all came home, after the kids had only been there for one day in Hawaii. Even Morris's half brother, Mike, sold his car—the only car he'd ever had—so he could go with them and cheer up Morris. I didn't even want Morris to know I was in the hospital . . . I wasn't that sick, and I would have been fine. It spoiled their whole trip."

Morris Blankenbaker had grown up in the icy winters of eastern Washington, and in Hawaii he felt like an alien in a foreign land. His world had been turned upside down and it wasn't better in Hawaii—it was worse. Someday he would have to accept that Jerilee was lost to him. It might as well be sooner as later. He missed his kids. He missed Yakima. He packed up and moved back home.

Morris found a big house on North Sixth Street, and he rented the extra bedrooms to some of his male friends. It wasn't the same as living with his own family, but he was a lot less lonely than he had been in Hawaii.

Morris was given a contract as a physical education teacher at Wapato Intermediate School. He was finally doing what he loved to do, but it was all ashes. Jerilee was gone. He only saw Amanda and Rick on sporadic visits. All the things he had worked for so long were gone.

His friends urged him to start dating—to stop being such a hermit—but he couldn't do it. When he tried, he felt as though he were an imposter. The only woman who meant anything to him was his wife—only she wasn't *his* wife anymore.

5

In September 1973, Jerilee Blankenbaker barely knew Gabby Moore; a year later she was divorced from Morris and married to him. Sometimes even she had trouble understanding how it could have happened.

At first, being with Gabby was romantic. There was no

question that he adored Jerilee. She liked his son, Derek, and she thought that probably she and Gabby could make their new his-and-hers family work, although it was only natural that it would take a while for all of them to adjust to each other. Where Morris had been easygoing and predictable, Gabby was moody and mercurial. That had been part of his attraction—in the beginning. The very excitement and the passion of being with this man whose emotions seesawed so wildly had drawn her to him. He had promised her so much. He had talked about their future and their love. His plans were grandiose and breathtaking. She had believed everything he told her. She had no reason not to—not at first.

In the mid-seventies Gabby Moore was still a very popular and respected man in Yakima. Townspeople crowded in to see his team's wrestling matches; he had put Yakima on the map with his wrestlers. He made a good salary; he had been at Davis High a long time, almost fifteen years. He was an institution, a tradition, and being his wife made Jerilee proud. Of course, there were those who whispered about how her second marriage had come about. But she held her head high. Her choice had been agonizing, but she had made it and she planned to stick by her new husband.

Even so, it wasn't long before Jerilee realized that some of Gabby's moods could be frightening. He revealed a side of his personality that she had not seen before. And many of his promises never came to fruition. He had led her to believe that he was very well fixed financially—and he wasn't. He had his salary, and that was about it.

In a sense, Jerilee was back where she had begun—married to a coach, raising a family, working full-time. Only the role of her husband had been recast.

One thing, however, was vastly different: Gabby Moore's consumption of alcohol. Morris had said something about it, but he had held back from telling her everything. Jerilee had not known that Gabby drank so heavily. Now she saw what she had not seen before. "He drank so very much. When he drank he became hostile toward anybody. . . . He yelled, and he grabbed hold of whoever was close and shook them."

Jerilee had never known anyone who could drink as much bourbon whiskey as Gabby Moore. In a voice still full of disbelief, Jerilee remembered how bad it became. "He even kicked his own family, *his daughter and his son,* out of the house on Christmas Eve.

"He drank very heavily," she would recall in her light, feminine voice. "Within a two- or three-hour period, he would drink a fifth of bourbon or whatever."

And Gabby's consumption of a bottle of whiskey in a few hours was not a sometime thing. Three or four times a week, he would sit with a bottle beside him, steadily downing shots until it was empty. Jerilee saw now that his moods had a direct correlation to the amount of liquor he put away.

"He loved you a lot one minute," she remembered ruefully. "And the next minute he would just kick you out of the house and I was getting a little bit scared of him."

Actually, Jerilee Moore was getting a *lot* scared of her second husband. Like most women married to alcoholics, she soon learned to chart precisely the progression from high spirits and loving sentimentality to suspicion and paranoia. When Gabby got close to the bottom of the whiskey bottle, he was a mean drunk. More than once, she found herself locked out of her own home. More than once, she must have wondered what on earth she had gotten herself into. Gabby could be insanely jealous. Perhaps he felt that she would leave *him* as easily as she had been lured away from Morris—that some other man could turn her head just as he had. He had stolen her; now he feared someone would steal her from him.

Three times, Jerilee did leave Gabby, even though she still felt a powerful attraction to him when he was himself. She was a woman torn by conflicting emotions. He could still make her cry when he put on his record that began, "Lay your head upon my pillow . . ."

But living in the center of a constant emotional hurricane was far different than the excitement of a rapid courtship, and Jerilee probably found herself longing for Morris's

ANN RULE

loving predictability. She saw Morris when he picked up Amanda and Rick or when she dropped them off. She talked to him on the phone, which was only natural since they still shared the responsibility for their children. They had such a long history together, and the longer she stayed away from Morris, the more Jerilee appreciated her first love and his steadfast devotion to her.

She had cut off so many ties that she almost felt obligated to make a go of her marriage. And that was not an easy task. When Gabby was out of control and full of rage he actually made her afraid for her life and for her children's lives. When he threw her out of the house, muttering the imprecations of a befuddled drunk, she had to find somewhere to run. To her family. To friends. Sometimes, she came back later in the night when she figured he would be asleep. Sometimes, she stayed away, hoping she would have the strength not to go back. Gradually, Jerilee began to make tentative moves away from Gabby. At first, she came back after a few days. Once, she managed to stay away for two weeks.

Each time Jerilee walked away from Gabby, he was instantly contrite. He turned on the charm and worked hard to convince her that he would never mistreat her again. She wanted to believe him.

It was a familiar pattern, but one that Jerilee had never had an occasion to understand before she fell in love with Gabby Moore. His tears and remorse were so utterly real to her. He knew her weaknesses and her tender heart. If he had been able to win her away from Morris and cut her neatly out of her marriage—and he had—he certainly was adept now at keeping her tied to him. He was her husband. Time after time, Jerilee believed his promises about a new start. Time after time, she went back to him.

All that spring of 1975, Jerilee vacillated. Outside, it was so like the spring a year before when she was falling in love with Gabby, when she was so transfixed by him and the way he painted their future together that she had forgotten everything else. But now, she was seeing the Gabby behind the charming mask and she was afraid.

42

Gabby had always been caught up in his coaching and his athletes. Having lived with Morris, Jerilee understood that. Coaches were a different breed. But Gabby didn't even care about sports any longer. Almost every other day, when he got home from work, he pulled a fifth of whiskey out of a brown bag. He usually drank it straight, out of a glass. Sometimes, he added a little Pepsi to the bourbon but it didn't keep him from getting drunk and argumentative. The worst thing was his unpredictability. Jerilee watched him warily, never knowing what to expect.

From the moment she fell in love with him, Jerilee had never even imagined she might want to leave Gabby. She had sacrificed her marriage for him; she had betrayed Morris when she committed herself to Gabby. But there came a moment when she listened to his importuning and only stared back coldly. She no longer believed that he was going to change. She had heard his promises too many times, and too many times had watched him turn and reach for his bottle of bourbon an instant later.

When all the periods of their actually being together were added up, it wasn't much time at all. Less than a year. Jerilee had married Gabby in September 1974. She left him for good in July of 1975. So when she filed for divorce this time, she would have two divorce decrees within eighteen months.

Jerilee Blankenbaker Moore had made an appalling decision when she left her first husband, and she saw that with the terrible clarity that the truth can bring. When she finally realized what she had done, she rushed to rectify her error. The longer she had been away from Morris, the more she had missed him and come to realize what a good man he was, that *he* was the man she loved. She had been momentarily bedazzled, but her eyes were open now.

In a sequence of events right out of a soap opera script, Jerilee left Gabby Moore's home and bed and moved back in with Morris Blankenbaker. It was a move that seared Gabby's soul, one that drove him nearly insane with jealousy. He drank to salve his pain, and drinking made him even more paranoid.

43

By 1975—if not earlier—Gabby Moore had come to a point where he saw everything that happened in the world in terms of how it affected *him*. He had no empathy, no sympathy. He had no rational or emotional ability to step back and view a situation from another person's point of view. If he had ever felt any guilt over betraying Morris, he fought it down before it could bubble to the surface of his mind. He could not now admit that Jerilee had been Morris's to begin with and that she had gone back to her husband and the father of her two little children. He could only beat his breast and cry out that he had been deeply wounded. The startling thing about Moore's position was that he believed that he was absolutely within his rights—that *he* was the injured party. He would have been astounded had anyone suggested otherwise.

His great love was gone, and he could not allow that to happen. The campaign that Gabby Moore mounted to win Jerilee back was prodigious—he used all of his considerable weapons.

When Jerilee and the children moved back in with Morris, he was still living in the big frame house on North Sixth. All of his roomers except for one had moved out, and he made plans to move soon. Morris, Jerilee, and the children occupied the downstairs until then.

If Jerilee had believed that Gabby would let her go without a fight, she soon found out she was mistaken. He called her every day—at the Pacific National Bank in Selah, Washington, where she worked and at the house where she lived with Morris. He made several trips to the bank to confront Jerilee at work. She had a good job as a loan interviewer, and it was embarrassing when one of her coworkers announced that Gabby Moore was waiting to see her.

She knew what he was going to say. He would ask her, "When are you coming back?" and "Won't you give me just one more chance?"

He told Jerilee that he wasn't going to make it without her, and she caught the manipulative threat. He was telling her that if he couldn't have her, he didn't want to live. When she refused to come back to him, he got more specific. He was going to kill himself, he said, and he wanted her to watch—to see what she had done to him.

Perhaps frightened by his threats of suicide, and worn down by his pleas, Jerilee may not have taken a strong enough stand with him. She may have agreed to meet him to talk more often than she would later admit to. There were those in Yakima who blamed her for being too "wishy-washy," and for not making the clean break that they felt would have kept Gabby Moore from pining after her.

Despite his drinking and his depression, Gabby had any number of people who loved him devotedly. His two daughters and his son came to Jerilee as emissaries from their father. Amanda and Rick had always followed Derek Moore around like puppy dogs, and they were thrilled when Gabby sent Derek over to take the children out for an ice-cream cone.

"I let them go," Jerilee said. "They thought a lot of Derek."

Gabby's daughters phoned Jerilee. They asked her what she thought she was accomplishing by leaving their father all alone. They blamed her for his pain.

"They asked me wouldn't I please go back and give their dad another try?" Jerilee recalled, and she said she simply could not go back to him again—ever.

She felt sorry for Gabby's children, and she could understand why they had come to her pleading his case. But there were things they didn't know. Once she was free of him, there was no way she was going back. She tried so many times to explain that to Gabby. She and Morris made plans to remarry shortly after her divorce from Gabby was final on November 10. They hoped to be married by Christmas. In time, she hoped that the whole episode with Gabby would be only a distant memory.

"I asked him very definitely to quit bothering me, [told him] that I was trying to start a new life; I wanted my family all back together and would he please quit harassing us."

Gabby had just stared at Jerilee as if she were speaking to him in a foreign language. He was never going to let her go. Didn't she know that? Whatever it took, he would do it.

Whatever she wanted, he would get for her. He would not accept that all she wanted from him was her freedom.

He just didn't get it. "He would say," Jerilee recalled, "'If it wasn't for Morris, you would be back with me.'"

But there *was* Morris, and she was grateful that he was still there for her. Nevertheless, she would not have stayed with Gabby even if Morris had turned his back on her. She could no longer live with Gabby's rages and his volatile moods.

In one of their conversations, Gabby told Jerilee—almost with a flourish—the depths to which she had made him sink. "I'm losing my job," he told her, "and it's because of you."

He told her that he had been asked to resign from Davis High School and that he had been told his contract would not be renewed after the 1975–76 school year. In June of 1976, he would be through. He told her that he had been fired because he'd lost his temper with some of the student drivers, that he'd grabbed them and shaken them when they were driving and made a mistake. *That* must have stunned both the students and the administrators. Gabby had always been the soul of patience with his driver-training kids.

Jerilee suspected that it was more than his behavior in his driver-training sessions that had led to Gabby's dismissal. Yakima was too small a town for the school administrators not to know about his drinking and his profound personality change. Even so, he was such an institution at Davis that it seemed impossible they would ever ask him to leave. He would have had to do something pretty bad to get fired. But, if Gabby had expected her to come back to him because he'd been fired, he was mistaken. *He* was the one who had ruined his career.

Jerilee was afraid of Gabby. He asked her to postpone their divorce date, to give him some time before she finalized it, but she was adamant that she was going ahead. When November 10 came, both Jerilee and Gabby were in the courthouse. One of the things she had requested in her divorce was that she have the name "Blankenbaker" back. When Gabby Moore heard that, he was visibly upset.

She had rejected even his name.

Jerilee got Morris's last name back and she got her divorce, but Gabby didn't go away. In fact, he became even more aggressive and insistent that he couldn't live without her *after* their divorce than he had been before.

It would be impossible to explain the siege Jerilee Blankenbaker was enduring to anyone but another woman who has had a man fixate on her. It is akin to being in a glass house where none of your movements are entirely free, where someone is always watching.

Both Jerilee and Morris were working; in fact Morris was working *two* jobs. He taught at Wapato Intermediate School and he worked three evenings a week at the Lion's Share Lounge as a bouncer. That meant leaving Jerilee alone at night, but they had "Hike," their big black Labrador who was very protective of Jerilee and the children.

Gabby had come three times to Morris's home in his desperate battle to get Jerilee to come back. Morris wasn't really worried that Gabby would do anything crazy. Despite everything, Gabby was still "Coach" to him. Morris figured that in time everything would work out.

Late one night in mid-November when Morris was working at the Lion's Share, Jerilee woke to hear someone walking around inside the house. There were no locks on the exterior doors. In a big city, that would have seemed foolhardy, but this was Yakima, where the crime rate was low. People didn't lock their doors, even when they lived— as the Blankenbakers did—only a few blocks from the downtown business district. Morris and Jerilee had a lock on their bedroom door though, to keep the kids from walking in.

Now, Jerilee, her children asleep beside her, lay frozen in bed as she heard heavy footsteps and crashing sounds. She was grateful for the bedroom door lock as she heard someone call her name and then unintelligible grumbling and muttering.

It was Gabby.

"He had been drinking," Jerilee remembered, "and he threatened if I didn't come out into the living room area

47

that he would kick in the door and come after me. He wasn't very rational at the time; he was quite drunk."

She had a phone in the bedroom and she reached for it quietly and dialed the number at the Lion's Share.

"Morris," she whispered, when he came to the phone. "Gabby's here. He's out in the living room and he's threatening to kick my door in."

Morris left the Lion's Share and headed for the house on North Sixth. It wasn't far; the bar was on Second Street.

Jerilee stayed quiet in her bedroom, listening, expecting to hear the crash of a foot through the thin bedroom door at any moment. She knew how Gabby could be when he was this drunk, and she was afraid, remembering some of the threats he had made.

It had become very quiet in the living room. Jerilee hoped that Gabby had given up and left. But then, suddenly, there was a banging crash on her window. Gabby was outside, yelling at her through the closed window. He was determined to get to her, to talk to her, to hold her in his arms.

Maybe this was the night he was going to kill himself in front of her. . . .

Joey Watkins* had known both Morris and Gabby for a long time. Seven or eight years before, when he was at Davis, Morris was an assistant coach on the teams Joey turned out for. Joey was a big guy—one of the heavyweights that Morris had helped coach. And, of course, Gabby was head wrestling coach when Joey wrestled.

Later, Joey, twenty-two, recalled the incident that night in November. "Well, I was sitting in the Lion's Share with Morris and we was talking, and like here the phone rang and a lady answers and said, 'It's for you, Morris,' and so Morris got the phone and it was his wife and she said that Mr. Moore was banging around on her house and stuff, and he said he would be over and he asked me to go with him, so I went over there with him. . . . Mr. Moore was 'bamming' on the windows."

It was apparent that Gabby Moore was drunk, and Joey Watkins half-expected Morris to start fighting with him.

After all, it was Morris's house, and Morris's woman, and she had sounded scared half to death when she called the Lion's Share.

"Morris got out of the car and went over there. But he said to me, 'Joey, you know what? I would hit him in the mouth, but he was my coach too. I can't do it.' So they just went over there and started talking. Mr. Moore and Morris was talking, and I guess Morris told him something and he just left."

Joey Watkins stared at his former coach. Gabby was so intoxicated that he had been staggering as he moved from window to window, beating on the glass with his fists. Like most of the young men who had turned out for sports at Davis High, Watkins had been flabbergasted at the change in Gabby.

"He was my football coach and wrestling coach ever since I was a sophomore in high school. . . . I seen Mr. Moore the first time [in a bar] when I was in the Lion's Share and he was wild, you know . . . like he just changed from the coach that we used to see because he was strict, you know, on us. He wasn't the same person. For one thing, his hair was longer and he just didn't dress like he used to."

After Joey saw Gabby in the bar the first time, he had seen him often. Gabby had always been with a crowd of friends, and he was drinking like there was no tomorrow. That just wasn't the coach Joey remembered. Gabby had always demanded that his athletes train hard. "If you got beat," Watkins said, "he knows why—because you didn't work out hard enough."

Joey Watkins couldn't hear what Morris had said to Gabby, but whatever it was it was effective. He saw Gabby stagger away, and then he heard the sound of a car starting up. He knew the sound of that engine; it was Gabby's little caramel-colored MG sports car.

Inside, Jerilee had listened to Morris's voice trying to reason with Gabby. She could make out only the faint mumble of deep voices and then the sound of a car leaving.

"Morris and Joey Watkins came into the house," Jerilee

said. "And then Morris called the police department and told them the story and they said they would send a patrol car just to go by off and on during the night. Morris went back to work."

And, apparently, Gabby went home to sleep it off. No one seemed to take the incident too seriously. Half the police department had taken a class from him, or played ball for him, or wrestled for him. Some had gone to school with him when he was a star himself. Gabby wasn't a threat—not really. Gabby was "Coach" and one of the finest teachers Davis High ever had.

He just had to get hold of himself.

6

Everyone who knew Gabby Moore believed that he would come to his senses. He had far too much to lose to let himself go over a woman. There were plenty of women in Yakima who would have been delighted to go out with him. But he wasn't interested any more than Morris had been interested when he was left alone the year before. When men fell in love with Jerilee, they didn't seem able to forget her.

That bitter fall, Gabby was living in an apartment with his son, Derek, out on South Eighteenth Street. He didn't want to live in the house where he had lived with Jerilee, and put it up for sale. The apartment he shared with seventeen-year-old Derek wasn't fancy, but it worked for two guys "batching it." Derek had the small bedroom off the kitchen. They ate what meals they took at home at the kitchen counter that separated that room from the rest of the apartment. Gabby turned the living room into a combination bedroom/living room by putting his bed in there and blocking the front door with a wardrobe. They parked out in back on the alley side and used the back door as the only entrance.

Gabby was still coaching and teaching although his contract would be up at the end of the school year. He was almost "phoning in" his participation at school, simply going through the motions, and mostly he didn't even bother with that. Gabby's wrestling team still turned out for practice and showed up at matches even if their coach wasn't the fireball he had once been. Sometimes it seemed they almost coached themselves, but they loved Gabby and covered for him.

In an unspoken pact, some of the athletes who had graduated from Davis started showing up after school to take over Gabby's duties. He had made his wrestlers champions and they would do anything for him. Between the alumni and the kids on the squad, the wrestling matches went on—mostly without Gabby.

Derek Moore was doing well in school, and he was a first team starter for the Davis High School "Pirates" football team. Any other time, his father would have been bursting with pride over his accomplishments in the athletic world. But now, nothing mattered to Gabby but getting Jerilee back.

Derek cut his dad a lot of slack. Like everyone else who knew Gabby Moore, he believed that things were going to be better in time. Derek was a strong kid who had a lot of emotional support—his grandparents, his mother, his new stepfather Larry Pryse, who was an assistant football coach at Davis.

At seventeen, Derek Moore's whole world was wrapped up in Yakima, in high school athletics, and in his girlfriend. Loyally, he lived with his dad and hoped for better days.

Dr. Myers, Gabby's former father-in-law, was extremely concerned about him. A.J. had been treating Gabby for hypertension for a decade, and he suspected that he wasn't taking his prescribed medication—a beta blocker and a diuretic. Gabby would take the medicine Myers prescribed all right, but then he would begin to feel better and, like many patients with high blood pressure, he would stop taking his pills. It was a vicious circle. Hypertension is a silent disease with few symptoms. A lot of patients die of strokes or heart attacks because they "feel fine" and they have no hint that the push of blood against fragile blood vessels has become critical. Sometimes, extremely high blood pressure causes headaches. Not often. The only sure sign of trouble is a nosebleed. If that happens, the patient is lucky. It is far better to bleed from an artery in the nose than to bleed, silently and lethally, from an artery in the brain.

Gabby was drinking heavily and he was stressed to the maximum. In addition, he wasn't taking his medication. Dr. Myers met him for lunch in November and tried to talk some sense into him. He warned him that he was going to blow out an artery if he didn't pay attention. But Gabby Moore didn't seem to care. All he could talk about was Jerilee. If he couldn't have her back, he didn't want to live, anyway.

Myers nodded. It didn't matter that his daughter was Gabby's first ex-wife since she was happily remarried. Now they were just two men talking as friends, and it was Gabby who was left out in the cold and in seeming agony over it.

Myers hoped it wasn't going to flat out kill him.

It looked as though it might, when on the 18th of November, a few days after the incident at Jerilee and Morris's house, Gabby showed up at Dr. Myers's office and asked for an appointment.

"He reported to me that he had had repeated nosebleeds for the past twenty-four hours—a total of four of them—which were difficult to stop," Myers said. "He appeared at my office following one of these. . . . Because of his blood pressure and the history of four nosebleeds in twenty-four hours, I decided to hospitalize him."

It wouldn't be the first time that Gabby's hypertension

became critical; Dr. Myers had been treating him for high blood pressure for ten years. He had had to hospitalize him for the same condition five years earlier, almost to the day. Now, Myers was really concerned; he could see that there was a clot on the arterial opening in the midsection of Gabby's left nostril. Gabby was going to be in trouble if he didn't get his blood pressure lowered and right away.

Gabby didn't want to go to the hospital; he just wanted Dr. Myers to give him something to stop the nosebleeds. Myers wouldn't listen to his arguments—not with such sky-high pressure registering on his sphygmomanometer. It didn't matter that Gabby was only forty-four, he was in danger of dying—and soon. With Gabby complaining all the way, Dr. Myers checked him into his own hospital, the Valley Osteopathic Hospital, at 3003 Tieton Drive.

From November 18 until November 22, Gabby Moore stayed in his hospital bed in a room just across the hall from the nursing station. He tried to check himself out earlier, but Myers would not allow him to go.

Jerilee knew that Gabby was in the hospital. His mother had called to tell her after he had been there for a day. Although she felt bad for his mother, she had disconnected emotionally from Gabby.

In a way, Gabby's illness and hospitalization made Thanksgiving a much happier day for Morris and Jerilee Blankenbaker. For two blissful days, he didn't call and he didn't show up to pound on windows or demand to be let in. They were back together for their first big holiday in this, the second phase of their marriage.

Thanksgiving meant so much more to them this year. They were fortunate to have salvaged what had been a good marriage, to be able to forgive and forget, and to start over.

Both Morris and Jerilee had to work on the day after Thanksgiving. He didn't have to teach, of course, because it was a school holiday, but he was due at the Lion's Share at eight that Friday night. Jerilee had to work all day at the bank, and Morris stayed home and looked after Rick and Amanda. He was so happy to have his kids back, to have her

53

back. They needed time, but they would regain the comfortable, secure world they had known before Gabby moved in with them.

While Jerilee didn't know if Gabby was still in the hospital, she hadn't heard from him and that was a good sign. "When I got home from work about six-thirty," she said, "Morris and the children and I went out to Shakey's for dinner, and Morris then took us home and dropped us off before eight o'clock."

Jerilee had planned to stay home all evening on Friday, but a friend, Helen Crimin, dropped by around nine and asked her if she wanted to go and listen to Helen's husband play in his band. He was an officer on the Yakima Police Department and he and some fellow policemen had formed a band that was playing at a cocktail lounge called the Country Cousin. Helen's invitation sounded like fun. Jerilee called her mother-in-law and Olive said she'd be glad to look after Rick and Amanda if Jerilee would bring them over to her mobile home. Olive had bought the double-wide trailer to use as an office, and now she made her home there.

"We stopped by the Lion's Share before we went to the Country Cousin so that I could tell Morris that I was going over there," Jerilee recalled. "We left about a quarter to ten. Then my girlfriend and I went down to the cocktail lounge and listened to her husband play . . . oh, probably ten songs."

Although she went to the clubs with some trepidation, Jerilee was relieved to find that Gabby wasn't in either of them. She and Helen had a good time and she began to breathe a little more easily. "We left and went to my mother-in-law's to pick up the children and then we went straight home to Sixth Street. It was about eleven o'clock when we got home."

When Helen Crimin's car pulled up in front of the Blankenbakers' house, everything looked normal. Still, Helen sensed that Jerilee was a little nervous, and she walked her and the children to the front door to be sure they got in all right, and that nobody was hanging around.

The house was quiet. Everything was just as Jerilee had

left it. Hike seemed calm as he padded around, following her as she got Amanda and Rick ready for bed, a good sign that nobody had been in the house.

Still, Jerilee felt a little jittery with Morris at work, and she tucked the children in bed with her. She could move them after two when Morris got home. She didn't set an alarm clock; she knew she would wake up when she heard Morris come home.

Something woke Jerilee at two. Some loud noise. She wasn't sure what it was, but she rolled over and looked at the clock next to the bed. It was right around two. "I realized Morris would be coming home soon," she said, "so I took the children out of the bed and put them in their own beds. Then I went back to bed myself."

It was cold, and she snuggled under the blankets. She didn't fall back to sleep because it was only a few minutes before she heard Morris's car drive in back in the alley, its tires crunching on the frozen ground. "I heard our car door shut. And then I thought that I heard two more car doors shut, and Morris didn't come in."

She wasn't worried. They had had three days without any trouble at all, and Morris had so many friends. Hike hadn't even barked, as he would if a stranger were outside. She assumed that someone had asked Morris to go out for a couple of drinks after work and that they had followed him home to pick him up.

She heard male voices coming from the back of the house someplace out toward the alley. They were excited sounding, high-pitched. She strained to hear what they were saying. It wasn't much—maybe ten words or so.

"I stayed in bed about a half hour," Jerilee remembered. "And then I got up and went to the back window and looked out, and I saw that our car was there. So then I went outside and went to the car and looked inside the car, and nobody was there so I went back in the house—went back to bed."

Morris had actually been driving *her* car that night—the forest green Chevy Malibu. It was parked there, and it looked just the same as always. She didn't expect Morris to be gone very long. While she was outside, Jerilee hadn't looked around very much; she was very nearsighted and she had removed her contact lenses, so it wouldn't have done much good to look around. But she did see her car parked in the back, and the Volkswagen that Morris usually drove was in the carport. They were both there, and that was enough to ease her mind.

It was dark and it was cold and she could barely see her hand in front of her face. Once inside, Jerilee shivered at the thought of going back outside. Vaguely uneasy, she read for a while until she fell back to sleep. The children slept peacefully in the other bedroom, and Hike snoozed on the floor beside her.

At five, Jerilee woke with a start. She was cold, and the other side of the bed was empty. *Where was Morris?* This wasn't like him. She tried to remember if he'd said anything about going somewhere after work, and she couldn't remember a thing. She was positive he had planned to come home after the Lion's Share closed.

She couldn't very well call the police. What would she tell them? That her husband was three hours late getting home? There were probably a lot of husbands in Yakima who were a lot later than that.

But Morris would have called her.

Jerilee dialed the number she had for Mike Blankenbaker, Morris's half brother. "I called Mike and asked him if he knew what Morris had planned to do after work," Jerilee said. "He said that he was going to come straight home to me. So then I was worried and I said, 'Well, the car is here but he hasn't come in.' And Mike said, 'Well, just stay where you are and I'll come down and check things out.'"

Jerilee was beginning to feel a little less nervous. She said that she would take Hike with her and look around outside the house. "I think it will be okay," she told her brother-in-law. He promised to wait on the phone while she checked.

Jerilee's hand was steady as she put her contact lenses in. There had to be a simple explanation for where Morris was. It wasn't like him to drink too much, but, if he had, he was probably asleep at a friend's house.

"I went out the front door and the dog ran ahead of me and started growling and barking at something on the ground. I couldn't tell right then what it was," she recalled quietly. "But when I got there, I saw that it was Morris. . . ."

Shock—the kind that congeals the blood and makes the heart race out of sync—also dulls the senses. When something bad happens, so bad that the world will never, ever be the same again, the human mind cannot take it in all at once. Jerilee Blankenbaker had not yet acknowledged that *her* world had changed forever. At that moment, as she moved toward the man who lay facedown on the snowy ground, she had the tremendous strength that comes with an adrenaline rush. He lay just inside the gate, his feet pointed back toward the alley. He had fallen forward in an almost perfectly straight line.

"I rolled him over," Jerilee said, speaking of a man who weighed 210 pounds. "And tried to pull him toward me. I felt his face and I thought I felt something on his face. I thought it was mud at that time. And he was really heavy. I mean, he didn't help me at all. . . ."

A long time later when she spoke about it, Jerilee Blankenbaker's voice had the thinnest layer of calm over the remembered terror of that moment. "I took a hold of his jacket on his right side and rolled him toward the house, which would be north, and then I pulled him into a sitting position toward me with his jacket. . . . And I think that I tried to hear a heartbeat . . . and then I laid him back down."

Jerilee remembered running inside the house and picking up the phone where her husband's brother still waited on the line. "Mike," she cried. "Come quick. Morris has blood all over him."

Within a few minutes, Mike Blankenbaker was on his way to help Jerilee, and, he prayed, to help his brother. And so were the Yakima police.

7

Dennis Meyers had been a patrol officer for the Yakima Police Department for six years, and he was working the early shift—four A.M. to noon—on November 22. He got a call from the police dispatcher at 5:03 that morning to proceed to 210 North Sixth Street "in regards to a subject at that location being covered with lots of blood."

That was all Meyers knew at that point. He half-expected to find some drunk with a bloody nose. He was seven blocks away from the location when he got the call, and he was there in a few minutes. Meyers saw a woman standing in front of the house. "She was standing there and crying."

The officer walked up to the woman who led him around to the south side of the house and showed him a man lying on his back. It was still almost dark and Meyers used his flashlight to examine the "man down." The fallen man wore jeans, athletic shoes, and an open down jacket. His right leg was crossed almost casually over his left, and his arms rested on the ground. There was a great deal of blood on his face and seeping into the grass and snow next to his left hand.

Meyers didn't recognize the man, but the woman told him that it was her husband: Morris Blankenbaker. Everyone in Yakima knew Morris, but it would have been hard for anyone to recognize him with so much blood on his face.

More police began to arrive and Meyers tried to calm Jerilee Blankenbaker, who was still sobbing and nearly hysterical, as Officer Terry Rosenberry knelt beside the supine man and checked for signs of life. None were discernible.

While Meyers and Rosenberry and Patrol Sergeant Pleas Green waited for Sergeant Robert Brimmer, the Yakima police's chief investigator of homicides and a nineteen-year veteran of the department, they did not approach the body. Time seemed to stretch into hours, but it was actually only fifteen minutes until Brimmer arrived. The patrol officers led him back to the body, and he noted that the blood on the ground was clotted; whatever had happened had occurred some time before the police were called.

It was an eerie scene in the gray half-dawn. An empty Budweiser beer bottle nudged the dead man's right foot and a section of Lincoln log lay near the body, left behind, probably, by the victim's small son.

A dark green Chevrolet was pulled up beyond the gate area, near the alley. Brimmer directed Meyer to check it out, and he found that Morris's keys were still in the car, dropped on the floor on the driver's side. His bank statement lay on the seat. Just as Morris had no locks on his exterior doors, he didn't bother hiding his keys. He had not expected trouble.

Don Washburn of the Yakima Ambulance Company was also a deputy coroner. Actually, the ambulance service had gotten the first call for help from the Blankenbaker house, and it was the ambulance company that had called the police. Washburn had driven in around 5:25 A.M. It was he who officially pronounced Morris Blankenbaker dead. He had been dead for hours; rigor mortis—the condition where a human body "freezes" into position after death— had begun. The victim's jaw and shoulders were already hard to move. It was difficult to be certain with so much blood, but he seemed to have been shot in the face. There appeared to be a bullet wound—an entry wound—through his upper lip.

It was the ambulance attendants who put a sheet over the body—not police procedure because evidence can inadvertently be transferred from the body to the sheet and vice versa. Brimmer wasn't happy to see this and removed the sheet carefully so that they could take photographs of the

59

body. Two decades later, sheets would be flung over the
bodies of Nicole Simpson and Ron Goldman. It is a natural
reaction to shelter the dead from prying eyes. Morris
Blankenbaker, Yakima's football hero and a friend to scores
of people, was lying dead, staring blindly as snowflakes
dotted his body. With his "wife" sobbing hysterically and
his small children inside the house, it had seemed the
decent thing to do. Then with the help of the investigators,
the ambulance attendants lifted Morris's body to a gurney
and put it in the ambulance for the short trip to the St.
Elizabeth's Hospital morgue to await autopsy.

The police at the scene searched the grounds for more
evidence. Brimmer, Rosenberry, and Lt. Bernie Kline
combed the area at the south side of the house, along the
wire fence between the yard and the apartment house, and
moved on to the back where Morris's car was parked, and
then into the alley itself. They had to use their flashlights at
first. Sometimes, the refracted beam of a flashlight can help
find minute bits of evidence as it hits the shiny side of a
shell casing, a bullet fragment, a key, something that might
lie hidden on the lawn or beneath a bush. The grass hadn't
been mowed and it was three or four inches high. They
searched trash cans in the alley in the faint hope that
someone had tossed the murder gun away in his—or *her*—
flight.

They found nothing.

They desperately needed to find some piece of physical
evidence that could lead them to Morris Blankenbaker's
killer. His executioner, really. They already had part of a
possible scenario. Morris Blankenbaker had arrived home,
stashed his keys on his car floor, and strolled through the
gate of his yard. Quite probably, the open beer bottle had
been in his hand. A man in fear of his life would not have
been carrying a bottle of beer. His ex-wife had found him
lying on his face and had somehow managed to turn him
over. It would have taken the kind of strength that lets
women lift cars off their children; Morris was a big man, a
solid man, and she was such a delicate woman.

The blood on the ground would have come from his facial

wounds; he had bled profusely in the moments before he died. In her vain attempt to save his life, Jerilee had managed to flip Morris over; the blood marked where he had lain.

Maybe an autopsy would give them some information. Maybe there was a bullet in Morris's head that they could trace to a gun. From the appearance of the wounds, Brimmer's long experience suggested to him that the gun had been a small-caliber weapon—possibly a .22.

Carefully, as a pale sun cast light on their cheerless work, Brimmer's team measured every inch of the Blankenbaker yard and the porch, and then measured again from one set point. Later, this would enable them to triangulate their findings and place the body and all the bits and pieces of evidence—so few—in the exact spot where they had been found.

Their precise work kept them from facing the terrible question that kept echoing. Who on earth would shoot Morris Blankenbaker? *Everybody liked Morris. . . .*

The word that Morris Blankenbaker had been murdered spread throughout town to almost everyone who had ever known him, and that was half of Yakima. Long before the headlines hit, everyone who mattered knew.

Olive Blankenbaker will never forget the way she heard the worst news of her life. From the moment he was born, she had worried about her only child, but she had fought her natural inclination to warn him to be careful. All through his football days, and then when he was in the service, and working in the mental hospital, and climbing telephone poles in all kinds of weather, she had worried, but she had determinedly kept her mouth shut. In the end she had raised a man's man, but a gentle sensitive man too.

Olive was asleep early on that Saturday morning after Thanksgiving. She didn't know that the police and Mike Blankenbaker were trying to locate the best person to inform her that her son was dead. "They finally went and got my sister. Hazel came and got me out of bed," Olive remembered. "She just said it right out, 'Olive, Morris has been shot.' And I said, 'Is he dead?' and she said, 'Yes.' I just wanted to know, to get it over with in a hurry. I knew he was dead from the moment she took ahold of my hand. I really thought that I was going to die right on the spot. I thought 'This is *too* bad. Nothing this bad has ever happened to me before, and I can't take it. I'm not going to survive this. I'm going to die tonight.'"

Wild with grief, Olive Blankenbaker asked silently why it had to be Morris, her only son. Why couldn't it have been someone else's son—someone who had ten kids—it might be easier for them. She knew that wasn't true, and that wasn't the way she usually thought, but she could not bear the idea of living her life out without Morris. She had no husband, her sisters had their own lives, the boss she'd loved to work for was dead in a plane crash. Now the future yawned ahead of her empty of everything she had ever cared about.

Olive had no idea who had shot Morris; she couldn't conceive how anyone could have wanted to hurt him, much less kill him.

Robert Brimmer returned to the police station, and he and his investigators started their incident report procedure. "At that time," he said, "we started contacting witnesses or people to talk to. They started coming in after eight-thirty that morning."

Brimmer, a tall, lanky, laconic man in his forties, whose smiles were infrequent, was in charge of almost every major crime that came into the Yakima detective unit: homicide, arson, assault, armed robbery. If he was occasionally short-tempered, he was always fair and he treated every man who worked for him equally.

Some of the information Brimmer had elicited thus far in the Blankenbaker case was no help at all, some might prove to be, and some was startling. It would take a while to check it all out, but first there was the postmortem examination to attend.

The word *autopsy* by definition roughly means to "see for one's self." Everyone who attended Morris Blankenbaker's autopsy would be there to see what had happened to him—medically, clinically, ballistically. They could not allow themselves to consider the emotional aspect of this crime. Not now.

Dr. Richard Muzzall was the Yakima County Coroner. In Washington State, counties can choose whether they want to have a medical examiner or a coroner. Yakima and many of the smaller counties have coroners who are medical doctors but have not had extensive training in the science of death examination. In the old days, some counties didn't even require that coroners be doctors. Muzzall, however, had more experience than most coroners. He had worked as a deputy coroner in the Minneapolis area before moving to Yakima. By the time he stood over Morris Blankenbaker's body, he had performed approximately 150 autopsies.

It was ten o'clock in the morning on November 22; Morris had been dead about eight hours, his body had been discovered only five hours before. Just the evening before, he had been laughing with Jerilee and their children as they ate pizza at Shakey's. Only two days ago, he had sat down to Thanksgiving dinner. And within the month, he and Jerilee would have remarried and the scars of the past two years would have begun to heal over.

Now that was not to be.

Three men stood in the autopsy room with Dr. Muzzall: Sergeant Brimmer, Eric Gustafson, a Yakima County Deputy District Attorney, and a young detective named Vern Henderson. Henderson swallowed hard and fought to maintain a professional distance from the dead man before him. It wasn't easy; Vern Henderson and Morris Blankenbaker had played football together at Davis High School. More than that—so *much* more than that—they had been best friends since they were thirteen years old. If any detective on the force had a special reason to want to find Morris's killer, it was Vern Henderson. Brimmer glanced covertly at Vern to see if he could handle this and, satisfied that he could, looked again at the perfect athlete's body on the table.

Vern Henderson had long since learned to hide his feelings, and his face was without expression. "I had been to a lot of autopsies by then, even to some where I knew the person. But I'd never been to one where the subject was such a good friend as Morris was. It was hard on me to go, but I wanted to know everything that had happened to him," Henderson said. "Because, see, I knew in my own mind that if they didn't find him [the killer] right away, I was going to have to look. I wanted to know what happened and you can only know if you go to the autopsy. I wanted to know the facts, so when I heard things, I'd know if it really happened that way or not."

Before the body was undressed and washed, photographs and measurements were taken. The four men took notes and observed minute details that would not have been significant to men in other professions.

Morris had always had a thick head of hair, and he had recently grown a mustache and a short beard. His face and beard were still stained with dried blood. When he was undressed and examined, it was clear that there were no injuries to his body. All the damage had been done to his head.

That he had been shot was evident both in the appearance of the wounds and in the gun barrel debris that was still present in his hair and on his skin. Muzzall pointed to the wound he felt had been the first, a shot fired while Morris was standing. It had pierced the upper lip at the center line and knocked out two front teeth before it embedded itself against the base of the spine just below the spot where the occipital portion of the skull joined the spinal column. The mouth wound itself, Muzzall felt, would not have caused death. However, the area where the spinal cord joins the brain is the control center of the human body. It regulates breathing and heart rate, and a bullet striking there might well have caused respiratory arrest. At the very least, this shot would have knocked the victim off his feet.

Morris had been lying on his face when Jerilee found him. Either the shooter had been in front of him, or the force of

A Fever in the Heart

the first shot had spun him around as he fell. Muzzall
pointed out the "freckles" of unburned gunpowder that had
tattooed the victim's face. Tiny black dots extended up to
the forehead, into the hairline and down into the beard for a
distance of about three and a half inches from the lip
wound. This meant that the killer had stood quite close to
Morris when he fired and hit him in the mouth.

The second and third wounds had been delivered when
Morris was down. They entered just behind the left ear and
traveled horizontally through the brain, causing fatal damage. The second bullet had lodged against the skull on the
right side, traveling at a slight upward angle. The third
bullet entered the head just below the second and traveled
forward and again slightly upward, ending in the frontal
lobe of the brain. This third wound had dark gunpowder
rimming it; it had almost been a *contact* wound. Each of
these two shots could be considered "execution style"
wounds. The killer had leaned over the prone man and held
the murder weapon very close behind the victim's ear. Each
was a fatal shot.

Whoever had shot Morris Blankenbaker had wanted to be
very sure that he was dead. Morris had probably seen the
first shot coming, if only at the last moment, Muzzall
explained. He lifted Morris's right hand. It was flecked with
dried blood. "This is blowback," he commented. "Here on
the back, side, and even the palm of his hand. I would say
the first bullet to strike him was the one to the mouth. . . .
He would have had to have been in an upright position, to
be raising his hand in front of his face, to get this blowback
of blood from the lip wound. If he had been shot behind the
ear first, he would have fallen on the ground, and his hand
would not have been in a position to catch this blowback."

Morris had no other wounds beyond a small scratch on
his nose, probably sustained when he fell. There was the
characteristic bruising around his eyes almost always present with a head shot—quite consistent with the brain
damage and bleeding behind his eyes. His knuckles were
smooth. He hadn't hit anyone. His clothing wasn't torn. All
he had time to do was hold up his hand in a futile attempt to

protect his head from the gun he saw in his killer's fist. Morris had been a tremendously strong man; given a chance, he would have put up an awesome fight for his life.

Vern Henderson knew that. He had never seen anyone take Morris—not in a fair fight. Morris was—*had been,* he told himself—as strong as a bull moose.

But he clearly had not been given any warning. Brimmer and Henderson knew that the victim was due home shortly after two, and that Jerilee thought she had heard his car about then. She hadn't heard gunshots—although others had—and had probably mistaken the shots for "car doors slamming." His dog hadn't barked. Whoever was outside was someone familiar to the victim's black Lab. Hike was a guard dog, but he was as friendly as a pup to people he recognized.

Someone must have known Morris's habits, or someone had followed him from the Lion's Share. Whoever it was, Morris hadn't been afraid when his killer came up to him. He was probably carrying the open bottle of beer in his hand, a bottle that fell at his feet when he was shot. He hadn't shouted out a threat or a warning. He hadn't called out for help.

Muzzall routinely took a blood sample, which he would send to the Washington State Toxicology Laboratory at the University of Washington in Seattle for analysis.

Muzzall removed some battered slugs and a number of bullet fragments from the victim's skull. Their combined weight suggested strongly that they were .22s. Robert Brimmer marked them into evidence and locked them in a file cabinet in his office until he could mail them to the Washington State Police Crime Lab for testing. The casings (or shells) that had once held them had not been found. If the murder gun was a revolver, the cylinder would have retained the casings until the shooter deliberately tipped them out. If the gun had been an automatic, it would have ejected the shell and slid a new bullet into firing position after every shot.

They couldn't be sure which kind of gun they were looking for. If the gun was an automatic, there should be shells at the crime scene. The investigators hadn't found any yet, but they had had to search in dim light in high grass with patches of snow on the ground. For all they knew, the bullet casings were still lying somewhere on the Blanken-baker's lawn.

Sergeant Brimmer had locked the Budweiser bottle and the Lincoln log in the evidence vault on the second floor of the Yakima Police Department. He dusted the brown bottle now with light fingerprint powder, but he could bring up nothing but smudges; there were no distinctive loops, ridges, or whorls that might give him the information that either the victim or the killer had held that bottle.

One of the most convoluted murder investigations the Yakima detectives had ever known—an intricate murder probe that *any* big city detective would have found baffling—was just beginning.

One of the people Brimmer talked to early on was a staff member at Davis High School. For the first time, he learned that there "was an indication of hard feelings between Morris and Mr. Moore."

It was like the first little wisp of smoke from a smoldering hidden fire. Brimmer knew Gabby, and he couldn't imagine the beloved coach would do something like shoot a friend in the face and the back of the head. But he would have to look into it.

When Jerilee came out of the worst of her shock and hysteria, she thought of the only person she knew who had resented Morris. As impossible as it seemed—even to her—she began to wonder, and she felt she had to mention her doubts to the police. Gabby had always told her that she would come back to him, if it weren't for Morris. She knew that Gabby didn't just love her; he was totally obsessed with her. He had let his job slide, he had let his athletes down, and his relentless drinking had made him turn on his own children. He blamed it all on her, and then on Morris.

She didn't even want to think what she was thinking. Gabby had threatened so many times to kill *himself* in front of her, but he had never said anything about hurting Morris. Morris had always been so kind to Gabby. Even after what she and Gabby had done to him, Morris *still* treated Gabby with respect. He still called him "Coach," and he had told

her he couldn't bring himself to hit Gabby a week before
when he had broken into their house.

No, she couldn't imagine Gabby Moore killing Morris.
But then, she couldn't imagine anyone else killing Morris.
Of all the things she had been afraid might happen, that was
one eventuality that had never crossed her mind.

Sergeant Brimmer called Gabby Moore and requested
that he come down to the police station, asking him to bring
any firearms he might own with him. Gabby did come to the
station on that first Saturday afternoon, but he did not come
prepared to talk to Brimmer. Instead, he said that anyone
who was interested in talking to him would have to talk to
his attorney. He had nothing to say.

8

Detective Vernon Henry Henderson had broken
through barriers of one kind or another all of his life. Like
Morris Blankenbaker, he had grown up in Yakima. But
Morris was *born* there, and Vern arrived at the age of five,
coming from the South to a world entirely different from
the one he had known.

"My mother, my sister, and I came from Shreveport,
Louisiana," Henderson said. "My grandfather was living up
here already, and he called and told us to come on up
here—that it was a better life. He owned some houses in
Yakima and told my mother she could probably get a home
up here. We moved up, and we *were* able to get a home."

It wasn't easy; Vern's mother, Leona, would work in a

Yakima cannery her entire life. She was everything to her son—just as Olive was all things to Morris. Henderson's sister, Joanne, died when she was only twelve, and he was working by that age thinning apples in the orchards, picking fruit when the trees grew heavy with ripe produce.

As hard as they all had to work, the move *did* bring Leona Henderson's family a better life. "When I was growing up, you could leave your house open," Vern recalled. "And no one would go in it. And if someone did, we all knew who it was. We *knew* who the bad people were. Later, when I was on [police] patrol, I *knew* who the bad kids were, but now, you *don't* know who they are, and that makes it real hard to investigate."

There was no father in Vern Henderson's world, and while Morris Blankenbaker did have his father, Ned, in town to go to in a pinch, basically both Morris and Vern were being raised by their mothers. Athletics and the friendship of two of his peers, Les Rucker and Morris Blankenbaker, filled in most of the empty spaces in Vern's life. They were *family* to him.

"I met Morris at Washington Junior High," Henderson recalled. "He showed up in either seventh or eighth grade."

That would have been when Olive left her court job in Vancouver, Washington, and headed back to her hometown. Vern said that Morris lived with his mother and his grandmother out near the river. Morris had always been blind to the color of anyone's skin. He had played with Indian boys when he was smaller, and if you had asked him what color Vern Henderson and Les Rucker were, he probably would have had to think a moment to come up with "black."

There weren't many blacks living in Yakima four or five decades ago. Vern remembered that he was one of only six at Washington Junior High and that there were eight black students at Davis High School when he attended.

Over the years, many races would move into Yakima, but in the midfifties, there were very few Mexicans and the Indian population mostly lived south of town in Toppenish on the Yakima Indian Reservation. At Davis High, when Morris, Vern, and Les attended, out of the three hundred teenagers registered there was a total of twenty mixed-race students: blacks, Indians, and, perhaps, two or three Chinese. Yakima was a typical small-town orchard and farming community where it was "normal" to be white, and unusual to be any other color, unless you happened to be there to harvest the fruit or work in the fields, and then move on to another migrant worker camp. But the migrant kids rarely got a chance to attend school; they headed south with the first cold snap.

While Morris treated everyone the same and didn't notice that his school was mostly white, Vern Henderson did; he had come out of the Deep South to a far better life, just as his grandfather had promised, but he was still aware that he was a member of a minority race, and that he was *truly* in the minority at Davis High School.

His mother had found them a house in the northeast area of town, an exclusively Caucasian section of Yakima. "Everything *north* of Yakima Avenue was white then," he said. "South was where other races lived. . . . I even played on a baseball team where I was the only black, because all my friends were white."

In Yakima, Catholic teenagers went to Marquette High School, and all the rich kids who went to public school went to Eisenhower High School. Jerilee, several grades behind Vern and Morris, would go to Eisenhower. Later, Vern Henderson remembered that she had lived in a big house up near Thirty-second and Inglewood. "There were *no* poor people up there."

Morris and Vern met Gabby Moore for the first time at Washington Junior High. He was the assistant wrestling coach then and they viewed him as the hero figure that most boys see in their coaches. They were twelve or thirteen, and Gabby was about twenty-one. The near-decade between them, of course, made a tremendous difference at that stage in their lives. Vern and Morris were awestruck by everything Gabby told them.

"I remember," Vern said, "that he taught us to always look our opponent in the eye to let him know what we were thinking, and that we weren't afraid of him, and that we could beat him."

When Morris and Vern moved up to Davis High School, Gabby was their coach there too; he had a better job, coaching on the high school level. "Morris and I both weighed one hundred eighty-five pounds," Vern said. "Gabby didn't need two of us competing in that heavyweight category, and he made Morris lose ten pounds so he could wrestle at a lower weight.

"Me and Morris were just about even," Vern said. "He was the only one I could go hand-to-hand with and come out even—anyone else, I could just tear apart."

Despite his prowess as an athlete, Vern Henderson never forgot what it felt like to be a kid who never had a father in the bleachers cheering him on, one who didn't have a dad to take him to the Father-Son banquets or to the awards ceremonies. Lots of times, Morris's dad couldn't come either, and both Vern and Morris had mothers who were working so hard to support them that they couldn't take time off. Vern and Morris and Les Rucker were a triumvirate against the world—more than friends—closer even than relatives.

"Morris and Les were always there for me," Vern recalled. "We were all there for each other."

Morris and Vern hung out together. You rarely saw one without the other. They didn't go to each other's homes that much, mostly because they were always playing football or wrestling or driving around town. Vern didn't have a car, but Morris had a little white Volkswagen that Ned Blankenbaker had bought for him. Olive laughed, remembering it. "Those great big boys weighed that car down so much when they were all in it, they looked like they were sitting on the street!"

Vern knew both Olive and Ned. "Morris's dad had the music store and sometimes we'd go over and see him at the store. He was a solid, stocky man." Morris's half brother, Mike, was just a little kid then, a kid who idolized Morris.

Like Morris, Vern belonged to the Lettermen's Club and was on the "A" Squad of the baseball and football teams, as well as turning out for Gabby Moore's wrestling squad. Vern and Morris were together so much that they actually could almost read each other's minds. "I knew what Morris was thinking and he knew what I was thinking." Vern smiled, remembering. "We could understand each other without talking. He knew if I was going to fight somebody, and he would walk up and stop me. And I'd walk up and stop him. We just knew each other. We *knew* each other."

Morris was not only a tremendously strong athlete, he also had an easygoing nature and reasonable turn of mind. He could always see the other guy's point of view. When he saw that Vern, who kept so much inside, was about to blow, he could step in and calm him down with a word or two.

Davis High School played in the AAA Football League and went up against Wenatchee and Richland, and, of course, Eisenhower. Vern played left halfback, Les Rucker played right halfback, and Morris played fullback. Dutch Schultz was their head coach, and Gabby assisted.

Even though the three musketeers would scatter—Morris and Les to Washington State University, and Vern to Central—Gabby Moore was a hero to all three through their high school years, and after. Lives in a small town are closely interwoven. Almost everyone knew each other and secrets weren't really secrets. Back then, Gabby seemed like the last man in the world to have secrets. He was a straight shooter, a good teacher, and a good coach whose athletes looked up to him. And he didn't live by a double standard. If the boys couldn't drink—and they couldn't—he didn't drink. If he ordered his wrestlers to diet, he dieted right along with them.

Vern Henderson and Morris Blankenbaker took his every word for gospel.

The friendship between Morris Blankenbaker and Vern Henderson only became stronger as the years went by. Vern laughed as he recalled that he was "serious about every girl I ever met—but not Morris," he said, suddenly sober. "I never saw him serious about anyone but Jerilee. Oh, he'd talk to girls at the movies or something, but Jerilee was the only one for him."

Vern and Morris both went off to college, working evenings and summers to pay for it. Vern married young, the first of their group to do so. He fathered two sons. He was working for the City of Yakima, driving a garbage truck while Morris was working nights in the state mental hospital.

They both had dreams. Morris had always wanted to become a teacher and a coach. Vern Henderson dreamed of being a policeman and one day a detective. "I always thought I wanted to be a policeman because I thought that would be nice—working and helping people," Vern recalled. "But I really thought that I never had a chance to be in law enforcement, if you want to know the truth. Back in those days, you didn't see any black policemen, not in Yakima. I wanted to work in the juvenile section; that's where I wanted to be, working with kids."

When Vern graduated from Davis and went to Yakima Valley Community College, and then Central Washington University at Ellensburg, he held on to that ambition. "A lot of my friends were becoming policemen. Jim Beaushaw—who was a quarterback and was a couple of years ahead of us—he became a police officer. And then a few others. Jim said, 'Vern, it would be a good job for you. You relate well with people.'"

Vern Henderson told Jim he would give it a try. He took the test for patrolman. "They had one opening," he remembered. "And the first time I took the test, I didn't pass high enough. And then I said to myself, 'Wait a minute. I can do better than this. I know these guys are not smarter than me.' I went back and I studied, and eight guys took the test and they had one opening again. This time, though, I came out number one."

That was in 1968. Chief Robert Madden hired Vern Henderson—the first black police officer ever in Yakima. It was the fulfillment of Vern's impossible dreams.

In 1968 Gabby Moore was bringing glory to Davis High with his wrestling squads. Morris and Jerilee had moved back to Yakima from Tacoma and she was pregnant with her first child. And Vern Henderson was a young patrolman, cruising the streets of Yakima.

Eighteen months later, Vern was sent "upstairs" to try out as a detective working in the juvenile section. "They were having a lot of problems with juvenile black gangs," he said. "They knew that I knew a lot of the kids. After I stayed there for three or four months, I went back down 'on the line.' But I was only there for thirty days. I'd made so many arrests in juvenile that they said, 'You're going back upstairs,' and that's where I was for the next ten years."

Over those years, Vern Henderson would work five years in juvenile, and then in the "regular" detective unit. He worked all manner of cases: burglary, auto theft, and homicides. His being black often gave him a leg up with many of the informants and suspects.

In the juvenile division, Vern could speak the same language as many of the kids who were brought in. "I understood them and I could talk to them. They knew I was serious when I said they could trust what I said."

Whenever there was a problem in the black community, it was Vern Henderson who was sent to represent the Yakima Police Department. He felt very confident then; it was only decades later that he marveled at his temerity in thinking he could handle the emerging gang problem single-handedly. It was decades later too when he would look back with some regret on a decision he had had to make—a decision that would weaken forever the link he had forged with members of his own race.

By 1974 both Morris Blankenbaker and Vern Henderson were almost thirty-two, and they had realized their goals. Morris was teaching sociology at Washington Junior High School and expecting to coach there too. The two men were still close friends, possibly closer than ever.

One day the Yakima City water line sprung a leak somewhere beneath the surface of the Yakima River. Someone had to dive down and try to locate the break. Both Vern and Morris were skilled SCUBA divers. "They couldn't pay me," Vern recalled, "because I was *already* on the city payroll, so I went and got Morris. We tied a rope around him and I stayed on shore and held on and he swam out and dove until he found the leak."

74

Morris was still strong as a bull, and a natural swimmer. Symbolically, one or the other of them was always holding the "rope" for the other, as if they could somehow keep each other safe.

Although Vern and his wife didn't socialize much with Morris and Jerilee, Vern had gotten to know Jerilee when he visited Morris, and he found her a gracious hostess, a pretty woman who kept a neat house. She seemed devoted to Morris. And Morris clearly adored her.

When Morris told him that Gabby Moore was moving in with him and Jerilee for a while, Vern didn't think much about it. Everyone knew that Gabby was having a rough time over his divorce from Gay. The word was that Gabby had begun to drink—something that none of his athletes had ever seen before. Vern was soon aware that Gabby became unreasonably jealous and suspicious when he drank, and heard the rumors that Gay Moore couldn't leave the house on the most innocent of errands without Gabby suspecting she was on her way to some romantic assignation. No marriage could survive long under that kind of pressure, and Gabby's hadn't.

It never occurred to Vern Henderson that Gabby would pose any threat to Morris's marriage. He was astonished when Morris stopped by the police station one day in the early spring of 1974 to see him. Morris didn't look very happy, and Vern led him to a quiet corner of the detective unit.

"You'll never guess who Jerilee's moved in with," Morris said.

Vern thought he was kidding. "What do you mean 'moved in with'? Jerilee isn't going anywhere."

But then the look on Morris's face stopped him. He was dead serious. "She's left me and moved in with Gabby."

"With Gabby?"

It was the most unlikely thing Vern Henderson could ever have imagined. He stared at Morris, expecting him to break into a grin at any moment and tell him that it was all a joke. Why on earth would Jerilee leave Morris for Gabby? Gabby was on the skids, and Morris was younger, handsomer, and

ANN RULE

more dependable. Morris would have given Jerilee the
moon if he could have pulled it down for her. Vern shook
his head, trying to picture Jerilee Blankenbaker living with
Gabby Moore.

In time, Vern accepted that impossible circumstance.
And, like all Morris's friends, Vern tried to cheer him up.
Nothing much helped, of course. Morris's wife and his two
little kids were gone from his home. His life had been
turned inside out, and now *he* was the one who was all
alone.

Vern Henderson was relieved when he heard that Jerilee
was back for a trial reconciliation with Morris. He expected
that it would work out for Morris after all. But then he
learned that she had gone back to Gabby. It seemed as
though the woman were torn between her first husband and
her second, and that her indecision was driving all three of
them crazy. Finally, in the summer of 1975, Morris told
Vern that Jerilee was truly back with him—that she had
filed for divorce from Gabby and that they were going to
remarry as soon as they could.

Vern Henderson was happy for his old friend. Morris had
always been so kind to everyone that it ate at Vern to think
of the pain his friend had endured. Vern was not so serene,
however, when he spotted Jerilee's car and Gabby's little
brown MG parked close together near a city park.

"There I am in a detective's car going up Lincoln Avenue
and I see Jerilee over in a parking lot on the West Side with
Gabby. They were sitting in one of the cars—talking," Vern
said. "And I'm saying to myself, 'Why is she talking to him?
What she was doing was giving him a ray of hope yet.' I saw
them a couple of times, and I thought, 'Can't the woman
make up her mind? She's got no business talking to Gabby
and giving him any kind of idea that she might go back to
him.'

"I didn't mention anything about seeing them to Morris.
For one thing, I didn't know what she was talking to Gabby
about. It wasn't my business. For another, I learned a long
time ago that you don't get involved in somebody else's

relationship. I liked Jerilee and I *loved* Morris. Me and Morris were kind of like brothers. . . . You side with one or another—or you tell what you've seen—and then they get back together, and they're *both* mad at *you*."

Everyone who had ever known Gabby knew by then that he was carrying a torch for Jerilee that could light up a whole street. Vern felt that Jerilee should have cut it off clean, and never agreed to meet or talk to Gabby. Vern knew how stubborn Gabby was; he had always taught his athletes never to quit. And Vern worried because it didn't seem like Gabby was about to let Jerilee walk away from him.

Still, it never crossed Vern Henderson's mind to worry that there would be any *physical* confrontation between Morris and Gabby. "There was never any thought that Gabby would do something at the house—not with the kids there. Morris still respected Gabby as his coach. Morris was not going to fight Gabby unless he had to. That's the way Morris was. He would never have hurt Gabby," Vern said. "And Gabby—he knew that Morris was so strong he would destroy him. He was too smart to ever take Morris on."

Vern could see that there might be more heartbreak on the horizon for his best friend and his former coach, but he never thought either of them was in danger.

Never.

Two decades later, a cloud passed over Vern Henderson's face as he remembered the night after Thanksgiving 1975. Apparently Morris had had more misgivings than he himself had had. Vern remembered a conversation he had with Morris, one he had sloughed off at the time. "Morris said to me about a month and a half before he died, 'If anything should ever happen to me, Vern, you be sure you check out Gabby.'

"I told him, 'Don't be talking this stupidness because this is not going to happen.' I didn't want to visualize anything like that happening. I said, 'You two guys—you gotta get straight with each other.'

"The thing is," Vern remembered, "I drove *right* by

Morris's house that last night. It was five minutes after one in the morning, and I drove by and I looked at the house because I'd heard Gabby had been coming over, but everything was fine. And an hour later, Morris was dead—shot."

One got the sense that Vern Henderson had lived with some unnecessary guilt, a vague feeling that if only he had stopped to see Jerilee that night, if only he had parked and waited for Morris to get home, if only . . .

When Morris Blankenbaker was buried on November 25, 1975, Vern Henderson was one of his pallbearers. So was Les Rucker. The service in the Shaw and Sons Chapel was conducted by Priest Charles Benedict of the Reorganized Church of the Jesus Christ of Latter-Day Saints, and the chapel was full to overflowing. Neither Olive nor Morris were Mormons, and many years later, Olive wasn't sure just why Morris had a Mormon funeral. That terrible week was a blur in her mind.

The news stories described Jerilee as Morris's ex-wife, but the funeral notices all omitted the "Moore" from Jerilee's name and listed her as Morris's widow, Jerilee Blankenbaker. And she would have been Morris's wife again within a matter of weeks if someone had not shot him execution style in his own backyard. Now, Jerilee was left in a kind of never-never land. She was legally free of Gabby, but nothing mattered much anymore. There would be no marriage ceremony and no future with Morris. Her children would have no father to guide them as they grew up.

Olive Blankenbaker didn't die, although her grief was so overwhelming that she wanted to. When Vern Henderson visited her to offer his condolences, she took his hand and looked into his eyes, "Vern," she said, "I know *you'll* find out who killed my son."

Vern looked back at her and made a promise he had every intention of keeping. "Yes," he said quietly and convincingly, "yes, I will."

The newspapers noted that there were "no suspects" in Morris Blankenbaker's murder. That wasn't technically true. The investigators were looking hard at Gabby. The very fact that Gabby Moore refused to talk to detectives and said he would not take a lie detector test made him a suspect in the investigators' minds. That didn't mean they could arrest him. Far from it. They had no physical evidence linking him to the crime scene, and they certainly had no eyewitnesses.

Since Vern Henderson was still with the Youth Division, he was not assigned to the investigation of his good friend's murder. Even so, Vern had been notified of Morris's shooting at five A.M. on the morning of November 22 by Sergeant Green. Pleas Green knew how close Vern and Morris were and he didn't want him to hear it on the radio.

Vern had steeled himself to be at Morris's autopsy. Vern owed Morris that—not that Morris knew any longer that his friend was there for him, just as he had always been. More than that, Vern Henderson had wanted to know *how* Morris had died, and then maybe he would know why. It wasn't his case, it wasn't his assignment, but he had left the postmortem knowing that there was a good chance that there might be some .22 bullet casings lying somewhere in Morris's yard or close by. He didn't know if the gun was an automatic or not. If it was an automatic, he didn't know if it ejected casings to the right or left. But he knew that casings ejected from an automatic would be left with very distinctive, individual marks both from the extractor and the ejector. That would be a start. Still, even if he found the casings, they would be of help only if they could be matched to a specific weapon.

A lot of people have guns, especially around Yakima. Most of them are unfamiliar with the science of ballistics and the damning evidence that can be detected in slugs, casings, pellets, wadding, gunpowder, the lands and grooves of a gun barrel. Bullets, once fired, are not unlike fingerprints, rife with unique individual markings.

If Morris Blankenbaker's killer wasn't arrested immediately and if a confession didn't follow soon after, it was likely that it would take direct physical evidence to find and convict the killer. And the only really compelling evidence Henderson hoped to find was a couple of bullet casings.

But Vern Henderson wasn't assigned to the Blankenbaker case and he didn't try to insert himself into other detectives' investigations. He went back to the Youth Division and the cases waiting for him there. But he didn't forget. In fact, the more time that passed, the more he remembered that Morris's killer was walking around free, perhaps smug in the belief that he had pulled it off.

9

Sergeant Robert Brimmer continued to direct the probe into Morris's death. He and his detectives learned from Jerilee that Morris had been working at the Lion's Share that Friday night. They checked to see if there had been any trouble at the tavern in the hours before Morris's murder. But there had been nothing unusual—just the regulars and a few quiet strangers. Someone thought that two young men had been asking for Morris or talking to him an hour or so before the Lion's Share closed for the night.

What Brimmer learned from Jerilee that was the most intriguing were the details of her brief marriage and quick estrangement from Gabby Moore. In talking with Jerilee, and with others, it soon became evident to Brimmer that Moore had been totally beset by his passion for Jerilee. The Yakima police investigators and the new Yakima County Prosecutor, Jeff Sullivan, thought it quite possible that he had killed Morris in a jealous rage. It wouldn't be the first time that they had seen jealousy spark murder.

But that theory lost some plausibility when Jerilee told

detectives that Gabby was in the hospital most of Thanksgiving week. She wasn't sure when he was released. Nor did she think he was capable of shooting Morris. Pressed, she said she just didn't know anymore.

The Yakima investigators knew that Morris had been shot at approximately 2:05 A.M.—give or take five minutes—on November 22. They were betting that Gabby Moore had been out of the hospital by then. They had witnesses who would testify that Moore had come to the Blankenbaker house a week earlier in the middle of the night in a drunken attempt to talk to Jerilee. Perhaps he had come back again.

It was easy enough to check on Gabby Moore's hospitalization. Brimmer and Sullivan went to the Valley Osteopathic Hospital and asked to see records on Moore's most recent stay there. Dr. A. J. Myers produced them at once.

"He was hospitalized on November eighteenth," Myers said, explaining that he was concerned about his former son-in-law's severe nosebleeds and he had advised him to go into the hospital until his blood pressure came down within normal limits.

"How long did he remain in the hospital?" Brimmer asked.

"Until November twenty-second."

For a moment, the detective's interest flared, but then he reminded himself that the twenty-second had been twenty-four hours long. Morris had been shot two hours into the day, in the wee hours of the morning, and most hospitals discharged patients around noon. He asked Dr. Myers just when Gabby Moore had checked out.

"He wanted to leave the night before—Friday—but I insisted he stay over to give me at least another night's rest on the blood pressure problem. So he went out on the morning of the twenty-second with my knowledge and permission."

"And what time *did* he check out?"

"I would say in the neighborhood of around nine-thirty, a quarter of ten o'clock that morning."

That meant that officially at least Gabby Moore had been a patient at the Valley Osteopathic Hospital at the moment

Morris Blankenbaker was shot to death. However, that didn't mean that he had not *left* the hospital sometime during the night and returned later.

Brimmer asked if Gabby had been confined to bed during his stay.

"A large part of the time. I would say the last thirty-six hours I got him up. I was trying to hold him pretty quiet because I was having difficulty getting the blood pressure down."

Dr. Myers said he had changed his patient's blood pressure medicine, but it would take ten days to see if it would be effective. The best thing he could do short-term was rest. "He spent most of the day reading and he was up to go to the bathroom. He visited the nurses at the desk, but most of the time he was reading or watching television."

"Did he have a phone in his room?"

"No. We have room service for a telephone. Phones can be brought to the bedside, but they are not left in the room."

There was, however, a public phone at the far end of the corridor near the emergency entrance. Gabby could have walked down there and used it, but he would have been observed doing so.

Bob Brimmer and Jeff Sullivan asked for a tour of the hospital, with a special trip to the room that Moore had occupied.

The hospital, which Dr. Myers had had built in 1952 and which he had remodeled four times, faced Tieton Drive to the north. On Thirtieth Avenue South, there was an emergency entrance and the Central Services Area with a waiting room and hospital offices. On the west side of the building, the patients' rooms opened off a wide corridor. There was an entrance from the waiting rooms on the south end of the hall, and a fire exit at the north end. There were a number of ways to get *out* of the hospital—perhaps even without being detected because no alarm would sound—but there were precious few ways to get back in. And all of those were monitored or alarmed.

They could see that no one could come into the area of the patients' rooms except from the waiting room. The fire exit on the north end of the same corridor was locked on the interior side with a bar. "There's no way to open this from the outside," Myers demonstrated, "with a key or otherwise." In case of fire, all a patient had to do was push on the door and it would swing open. But then the bar lock inside would click back in place.

There was another door to the outside through the kitchen and dining room area, but that too was locked unless an actual delivery was being made.

"The nurses' desk is here at the apex of the ell in order that all of the rooms are under observation from the nurses' desk—in addition to communication—so that there is an unobstructed view to the waiting room's inside door," Myers pointed out. "And an unobstructed view in this direction down to where you go out of the exit."

"Where was Mr. Moore's room?"

"His room was directly across from the nurses' desk," Myers said. "This just happened to be a vacant bed I put him in."

Myers said that there had been three nurses on duty on the night of November 21–22, at least one of whom would always be at the desk. It began to sound almost impossible for Gabby Moore to have left his hospital room without a nurse or hospital employee observing him. The corridors were brightly lit and well within the nurses' line of sight.

"What about the emergency room door?" Brimmer asked, speculating on another egress and reentry for the suspect.

Dr. Myers said that they had had a problem with theft of equipment when the ER door was left open. "That's locked now throughout a twenty-four-hour period, and it's not opened except by signal. There's a two-way speaker there. That door can be opened immediately from the inside, but not from the outside."

The visitors' room door was locked after 8:00 P.M. and no one could get *back* into the hospital from the outside after 8:00 P.M.

Myers repeated that it would be highly unlikely that a patient could slip out. "With three nurses on duty, you have one at the desk to watch the monitoring equipment and for patient calls, to write orders as they are telephoned or brought in, to chart the care . . . this desk is seldom unoccupied."

The investigators reasoned that *even if Gabby somehow managed to leave the hospital unobserved, there was no way he could have gotten back in without someone seeing him. No possible way.*

If Gabby Moore had wanted to get out of the hospital, it looked as though the only way he could have done it and be sure he wasn't observed would have been to go through the window in his room. But that proved to be impossible too; when Brimmer checked the outside of the hospital, he saw that the patients' windows were locked from the outside with a cylinder that slipped into a slot and was then held firmly by a screw.

Unless Gabby Moore had perfected the art of astral projection, the most viable suspect in the murder of Morris Blankenbaker had just been eliminated from the list of possibles. Gabby might have resented Morris and blamed him for Jerilee's departure, and he might have refused to talk to the police, but he couldn't have pulled the trigger on the gun that killed Morris; he had been in the hospital under medical watch at two A.M.. on November 22. He had been there until 9:00 or 9:30 the next morning, seven hours after the murder.

Jerilee and her children moved in with her parents. She couldn't imagine staying in the house on North Sixth, not with the memory of Morris lying there in the snow, his blood staining the ground.

As far as Jerilee was concerned, the fact that Gabby had been in the hospital when someone killed Morris didn't lessen her suspicions one bit. But as much as she thought about it, she couldn't come up with one person, other than Gabby, who had a reason to want Morris dead. He had said often enough that Morris was the only reason she wouldn't come back to him.

Morris had only been dead a week when Jerilee learned

that Gabby was trying to manipulate people so they would convince her to come back to him. It was as if he didn't care that Morris was dead. He couldn't even wait for a decent period of mourning. It didn't really matter to Jerilee how long he waited, though; she was never going back to him. Somehow, in some way that she didn't yet understand, she knew that Gabby was the cause of Morris's death. She would never forgive him, much less consider being with him again.

The thought made her skin crawl.

Jerilee's sister Kit* owned the apartment where Gabby was living with his son, Derek, and she lived close by. There wasn't even a proper street that separated their residences; it was more of a "lane," and Kit could not avoid seeing Gabby. It seemed as though he were always there, wanting to talk to her.

Moore wanted Kit to reason with Jerilee. He asked her all the time to try to persuade her sister to reconcile with him. When she stared at him, appalled, he looked back uncomprehendingly. Both Kit and Jerilee were horrified at Gabby's easy assumption that it was completely logical Jerilee should come back to him now that Morris was dead.

Gabby had a theory which he propounded to anyone who would listen. He suspected that someone wanted both him and Morris out of the picture. He said he had had unsettling incidents himself—odd phone calls at all hours of the day and night. He said he couldn't identify the voices. Some sounded Caucasian and some sounded black. But the gist of the calls was plain enough; the voices threatened him with death.

He told people that he had found a windowpane shattered and it looked as though the damage were done with a bullet.

Gabby told his intimates that *he* intended to find and expose Morris's killer, and that he figured he must be getting awfully close because someone was trying to silence *him* before he "scored." He was especially worried, he said, that one of his daughters had gotten a threatening call, and so had his mother.

That was much too close for comfort, and he said he didn't know what would happen next. He was a fatalist. He was going to do what he had to do without giving in.

Gabby even went into great detail with his older daughter about plans for his funeral in case the person who was stalking him succeeded in killing him. Gabby described what kind of funeral he wanted, but when his daughter started to cry, he would laugh, as if he had been kidding all along. One can only imagine the emotional impact on a teenager who loved her father.

Jerilee wasn't buying any of it. "*I* thought he had something to do with killing Morris," she recalled. "Just from different things he said. He had told my sister that he knew people that would do anything for him. All he had to do was ask. I just felt that *he* felt that if Morris wasn't there, I would be back to him; he was very confident that I would be back."

Gabby Moore was so confident, in fact, that he continued to phone the now-widowed Jerilee as the Christmas season approached. He wanted her back. He needed her, and now, he pointed out, she really needed him too. Jerilee refused to talk to him. She would have her mother or someone else answer the phone and tell him that she was unavailable.

Sometimes, Gabby would have his mother call. Jerilee would talk to her. She had nothing against Gabby's mother. But then the older woman would say suddenly, "Just a minute, Glynn wants to talk to you."

And then Jerilee would immediately say, "I'm sorry," and hang up. Always before, Gabby had been persuasive enough to get her to meet him "just to talk." No more. He had tried to confuse her in his campaign to get her to leave Morris. She was no longer confused; the bleak specter of Morris's death had made everything all too clear. She could not afford to talk to Gabby.

Finally, he stopped calling her parents' home and her office every day. He no longer tried to speak to her in person, but she knew he hadn't given up because he continued to send messages through his family.

Only once after Morris's murder did Jerilee agree to speak to Gabby on the phone. It happened approximately two-and-a-half weeks after Morris's murder—in the middle of December. Gabby told her that the police were bothering him, that they had asked him to take a polygraph test. He didn't tell her that he had hired an attorney.

Jerilee couldn't hold back her feelings. She told Gabby flat out that she believed he was involved in Morris's murder.

"He said he couldn't have done something like that," she recalled. "He insisted that he just couldn't have done it. I didn't believe him."

She told him it didn't matter anyway. She would never come back to him, and he had to accept that. As always, he countered with what he wanted her to believe. He told her that he could *prove* to her that he had absolutely nothing to do with the murder. Before he could begin to expand on the weird threats he was receiving, she cut him off.

She told him again that made no difference. She wasn't coming back to him. He kept repeating that he could prove what happened to Morris might be connected to him, but that it had nothing to do with his feelings for her. He *loved* her. He suspected that there was someone who had been after *both* him and Morris, and he had reason to fear for his own life. Something strange was going on.

Jerilee hung up. That was the last time she spoke to Gabby before Christmas. He sent messages through her sister, or through his relatives, but she would never speak to him again.

After Christmas, everything in Jerilee's world would change once more. It was as if she had entered a "House of Horrors" at the county fair—only it was all real. With every step she took, something even more ghastly popped up.

Bright lights lit up houses and lawns all over town, and deep snow fell. It got colder and the icy wind blew across the hills and plains of Yakima County, howling like the hounds of hell.

There *was* someone following Gabby Moore, someone just beyond his awareness. It wasn't anyone for Gabby to fear—at least not physically. But Vern Henderson was curious about Gabby Moore. He thought he had known the man; now he was not so sure. Although Vern wasn't officially working Homicide, and he was not assigned to Morris's case, he had promised Morris's mother he would find her son's killer.

In his own mind, he had promised Morris too.

From time to time, Vern spotted Gabby's MG or his Jeep weaving through town. Sometimes, Vern followed him. On two occasions, Vern followed Gabby as he drove up to the Tahoma Cemetery where Morris was buried. While Vern watched undetected, Gabby stood looking down at Morris's grave, his face a blank mask. What was he thinking? Vern wondered why he had come here to stand silent in the cold.

"He looked as though he felt bad," Vern remembered. "And I wondered if he had really loved Morris, his old friend, but maybe he'd wanted the woman more."

Inside the apartment Gabby Moore had rented with his sixteen-year-old son, there were no Christmas decorations. The two had been batching it for two months in an apartment that was nothing like the comfortable homes they were both used to. This was not a home; it was a stopping-off place for two males on their way to someplace else. They both had sports practice after school and games and wrestling matches. But Derek had a girlfriend, and his father had no one.

When he was alone, the sound of Gabby's stereo echoed through the empty rooms. He played the same record over and over and over again.

"Lay your head upon my pillow, put your warm and tender body close to mine. . . ."

It was one of the saddest—and most popular—of the country-western hits that year, Ray Price singing of lost love. The lyrics were far more accepting that the love affair was over, however, than Gabby was.

"I'll get along; you'll find another," Ray Price sang, "and I'll be here in case you ever need me. Let's just be glad we had some time to spend together. We don't have to watch the bridges that we're burning . . ."

Gabby had played "For the Good Times" so often that

the record sometimes skipped where the needle had worn deep grooves. He was living almost entirely in the past, but he was planning for the future he was determined to have with Jerilee.

10

Although Jerilee could no longer be counted among that group, there were still many, many people who loved Gabby Moore. His three children tried to help him deal with his lost love. His ex-in-laws made him welcome, and Dr. A. J. Myers made an effort to keep track of Gabby's health. Looking at Gabby's bloated body and flushed face, Myers worried. He was clearly drinking too much and not eating right, and he didn't appear to have been taking his medication. He looked like a heart attack looking for a place to happen.

Perhaps more than anyone, Gabby's athletes—past and present—kept close tabs on him, making sure he wasn't alone for too long, trying to stop by and visit with him. He was "the man" to his boys. He was the coach that had lifted many of them from mediocrity and made them champions.

When Gabby was too distraught or too ill or even too intoxicated to show up for wrestling practice and wrestling matches, some of the star wrestlers who had graduated from Davis made sure that *they* were there to see that things ran smoothly. It was getting pretty bad. They had seen Gabby step out of the gym and go to his car and take a swig out of a bottle he kept there. They had often smelled alcohol on his breath inside Davis High School at practice.

Still, not one of them could believe that the Davis High administrators would really fire Gabby. Sure, he said that he wouldn't be teaching or coaching at Davis after next graduation, but that seemed impossible. When push came to shove, it couldn't happen. Gabby was part of Davis, and Davis was part of him.

Gabby was as low as they had ever seen him. He was getting more reclusive, and he spent a lot of time in his apartment. Gabby's boys didn't see him around town in his snappy little MG sports car as much as they used to. Sometimes he showed up at the bars and the lounges, but not often. He bought bottles and took them home to drink. Gabby urged his former athletes to come over to his apartment. That meant they would have to have a drink with him and listen to him talk about Jerilee. They had heard about how wonderful Jerilee was and how beautiful and how she was meant to be with Gabby so many times that they could practically recite chapter and verse, but they listened attentively and tried to say something that would make their old coach feel better. They urged him just to "give the woman some time," because he wouldn't listen to them when they suggested he should forget her and find a woman who appreciated him. He would not allow them to say one word against Jerilee.

Nothing could make him feel better. Gabby wallowed in self-pity and in his memories. He had albums full of pictures of himself and Jerilee when their lives together were happy, and he had the record of their song. At some point during the long evenings, when he had just enough bourbon in his system to blur the emotional pain he felt, he would pore over his photographs and tell himself that Jerilee *would* be coming back. She didn't have any reason not to now. She had no husband, and no other boyfriend. Gabby still believed she was meant to be his.

On Saturday, December 13, Yakima Officer Michael Bartleson received a radio call to an address on South Fourth Street. It was one A.M. He was to meet officers in a two-man unit at the address. En route, they got a second complaint, "Possible child neglect at this address."

The officers had had calls to this address before and they knew that a teenage girl was baby-sitting her younger brothers and sisters while their mother was at work. When the girl answered the door, she appeared to have been drinking.

"Everything's all right," the girl mumbled.

"Is there anybody else in the house besides you and your brothers and sisters?" Bartleson asked.

"Maybe two . . ."

"Does your mother know that?" he asked.

"Yeah, she doesn't care," the girl said.

Bartleson doubted this, and he asked the station to call the mother and tell her that things didn't look good at home. She said she was on her way. The worried mother arrived after the patrolmen had been there for about half an hour. She wanted to go inside, and Bartleson went with her while Officers Ehmer and Beaulaurier circled around and waited at the back door on the alley side of the house.

As Bartleson and the mother went through the front door, they heard loud running sounds headed for the back door and something crashing in the rear of the house. "The two subjects—three subjects actually, were stopped at the back door by Ehmer and Beaulaurier," Bartleson recalled. "There was one young white male about fifteen or sixteen who was a cousin of the family, and a Kenny Marino* and a Glynn Moore—known to us as 'Gabby.' "

Marino was carrying a half-gallon of Ten-High whiskey, and the coach the officers all knew well was so under the influence that he didn't recognize them. "He was very intoxicated," Bartleson said with regret in his voice. "Leaning against the side of the house. He had no shoes on, in his stocking feet; there was snow on the ground. His pants were unbuckled, snapped at the top and unzipped . . ."

Inside the house, the teenage girl had gone to bed in the basement. She was fully dressed, and there was no indication that she had been harmed.

Still, it was a disturbing incident. It was just one more step down for Gabby Moore, shocking to the officers who had confronted him.

* * *

Jerilee tried to pull some kind of Christmas together for the children. They knew their father was gone, but they were far too young to understand that he was never coming back. Their grandparents tried to help, even though everyone was heartbroken. There is never a good time to lose someone to a senseless murder, but the holiday season is somehow worse than any other; none of them would ever see a Christmas tree again or a Thanksgiving turkey without thinking of Morris. Morris should have been with them for another fifty years.

Christmas Eve was the hardest. For everyone. The year before, Gabby had been with Jerilee, their only Christmas together. And now he was alone again. On Christmas Eve afternoon, Gay—Gabby's first ex-wife—came over to the apartment on Eighteenth Avenue and cleaned it up, doing the dishes, vacuuming, and trying to make it look a little more livable. Her son lived there too, of course, but even she felt sorry for Gabby. Gay had gone on with her life, but Gabby still seemed to be caught up in his obsessive jealousy; only the object of it had changed.

The Christmas before, Olive had had her son; the holidays had always been a happy time for her because Morris had been born just before Christmas.

Derek Moore stayed home with Gabby and watched television during the early part of Christmas Eve. Gabby had no plans to celebrate the holiday, but Derek was going to go to his girlfriend Janet Whitman's family to join in their Christmas Eve festivities. Her grandmother lived in the hamlet of Union Gap, a ten-minute drive from Derek's apartment, and Janet had arranged to pick Derek up in her car around eight.

Derek wasn't sure what his dad was going to do. He probably would call Derek's sisters who would be over at their grandparents, the Myers.

When Derek and Janet left the apartment, Gabby was alone. Later, when Derek tried to remember, he said he didn't think his father was drinking. It was kind of sad, though, leaving him behind in the apartment. No Christmas tree. No decorations. It could have been any other night in the year.

No one in the family heard from Gabby that evening until sometime between eleven and midnight when he called over to Dr. Myers's residence and talked to his eighteen-year-old daughter, Kate. They spoke for about fifteen minutes, a conversation that obviously upset Kate. After she hung up, she tried four times to call her father back. Each time, the line was busy. She wasn't looking at the clock, but it seemed to her when she tried to remember later that her last attempt had been at about 12:15 A.M.

What Kate didn't know was that her father had called her back after their first conversation, and that her grandfather had picked up the phone. He expected it to be his son, who was late in arriving for their Christmas Eve festivities, but when he heard Gabby's voice, he decided to talk to him to forestall any scenes. He didn't know until later that Kate had already talked to her father.

All over America, families were tiptoeing through the holidays, avoiding confrontations about old resentments and grudges. Alcohol only adds to the potential for trouble, and Gabby Moore's drinking was scaring his family.

"I decided to occupy his time on the telephone with me, rather than to have any problem . . . to disturb Christmas Eve," Dr. Myers remembered. "I visited with him and we made a date for the day following Christmas for him to appear at my office—it would be closed. . . . I wanted to examine him, and I suggested that I take him to lunch."

Gabby hadn't asked for Kate and he thanked Dr. Myers for remembering his birthday three days before. Dr. Myers assumed that that had been the purpose for his call. As close as Myers could tell, it was about 11:30. He was becoming quite concerned about his son, worrying that he might have had car trouble or a flat tire, so he had been glancing at the clock.

Myers couldn't be sure if Gabby was drinking. "He generally hid that pretty well from me. . . . He told me he wasn't drinking and I rather suspected that he might be bending the truth a bit with me," Myers recalled. "That particular night, he gave very little trace of drinking except toward the end of the conversation. And I asked him then, and he said, 'Oh, just a little bit.'"

If Gabby had been imbibing, he did an excellent job of hiding any slur in his voice. It was easy for Myers to believe that he had had only a few drinks and that things would be all right. He would get Gabby into his office, check his blood pressure, take him out for a good lunch and they could talk things out. Gabby wasn't even forty-five; he had so many good years ahead of him. He would pull out of this depression and get his life together.

That night there were no more calls from Gabby Moore.

Derek Moore and his girlfriend, Janet, had a great time at her family's Christmas Eve, and it was late when they left Union Gap to head back to Derek's apartment. Derek was driving Janet's car and he estimated that he pulled into the backyard parking spot sometime between one and one-thirty.

They noticed right away that the back porch light was off; Gabby *always* left it on.

"Derek," Janet said, "I think something is wrong."

"We better get out of the car," Derek answered. He had seen that both his dad's MG and his own Jeep were parked in their usual spots. "I'll look in the house," he said, while Janet reached in the backseat to gather up his Christmas gifts.

As Derek walked up to the back door, he noticed that the screen door in the back, which Gabby hadn't gotten around to replacing with a storm door for winter, was propped open, held by a white brick.

It hadn't been that way when they left.

Derek saw that someone had closed the kitchen window blinds during the time he'd been gone. They were always open, but now there were just thin slices of light coming through. Vaguely uneasy, he peered through the glass in the back door, and then he spun around with a premonition of trouble, and yelled to Janet who had been waiting tensely in her car. "My dad's not in there!"

"Then he looked at the floor," Janet remembered, "and he said, 'Janet, Janet! Come here!'" As Janet rushed up the steps to join him, Derek cried, 'My dad is laying on the floor!'"

Janet looked in and saw Gabby lying there. They both acknowledged that Derek's father drank a lot, but they had never seen him on the floor and that frightened them.

"We didn't know what the deal was . . . we didn't know that he was passed out or anything," she said. "We just kind of stood there, didn't know what to do, and then Derek said, 'Come on, I'm going to my mom's—to get her to come down with us,' so we went to his mom's and she wasn't home, so we went to the assistant wrestling coach at Davis—to his house—and *he* wasn't home, so we went to the Seven-Eleven and I called the police."

Most people don't have to work on Christmas, but cops do. Police departments never close down—especially not during the "amateur drinking" season when holiday parties send intoxicated drivers out on the roads and trigger family brawls. Patrolman John Mitchell was working one of the least desirable shifts that Christmas in Yakima. Third shift—from eight on Christmas Eve until four o'clock Christmas morning. It was very cold, the ground was covered with snow and the streets were a glare of ice.

It was nearing two A.M. that Christmas morning when Mitchell's radio suddenly crackled, "Respond to eight-one-six South Eighteenth Street . . . Unattended death . . ."

It was an especially sad call at Christmastime. An unattended death. Probably some elderly person, alone and ill, who had died all alone on Christmas Eve. It was a police matter in a sense, but it would probably prove to be a natural death. A stroke. A heart attack. Mitchell drove toward the address on South Eighteenth but he didn't use his whirling bubble lights or siren and he didn't speed over the slippery streets. Whatever had happened had already happened and there was no need to rush. He pulled his police cruiser up in front of the small frame house. He had been told someone would meet him there and he saw a young couple waiting in a parked car. They introduced themselves as Janet Whitman and Derek Moore.

They appeared to be in their teens and they both looked frightened. The boy said, "I think my father's dead. We have to go around to the rear to get into our place."

Mitchell followed Derek Moore's car as he drove around to the back alley and parked. The screen door in the back of the place was held open by a large brick or building block.

"He's in there," the boy said.

Mitchell walked up the steps and peered through the window in the door. There was a light on in the kitchen just beyond the door. A counter, which seemed to serve as an eating area, ran parallel to the back wall. Mitchell could see a man lying on the floor. He had fallen just where there was a passage between the counter and the wall, and his legs were toward the back door. Mitchell couldn't see the upper portion of the man's body because it extended into some room on the other side of the breakfast bar.

Cautiously, the officer stepped into the kitchen. The apartment was quiet. He leaned over the fallen man, who was lying on his left side. Mitchell touched the side of the man's neck, just over the carotid artery. There was no encouraging pulse there, and the skin beneath his hand was already faintly cold. There were no signs of life at all. It looked as though the man had suffered a seizure of some sort and fallen forward, probably dead when he hit the floor. There was no blood, and no sign of struggle.

The call seemed to be as the dispatcher had said, "an unattended death."

Mitchell stepped outside and saw that the young girl—Janet—was waiting close by, while the boy was standing back by their car. "I'm afraid Derek's father is dead," he said quietly, and then he watched while she went over to the boy, put her hand on his arm, and spoke to him.

John Mitchell was startled to hear Janet Whitman say, "Derek, they've shot your father."

Why would she say that? As far as Mitchell knew, the man inside had died a natural death; he certainly hadn't seen anything to indicate that there had been a shooting. Janet was probably on the thin edge of hysteria, and, like all kids, she had undoubtedly seen too many violent movies.

Mitchell didn't know at that point that Gabby had been telling everyone around him that he feared for his life, that someone was threatening to shoot him just as they had Morris Blankenbaker.

Mitchell walked up to Derek Moore. The boy was shocked, but he was able to answer questions.

"Did your dad have any medical problems that might have caused his death?"

Derek nodded his head slowly. "He had high blood pressure, but he was feeling fine tonight when I left. He was in good health . . ."

Puzzled, Mitchell went back into the kitchen. He looked around the room and he caught a glint of light reflected from something on the floor. Leaning over, he saw that it was a .22 caliber brass cartridge. He didn't touch it. He looked beyond the kitchen counter into the living room and noted that the telephone receiver was off the hook, and that a glass next to it had been tipped over.

Still, the place seemed fairly normal. The dishes had been done and the rooms looked neat. Mitchell glanced around the kitchen. There was a broiler pan on the kitchen counter, but it wasn't sitting flat; it rested on a pair of eyeglasses.

That was odd.

Back outside, Mitchell learned that the man who lay dead on the kitchen floor was Glynn "Gabby" Moore, the coach from Davis High School. That made the second coach in Yakima to be found dead at two A.M. in less than five weeks. What were the chances of that happening? Mitchell radioed for his sergeant, Mike Bamsmer, to respond to the scene. While he waited, he advised the watch commander, Lt. Roy Capen, that he thought he might have a possible homicide and requested a detective team too.

Since Moore was lying there in a white T-shirt and there wasn't a speck of blood on him, Mitchell still believed that Gabby had died of a heart attack. The bullet casing on the floor was a little out of place, but it could have been lying there for a long time. The phone off the hook and the glass being knocked over didn't concern Mitchell. If Moore had felt the first twinges of a coronary, he might have tried to call for help, left the phone off the hook, knocked over the glass, and then staggered toward the kitchen—maybe to open the door for the ambulance attendants. Of course, he *had* fallen with his head in the living room and his feet toward the back door, and it seemed as if he should have fallen in the other direction if he had been coming from the living room.

During the fifteen minutes it took for the detectives and his supervisor to arrive, Mitchell planted himself at the back door to keep the scene from being contaminated.

Sergeant Robert Brimmer and Detective Howard Cyr had been wakened from sleep and they had hastily thrown on their clothes to get to Gabby Moore's apartment as quickly as possible. When they arrived at 816 South Eighteenth Avenue, they saw Sergeant Bamsmer and a Dr. A. W. Stevenson standing out in the street on Arlington on the south side of the residence. Stevenson was very active with the athletic teams in Yakima, and Derek Moore had called him to tell him that his father was dead. He had gotten dressed and come over to help in any way he could.

Bob Brimmer stepped into the kitchen and observed Gabby Moore lying on his side between a counter and a wall in the kitchen. His feet and legs were up against the south wall of the kitchen and his back was against the end of the counter. There was a small throw rug beneath his body.

As Brimmer started to enter the kitchen, Mitchell warned him not to step on the shell casing lying on the floor just inside the door about two feet from Moore's feet. The casing was already slightly crimped as if someone had accidentally stepped on it. Mitchell was sure he had not. It was impossible to say how long the casing had been there.

The death scene was photographed, a not entirely silent tableau, because Brimmer became aware of the sound of a record someplace in the apartment, a record that had come to the end, with a needle still wobbling on it: *bi-bipp . . . bi-bipp . . . bi-bipp . . .*

The apartment looked like any bachelor pad that lacked a woman's touch. One end of the living room was being used as a bedroom, blocked off from the rest of the room by a chest of drawers. The king-sized bed was unmade, and a television set and a pair of trousers with the belt still in the loops rested atop the tangled covers.

Brimmer saw that there was a photo album lying open on the floor beside the bed. Bending closer, he recognized pictures of Gabby Moore and Jerilee Blankenbaker Moore. Someone had apparently lain on his stomach on the unmade bed and gazed at the photographs of a once-happy couple—as a record played.

As Brimmer's eyes and camera swept over the room in segments, recording everything, he saw a series of file cabinets that were stuffed with wrestling records and coaching plans. There was a solid cabinet blocking the front door, an overstuffed chair, a couch, a small coffee table. There was a single bathroom, and a small bedroom near the kitchen where sixteen-year-old Derek Moore apparently slept.

The wallpaper was patterned like a simulated old-fashioned piecework quilt, and there were knickknacks here and there and a few prints on the walls; the decor seemed to be a combination of what a previous tenant might have left and the necessary items that Moore and his teenaged son had moved in. Above the bed was a Renoir print of a long-ago Parisian woman with a shadow-box of miniatures beside it—hardly something Gabby would have placed there.

There was a concrete building block beside the rumpled bed, with a box of Kleenex on it, a shoe rack with men's shoes lined up with a precision that seemed ironic now, an alarm clock, and a stack of paperback books.

The phone receiver was on the floor. A portable stereo sat on a table in a corner. The record still revolved, but the arm and needle were at the inside center groove, so that no music played any longer. The record on the turntable was Ray Price's "For the Good Times."

Brimmer found two guns in the bedroom section of the living room. A loaded shotgun leaned against the wall, and a 30-30 lever-action rifle, a Marlin, was lying under the bed. It too was loaded.

"I unloaded both of the weapons," Brimmer said later. "I smelled the barrels. There were no empty rounds in the chambers, and there was no odor of fresh burnt gunpowder in either."

All the while the detectives moved around the Moore apartment, taking pictures, measuring, Gabby Moore's body lay on the little throw rug. They all assumed he had suffered a fatal heart attack. But, because of the recent murder of Morris Blankenbaker, they were taking extra care as they processed the apartment.

They looked in a trash can in the kitchen and saw the Ten-High whiskey bottle with perhaps a "finger" of liquor in the bottom. Brimmer was unable to bring up any usable prints, only prints on top of other prints that left unreadable smudges.

Brimmer and Detective Howard Cyr stood over Gabby Moore's body. He looked quite peaceful now in the darkest moments of the long Christmas Eve-Christmas Day night. Whatever had killed him, he had died, it appeared, almost instantly. It was time to have his body removed. Chances were that there might not even be an autopsy—not with his history of high blood pressure. Brimmer knew, of course, that Gabby had been hospitalized for hypertension only a month before.

"We had taken measurements, we photographed the scene, and there was absolutely no evidence," Brimmer recalled, "and then I got down on my hands and knees and I was looking at this small rug on which he was lying—and *I detected a small spot.*"

Brimmer enlisted Cyr to help him roll Gabby's body over so that he could investigate the speck of red on the rug. Probably catsup or something.

"We moved Mr. Moore from his original position," Brimmer said. "At that point in time, a quantity of blood oozed from the body through this opening in the left shoulder area."

The detectives, who were rarely startled by anything, were shocked. Even with their combined years of experience in investigating deaths, they couldn't believe that there could be this much free blood and not one spot on Gabby Moore's white T-shirt. They could see now, however, what had happened.

Gabby Moore had been shot in the side beneath his left armpit. As long as he lay on the cold linoleum floor of his kitchen with his own considerable weight compressing the wound, the blood was walled back. There had been no sign at all that a bullet had pierced his body. But once they changed the position of his body, the huge amount of blood inside his chest had begun to seep through the wound beneath his left shoulder. It didn't gush as it would from a live person whose heart's beating would pump it out in geysers. The blood only leaked as any fluid would through an inanimate object with a hole in it.

Somewhere along the way, the tangled skein of Gabby's and Morris's personal relationships seemed to have caught them up and trapped them until they had come to a place where they could not get free.

And now neither of them ever would.

11

It was eleven A.M. on Christmas Day. But it did not seem like a holiday in the clean white room where a bright light illuminated the metal table and the air smelled of dried blood and disinfectant. Dr. Richard Muzzall bent once again to perform an autopsy on a most unlikely murder victim. Thirty-three days to the hour since Morris Blankenbaker's postmorten exam, it was Gabby Moore's turn.

Some of the men in the room had been there on November 22: Besides Muzzall, there was Sergeant Brimmer and Detective Vern Henderson. Detective Howard Cyr was there too, and Jeff Sullivan joined them now. The young prosecuting attorney had been elected to office the year before. He and his seven deputy prosecutors took turns being on call to attend autopsies. Sullivan knew it was vital that someone from his office be present at postmortems. When Bob Brimmer had called him before dawn on this Christmas Day, he had elected to forego a celebration with his family. Moore's death astonished him as much as the rest of them.

"Up to that point," Sullivan recalled, "I felt that Gabby was somehow involved in Morris's death, but I'd been out to the hospital and I knew he couldn't have done it himself. We figured maybe he had hired someone to do it. When Gabby was shot too, I didn't know *what* to think."

All of them watched intently as Muzzall lifted his scalpel and made the initial cut. Muzzall's first gross examination of the body of Gabby Moore, forty-four years and three days old, was that he had sustained a gunshot wound to the left posterior, lateral chest. That was all; there were no other injuries.

Muzzall made the first Y-shaped incision from shoulder to shoulder, and at the midpoint, a vertical cut down to the pubic bone. There had clearly been tremendous damage to the organs in the upper part of Moore's body and it was necessary to remove the front ribs and the breastbone so that the coroner could examine the dead man's heart and lungs.

Gabby Moore had died from a massive hemorrhage "secondary to a bullet wound passing through both chest cavities and the heart," Muzzall explained. "After entering the muscles of the left posterior chest, the bullet struck the fourth rib—here—on the left," he said, pointing. "Then it deflected. That changed the angle of its course so that it traveled transversely through the chest passing through the left lung, entering the left side of the heart—what we call the pulmonary outflow tract where the right ventricle pumps blood into the lungs."

Seldom had any of the men in the quiet room seen such damage from a lone bullet. Muzzall showed them where the slug had passed out the right side of the heart and through the right lung, lodging finally underneath the fourth rib on the victim's right side.

"There are approximately two thousand cc's of blood in

the left chest," he said. "That's about four pints. I'd say fifteen hundred cc's—three pints—in the right chest, and another three hundred cc's in the pericardial sac—the membranous sac that surrounds the heart."

Half the blood in Moore's body had gushed out into his chest cavities, and yet only a slight fleck of red had stained the rug beneath him. Muzzall likened the bullet's effect on Moore's heart to cutting a garden house with an ax. "You hemorrhage out exceedingly rapidly," he said. "I'm sure that he lost consciousness within less than a minute and was probably dead in three or four at the most."

Pathologists often use metal probes to figure the angle at which a bullet enters a body. Dr. Muzzall inserted the probe and showed the investigators watching that the bullet had entered directly below the victim's left armpit at the fourth rib, a shot into his "side" in laymen's terms. Had the bullet continued down at the angle it entered, forty-five degrees, Muzzall said that he doubted that it would have been a fatal wound. It probably would have gone through a portion of the left lung, but in all likelihood would have missed the heart and come out somewhere in the front of the chest. However, once it hit the fourth rib, it deflected. The probe went horizontally across the chest, following the path of the bullet that had penetrated the heart and both lungs.

At this point, Muzzall's conclusions didn't seem as important as they would later. What did it matter the angle at which a bullet had entered? Or that it had traveled inside the body? Gabby Moore was dead; he had been dead almost from the moment he hit the kitchen floor.

Muzzall retrieved only one bullet, a .22 caliber slug, that was very distorted after it had smashed into the fourth rib on the left. These bullets are notorious for their unpredictability. They are small caliber and if they pass only through soft tissue, they do minimal damage. However, .22s cut through the air with such velocity that they have been known to kill a target a half mile away. A larger caliber bullet stops a victim in his tracks and knocks him down, doing tremendous damage. The speeding .22 slug is given to tumbling when it hits a bone and is far more likely to ricochet than a larger bullet. A .22 slug that comes into contact with a bone is like a car without a driver—bouncing heedlessly from one obstacle in its path to the next.

Gabby Moore had been alive at eleven P.M. the night before—Christmas Eve. He had been alive, according to his former father-in-law, at 12:15 A.M. when Dr. Myers talked to him on the phone and the two planned a lunch date for December 26. He was dead when his son came home an hour to an hour and a half later.

What had happened during that vital and mysterious time period? Had someone forced his—or her—way into Gabby's apartment, pulled down the blinds to hide what was going on inside from the neighbors, leaving the back door propped open with a brick to assure a quick and fluid getaway?

Ever since Morris Blankenbaker's murder, Gabby Moore had been telling intimates that someone was stalking *him* too, and that he was afraid for himself and his family. No one had taken Gabby very seriously when he insisted that someone was trying to get to him, just the way they had got to Morris. He had tried to tell Jerilee about it, to convince her that not only was he innocent of any implication in Morris's death, but that he was in danger too. He had sworn to Jerilee that he would prove to her he was not involved in any collusion in Morris's murder. Had he had to die to prove his innocence to her? Or was it possible that the real answers to two seemingly senseless murders were more bizarre than anything a fiction writer could possibly dream up?

Now Gabby was dead too, murdered too. The answers were not going to come from him.

Although both of the victims were coaches, both had been shot with a .22 caliber gun, both had been married to the same woman, and both had been killed during the holidays, there were dissimilarities too. Just as he had during the Blankenbaker autopsy, Dr. Muzzall had removed a blood sample from Gabby Moore to check for any alcohol content. Morris had had no percentage of alcohol at all in his blood; Gabby's reading was almost .31. In Washington

State, as in most states, .10 is considered evidence of intoxication.

Gabby Moore had done a remarkable job of convincing Dr. Myers that he had had only a "little" to drink. It was amazing that he was still standing when he was shot. For a person unused to drinking, much beyond .30 is life-threatening; Gabby had undoubtedly developed a tolerance to liquor over the past few years, but even so, .31 was startling.

The killer had had the advantage over both victims; Morris had quite likely been taken by surprise. Gabby would have been too drunk to fight back.

On Friday, December 26, the *Yakima Herald-Republic* headlined the news that another popular local coach had been murdered: "Tied to Blankenbaker Slaying? Davis Mat Coach Moore Shot, Killed."

Dr. Myers was as shocked as anyone. After all, he had spoken to Gabby within an hour or so of his death. Now, he remembered an odd question that Gabby had asked him once—something that had no meaning at the time. Gabby had wanted to know if there was any place on the human body where a person could be shot—not in an arm or a leg, but part of the torso—where it wouldn't be fatal. Myers had pondered the question for a moment and then said that most people could probably sustain a gunshot wound in the shoulder blade and it probably wouldn't hit any vital organs. From what he understood, Gabby had been shot somewhere near his shoulder. It was odd and troubling to think that what he had taken to be a casual conversation might have had a purpose, although for the life of him he couldn't imagine what that purpose might be.

To the media's frustration, Prosecutor Jeff Sullivan was playing his cards very close to his vest, and anyone outside the investigation was getting very little information. "It's a real tragedy," Sullivan said. "I'm very concerned. The police are working on it. So far we have nobody in custody, no answers."

And, indeed, there did not seem to *be* any answers. From

all reports, Gabby Moore had been his own worst enemy. Neither the Yakima Police nor the Yakima County Prosecutor had any idea who had reason to kill him. He had lost a lot of his credibility but not his popularity. Revenge for Morris's murder seemed an unlikely motive. Everyone who knew Gabby well knew he had been in the hospital when Morris died. It seemed unlikely that anyone would be so convinced that Gabby had a finger in Morris's murder that he had murdered Gabby in reprisal. Moreover, Morris Blankenbaker's friends were good solid guys—athletes— some the men who had worked climbing telephone poles with him, some who had gone to school with him. No, detectives couldn't believe that any of them had killed Gabby for revenge. They had no proof. Even if they had had evidence linking Gabby to Morris's murder, they would have gone to the police and not taken justice into their own hands.

The obituaries for Gabby Moore were all glowing, reminding Yakimans of what he had done for sports in their town. No mention was made of the fact that Gabby Moore had been asked to leave Davis High School at the end of the school year. In death, he had somehow regained the respectability that he had lost in life. The quotes from his superiors made it sound almost as if the administration regretted firing him.

Yakima School Superintendent Warren Dean Starr told the press, "We're shocked. He's been a fine employee and an outstanding wrestling coach. The administration is just sick about it."

Funeral services for Gabby Moore were held on December 29, 1975, in the Central Lutheran Church in Yakima. Dr. Charles Wilkes of the First Church of the Nazarene officiated. Gabby's family suggested that memorials be given to the Davis Wrestling Team or Yakima Youth Baseball. There was a decent-sized group of mourners, but not nearly as many as those who had come to pay their respects to Morris Blankenbaker five weeks before.

The apartment on Eighteenth Street that had become a shrine to Jerilee was vacated. Derek Moore went to live with his mother, sisters, and stepfather.

Jerilee Blankenbaker looked for a way to pick up the fragments of her life. If she was afraid, few would blame her. Both of her husbands had been murdered within five weeks, and the police had no idea who the killer was. It was easy to imagine all kinds of frightening scenarios. She wondered sometimes if she *did* have a phantom admirer, someone even more obsessed with her than Gabby had been. What if there was still someone out there who was watching her, now that the men in her life were dead? What had happened already was beyond comprehension. She could no longer believe in a safe, protected existence; she knew that the whole world could blow up without warning.

For her, it had done so. Twice.

Two coaches. Two murders. One at Thanksgiving. One at Christmas. There was no way that anyone was going to write this off as coincidence.

What on earth did it mean? Who would have a reason to hate both of the dead men enough to kill them? A disgruntled former athlete? Some other man who was fixated on Jerilee—from a distance, perhaps—and seethed to see her with Morris and Gabby? No, that was fictional plotting. It didn't fit in Yakima, and it didn't fit with Morris Blankenbaker and Gabby Moore. That didn't stop the rumor mills from churning out motives both plausible and utterly ridiculous.

One tale that circulated around Yakima County was that there was a "drug connection," that both of the victims had known too much about illegal narcotics operations in the area. Another strong rumor was that "organized crime" was involved.

Lt. Bernie Kline told the press that the Yakima police had found nothing that suggested either motive. Nor had they found any connection at all between Morris and Gabby's murders and the shooting death of Everett "Fritz" Fretland, a restaurant owner in nearby Selah, Washington, who had been found shot to death on September 6. Aside from the parallels in time and place, Fretland's murder had nothing at all to do with those of the two coaches.

Kline would say only that Prosecutor Jeff Sullivan and the

police were making progress on Blankenbaker's and Moore's murders, although neither would give any details. "I have every confidence that both killings will be solved," Sullivan said. "The investigation is proceeding and progress is being made. We are looking into a number of possibilities. It is just a process of putting them together."

12

In truth, Sullivan and the others were baffled—but only for a short time. Then they dug in hard to solve this seemingly insoluble double-murder case. In the years ahead, Sullivan would prosecute dozens of felonies and supervise many times that number, but he would never forget this case, a baptism of fire.

In 1976 Prosecuting Attorney Jeff Sullivan was thirty-two years old, the same age as Morris Blankenbaker. Indeed, they both graduated from high school in Yakima in 1961, but Morris had gone to public school at Davis and Sullivan had attended parochial school: Marquette. Basketball was Sullivan's sport; football was Blankenbaker's. Sullivan would come to know Morris Blankenbaker—and Gabby Moore—better in death than he had ever known them in life.

Jeff Sullivan was very handsome, a tall man with a thick shock of blond hair, who bore more than a passing resemblance to John F. Kennedy. After winning the election in November 1974, Sullivan was just embarking on the first of six terms as the elected prosecutor of Yakima County. He

was a native Yakiman, the son of a family who had run a dry
cleaning business in the area for many years. Sullivan had
worked long and hard to achieve the responsible position he
held at such a young age. His BA degree was from Gonzaga
University in Spokane; he had a Bronze Star from his
service as a first lieutenant in Vietnam where he was
platoon leader and executive officer.

Returning from Vietnam, Sullivan, who had a wife and
two children by then (a family that would swell to four
children), worked a full-time job as a trust officer of a
Spokane bank during the day and attended law school at
Gonzaga at night. Despite his punishing schedule, he graduated third in his class in the spring of 1971. Two months
later, he was a deputy prosecutor in Yakima. The next year,
he changed hats and worked as a public defender.

The first case that Sullivan won was against J. Adam
Moore (no relation to Gabby). He managed to get the
second-degree murder charges against his client reduced to
manslaughter. "Well, *I* think I won." Sullivan laughs.
"Adam Moore claims he won."

Adam Moore and Jeff Sullivan would continue to meet on
the legal battlegrounds of Yakima County over the next
three decades.

During trials, their friendship was always there—but on
hold. Sullivan considers Moore "the premier defense attorney in Yakima County—probably in the whole state of
Washington."

The two attorneys had no way of knowing in December of
1975 how challenged both of them would be by the Morris
Blankenbaker–Gabby Moore homicide case.

Gabby Moore's death left a huge void in the lives of his
current and former athletes. His connection to them had
been so much more than that of a teacher to his students.
Coaches—good coaches—shape the lives of their athletes
forever after. They are often the father figures that some
boys and girls never had. They can instill a sense of self-
worth and an inner confidence that lasts a lifetime. Teenagers may be cocky on the outside, but most of them are

unsure of their own capabilities, tough or sullen because they are scared inside. Sports bring discipline and the courage to keep going when it looks as though the athlete has no more heart, muscle, or breath left.

For most of his life, Gabby had been a superlative coach; only the last few years had sullied that image. Gabby had coached both football and wrestling, but, like most coaches, he excelled in one—and that was, of course, wrestling. Wrestlers have to practice more self-denial than participants in almost any other sport. In order to "make their weights," most wrestlers diet or fast the last few days before a match. They may also "sweat out" water weight in saunas. A football player can still play his position if he goes into a game weighing 195 instead of 190; a wrestler cannot. His sport is one-on-one; in a match, he is on his own: just the wrestler and his coach against another team's wrestler and *his* coach. And, of course, almost to the end of his life, Gabby Moore had been there with his boys all the way.

Gabby had recruited his wrestlers when they were in junior high. In Yakima, many of them had the choice of attending either Eisenhower or Davis High School, and Gabby had scouted for up-and-coming young athletes when they were way back in the seventh or eighth grade. With his chosen boys, he became a large part of their lives from that moment on. Little wonder, then, that his murder left dozens of young men shocked and grieving. Gabby Moore had been invincible to them, the strongest, toughest man they had ever known. If something could happen to Gabby, their own mortality suddenly stared back at them when they looked in their mirrors.

Hurting the most were the handful of young men who had counted on Gabby for advice and inspiration and friendship, who had continued to see him on an almost daily basis, even when his life had blown all to hell over a woman who didn't love him anymore. Now they were left free-floating with no anchor.

All of the massive media coverage of Gabby's mysterious death and his obituaries had mentioned that his Davis wrestling team took the Washington State Championship in

1972. That was his dream team. The stars were Kenny Marino, Greg Williams, J. T. Culbertson, Mike McBerb, and Angelo Pleasant. Angelo was probably the most outstanding athlete Gabby had ever coached. Together, that 1972 team had shown what small-town athletes with a superb coach could do. Those were glory days, days that none of them forgot.

And now all the glory was ashes.

Angelo Pleasant was the shining star of the 1972 Davis wrestling squad. His family was proud of him, just as he was proud of them. The Pleasant family had carved a place for themselves as one of the most respected families in Yakima. Coydell Pleasant and her husband, Andrew, ran the Pleasant Shopper Market on South Sixth Street. In order to make ends meet and see that his children all had a good education, Andrew also drove a garbage truck for the city of Yakima. In the summer, when Vern Henderson was between college terms, he and Andrew Pleasant had worked together on the garbage routes, and the two became good friends.

The Pleasant Shopper Market was a typical neighborhood grocery store with a little bit of everything from canned goods to dairy products to produce, and even had a small line of clothing. The Pleasants' strength was that they gave a lot of personal attention that customers didn't find at chain supermarkets. They went out of their way to help customers find what they wanted, they were unfailingly friendly and they were just plain nice people. A black family in a small town populated mostly by Caucasians and a few Hispanics, the Pleasants worked long hours themselves and so did their three sons and three daughters. A close family, they were highly respected for what they had achieved.

"We were always close," Coydell recalled of the good days. The two younger boys, Angelo and Anthony, who were two years apart in age, were especially tight. "They never really fought much. . . . They did things together," Coydell remembered. "They hunted, they fished, picnicked . . . bowling."

The boys were always tussling around and wrestling with each other. They were in Boy Scouts together—in Pack 22 to start with. Later, they both wrestled for Gabby Moore.

One of the things the elder Pleasants preached over and over to their children was the value of education. "I have always taught the kids," Coydell emphasized, "to listen and do what their teacher tells them because the teachers that's teaching them have their education, and they [the kids] are there to try and get theirs. . . . We were really wanting them to go and get an education and that was the only way to do it. They would have to listen to their teachers and learn."

By 1975 the Pleasants had been in business for a decade and their children were just about grown, ranging in age from eighteen to twenty-nine. They had all either completed their higher education or were in the process. The boys all had *"A"* names: Andrew, Jr., Angelo, and Anthony. The girls had pretty *"S"* names: Sarita*, Sondra*, and Selia*. Andrew, Sr., and Coydell were proud of all their children, but it was Angelo who had truly excelled in sports. Andrew and Anthony were good, but Angelo was championship material. Gabby Moore had dropped by the store and told the elder Pleasants that he couldn't see that anything would keep Angelo down; in fact, he figured that Angelo might even make the Olympic Team.

Angelo worked hard in the store. His parents loved to fish, and when they took short vacations, he took over the market and ran it for them. He was an energetic shelf stocker too, and good at getting his friends to help him. Angelo was the kid with the biggest smile and the broadest shoulders. But it was Angelo who had given his parents the most grief too. Every family with more than one child has its problem kid—or *kids.* If one of their children was going to be in trouble, the Pleasants knew it would be Angelo. He was tremendously strong and he was as quick to fight as he was to laugh. He did a lot of both. Schoolwork was harder for him than it was for his older brother, Andrew, or for his sisters. And it was Angelo who chafed most at his father's strict guidelines for behavior.

To his everlasting regret, it was Angelo who once raised his fists to his own father.

Eventually, all three of the Pleasant sons went out for wrestling at Davis High School and wrestled under Gabby Moore's tutelage. Angelo and Anthony admired their older brother, Andrew, and they wanted to follow in his footsteps.

In keeping with his pugnacity, Angelo had a nickname that made his complete name sound like an oxymoron; everyone called him "Tuffy"—Tuffy Pleasant. Only on formal occasions did anyone call Angelo anything but Tuffy.

Tuffy was a good-looking kid with a wide smile. You had to like him when he grinned. He was born on January 28, 1954, in Yakima and spent most his school years there.

"I was in the sixth grade at Adams Elementary School," he remembered, "when my parents went into the grocery business."

Tuffy Pleasant went on to Washington Junior High, and that was where he first met the man who would become his hero. Tuffy was in the ninth grade. Everyone knew Gabby Moore, and when he showed up in the gymnasiums of middle schools, it was like a Broadway producer showing up at a college play. There was a buzz.

"The season was about half over," Tuffy remembered, "and I saw him at certain matches, but I still wasn't wrestling varsity until after Christmas. I finally made the first string and then a couple of people on the team told me that he was the coach at Davis High School and he was down looking for prospects for the years coming."

Tuffy had planned to go to Eisenhower High, but Gabby changed that. "He was down there to talk to me as a coach and asked me to, you know, wrestle for them—that I had potential and to give him a chance as a coach."

Actually, Gabby wasn't the first coach who had tried to recruit Tuffy Pleasant. Even in the ninth grade, the kid had something extra. It wasn't that he was that big; he grew to be 5'7" and he only weighed 138 pounds in his sophomore and junior years in high school, but even way back then he just wouldn't quit.

From the beginning, Tuffy liked Coach Moore. Gabby seemed to take an interest in his wrestlers not just as athletes but as *people*. "You know, it kind of went beyond a coach and a student. It's kind of hard to explain," Tuffy said

113

many years later, half-smiling. "But [it gets so] you know you are pretty good . . . you *are* pretty good, and you just get pretty tight with that coach, especially if you're one of the main starters and he had a lot of interest in you. . . . You want to do good for your coach and your school."

Tuffy did remarkably "good" for his school *and* his coach. He and Gabby had a truly symbiotic relation. Gabby could see that Tuffy was the most outstanding wrestler on a squad of top-grade athletes and that Tuffy would represent him well. A coach's "work product" is the athletes he brings along. Tuffy Pleasant had one of the best wrestling coaches in the state, and a friend/father-figure who had been there for him for years and who would continue to be there. Tuffy already had a wonderful father in Andrew Pleasant, but Gabby painted pictures of a future for Tuffy that Andrew might never have imagined. Gabby promised Tuffy the whole world.

Gabby was Tuffy's football coach too. "He was our head coach on defense." Tuffy had the most challenging position on the football team. "I played 'monster back,' the toughest position on defense," Tuffy remembered. "You can get trapped sometimes. They double-team you, they *triple*-team you—and you got to be tough to handle the position. . . . I was mostly on the off-side of center—either on one side or the other of our defensive tackle."

Tuffy played football two years at Davis High School, but wrestling was his real love, his avocation, the very center of his existence. He didn't mind the strict training rules Gabby Moore laid down.

"No drinking," Tuffy recited the forbidden activities. "No late hours whatsoever, and, if you can restrain yourself from it, no 'physical contact' with any type of lady."

Gabby didn't like his athletes to have girlfriends. "I tried to observe his requirements," Tuffy said with a grin. "To the best of my ability." Since Tuffy had always been a ladies' man, the "best of his ability" was none too pristine when it came to sex.

It was probably natural that Tuffy Pleasant and Gabby Moore were already more than coach and athlete while

Tuffy was in high school. Gabby visited a few times at the Pleasant family home, and he still dropped by the Shopper Market often. The man and the boy went out to dinner where Gabby preached to Tuffy about what his future could be. "He talked to me," Tuffy said. "He told me to keep on moving. 'Don't let your education stop here,' he said. He told me to carry it on through, and I could probably be the head coach here at Davis myself."

Head wrestling coach at Davis! The very thought of something so wonderful made Tuffy's chest swell. That became Tuffy's ambition, the goal he looked toward all through college. One day, he would pick up the torch that Gabby handed down.

Looking back, Tuffy said he considered Gabby a "second father," who was always there for him. "I would go over to his house. I would get the best treatment, and I felt like he just treated me like one of his own kids."

During Tuffy's senior year in high school, he was wrestling in three or four matches a week. Gabby, Gay, and their three children shared a big two-story house, and Tuffy was often invited to stay in the basement guest room. There was a wrestling mat down there, and after a workout, the young champion and several of the others on the squad—Kenny Marino and Joey Watkins, and some of the others—would head for Gabby's house where they would go through another workout. They were young, in peak form, and tireless. They *and* their coach were eating, breathing, and sleeping wrestling.

There was no drinking. Not even beer. The teenagers on his squad got caught drinking beer once and Gabby had a fit. "He just wouldn't allow it," Tuffy said. "Because you get to messing with all of that stuff and you can't get in as good a shape as you need to be for that type of sport."

Gabby himself wasn't drinking then either. None of them could even picture Gabby drinking. When his boys had to "cut weight," he did too. Tuffy smiled again, remembering. "He would have him a little stomach too, you see, and he would lose weight right along with us. We had to have our hair cut; he would cut his."

Sometimes the wrestlers, including Tuffy Pleasant, had trouble with their grades. Gabby saw to it that they had tutors to help them. And if they needed extra credits, he made them "assistants" in his driver-training classes. How much actual work they did is questionable, but they made up for lost credits. It wasn't that he made life too easy for them though. It was more that he was always there to solve their problems, to make them feel confident, to tell them that their hopes for the future *were* attainable. He was a benevolent tyrant, far more benevolent than tyrant.

In 1971 and 1972 Gabby Moore seemed to his athletes to have it all, everything that they hoped to have one day. He had a beautiful wife and a long-standing, apparently happy marriage. He had three great kids and a nice house. And he had the job that most of them thought would be the best job in the world.

Most of them wanted to be just like him.

The peak experience of Tuffy Pleasant's life and his athletic career to date was in the summer of 1972. He had just graduated from high school and was looking forward to college. Four wrestlers—the best in the state of Washington—would be chosen to go to Japan and Hawaii in the exchange program that Gabby had worked so hard on. Tuffy yearned to be one of them.

Tuffy had put on some weight—not much. By his senior year, he was wrestling at 158 pounds. There would be only one wrestler in that weight category chosen for the Japan trip. It was going to be difficult to pick *the* best from the whole state of Washington. All the contenders went to wrestling camp in Moses Lake, Washington. Tuffy roomed with his best friend and teammate, Kenny Marino, knowing how much both of them wanted to win the trip to the Far East.

Kenny made it to the semifinals and then he was dropped. Tuffy made it all the way. He was on top of the world. He had a memorable time in Japan and Hawaii, and then came home to a hero's welcome in Yakima.

He was proud—and happy. No matter what happened to him later in his life, he would always talk about his shining moments in the summer of 1972. "[I was] very happy and always will be too," he would say, almost defiantly.

Tuffy soon came back to earth after the glory of his triumph in Japan. The rest of the summer of 1972 he worked for the Yakima City Sanitation Department hauling brush, to save money for college. With Gabby's hearty recommendation, he had been recruited by the wrestling coach at Columbia Basin College in Pasco, Washington.

Tuffy attended Columbia Basin from September 1972, through the winter quarter in 1975. His best friend, Kenny Marino, started *his* freshman year at the University of Washington in Seattle. Tuffy's brother Anthony was still in high school.

Gabby kept track of his "boys" even after they were in college. "He would come down and see me," Tuffy said. "He was interested in how I did. When I left high school, he called my college coach and asked 'How's Pleasant doing?' If 'Pleasant' was not doing this well, [he'd say] 'Have him do this,' or if 'Pleasant' is not responding to that, 'Well then, have him do that—and he'll respond.' "

It was as if Tuffy had team coaching. Gabby was always around or on the phone to be sure that he was wrestling to his peak ability. It made Tuffy happy to know that his old coach was still guiding him. They were as tight as ever.

Tuffy had not cut himself off from Yakima ties, even though he was living in Pasco. He made the 160-mile round trip twice a week—once in the middle of the week, and again on the weekends.

Kenny Marino, who hadn't gone back to the University of Washington after his freshman year, was living in Yakima. "As soon as I would hit town, he [Kenny] would probably be the first person I would look up," Tuffy remembered. "Before I even went to see my family."

Kenny Marino was like another brother to Tuffy. "I loved him just as much," he said. But neither Kenny nor Tuffy's brother Anthony seemed to have the ambition that Tuffy did. He and Kenny Marino had a social life together, but they didn't talk much about the future. And Tuffy saw that his younger brother Anthony's main ambition was to "become another Jimi Hendrix." Anthony was very good with the guitar, but Tuffy knew what the odds were and sometimes he thought his younger brother was a dreamer.

Anthony had dropped out of school, and both Tuffy and Gabby were trying to get him back in. "Gabby was talking to the principal and some of his teachers trying to get some of his grades straightened out, and the classes straightened out."

In college, Tuffy's road suddenly developed detours. Although he had been a phenomenon in high school, Tuffy Pleasant never quite saw his dreams of wrestling championships in college come to fruition. "I did good," he said of his career at Columbia Basin. "Except that I never did finish up at 'State' because every time it got right down to it, something all the time happened to me—not grades—it was either injury or sickness."

But his grades weren't superior; Tuffy had a hard time in college, and he didn't have Gabby close by to find tutors for him.

In the spring of 1975, as Jerilee Blankenbaker Moore was trying to get up her courage to leave Gabby, Tuffy Pleasant had decided to drop out of college for a quarter. He stayed on in Pasco, though. He had a job with the Washington Fish and Game Department. "We planted fish, salmon, steelhead at certain dams," he explained. "We would go up the river and plant fish, and then we would go down the river to a lower level dam and wait and count how many came through."

Tuffy planned to continue his college at Central Washington University in Ellensburg. He had enough credits to enter as a junior. He planned to bring his grades up so that he really would have a shot at being a teacher and coach back in Yakima. Gabby had told him he could do it. In September 1975 Tuffy would move to Ellensburg and share an off-campus apartment with two roommates at 1501 Glen Drive.

With the new freeway between Ellensburg and Yakima, Tuffy could be in Yakima in thirty-five or forty minutes.

And he had a number of reasons to make the trip often. For one thing, he had never been able to adhere absolutely to Gabby's "no girlfriends" rule. Tuffy was engaged to a young woman named René Sandon*. *More* than engaged, really. They had a three-year-old daughter and René was pregnant again by late fall 1975, due to deliver in June.

Tuffy's second reason to travel often to Yakima was that he realized that Gabby Moore needed him. Gabby had been keeping an eye on Tuffy's college wrestling, but Tuffy had not visited Gabby's home as he used to. He knew that Gabby and Gay were divorced, and he knew about the merry-go-round involving Morris and Jerilee and Gabby, but he was shocked when he moved back closer to Yakima to find that Gabby had completely fallen apart after Jerilee left him.

Beginning in August 1975, Tuffy saw Gabby more often. "Usually," Tuffy said, "I started seeing him other summers toward the end—seeing how he's doing and talking to him about his team for the coming year, and about football."

But this summer was different. Sometime in August, Tuffy went by the house that Gabby had bought to share with Jerilee and her children. He was surprised to find that Gabby didn't live there any longer. He set out to find him.

"I kind of felt he would be the same old Mr. Moore," Tuffy recalled. But he had heard rumors that Gabby's teams weren't doing well at all, and some of the wrestlers had told him, "It's Mr. Moore—it's not us."

Tuffy had wanted to see for himself, and he found that the scuttlebutt was all true. Gabby was doing a lot of drinking, sitting there in front of Tuffy and the other guys and pouring one drink after another. Gabby had always told Tuffy and the other athletes, "I don't care what you do out of season, but *during* season I care a lot what you do."

Now, Tuffy tried to tell himself that it wasn't as if school had started. Gabby wasn't really coaching yet, and when September came and the wrestlers turned out, he would shape up. Tuffy was sure Gabby would quit drinking then.

From the moment Tuffy Pleasant renewed his contacts with Gabby Moore in the summer of 1975, he saw him every day for a month. It seemed essential to Gabby that Tuffy be there—to listen. Gabby was morose; all the old spark had gone out of him. He told Tuffy that he was selling the house he had just bought the year before. No reason to keep it. He had only bought it for Jerilee and her kids. He couldn't live in it alone. He thought it would sell quicker if he put in a concrete driveway. Laying concrete was at least something solid Tuffy could do to help Gabby, so he and a couple of his cousins put the driveway in. "We finished it off after Labor Day."

School started and Gabby kept right on drinking.

Tuffy and Kenny Marino and some of the other members of Gabby's earlier teams talked it out and set up a schedule where they could cover for him at after-school practice and even at wrestling meets. They knew that if they weren't there to oversee things, the school administration would see how bad things really were with Gabby.

There are few things more shocking for the very young than to discover that their heroes have feet of clay. Gabby Moore had been everything to them, and he had had it all. Now, their old coach didn't have the perfect life any longer. Both his marriages were history. His first wife, Gay, was married to one of the football coaches at Davis. Gabby's marriage to Jerilee had been over before it began. And soon his athletes heard that, despite their help, Gabby's job was in jeopardy. This news only made them redouble their efforts to save it for him.

Sometimes Gabby showed up for practice, and sometimes he didn't. It was really better when he *didn't*—better than the occasions when he had liquor on his breath, or when he went out to his car to sneak a drink from a bottle he kept there. He just hadn't seemed to care anymore about anything except getting Jerilee to come back to him.

Gabby's athletes had tried to save him. If it was a matter of trying and wanting and wishing on their parts, he would have somehow come around to being his old self again. Right up to the end, they had been visiting him and trying to cheer him up.

But now Gabby Moore was dead, and none of that mattered anymore.

13

Vern Henderson had not been officially assigned to the Morris Blankenbaker murder case, but now, with Gabby Moore's murder, Vern was transferred to the homicide team investigating both the Blankenbaker and Moore murders. There was no way that Vern could keep from working on the growing mystery. He couldn't stand on the outside any longer. He had to be there to find the answer to what was proving to be a more and more inscrutable puzzle. But first, he needed some key to find his way in—some piece of physical evidence that could start him in the right direction.

The loss and grief Vern had felt when Morris Blankenbaker was murdered had not diminished, and it never would until he found his friend's killer. "I don't have many friends," he said. "No, that's not what I mean—I *know* lots of people—but people who really *know* me, know how I'm feeling, no . . . I don't let many people get close to me. Morris was like that. Rucker was like that too. We had *bonds.* Just some people you get the feeling with and others you don't. . . . I always learned you *can't* let people get that close to you because then they know your weaknesses. In a fatherless home, you learn to grow up quick; you don't really have a childhood. . . . Morris's mother and my mother kept telling us, 'You gotta do something with your life. You can't just be running around the streets.' "

Both Morris and Vern had been aware that people said mothers couldn't do a good job of raising sons, and they strived to excel to prove them wrong. "I always wanted to

121

do something to make my mother proud of me," Vern Henderson said.

Now Vern would never be proud of himself, not really, until he found Morris's killer. Morris had been so kind to everyone. "If Morris Blankenbaker liked you, he would do anything for you. He was like a bull on the football field," Vern said. "He could run right over anybody. He could have whipped half the school, but he wasn't a bully; he wasn't like that."

Everyone on the Yakima Police Department wanted to solve the bizarre double murders of the two popular coaches, but not one of them felt the impetus to do so in his gut the way Vern Henderson did. In that dismal period between a bloody Christmas and a cheerless New Year, Vern thought about all that had happened and wondered where to start. Which brick could he remove from the wall that a killer had built up around himself? How could he make that wall tumble?

Bob Brimmer was Vern's sergeant upstairs in the detectives' office. He was an old-school investigator with decades on the job. He would work the case his way, and Vern would work it his. He knew what his strengths were. He was a "listener" and he had spread out a network that snared information during his years investigating juveniles. He counted on his network now. Yakima was a small town, and people talked. Sooner or later, some names were going to work their way back to Henderson. At a time when he had the *least* inclination to be patient, that was just what he was going to have to be.

Vern Henderson, always taciturn, became doubly so as the old year passed away and 1976 dawned. Somebody knew who had shot Morris and who had shot Gabby. It might be the same man—or woman. It might be two different men—*or women*.

Even though Gabby Moore had begun as the prime suspect in Morris Blankenbaker's murder, Bob Brimmer and Howard Cyr had established that he could not have killed Morris—not with his own hands.

But then who had?

When Vern Henderson said everybody in Yakima liked Morris, he wasn't overstating it. Everybody had.

It's an old rule of thumb in homicide investigation that detectives look for the killer among those closest to the victims. Family first. Then friends. Then coworkers, and out into a continually widening circle. There had been no obvious reason at all for strangers to kill either Morris or Gabby. They hadn't been robbed. Neither had been involved in a fight or altercation with anyone. Their only "enemies" were one another.

And their main "connection" was Jerilee. All of the witnesses who had seen Jerilee the morning she found Morris's body agreed that this was a woman in deep shock and excruciating grief. She was never a serious suspect. Why should she be? If she had wanted to be free of Morris a second time, he would have let her go as gently as he had the first time. But she hadn't wanted to leave the father of her two little children; she loved Morris, and she was looking forward to remarrying him.

She had no gun.

She had no gun debris on her hands.

Her recall of events of the night/morning of November 21/22 dovetailed perfectly with witness statements and with the detectives' reconstruction of events.

Morris had stuck close to home when he wasn't teaching, coaching, or moonlighting at the Lion's Share. Gabby had stayed in his apartment in the last weeks of his life. His closest companions had been his son, his daughters, and the former athletes who had tried to comfort him and to cover for him so he wouldn't lose his job.

Even in the weeks when he had not been officially assigned to the Blankenbaker case, Vern Henderson had gone over Morris's last moments a hundred times in his mind. "He knew who it was," Vern said. "The reason I know Morris knew who it was was because there were no defensive wounds. I looked for that when I was at his autopsy."

Vern Henderson knew Morris's habits almost as well as he knew his own. Morris would have driven into the alley behind his house, parked his car next to the carport, and headed for the side gate.

"He had gotten through the gate," Henderson surmised. "And he was probably shutting it, and someone called, 'Morris!' and he turned around. He knew who it was. As good as Morris was, you might have killed him, but not without his having some defensive marks, unless he knew who it was. As close as the shooter was, it made me know it wasn't an 'enemy' who shot him, to get that close to Morris—because Morris was too good at hand-to-hand combat. No, he knew him."

There would always be times when Vern Henderson regretted that he carried the visual memory of Morris lying on the autopsy table, but that was the price he had to pay. He had needed to *know* that there were no defensive marks on his friend at all, to *know* how close the shooter had gotten to Morris. It helped him to picture who he was looking for. "I knew that Morris not only knew the person who shot him—he had to have trusted him—to let him get that close."

Now, at last, Vern was right in the middle of the investigation not only of Morris's murder but also of Gabby's. He had watched Gabby from a distance during the last weeks of his life. "I expected that Gabby had had something to do with it," he said. "I knew he didn't shoot him [Morris]—as far as that point, but naturally he was a suspect."

One encounter kept coming back to Vern. After Morris's autopsy, he had been downstairs in the radio room just as Gabby Moore was coming down the hall headed for Brimmer's office on the second floor. "He was coming around there and I wanted to see him, because that would tell me something for my own self.

"He came down the hall and I'm standing at the end of the hall waiting on him. And he kept his head down. He would not look up at me," Vern recalled. "And he got right even with me and he says, 'Vern, I . . . I . . . just didn't do it,' but he never would look up and look at me dead in the face. And he went on and I kept looking at him. I said, in my own mind, I *know* he didn't shoot him, but he had someone do it."

Vern Henderson shrugged. "And there was no evidence. And all I could think of was when we were back in junior high school and he was our wrestling coach. How he always said, 'Look your opponent dead in the eye. Let him know what you're feeling, and that you're going to beat him.' But Gabby wouldn't look at me."

Sometimes now, Vern wished he had gone up to Gabby as he stood over Morris's grave and asked him some questions. Vern hadn't known how short the time was. He had always thought that there would come a time when he could talk to his old coach—where maybe careful conversation would allow the whole truth to come out. He remembered the old Gabby, and how he had loved his athletes—how he had loved Morris. He had figured that somewhere deep inside, Gabby had to be feeling pangs of conscience. That was why Gabby had driven up to the cemetery in the bitter wind of winter. That was probably why Gabby had increased his prodigious consumption of alcohol. At the end of his life, Gabby Moore had been as self-destructive as any man Vern Henderson had ever seen. Whatever had happened on Christmas Eve, there would never be a time now for Vern Henderson to sit down and talk with Gabby Moore. He would have to figure out a way to tap into the minds of the killer or killers, living or dead.

How were Bob Brimmer and Vern Henderson and the rest of the Yakima detectives going to find the concealed fragments that made up the crimes? How were they going to get solid evidence that Jeff Sullivan could take into a murder trial? Tips and leads were called into the office, and Brimmer fielded those. Henderson was more a believer in the gifts of information that could be gleaned out in the streets.

Henderson had made a point to find out who Gabby's closest associates were when Morris was killed. Now, the Yakima investigator set out to see who Gabby Moore had spent his time with in the last week or so of his life. It didn't take long for him to find out that Gabby had had almost daily visits from a number of his athletes. Names mentioned to Vern Henderson and Bob Brimmer were Joey Watkins, Angelo "Tuffy" Pleasant, Tuffy's younger brother Anthony, and Stoney Morton*.

Joey Watkins told Brimmer and Henderson that several of the guys had visited Gabby often in December. He knew for a fact that Tuffy and Anthony Pleasant and Stoney Morton had stopped by to check on him on Christmas Eve.

Vern couldn't believe that the Pleasant brothers or Joey Watkins or Kenny Marino would have hurt Morris. They were Morris's friends. Vern had seen Morris teach Tuffy some wrestling moves, and the Pleasants and Joey sometimes visited at the house on North Sixth Street.

"I called all my friends," Henderson said, "and asked if they had heard any rumors, and my one friend said he had heard that Joey Watkins and Tuffy Pleasant had been in the Lion's Share talking to Morris a little while before he got off work."

That information didn't make much of an impression on Henderson. He knew that both Watkins and Pleasant often stopped by the Lion's Share; it wasn't as if they had suddenly shown up someplace where they had never been. In fact, it was Joey Watkins who had gone home with Morris to back him up the night Gabby broke into Morris's house while he was working and Jerilee had been frightened.

When Vern checked at the Lion's Share, he learned that Tuffy and Joey had been in on Friday night, probably between nine and eleven, at least two hours before Morris got off work.

Tuffy Pleasant interested Vern more than Joey Watkins, though. "I thought, 'Now Tuffy hung around with Gabby all the time.' I'd seen him driving Gabby's little MG around town."

Back in November, Vern had turned that information over in his head but he never could make it fit. Sure, Tuffy had two sides to him. He could be the kid with the wide-open grin who was everybody's friend, but he could also be a fighter. Vern knew that Tuffy had put his own father in the hospital once. "His dad never turned him in," Vern recalled. "But I knew about it because we worked on the garbage trucks together way back and we got to be friends."

Joey Watkins was a big guy, but Vern had never known

him to be threatening off the wrestling mat. Naaww . . . he couldn't see either of those "fools" shooting Morris. He put it out of his mind and concentrated on his own assignments.

But now he was working two homicides and on occasion his thoughts turned back to the tight relationship Gabby and Tuffy had had. Vern wondered if Tuffy had wanted Gabby to be happy bad enough to shoot Morris. That conclusion was too mind-boggling and Henderson shook it away. Tuffy was a hothead sometimes, but Vern couldn't picture him as a killer.

And then there was the question of who had shot Gabby. Tuffy Pleasant owed everything to Gabby Moore. He loved his coach and his friend. There was no way he would have harmed a hair on Gabby's rapidly balding head.

Vern Henderson always ended up right back where he'd started with his maddeningly circular theorizing. When it came right down to it, he had no idea who had killed either Morris or Gabby.

Bob Brimmer and Vern had gone to the Pleasants' South Sixth Street grocery store several times. They now asked Tuffy's mother, Coydell, if she would have Tuffy contact their office.

On Saturday, January 3, 1976, Tuffy Pleasant came into the Yakima Police Station for an interview. He was not read his rights under Miranda because he was not considered a viable suspect. Yes, he said he had visited with his former coach early on the evening of Christmas Eve. He said he had asked Moore if he'd like to go out someplace and have a couple of drinks and Gabby Moore had agreed and started to clean up. But then, Gabby had received two phone calls and whoever it was had seemed to upset him. Tuffy said he had changed his mind about going out. He wanted to stay in his apartment and have some drinks. And so Tuffy had left to go to some of his own family's Christmas celebrations. When Tuffy left, he said Gabby had been fine. Tuffy had apparently been as shocked as everyone else to learn the next morning that Gabby was dead. ·

Pressed, Tuffy admitted that Gabby had been talking kind of crazy about getting rid of Morris Blankenbaker earlier in the fall. He had told Tuffy that he would be willing to pay five hundred dollars, or even more, if someone would shoot Morris. Tuffy had said he wouldn't even consider killing Morris. To get Gabby off the subject, to placate him for the moment, he had suggested a name he plucked out of the air as a possible hired killer, someone who could furnish "a cold gun." He said he had described this potential hired gun as someone who "likes leather clothes."

"The whole idea behind the [proposed] shooting of Morris," Tuffy told police, "was for the love of Jerilee."

Gabby was up and down emotionally all fall, Tuffy said, but he seemed to be at his lowest ebb a few days before Christmas. Tuffy told Brimmer and Henderson that he had a strong alibi for the night Morris Blankenbaker was shot, although he couldn't say just what Joey Watkins had done that night.

He said that he and Joey had gone to the Red Lion and then Joey "split" and went off by himself. Tuffy said he had stayed all night with a girl at the hotel, and then had gone to an address on North Fourth in Yakima and spent the rest of Saturday and Saturday night with the girl there. On Sunday, he said he had moved his belongings out of Joey Watkins's house and that was the last time he had had much to do with him.

Although the Yakima detectives were not entirely convinced that Tuffy had told them the truth or *all* of the truth, they had no evidence to tell them differently. Tuffy left their offices.

Tuffy Pleasant's whereabouts on the night Morris Blankenbaker was shot had to be traced. Hard facts were essential, even though Tuffy made an unlikely suspect. No matter how many questions the Yakima detectives asked, they couldn't find anyone who said Tuffy had anything against Morris. It was common knowledge that Gabby had been his hero, his mentor, for years.

Bob Brimmer and his detectives had gone over the yard where Morris Blankenbaker had been shot a number of times. They figured that, with three shots, there should be three bullet casings lying somewhere in the area, unless the death gun had been a revolver. An automatic or a semiautomatic would eject the spent casings once the slug had been fired at a target. Morris hadn't mowed the grass before the snow fell, and there were also tall weeds in a lot of spots. It wasn't likely that the killer had taken the time to stop and look for bullet casings so he could pick them up before he fled down the alley. The detectives had even used metal detectors, painstakingly working over the grass and parking area in a grid pattern.

And they had found nothing.

With Gabby's murder, they *did* have a bullet casing. The .22 shell was crimped on the open end, probably where the killer had stepped on it as he left by Moore's back door. The casing's worth was minimal *unless* or *until* they found a gun to match it to, or they found a casing from the Blankenbaker shooting to compare to it. At least they knew now they were looking for an automatic .22 caliber weapon.

If they were lucky enough to find a casing on the Blankenbaker property, they could establish what everyone involved in the probe already believed—that both Morris and Gabby had been shot with the same gun. If they could prove that, and if they could somehow locate that gun—a tremendously big "if"—they might just be back in business.

In the meantime, Vern Henderson continued his "playing tag," as he put it. He talked to his friends who had talked to their friends who had talked to others. Everyone seemed to have his or her own slightly unique hypothesis about who the killer was.

Vern kept hearing Joey Watkins's name. Vern's gut still told him that it wasn't Joey Watkins he was after. Joey was talking too much for a man trying to hide something, and Vern just couldn't see him as a double murderer.

But Joey Watkins and Tuffy Pleasant were friends, and they had occasionally shared living quarters. In fact, they had lived together right up to the night Gabby died. Tuffy and Gabby had been "tight." Both Tuffy and Joey Watkins had been seen with Morris within hours of his murder, and over the last few months of his life they had been regular visitors to Gabby's apartment.

Joey Watkins and Tuffy Pleasant had been close friends

since grade school. Joey nodded when Vern asked about that. Yes, Tuffy had lived with him on and off during the previous autumn when Tuffy came home from college on the weekends, except when he was staying at his girlfriend's house. Joey told Vern Henderson that he *was* with Tuffy for the first part of the evening on November 21, until Tuffy joined some people at the next table in the Red Lion—two women and a man.

Joey said he had gone home, visited with his girlfriend, and then gone to bed. He said he really didn't know *when* Tuffy came home, or *if* he came home during the night. Tuffy often went to his girlfriend René's house to stay overnight. He had his own key to Joey's place, so Joey couldn't say yes, no, or maybe about where Tuffy had been after he last saw him at nine P.M. on the night of November 21.

However, Vern found it interesting that by Christmas Eve, Tuffy no longer stayed with Joey Watkins on weekends. In fact, Joey said, they rarely saw each other after Morris's death.

Joey agreed that he had seen Gabby Moore on Christmas Eve. Moore had come over to his house around 6:30 or 7:00 that evening. He had been looking for Tuffy and Kenny Marino because they had his sports car. The coach had sat down and watched a football game with Joey for a while, and then Joey said he had driven Moore down to North Fourth Street where Kenny Marino lived. "Gabby's car was parked out there."

Joey said that was the last he saw of Gabby; he had picked up his girlfriend and gone out to Harrah, a tiny hamlet south of Yakima, where she worked at a halfway house for mentally disturbed adolescents. "We stayed there until Christmas morning," Watkins said.

Joey said he had no idea that Gabby Moore had been shot until the next morning. "I stopped at Mrs. Pleasant's store and I was going to get something to eat and I just saw his picture in the headlines."

In January, Sergeant Richard Nesary, the Yakima Police Department's polygraph examiner, ran four lie detector

tests on Gabby Moore's associates—including Tuffy
Pleasant—in an effort to see if red flags might pop up.
Nesary read the resulting strips and came up with only
inconclusive readings.

Despite Tuffy's protestations that he had no idea who had
shot Gabby Moore, Vern Henderson had heard enough
through the grapevine to be more interested in the results of
Tuffy's polygraph than in the others. Tuffy had been the
closest to Gabby Moore by far. Tuffy Pleasant had always
called Gabby Moore "The Man." And that was exactly
what Gabby had been to Tuffy for the greater part of their
relationship—the perfect example of what a man should be.
If Tuffy had wanted one thing in this world, it was to go to
college and graduate and be just like Gabby Moore. Vern
heard that often enough as he asked around town. "It wasn't
Joey Watkins who was driving around in 'The Man's' car all
the time," Vern said. "It was Tuffy in that little MG."

Then how *could* it be Tuffy who had killed his hero?
Everyone Vern talked to said that Tuffy would have done
anything to help Gabby. Vern Henderson realized *that*
might be the answer to only half of the puzzle, and that if
Tuffy had killed Morris for Gabby, it made some kind of
bleak sense. The other half didn't make any sense at all.
Tuffy might have killed *for* Gabby, but he would have died,
Vern thought, before he would kill Gabby himself.

Vern had begun following Tuffy's car occasionally as he
drove through Yakima. He knew that Tuffy had gone up to
Gabby Moore's grave—just as Gabby had been seen standing silently over Morris's grave. Was Tuffy's grief a normal
sense of loss or was it combined with regret and guilt?

Polygraph examinations can produce all kinds of results.
Four recording "pens" glide smoothly along moving graph
paper at the rate of six inches a minute. A subject's blood
pressure, respiration (number of breaths per minute), galvanic skin response (sweating), and pulse are generally good
indicators of reactions to stress-producing questions. All
polygraph questions are answered either "Yes" or "No,"
and the operator establishes his subject's "normal" re-

sponses by asking innocuous questions such as "Do you live in the United States?" "Is it Wednesday?" and "Is your shirt green?" He often will ask a deliberate lie question to check to see how a particular subject will react when he gives a dishonest response.

With every decade, polygraph machines become more sophisticated just as their operators learn to look for more subtle signals. Beyond the accepted physiological reactions, there are minute chemical changes that today can alert a polygrapher that a subject may be evading the truth.

When Tuffy Pleasant went on the polygraph on January 10, 1976, Dick Nesary was using what was then a near-state-of-the-art system: a 1971 Arthur II polygraph machine. Nesary always double-checked the machine beforehand. Nesary explained his check-out procedure. "Well, it's very simple. You take a pop bottle and wrap the blood pressure cuff around it, pump up the pressure to eighty and leave it sit for five minutes and see if the pressure goes down. If it doesn't, then there's no leaks in the system."

On January 10, as Nesary gave the lie detector test to Tuffy Pleasant, he built up gradually to the vital questions: "Did you shoot Morris Blankenbaker?" and "Did you shoot Gabby Moore?"

In Nesary's words, the results were "unreadable."

"My opinion was that he had knowledge of the situation, but I could not arrive at an opinion as to whether or not he was the actual one involved in it."

Those January results dampened Vern Henderson's enthusiasm for Tuffy Pleasant as a viable suspect, at least until he talked again to Joey Watkins. Watkins wasn't happy about becoming even a long-shot murder suspect, and he was quite willing to talk with Vern. He pointed out that *he* was not the one who had always been seen with Gabby Moore—that it was Tuffy who was Gabby's buddy. "Who do you think was running around with Gabby?" Watkins asked Henderson. "It was Tuffy, not me. I didn't run around with that man."

"That's true," Vern agreed. "You didn't."

Vern Henderson realized, however, that Joey Watkins might be the vital link between himself and Tuffy Pleasant.

With every meeting he had with Watkins, Vern learned more. "Tuffy didn't know what Joey Watkins was saying to me," Vern recalled. "But from talking with Watkins, I knew that when I eventually got to Tuffy, he would be able to tell me what had gone on."

Joey Watkins had taken his time about trusting Vern Henderson, and he had debated how much to tell him. Finally, he blurted out information that was of tremendous importance to the double-murder probe.

Vern remembered the moment. "Joey said, 'Hey, look— Tuffy—I saw Tuffy with a *gun.*' And I said, 'What kind of a gun?' and he said, 'A German-type twenty-two with a long barrel and a long handle that was wrapped with tape.'"

Vern asked Watkins if the gun had been an automatic, and Watkins nodded. "Yeah, one of those German Luger type guns."

"But I heard *you* had a gun like that," Vern hedged.

"It was in my house, all right," Watkins agreed, "but it wasn't mine. It belonged to Tuffy."

Watkins said he didn't know where the gun had come from and he had no idea where it might be at the present moment.

Although he desperately wanted to solve Morris's and Gabby's murders, Vern Henderson had been halfway hoping that he wouldn't hear information that placed Tuffy Pleasant squarely as the focal point in his investigation. He would far rather have had the suspect be a stranger. There were too many ties between them, these two young black men in a town where they were in such a minority. Vern and Tuffy were both athletes who had excelled and made their school and their town proud. Vern liked Tuffy, even though he could be a wiseguy at times, and Vern deeply admired Tuffy's father, Andrew Pleasant, Sr. The last thing Vern wanted to do was humiliate and grieve that man who had struggled so hard to see his children do better in the world than he had. Andrew had worked two jobs all his life and he had just about seen his dreams come true; all but one of Andrew and Coydell's children were in college by the midseventies.

But the word was out that Tuffy Pleasant might be a suspect in the two shootings—not officially, but in an undercurrent of gossip—and Andrew, Sr., came to Vern, just as Olive Blankenbaker had once come to him. They were each pleading for justice for their children, and their requests left Vern Henderson torn in two.

"When Morris's mother asked me to find who had killed him, I told her that I would," Vern said. "I didn't know what else to say. It was very emotional, and I just wanted to hug her. It was the same with Tuffy's father.

"Tuffy's father came to me and he said, 'Look, Vern, you're working this case. I want to know if my son actually did this or not. I know we can trust you.' I knew right then that I was going to be in trouble because who *really* wants to know that his son committed murder? I knew right then that if I found out Tuffy had something to do with it, our friendship would be over."

It was a solid friendship going back to when Andrew Pleasant came to watch Vern play football and continuing when they worked in the Sanitation Department while Vern was going to Yakima Valley Community College.

Vern didn't know Tuffy Pleasant as well as he did Tuffy's father, but he was about to. He drove up to Ellensburg and went to the rooming house where Tuffy was living while he was going to Central Washington University. Tuffy met him outside, and the two began what would be a tentative, edgy, continuing dialogue.

From that point on, Tuffy Pleasant would always sense that someone was waiting and watching his movements. He could count on seeing Vern Henderson often. He suspected—correctly—that Vern was somewhere around, even when he didn't see him. It didn't matter that Tuffy had walked out of the lie detector test with an unreadable graph, leaving the polygrapher Dick Nesary shaking his head. It didn't matter that Tuffy felt he had aced his meeting with Brimmer and the other detectives in January. He still felt uneasy. It seemed to Tuffy that Vern knew too much about him, and that he wasn't ever going to leave him alone until he proved it.

The hell of it was that Tuffy kind of liked Vern Henderson. In other circumstances, he would have been glad to talk with him, but, for the moment, Vern made him nervous.

And that was exactly the reaction Vern was trying for.

14

Morris's big old house on North Sixth Street had renters again, and life went on. Every time Vern Henderson passed the house, memories came back, good memories of visiting with Morris and Jerilee, of being welcome in their home and of his own pleasure at seeing Morris happy again. But in the end the bad memories always prevailed. Vern had not seen Morris lying there in the snow on that awful night when he died, but he had seen the pictures. He could half close his eyes and see just the way it had been. There had to be some evidence left in Morris's yard or in the alley, something that hadn't been found yet.

The pressure to come up with enough evidence to charge a suspect had been incredibly hard on Sergeant Bob Brimmer. It was Friday, January 16, when he took his first day off in a long time and prepared to go fishing for three days just to get away from the case for a short time.

Sitting in the detectives' office alone, Vern Henderson felt an overwhelming urge to do *something*. He threw on his coat and headed out to North Sixth Street. He knew from talking with Joey Watkins that Tuffy Pleasant had had the German automatic in his possession during November and December. *If* Tuffy was the guilty man, and *if* he had used that gun to shoot Morris, there would have to be some casings somewhere near where Morris had fallen. Henderson decided to literally put himself in the shoes of the shooter.

He walked south from Lincoln down the alley behind the apartment house at 208 North Sixth Street where Gerda Lenberg had heard the sound of someone running the night after Thanksgiving. Her duplex was right where the sidewalk on Lincoln met the alleyway.

Several houses down, Vern came to the parking area behind what once had been Morris's house. The little Volkswagen would have been in the carport, and the Chevelle that Morris had driven to work that night had been pulled right up onto the grass of the backyard. There were different cars there now, but Vern saw only the way it had been in November.

The new apartment house where Rowland Seal and Dale Soost lived was very close to Morris's yard, probably not more than ten feet from the property line.

"First, I walked up to the fence where I knew—where I thought Morris would have been standing," Vern remembered, his eyes focusing on some time long ago. "I knew how the body was, because I knew how the bullets had entered—from seeing the autopsy . . . and I'd seen the photographs."

Now Vern Henderson *became* the shooter. He never doubted that there had only been one killer; Mrs. Lenberg was positive she had heard only one set of feet in clunky shoes running down the alley, and then, after the "firecrackers," back up the alley. Vern stood where the man whose face he couldn't yet know had stood facing Morris.

It was almost as real to Henderson at that moment as if he had actually been there two months earlier. "I knew it was an automatic. I said to myself, those guns will kick to the right. I'd read in a book that the casings could kick up to fifteen to twenty feet when they eject out of that thing depending on what kind of spring it had in there. That shell could pop fifteen to twenty feet and it could go in either direction, directly back or out to the side. Well, so I said to myself, let's do a triangle. You're standing here when you shot him, so it went over to the right."

Vern turned his head slowly and looked to the right. He saw the four-foot-tall chicken-wire fence that separated the apartment grounds from the lawn of Morris's house. There was a cement path with a curb just beyond the fence. He figured the fence was about ten feet from where he stood. Almost as if some hand were guiding him, Vern drew an imaginary arc in his mind to the right, and then he walked over to the fence. To himself, he muttered, "It should have landed right here."

He looked down at a spot between the path and the fence on the apartment house side. And there it was. The shell lay in a puddle in the shadow of one of the cement posts, its shiny surface dulled now from lying out in the weather.

Vern Henderson felt his heart beat faster as he crouched and picked up the single shell casing. It was more precious to him than if it had been made of solid gold. He knew in his gut that it had been there all along—from the very moment Morris died. The slug from this casing had entered his best friend's head and shattered, and the casing had sailed through the freezing night air and landed so that it was hidden in plain sight.

Cradling the shell carefully, Vern Henderson slipped it into an evidence envelope and drove to his sergeant's home. There, Bob Brimmer looked at it and said that he thought it would turn out to be almost identical in make and in markings left by the firing pin, extractor, and ejector to the casing found on the kitchen floor of Gabby Moore's apartment on Christmas Eve. They would have to send it to the state lab to be sure.

Both men were excited but cautious. They didn't have a gun yet, but if the casings matched, they would know that the two shootings were connected. However, they still wouldn't know whose gun had fired them.

Vern Henderson took the shell back to the Yakima Police Department. He compared it to the casing from the Moore murder. That shell was shinier, but that didn't matter. What mattered were the extractor and ejector marks made by the gun mechanism—and the firing pin mark.

"They both had that moon-shape on the bottom," Vern remembered. "Just alike."

He tagged the casing from the apartment fence and locked it in his desk. On Monday, Bob Brimmer would send it to the lab to verify what both he and Henderson had seen with their naked eyes.

When—and *if*—the murder weapon was located, the casing from the bullet that had killed Gabby Moore could be matched to the lands and grooves inside the barrel. Not so with the weather-beaten shell Vern had found ten feet from where Morris died. But the marks left by the gun on its base would be enough.

Henderson suspected that the other two casings from bullets fired at Morris had ejected to the right too, but had traveled farther than this one; they probably had landed on the well-traveled path and been stepped on or kicked aside long ago by residents of the apartment house. He didn't need them. Even so, he and another detective returned to North Sixth Street with a shovel and a screen. They pulled up grass and weeds and dug up shovelfuls of dirt and sifted them through the screen on the off-chance they would find the other shell casings.

They didn't find them. They never would.

The chance of finding the gun that had killed both Morris Blankenbaker and Gabby Moore was minute. Whoever the killer was, he would have been a fool not to have gotten rid of it after the second murder. There were so many places around Yakima to dispose of a weapon. Canyons, endless miles of barren desert, mountains, rivers. There was a huge military training reservation east of town where thousands of Washington State National Guardsmen, reserve officers, and troops from Fort Lewis went on maneuvers. For that matter, the gun could have been sold or given to someone on "The Coast"—a term residents of eastern Washington use when referring to Seattle.

The latter assumption seemed the most likely. The *Yakima Herald-Republic* reported that Yakima County authorities were arranging for divers to search for the missing .22 in rivers and lakes on "The Coast."

As it turned out that wasn't necessary. Some unseen force

seemed to be dictating that there would be justice in this murder puzzle. The discovery of the missing weapon was too perfect; any editor in his right mind would have penciled it out of a fictional murder mystery. But this was real life.

On February 21, five weeks after Vern Henderson had walked unerringly to the shell beneath the fence, John and Paul Klingele, aged fifteen and sixteen, went off to pursue their favorite hobby—fishing. They headed for the Naches River just where it flowed into the Yakima River right under the Twin Bridges, two double green steel arches over both the north and south lanes where Interstate 82 now heads north toward Ellensburg out of Yakima, or south into Yakima itself.

John Klingele would remember that day for a long time, not because of the fishing, but because of what he found in the river. The rains and melting snow runoff had been heavy that winter and the river had actually rushed in a tumult over a little island that sticks out into the Naches beneath the Twin Bridges. But now, the water had receded until it was very shallow and John was able to wade underneath the bridges from the west side to the east. It was about noon when he looked down and saw a cylindrical metal object in the water. Peering closer, he realized it was the long barrel of a handgun. He called to his brother, Paul, who was fishing about fifteen feet away.

The boys pulled the gun from about three inches of water and saw that the grips were wrapped with white masking tape. The gun was a .22 caliber automatic. They washed it off in the river and Paul checked to see if it was loaded. The clip was empty. Still curious, they unwound the tape.

John Klingele was more interested in fishing than in guns, and he gave the .22 to his brother to take home. They would ask their dad about it when he came home for lunch. Wayne Klingele, a printer for the *Yakima Herald-Republic,* knew a lot about guns. He was a hunter and·a trapshooter, and he kept his own guns in good shape.

The elder Klingele was not too happy to hear that his

teenaged sons had been fiddling around with a gun. He looked at it, saw it was unloaded, and recognized it as a .22 Colt Woodsman with a six-inch barrel. It was an older model, somewhat rusted from being in the river. He supposed it could have been in the Naches for years.

Klingele had to go back to work, but he was dead serious when he instructed Paul to put the gun high up on the Klingele trophy shelf and to remember that neither he nor John were to touch it. Wayne had no idea where it had come from, but he knew what he was going to do about it. Wayne Klingele kept guns in the house—shotguns and rifles— because he was such an avid trapshooter. In fact, he would be trapshooting the next day, Sunday, with Jack La Rue, the chief of police of Yakima.

When Klingele mentioned the gun from the river to La Rue, he found the chief was extremely interested in seeing it. Klingele promised to bring it to the station the next morning. "I took it down on Monday morning and Chief La Rue was waiting for me and took me right up to the second floor to see Sergeant Brimmer. I handed the gun to him."

Brimmer and Henderson were fascinated with the gun that had lain in three inches of water where the Naches lapped up over the island. The caliber was right. The long barrel was right. It was an automatic. When they heard that the Klingele boys had unwrapped white tape from the grips, they began to grin. But cautiously.

Now they had two casings from two murder scenes— casings that had tested as having been fired from the same gun—*and* a .22 caliber, long-barreled, automatic Colt Woodsman with vestiges of white tape on the grips. The crime lab would be able to tell them if the river gun had fired those bullets.

They also had to try to trace the peregrinations of that weapon before it landed in the river. Whoever had tossed the gun into the Naches had probably been headed toward Ellensburg or was coming back from Ellensburg. And they surely had not known about the way the little island below projected out into the river. Had they known, they would have pitched the gun with a lot more force.

Instead, the rusty old gun had just been waiting there for

someone to find it, its barrel moving slightly with the tug of the current. It was almost eerie, when one considered how the bullet casing had been waiting for Vern Henderson to discover it. And now the gun had been found almost as easily. Murder sometimes does will out, after all.

In this case, it was beginning to look as though luck were walking with the Yakima police. Still, the detectives had no way of knowing how convoluted this case would become. They had some promising ballistics evidence. They had a lot of rumors, but they had no idea what the motive behind the two murders was. That had all blown up on Christmas Eve when their likeliest killer had turned out to be their second victim.

15

Prosecutor Jeff Sullivan met with Bob Brimmer and Vern Henderson. The gun might prove to be vital to the case. At this point, they had no idea who that gun belonged to or through whose hands it might have passed. But they suspected someone out there would be sweating if he—or she—knew that the weapon was now in the hands of the Yakima police. Most people have seen enough television mysteries to know that guns can be traced, but they don't understand the finer points of forensic ballistics.

For the moment, the gun was mentioned to no one outside the investigation. But when a reporter from the *Yakima Herald-Republic* made his usual police department rounds on that Monday, February 23, he asked, as always, whether there was anything new on the Blankenbaker-

Moore case. There wasn't much, but Chief Jack La Rue casually mentioned that someone had brought in a .22 that had been found underneath the Twin Bridges.

That news story galvanized at least three readers into a panic. Each felt that the police would know who had thrown the gun in the river as surely as if they had scratched their names and addresses on the side of the barrel.

In the meantime, Vern Henderson was wearing a groove in the road up to Ellensburg. Tuffy Pleasant was growing used to looking up and seeing Vern heading his way. It bugged him that Vern seemed to know what was going on in his head. And the detective had picked up a lot of things on the streets in Yakima, rumors and remarks made by some of the guys Tuffy ran with.

Henderson had felt for weeks now that Tuffy was somehow connected with the two shootings, but he wasn't sure how or why. When they talked, they talked in circles, fencing and feinting. Sometimes, Vern thought he saw sweat bead up along Tuffy's forehead, especially when Vern confirmed that they had, indeed, found a .22 in the Naches River.

"I told him how much we could tell from a gun," Henderson recalled. "He didn't know we couldn't trace it unless someone came forward, and he believed me that we were right next door to knowing who the killer was."

Tuffy had brazened it out. He told Vern that he had talked to a lawyer, and he "knew his rights. I don't have to talk to you or Brimmer if I don't want to."

"That's right."

"What would you do if you were in my position?" Tuffy asked suddenly.

"Well," Vern Henderson said slowly, "if I was in your position, I don't know just what I would do. I might—I *would* get myself an attorney and I wouldn't say anything."

Henderson figured he'd just put his foot in his own mouth, but the kid asked him, and he answered him straight. Tuffy stared back at him, weighing something in his mind.

"No," Tuffy said. "I want to talk with you. I want to help clear this up."

And they kept talking until it grew cold and dark and Vern had to head back to Yakima. Whatever Tuffy had been about to say, he didn't say anything definitive. He just wanted to know more about what police could tell from a gun.

Driving home, Vern was convinced Tuffy knew who had killed both Morris and Gabby. He wondered if Tuffy had done it himself. And then, as always, he wondered, if he did, *why?*

Actually, the Yakima investigators were both further and closer than they suspected from finding the gun's owner. They didn't know it yet, but the old Colt had come back from Vietnam and there was virtually no way to trace it. It was of no more use than a "drop gun," a gun deliberately left at the scene of some crimes to throw police off because the person who left it behind knows it has no identifying marks. They might be able to show that the deadly bullets had been fired from the gun in the river, but unless the investigators could find a link between the gun and Tuffy— or whoever the shooter was—they couldn't prove he had used it to commit murder.

During that third week in February, a very attractive twenty-seven-year-old woman named Loretta Scott* read the paper and felt her heart constrict. She had been panicky since Christmas Day, worrying about that gun, although she had nothing whatsoever to do with killing Morris Blankenbaker or Gabby Moore. She hadn't even known them except by sight.

But Loretta Scott had been drawn into a most bizarre sequence of events, all because she wanted to help out a relative. Now Loretta was apprehensive as she contacted a public defender and said she might have a legal problem. She told him that she might know something about a gun that had possibly been involved in a murder. She didn't want to believe that it was, but she confessed that she and her brother had thrown it into the Naches River.

"Could I be in trouble?" she asked.

The public defender pulled no punches. "You could. I think you should tell the prosecuting attorney what you know."

First, though, the attorney from the Public Defender's office placed a call to Jeff Sullivan and gave him the plot of a theoretical set of circumstances involving a bystander who had inadvertently become involved in a murder—or two murders—"after the fact."

The Yakima County prosecutor understood immediately what he was hearing. They had just hit paydirt. He asked the attorney to bring his client into the courthouse.

Together, Loretta Scott and her attorney appeared at Jeff Sullivan's office in the Yakima County Courthouse. Tall and slender with huge sloe eyes, Loretta could have been a model. But not on the day she came in to tell her story; she was trembling too badly.

Loretta Scott explained that she was Tuffy Pleasant's first cousin on his father's side. For seven months of the previous year, she had lived with her three small children in Walla Walla, Washington, over a hundred miles southeast of Yakima. She said that she and Tuffy had been close growing up but she had seen little of him in the past few years. The Pleasant clan was large and cherished family loyalty, but Tuffy hadn't been around much, and then she had moved out of Yakima for a while herself.

Loretta said she had been surprised when Tuffy visited her in Walla Walla around Halloween. He had not called her first; he just showed up on a Thursday afternoon. She was startled, but she was happy to see him too.

"We sat down and rapped and went to the store and got some food and ate . . . and then," she continued, "and I don't know how the conversation really came about—he asked me, 'Hey, Cuz, do you have any weapons? Do you have a gun?'

"I said, 'Yeah, I have a gun,' and he asked, 'Can I see it?'"

Loretta Scott said she had an old .22 that someone had given to one of her brothers and then he had given it to a friend, who had given it to her. She had been having trouble with an old boyfriend who wouldn't let go. Having the gun around made her feel a little safer. She had no idea where it had come from in the beginning. When she had bad times with her ex, somebody gave it to her. When Tuffy asked about a gun, she retrieved it from where she kept it hidden from her children and showed it to him.

Asked to describe it, Loretta remembered that the gun had a long barrel and some kind of white tape around the grips. Tuffy had told her that he might buy it from her, but he would have to test it first. He told her that he needed it for "protection."

"You can have that old gun for thirty-five dollars," Loretta told him.

Tuffy had played with her kids and visited and then stayed the night at her home. Just before he left for Yakima the next day, he asked her if he could try the gun out. Then he asked for a potato. She had looked at him as if he were crazy, but she handed him one.

"And so we went out into the backyard," she said, "and he took the potato and held it in his hand and he fired the gun off into the potato to see how much power it had."

"What happened to the potato?" Prosecutor Jeff Sullivan asked.

"It went all over. It hit me in the eye."

Tuffy had tried shooting a potato twice and then, satisfied, he said he would buy the gun. He didn't give her any money at the time, but offered to pay her later. Loretta didn't know what he needed a gun for, and he didn't offer any explanation. He was a good kid who'd never been in any trouble, so she wasn't concerned.

Loretta said she had never checked for a serial number on the gun, but she remembered it had a clip in it, and that she had given Tuffy some bullets that came with it.

On November 10, Loretta Scott had moved back to Yakima. Sometime in the next few weeks, she had seen Tuffy again over at her sister's house. He didn't have the gun with him, and he had never paid her. Thirty-five dollars wasn't that much, but he *had* promised. On November 29, Loretta decided to confront him about getting either the gun or the money back, and she went to the apartment he shared with his girlfriend when he was home from college.

Tuffy was outside working on his car when she drove up and he grinned at her and sauntered over to her car.

"I went over there and I said could I have it back?"

Loretta said. "He gave the gun back. He went to his car and wrapped the gun up in a cloth and gave it to me."

Loretta said she had stuck it in her purse and then put it in a closet at her apartment. That seemed to be the end of the matter. She wasn't mad because her cousin hadn't paid her for the gun and she had it back. As far as she knew, he had just wanted to carry it to look like a big man. He was going to college, he wasn't in any trouble, and the whole transaction was no big deal.

Loretta Scott paused as she answered the detectives' and the prosecutor's questions. She was still nervous, but she felt better now that she'd started to tell the story.

"Okay," Jeff Sullivan asked her, "did Angelo [Tuffy] ever come to you again asking for the gun?"

"Yes, he did," she said. "On the twenty-fourth . . . Christmas."

It was Christmas Eve and she and her sister were alone when he came over and said, "Can I get that from you again, Cousin?" He didn't say the word *gun* at first but she knew what he meant. She asked him what he wanted it for, but he didn't really answer. All he would say was, "You'll read about it in the paper."

She stared at him. That didn't sound so good. But he seemed to be in a hurry, and he was Tuffy—her "Cuz," her longtime friend. She gave him the .22 again and he asked about ammunition. "I told him I only had one bullet left— in the bathroom in the medicine cabinet. We were in there already and I just had to turn around to get it for him."

She remembered that she had put the lone bullet in a medicine vial when she cleaned the cabinet. It was there with a single aspirin, a bobby pin, and a penny.

When Tuffy left, her sister had looked at her and shook her head. "You shouldn't have done that, Loretta," she said flatly.

Loretta had wondered briefly why her sister hadn't objected while Tuffy was in the house. Whatever he wanted the gun for, it was too late now. She moved about her kitchen, getting ready for a family Christmas Eve party.

All over Yakima, people were celebrating the holiday.

The first time Loretta Scott had given Tuffy her gun, she

had had to go and ask for it. That's probably why Loretta's sister had told her she had done a dumb thing. Oddly, she didn't have to ask for the gun this time. Tuffy was back before she knew it.

Loretta had been bewildered to see Tuffy again at about 1:30 A.M. Christmas morning. Her Christmas Eve party was in full swing when he and his girlfriend, René, showed up unexpectedly. But he hadn't come to the party; he had come to give her the .22. She thought that was kind of strange—his bothering to come to her house on Christmas Eve.

"Did you have any conversation with him?" Jeff Sullivan asked Loretta.

"No, he just gave it to me. I put it in a drawer."

Loretta had no idea what Tuffy had wanted with the gun that he had kept for only five hours. Not, at least, until Christmas morning.

"We had opened our Christmas gifts and we were supposed to have dinner at my mother's house," Loretta said nervously. "When I came in the door, my sister said, 'Loretta, I have something to tell you.'"

Loretta Scott had thought her sister was just joking and she moved toward the buffet to fill her plate. But her sister was adamant that she stop and listen to her news before she ate.

"Okay," Loretta said. "Before I fix my plate. *What?"*

"Mr. Moore is dead."

"Aww, girl, go on." Loretta laughed.

"No," her sister said urgently. "He's dead. He was shot last night."

Suddenly, Loretta Scott had lost her appetite and any Christmas spirit. *"He was shot last night?"* she whispered.

"Yeah, he was shot last night with a twenty-two."

"With a twenty-two?" Loretta repeated like an automaton. She kept hearing Tuffy say, "You'll read about it in the paper."

She stayed at her mother's house so her children could enjoy the day, but her mind had been going ninety miles an hour. She could not believe that Tuffy had had anything to do with shooting Mr. Moore. Mr. Moore had made Tuffy a champion. Still, on Monday, she was waiting for the paper boy at five. She took the paper in carefully but was afraid to open it. She set it down on the kitchen table. "I let it sit there until about eight-thirty and I started thinking. I was trying to get my mind clear."

Loretta still could not imagine that Tuffy would hurt anyone, much less Mr. Moore. She turned to her boyfriend, "G," and the look on her face made him ask, "What's *wrong?*"

"I've got a gun," she answered. "And I've got a feeling something is wrong."

Loretta picked up the paper and started reading about Gabby Moore's murder. "When I got to the twenty-two-caliber part, I panicked."

The paper said the bullet had been a .22 caliber long bullet, and that was the same kind of bullet she had given to Tuffy. She asked "G" if she could borrow his car, a brand-new Oldsmobile.

He handed her the keys. Whatever was going on, he didn't particularly care to know the details.

"I went to my mother's house," Loretta told the investigators who were listening to her recollections avidly. "I had forgotten that she had left and went to Seattle, and there was no one there but my brother, Charles. He was having a little party. I called him into the bedroom, and I said, 'Chucky, I did something terrible. I don't know what to do about it. I'm panicky and I'm scared and I don't want to believe it. I think it's a dream.'"

Seeing how upset Loretta was, Chucky Pleasant was scared too.

"He panicked right along with me," Loretta said. "We started talking about, 'Let's bury the gun,' and we started acting like Columbo—trying to pick apart a puzzle and everything. And so we got into the car and so we decided to throw it in the river."

"Where did you throw it in the river?" Jeff Sullivan asked.

"The Naches."

They had been heading south toward Yakima when they approached the Twin Bridges. If they hadn't been so frightened and if the reason for their mission hadn't been so deadly serious, their efforts to get rid of the .22 might have been humorous. It was like a snake lying between them on the car seat, and neither of them was adept at stealthy games.

Chucky Pleasant, nineteen, who was also Tuffy's first cousin, had flung the gun from the car, aiming at the Naches River. Instead, he hit the bridge railing and the gun bounced back into the road. Loretta told him to get out and throw it far, far out into the swiftest, deepest part of the river. She would circle around and pick him up on the other side of the road.

It was very dark and cold. December 26. They were both scared to death that someone would see them. They didn't want the gun, but they didn't want to implicate their cousin in a murder. It was almost as if they could throw the gun away, the whole ugly business could be over and forgotten.

Chucky picked up the gun and threw it where it looked like the river was deep and running fast. He didn't know that he had only tossed it onto the little island below the bridge where the water would not be deep for long.

It was ironic, Jeff Sullivan realized. If Chucky Pleasant hadn't missed with his first throw, the gun *would* have gone into such a deep part of the river that no one would ever have found it. The second throw was the one that hit the water over the island.

Loretta Scott was still afraid as she poured out her story, but telling it to the police and the prosecutor made her feel a little better. She still fully expected to go to jail.

She said her brother hadn't told her exactly where he had thrown the gun, but he had assured her it was "deep."

"What did you do after you threw the gun in the river?" Sullivan asked.

"I went home and went to sleep."

Loretta had read the papers, seen all the stories about Mr. Moore and Mr. Blankenbaker, but she had tried to put it all out of her mind. She didn't want to know what had happened. It was exactly two months later—a few days before she came to the prosecutor—Loretta said, when her cousin Tuffy had showed up at her new apartment.

He was the last person she wanted to see. He seemed jittery. He *was* jittery, and that just wasn't like Tuffy. He

ANN RULE

always had fun and saw the happy side of things. But he had been having too many visits from Vern Henderson, and Vern had told him how much the police could tell if they ever found the gun that shot Gabby and Morris. And Tuffy had read about the Klingele boys finding a .22 automatic in the Naches River. He wanted to make sure that it wasn't *the* gun.

Tuffy and Loretta talked around the subject. They had known such happy family times together in the past, and each of them wanted so much to go back to those days. But it was too late. Finally, Tuffy blurted out a question, "Where's the gun?"

Loretta studied his face, and she knew she had to find out what had really happened to Mr. Moore. Feeling a little guilty, she told Tuffy a lie. "Oh, I gave it to some dude who lives down in Florida. I just gave it to him."

Instantly, Tuffy's face gleamed with relief. "Oh, Cousin, thank you," he said. "I love you for what you did."

Tuffy asked her if she had read in the papers about the little boy who had gone fishing and had pulled a gun from the river. He had been so worried when he read that, afraid it was the .22 she had loaned him. But now he was relieved.

Softly, Loretta continued her story to the Yakima investigators. "I saw the joy and the love he had for me on his face because he thought I had done this [sent the gun to Florida] and I said, 'No, Cuz, that's a lie I told you.' And I sat him down on the couch and I said I had thrown the gun away in the river."

All the relief had drained from Tuffy's face, Loretta said.

"How did he act when he found that you *had* thrown the gun into the Naches River?" Bob Brimmer asked.

"Time . . ."

"I don't understand."

"Time. He was talking about, you know, what he was going to have to go through."

"Go through?"

"Time" meant time in prison. Vern Henderson had convinced Tuffy so completely that if that death gun should ever be found, it could be traced directly back to the man who shot Morris and Gabby. And at this moment, Tuffy

Pleasant was reacting as if all of his dreams of glory in wrestling, all his hopes and plans to be a teacher would evaporate.

"All he could see was hard time," Loretta said.

Loretta said that Tuffy had told her that a "white boy" had shot Mr. Moore as part of a plan that was supposed to pay off five thousand dollars. She didn't know if the shooter was supposed to get the money or if Mr. Moore was supposed to—because Mr. Moore wasn't supposed to be killed; he was only supposed to be wounded.

The men listening exchanged glances. It sounded like a peculiar plan indeed. Tuffy had mentioned Joey Watkins and Kenny Marino as part of the plan, and he had said Mr. Moore was supposed to sign a piece of paper and give somebody five thousand dollars.

Tuffy had never admitted anything incriminating to Loretta. He hadn't told her that *he* had held the gun himself or that he had shot it at anyone.

And *who* did he mean by the "white boy" who had shot Mr. Moore? Kenny Marino? Or someone they had never considered before?

It was time for more lie detector tests.

16

Olive Blankenbaker tried to keep busy, but the walls of her mobile home were closing in on her. She waited for Vern Henderson to come and tell her that he had solved Morris's murder. It wouldn't bring Morris back, but it would help some.

Morris's half brother, Mike, who resembled Morris and Ned, their father, so much around the eyes that he made Olive catch her breath whenever she saw him, was very good to her. He stopped by often to see if she was managing all right, even though he knew she would never really get over losing her only son.

In the early months of 1976, Olive thought about how Mike had sold his car so he could go to Hawaii and comfort Morris when Jerilee divorced him. *When was that?* It seemed to her that a dozen years had passed, but she realized it had been less than two years ago. That was hard to believe when so much had happened.

Olive arranged to buy Morris's Volkswagen from his estate. She wanted Mike Blankenbaker to have it; it would make up for his giving up his first car for Morris, and it would be something of his big brother's that he could cherish.

Jerilee Blankenbaker-Moore-Blankenbaker, in some ways a double-widow now, kept working at the bank. If she moved through her days in a blur of shock, no one could fault her. She was brilliant on the job; it was a way to shut the world out for a while. Her children were small and they needed her, her own family was supportive, and so the months rolled by. She was very lonely at first, adrift really. She had been married since she was eighteen years old, albeit to two men, but she had never been truly "single" during the past dozen years. One marriage had moved so seamlessly into the next that she had never learned to live alone.

There was—there *had* to be—a distance between Morris's family and Jerilee. Although no one ever said it aloud, the thought was always there: If Jerilee had not fallen in love with Gabby and gone off with him, if he had not become obsessed with her, Morris's family believed that Morris would be alive. They had no proof. Even the police had no proof. But it was just common sense. Except for the normal problems everyone has from time to time, all of their lives had moved along so smoothly until Gabby Moore moved in with Morris and Jerilee. In time, maybe they could work out their differences with Jerilee, but it was hard for Olive to look at her and not think of losing Morris.

Olive didn't know exactly what had happened, but she vowed she would find out before she died. And Olive had learned that she probably *would* die soon. At sixty-five, she had been diagnosed with lung cancer. Wasn't that just her kind of luck? She didn't even smoke. Sometimes Olive wondered why she had had to take so many heavy hits in her life. She had lost her only husband, her only child, the best friend-and-boss she had ever had, and now it looked as if she were going to be one of the small percentage of nonsmokers to die of lung cancer.

Yet there was a strength in Olive Blankenbaker that few women have. Maybe it was rage, and maybe it was only an ability to accept the unthinkable and go on. She planned her little garden for spring and was pleased that her cat was going to have kittens.

Olive loved life and she was not going to give up easily. She knew what the odds were—the doctors had told her—but it didn't matter that much to her any longer. "I just figured I wasn't going to live to be an old woman," she said quietly.

Olive was determined, however, to stay alive long enough to attend the trial of Morris's murderer—whoever that turned out to be. Vern Henderson wasn't telling her anything specific; he just kept reassuring her that he was working on the case, and for her not to worry.

"I didn't sit around and cry," Olive said. "I went back to work. As it turned out, I worked for years after Morris was killed. If I hadn't had my work, I don't know what I would have done because when I wasn't busy, I sat around and thought about Morris. I went back to work as a court reporter in federal court cases. They brought a lot of them down from Spokane, and I was kept busy."

Olive was completely unaware that Jerilee had begun to date again. Had she known, she would have been shocked, even though she expected that one day, in the future, Jerilee would remarry since she was only thirty. Olive certainly did not consider that her ex-daughter-in-law would even think of another marriage anytime soon.

While the *Yakima Herald-Republic* was barely mentioning the Blankenbaker-Moore murders anymore, there had been a great deal going on below the surface. District Attorney Jeff Sullivan, Sergeant Bob Brimmer, and Detective Vern Henderson had been working feverishly to build the strongest case possible against the man they now believed to be the shooter in at least one of the murders. And that was the man who had borrowed the death gun shortly before each of the killings: Angelo "Tuffy" Pleasant.

Brimmer, Henderson, and Jeff Sullivan were about to make a move. With the visit from Loretta Scott and her linking of the .22 to her cousin, Sullivan agreed that they had probable cause now to arrest Tuffy Pleasant. On February 27, 1976, Sullivan issued a warrant charging Tuffy with aiding and abetting first-degree murder, and for commiting second-degree murder.

The warrant was sent up to the Ellensburg Police Department with a request to arrest Tuffy Pleasant and to inform Yakima County detectives when he was in custody. It didn't take long. Tuffy wasn't hiding. He was going to class during the week, and he was coming home to be with his friends on weekends. It was that same Friday, in the late afternoon, when word came that Tuffy Pleasant had been arrested and was being held in the Kittitas County Jail in Ellensburg.

The weather was bitter. Snoqualmie Pass, the main route through the Cascade Mountains between Seattle and Yakima, had already been closed down twice and motorists who were finally allowed to risk going through were warned to watch for avalanches and rolling rocks. There were twelve inches of snow on the ground in Yakima and more coming down.

Bob Brimmer and Vern Henderson checked out a city car and headed north in the roaring blizzard to pick up their prisoner. When Tuffy saw Vern and Brimmer, he half shrugged. Whatever the game was, it was over—or it had entered another phase. Brimmer advised Tuffy of his rights under Miranda. *This* time, Angelo "Tuffy" Pleasant *was* a suspect. He got in the backseat of the patrol unit with Vern Henderson while Brimmer drove. The snow was so thick as it pointed icy darts at the headlights that it was hard to see the road. But all of them were used to this kind of weather. It was a typical February in eastern Washington.

Just to be doubly sure that his prisoner understood his rights, Vern pulled the little Miranda card from his pocket and read the warnings again. Tuffy nodded that he understood he didn't have to talk to them, but he was willing to do so.

As a cop, Vern Henderson was elated; they had hooked a big fish. As an athlete, a black man, a human being, he pondered how sad this all was. Andrew Pleasant had been so proud to see his son get a hero's welcome when he came back from Japan in 1972. Tuffy Pleasant was never going to make "State" now, and he was never going to the Olympics. He wasn't going to get a college degree in education and become head wrestling coach at Davis High School. He had had the whole world almost in his grasp.

That was all gone now.

"I didn't shoot anyone," Tuffy told Vern. "The only thing I did was furnish the gun."

"Who did you give the gun to?"

"To Gabby. I picked it up from him a week after Morris was shot."

"What about Christmas Eve?"

"I . . . I went and picked the gun up again and gave it to Gabby."

Vern Henderson asked him how he got the gun back after Gabby was shot, and Tuffy said that the "shooter" and he had agreed on a "rendezvous spot" where he would retrieve the gun on Christmas morning.

"And where was this rendezvous spot supposed to be at?"

"Over by Eisenhower High School by the golf course."

Vern said nothing, but none of it made any sense. All that nonsense about Tuffy running around borrowing a gun and picking it up and borrowing it again. And why was Gabby Moore sending out for a gun to have himself shot, and then arranging to have Tuffy pick it up? Why would he care *what* happened to the gun after he was dead? Had he so wanted to convince Jerilee that he too was the victim of an unknown stalker that he was willing to literally *die* to do it?

The winter wind howled around their patrol car and it felt as though they were being lifted off the road and set down again. They barely noticed; the questions on their minds preoccupied them. But Vern Henderson and Bob Brimmer were going to have to wait to find out the rest of the story—if they ever did. Tuffy didn't want to talk about the murders anymore.

Ordinarily, they could have made the drive back to Yakima in about half an hour, and it took them only a little longer in the snowstorm. Tuffy stared out the window at the white on white on white. Vern wondered what he was thinking about.

Time, probably. That's what his cousin Loretta said he was afraid of, *doing time.*

And he had good reason to be afraid.

As they drove into Yakima, Vern realized that it was too late for Tuffy to get anything to eat at the Yakima County Jail. He asked his prisoner if he was hungry.

"Yeah . . ."

"Well, the best you might get in the jail this time of night is a cold sandwich," Vern said. "You got any money on you?"

Tuffy shook his head.

"The only people I treat to free meals are pretty women, and that's not you," Vern kidded him. "I'll *loan* you the money for a hamburger and a Coke."

They stopped at a drive-in and Vern bought the food for Tuffy. It was dark and late when they booked him into the Yakima County Jail. It was too late to start an interrogation into what they knew were two very complicated murder cases. Tuffy was placed in a single cell.

Brimmer and Henderson had waited three months to find out why Morris Blankenbaker had been murdered, and two months to solve the riddle of Gabby Moore's death. They felt they were right on the brink of knowing, but one more night wouldn't make any difference.

"You want to call anyone, Tuffy?" Vern asked.

Tuffy shook his head.

The two detectives left him there and walked away from the jail smells of stale cigarette smoke, sweat, urine, and Pine-Sol disinfectant out into the blessedly cold, clean air. Their feet crunched on the snow. They didn't talk. Both Brimmer and Henderson felt as if they were in a state of suspended animation.

Tomorrow would—tomorrow *might*—bring the explanations that had eluded them. They both felt they had the right man—at least on Morris's murder. They still didn't believe that Tuffy could have killed his hero, Gabby Moore, but they figured he knew who had.

17

At 9:30 on Saturday morning, February 28, Bob Brimmer and Vern Henderson took Tuffy Pleasant from the Yakima County Jail back to their offices. Again, Brimmer read him his rights and explained that Tuffy could waive his rights to have an attorney present during questioning. The detective sergeant was careful to assure himself that his prisoner understood what "waive" meant. Tuffy did and said he wanted to talk with Brimmer and Henderson.

But if they had expected that he would tell them what they had waited so long to hear right away, they were disappointed.

Since January 3, they had both been convinced that Tuffy knew the motivation for the two murders, and now they knew from talking to his cousin, Loretta Scott, that he had arranged not once, but twice, to furnish the death weapon. What they wanted to know was the entire story, and the name of the actual shooter.

Tuffy talked around the subject for an hour or more. It was obvious that he wanted to tell them the real truth after all the false starts and half truths he had told before. It was also obvious that he knew that once he told them what was fighting to get out, there would be no going back.

Half an hour past noon, Tuffy Pleasant agreed to dictate a statement about the death of Gabby Moore. The long descent of what had once been the finest example of a coach-athlete relationship into a sinister manipulation would be caught on the slowly turning tape recorder.

Tuffy gave his birthday, January 28, 1954, and his address, 1501 Glen Drive, Ellensburg, Washington, Apartment 12, Executive House.

He listened quietly, poised to speak, as Vern Henderson once more read him his Miranda rights. As the last clause echoed in the room, and after Tuffy had indicated that he understood every one of his legal options under Miranda, he declined to have his attorney present. He looked at Vern Henderson and he began to talk.

"Christmas Eve night," Tuffy said, "after I did a little visiting, I decided, you know, to go up and see Mr. Moore. . . . Okay, so apparently he had just gotten home. He just got home so we just started talking and I asked him if he would like to go out—you know, get a drink, go visit, whatever. And he said, 'Yeah'—we'd go check it out after he got cleaned up. But then the phone rings. I think it was Kenny Marino on it and he said I was there. . . . Okay, then he hangs up and we start talking . . . about everyday things, mainly about wrestling. About half an hour later, there is a second phone call. And then I notice something pretty strange about it."

Tuffy explained that Mr. Moore usually told him who was on the phone, but on this night, he hadn't explained anything about the second call, and the call had seemed to upset Moore.

"Then," Tuffy continued, "he started acting strange and then he broke out his bottle. He started drinking—drinking everything straight. Then he started to talking crazy. He started saying, 'Tonight's the night.' He asked me if I could go get the gun. . . . I told him no. Then he said, 'Look, if you don't go get that gun, I'll see to it that your neck is on the chopping block for Morris Blankenbaker's death.' And I says, 'It don't make no difference because I didn't do it.'

". . . Then he ran it down to me. He said, 'It's not that you did it or not; it's just that you did have a part in it because you committed [sic] this gun to me the first time.' And unaware, *myself* unaware the gun was going to be used."

Tuffy said he had resisted Gabby's plan. "So then I says, 'Well, look—that gun is a long ways from here.' And he says, 'Well, can you get it tonight?' and I says, 'No.' He says, 'Well, we can gas up my car and we can go get it wherever it's at because I want to have it tonight.'"

Tuffy Pleasant's face glistened with sweat as he relived that last ghastly Christmas Eve in Gabby Moore's apartment. "And then I told him I wasn't going to do it. But then he threatened me again, and he showed me the police department's number on the phone book, and he dialed all four numbers—four, five, and then four numbers—and he said, 'You sure you don't want me to dial this last number? Think about it.' And then he went on and dialed that last number."

There was remembered desperation in Tuffy's voice as he stared at Vern Henderson. He sighed. "Then I told him I could get the gun. That was the end of the phone call to the police department, so he said, 'Well, you go get that gun.' He gave me fifteen minutes to get that gun."

His coach, whose word had always been law to him, had ordered him to do something he dreaded doing. But Tuffy had finally said "All right." Gabby told him to get the gun and come back with it. "I was supposed to come back and honk twice—to let him know I had the gun."

Vern Henderson thought he knew what was coming next; Loretta Scott had told them about Christmas Eve, but he wanted to see if Tuffy's version of the evening meshed with her recall.

Just at that instant, the tape recorder ground to a halt, and tensely Henderson and Brimmer checked it out, while Tuffy waited, wanting—and not wanting—to continue his statement.

"We got everything going again, now," Vern told him.

"Okay," Tuffy continued. "So I went and got the gun. I went to my cousin's house. She was having a little party, so I had a drink or two and then I asked her if I could get the gun and she didn't ask me for what or nothing. You know, my cousin is unaware of what is going on.

"So I got the gun from her and I went back by Mr. Moore's place and I honked twice. He was supposed to be ready, see, and he was supposed to come to the door, drunk, you know—trying to get drunk so he wouldn't feel too much pain."

Henderson was hesitant to slow down this outpouring of confession, but he wanted to be sure that he understood what Tuffy was talking about. Why would Gabby have wanted Tuffy to shoot him in the first place? He had to have known it was going to hurt like hell.

Tuffy Pleasant had known about Gabby's plan to make Jerilee believe that someone was after him, trying to kill him—just as they had killed Morris. Gabby had seen that she suspected him of being behind Morris's murder, and he believed he had to convince her otherwise or she would never marry him again. Tuffy knew that Gabby had told Jerilee about mysterious phone calls and broken windows. He knew she hadn't believed a word of it, and that she had hung up on Gabby, making him more despondent.

On Christmas Eve, in his obsessive, desperate fool-for-love state, Gabby had demanded that Tuffy help him carry out a wild, ill-conceived, tragic plan.

Gabby had had it all figured out. If he were to be shot—not actually *killed*—but just injured by a bullet fired from the gun that had killed Morris, then he was sure Jerilee would relent. He would become a victim himself, and no longer a suspect. He didn't care how much it hurt; nothing could hurt him more than being without Jerilee. Besides

Gabby planned to drink enough while Tuffy was picking up the gun so that the pain wouldn't get to him.

Jerilee. Jerilee was why Gabby had threatened Tuffy and sent him out into that icy Christmas Eve to find the .22 that had killed Morris. If Loretta hadn't moved from Walla Walla back to Yakima the month before, it would have been impossible to carry out Gabby's plan. Walla Walla was at least a four-hour round trip. Tuffy could never had retrieved the gun and come back to Yakima before Derek Moore got home from his date.

But Loretta was only blocks away, and Gabby had convinced Tuffy that he would turn him into the Yakima police and say he had shot Morris *unless* Tuffy did exactly what he ordered.

Vern Henderson could sense that Tuffy Pleasant must have been driven by two tremendously compelling and powerful emotions that night. He loved Gabby Moore—his coach, his alternate father, the man who had told him he could do anything and be anything he wanted to be, the man whose guidance had already taken him to heights of glory he could never have imagined. He must have wanted to bring back the old Gabby again, the happy, joking, confident Gabby. He had seen the man's heart break over the loss of Jerilee, and he wanted Gabby to have her. After months of listening to his coach talk about Jerilee and break down in tears, Tuffy had finally believed that *nothing* else was going to make him happy. Tuffy couldn't see it, he'd said, but Gabby Moore was a one-woman man.

Tuffy's second emotion was probably even stronger—the instinct to survive that bubbles to the surface of any human being in danger. Gabby had scared him when he picked up the phone and dialed the police. If Gabby turned him in and said he had shot Morris, Tuffy knew they would come and arrest him, and he would do heavy hard time.

When Gabby was drunk, there was no telling what he would do. And he was drinking heavily on Christmas Eve.

And so, Tuffy had gone to get the .22 from his cousin Loretta. He explained Gabby's plan in more detail.

"He was trying to get drunk so he wouldn't feel too much pain. [He would] come to the door, and I was supposed to hit him in his left shoulder. I was supposed to hit him—just *nick* him in his left shoulder." (Tuffy had no way of knowing about Gabby's conversation with Dr. Myers. He didn't know Gabby had researched just where the bullet should go in so it would wound but not kill him.)

There were tears in Tuffy's eyes as he moved through the scene in Gabby's apartment on Christmas Eve in his mind. He shook his head almost imperceptibly as he brought it all back, as if he could not believe that it had really happened.

"So I banged on the door," Tuffy remembered. "But it didn't come to that. What happened was I *couldn't do it.* I couldn't do it and I tried to talk to the man. I tried to talk to him, so we went inside. He had a few more drinks and I kept telling him—talking to the man. I said, 'Look, *I* can't do it.'"

Vern Henderson tried to picture what it must have been like. He knew that Tuffy was a womanizing, party-going mischief-maker. He knew he had given his parents any number of gray hairs. But Tuffy wasn't naturally a mean guy, and he had loved Gabby Moore like he loved Andrew, like he loved his natural father. Could Tuffy have fired a bullet into his own father? *No.* Could he have fired a bullet into Gabby?

Maybe, but it must well-nigh have killed him to do it. Vern waited while Tuffy took a deep breath and kept talking and the tape recorder lead circled around and around.

"He said, 'You are *going* to do it, whether you like it or not.'"

"But what it was supposed to be," Tuffy said desolately. "It was supposed to have just been a hit and a miss, and therefore the hit and the miss [would have meant] he could get to the phone and call up his girlfriend named Cathy so she could call the ambulance and then things start from there. There was supposed to have been only an *attempt* made on his life."

Tuffy said that Gabby kept insisting that he had to shoot him, and that he realized his own neck was "on the chopping block" for Morris Blankenbaker's murder.

"So, therefore, I took the gun, you know . . . I shot him, you know. I pointed the gun, you know. As soon as he turned his back—right here in his left shoulder. . . . As he turned, I shot him in the shoulder, high in his left shoulder. Okay, well, it happened he turned and stumbled, but then I guess I hit him low and then that was it. I just left and took the gun back to my cousin."

Tuffy Pleasant made a point of releasing his cousin Loretta from any complicity in Gabby's death. He stressed that she knew nothing at all about it.

Henderson believed him. It was odd, he thought, the points of honor in the delicate dance around the crime of murder. The detective did not believe, however, that he had heard the true version of Gabby's death. Tuffy had waffled too much over the sequence of events. He offered him another cup of coffee, and they changed the tape on the machine.

There is a rhythm to an effective interrogation. Henderson fell back now into simple questions and answers. The emotion in the room was about to choke them both. He would have to back off and let Tuffy build up to the actual killing again. Bob Brimmer sat back, silently; he could see that Vern Henderson was doing a good job of drawing out Tuffy's confession.

"Okay, Angelo," Vern said, "going back to the beginning of your story. You were talking about being over there Christmas Eve, the twenty-fourth. You were at Mr. Moore's address on Eighteenth Avenue, right?"

"Yes."

"How did you get there?"

"My car. I drove."

"Where did you park?"

"I parked out front on the street."

"The reason I ask you this is isn't it kind of normal that everybody comes around and parks in his backyard? Is that right?"

"Yeah."

"A lot of people?"

"Yes."

"Students?"

"Yes."

"Now, during the time that you were sitting there talking to Mr. Moore, did anybody else come and go from there?"

"Yes, my brother Anthony and Stoney Morton."

The story was already changing slightly. Vern Henderson's voice betrayed no surprise.

"About what time were they there?"

"I would say they were there between nine-thirty and ten-thirty."

Tuffy said that he had stayed on visiting with his coach after the other two left.

"Now had you already gone and got the gun by the time your brother and Stoney got there? Was the gun in the house at that time?"

"Uh . . . yes."

"Where did you put it?"

"It was on the other side of his daveno—in back of it."

"Okay. Now then, did you go out in your car and toot the horn or had you already done that?"

"That was already done. It was supposed to come down after I honked the horn twice. I was supposed to wait five minutes and then knock on the door, and he was supposed to come to the door and then I was supposed to shoot him."

"Okay. Now what happened in the kitchen? There was a curtain pulled loose and the screen door was propped open by a cement block. How did this all come about?"

"He did it."

"He wanted to make it look like a big deal?"

"Yes, he did that himself."

"Did he ever say he had made any phone calls to himself or to his relatives about being threatened. Did he ever tell you anything?"

"Yes," Tuffy said. "He told me he had. There were a couple of phone calls about threats being made on his life."

But Tuffy said he really didn't know if Gabby had made the calls himself or not.

On Christmas Eve, Tuffy thought there had been a phone call for Gabby about 10:15. Vern knew that would have been Gabby's daughter, but believed she had called him a little later.

They were approaching Gabby Moore's horrific death again, and the room crackled with tension.

"Okay then," Vern began, "did you go over and pick up the phone after you shot him?"

"No. He took the phone off the receiver."

"He did? This was *before* you shot him? Why? So there wouldn't be any phone calls or something?"

"I don't know. I don't know," Tuffy said, distressed. "But I think it was because that way it was off the receiver and all he had to do was dial the number like he planned. He could take the shock and just crawl to the phone and just dial with one hand. That way he wouldn't have to fumble with the receiver. . . ."

It wouldn't have worked, of course. After twenty seconds or so, the phone would have lost its dial tone and Gabby would have had to hang it up. That would have been harder for him than to leave it on the hook all along. It sounded crazy, but maybe he didn't want the sound of a phone jangling as he braced himself for the bullet he had apparently ordered Tuffy to fire into his body.

But Vern knew that Gabby had done one more thing before he prepared to stop a bullet. He had turned on his stereo, set the needle on his record of "Lay Your Head Upon My Pillow," and turned the volume up high. Ray Price's words of lost love had floated through his apartment long after he died—until the needle wore a groove it couldn't get out of.

"The whole plan revolved around the fact that he wanted Jerilee to come back?" Vern asked again. "Is that right?"

"Jerilee." Tuffy Pleasant made the name sound like a swear word. "Yes. He wanted to prove the fact that he had nothing to do with Morris Blankenbaker's death and that he wanted her that bad—enough to go all the way."

"After you shot him and he fell to the floor, how did you leave the place?" Henderson asked.

Tuffy looked down at the floor. Then he gazed straight into Vern's eyes. "Uhhhhh. I didn't shoot him and he didn't fall on the floor. I shot him when he was already *on* the floor in what we call in wrestling terms the 'referee position,' both hands on the floor with your palms down."

The room was silent for a full minute. What a travesty of everything that the shooter and the dead man had been to each other and to the sport they had both loved. Gabby Moore had taught Tuffy everything he knew about wrestling. In the end, in the last moment of time they would spend together in this lifetime, Gabby had dropped to his hands and knees, drunk from a full bottle of whiskey, and assumed the "referee position"—after instructing Tuffy exactly where to shoot.

It made an awful picture, but it explained more how Gabby could have lain there without so much as a tiny spray of blood on his T-shirt. The .22 that went in beneath his left armpit had done its damage as he dropped the last few inches to the floor and his full weight compressed his chest, holding back the quarts of blood that were already drowning his ruined heart and lungs.

"How far away were you when you shot him?" Henderson asked.

"How far is that table, there?"

"Two feet," Vern answered, and then understanding what Tuffy meant, he asked, "You mean from where you are sitting from the wall of this room? Oh, we are talking about seven feet—or something."

Tuffy indicated that he had been six or seven feet from Gabby when he pulled the trigger, with Gabby's voice repeating, "Shoot . . . shoot . . . *shoot* . . ."

"Did you point the gun, aim the gun, or just pull it up and shoot?"

Vern knew that Tuffy had had only one bullet. Only one. If he had missed, in all likelihood Gabby would still be alive.

"I pointed it at his shoulder," Tuffy said. "But then he moved. . . . I believe he fell against the refrigerator . . . I guess from the effects of the alcohol."

"Are you sure he was down on his hands and knees?"

"Yes."

"Did you try to bend over to shoot him?"

"Yes."

"You didn't just walk up and shoot straight down, did you?"

"No . . . I was off to the side."

"And did he just fall to the floor?"

"Yes."

"Did you say anything to him?"

"No."

"You just got out of there?"

"Yes."

"Was this the plan after you shot him? You were to run out of there and leave?"

"Well, it wasn't a plan. I just did it."

Vern Henderson asked the next question quite deliberately. He needed to know which emotion had prevailed in the end: Gabby's power over Tuffy, or Tuffy's own fight to survive as a free man? "Now, did you do this because he had you up against the wall or did you do this because this was the plan he had?"

"I mainly did it because he had me up against the wall. I really believed he had me. . . ."

With those words, Tuffy Pleasant probably sealed his own fate. When Tuffy left Gabby's apartment, he could not have known if Gabby was alive or dead. He ran into the frigid night with the music still playing behind him, "Don't look so sad . . . I know it's over. Let's just be glad we had some time to spend together. There's no need to watch the bridges that we're burning. . . ."

Vern Henderson and Bob Brimmer knew what had happened; they had been present at Gabby's autopsy. That single .22 bullet had hit a rib and gone crazy. All of Gabby's planning and careful questions to Doc Myers had been for nothing; you can't trust a .22 slug to go where it's intended anymore than you can throw a knife with your eyes closed and expect it to hit a target.

Tuffy Pleasant was drained. He knew that he would have to tell Bob Brimmer and Vern Henderson about the night that Morris Blankenbaker died.

But that could wait until tomorrow. In his mind, he had to be seeing the kitchen where Gabby Moore lay, unmoving, and hearing that song again, over and over and over . . .

18

Even under ordinary circumstances, February 29 is a special date, but on this Sunday, February 29, Vern Henderson and Bob Brimmer were about to experience—at least, they hoped they were—the culmination of an intensive investigation, the last answer to the last question. Who had shot Morris Blankenbaker?

Angelo "Tuffy" Pleasant sat once more in the interrogation room of the Yakima Police Department. They began by talking, the pas de deux that takes place in every well-orchestrated interrogation. Almost always, everything in the suspect makes him want to keep silent. Often he is appalled at what he (or *she*) has done. It is difficult when the words finally burst forth, to be frozen forever on a tape recorder. Tuffy's confession to shooting Gabby Moore had been hard, but it was obvious that he had been cajoled, ordered, blackmailed, and threatened to shoot by the victim himself. There was every reason to think that he had shot in the belief that he would only wound—that he never intended to kill his hero.

When Tuffy Pleasant had confessed to shooting Gabby Moore, he had conveyed his shock and his grief. When he said that Gabby had had him "up against the wall," it was apparent that Tuffy meant just that. At the time of the shooting on Christmas Eve, he had felt he had no other choice.

But Morris's death was something else again, something to be ashamed of. The victim had not participated in his shooting, and he hadn't braced for the bullet. Vern knew from the blood "blowback" on Morris's hand that all he had had time to do was throw up that hand, a flesh-and-blood barrier against death, and he only did that at the last moment when he finally recognized his enemy. Morris's murder had been the result of a cowardly and treacherous plot.

It had been the ultimate act of poor sportsmanship, something that both Vern and his prisoner deplored. It was no wonder that this was the murder that was hardest for Tuffy to discuss.

They took their positions across the table from one another: Vern on one side and Tuffy on the other. Way back in the beginning of the probe, Vern had told Tuffy that he would eventually find out the truth, and he had compared their verbal jousting to a "game." It was a game of deadly seriousness, and they had now come to the last period of play.

Once again, Vern would do the questioning. All three of the men in the room acknowledged why Tuffy had shot Gabby Moore. It was simple and terrible: Gabby had had Tuffy backed into a corner. Tuffy had told them the day before that he feared he would take the fall for Morris's murder, even though he hadn't done it.

Well then, *who* had? Maybe now they would know. Vern thought he already did. "I was always honest with Angelo," he recalled. "I told him the things that I knew to be true, and I said, 'This is how I knew you did it.'"

Off the tape, Tuffy admitted that he had tried to tell Morris to leave Jerilee alone—for Gabby's sake. He had confronted Morris that night in his yard and tried to reason with him. "He told me he wasn't going to leave her alone," Tuffy said, "because Jerilee was *his* wife."

He told Vern that he had lied to Morris and told him that he had run out of gas. Tuffy was edging closer and closer to the whole story, and he had not yet mentioned that anyone but he and Morris had been present when Morris died.

Even so, it took two and a half hours before Tuffy was finally willing to commit his statement to tape. At 12:20, Bob Brimmer set the tape recorder up.

"Okay," Vern said, "let's go back to the beginning of a situation which involved Morris Blankenbaker. Angelo, you tell us in your own words how it came about, and what happened on that night, please."

Henderson had to remind himself that this was his job, an interrogation about a murder. He couldn't allow himself to think of the Morris he had known, of all the football games in the autumn nights, all the problems and the confidences they had shared, of riding around with Morris and Les Rucker in the little white Volkswagen. Whatever he was about to hear, he had to remember that it was over. It had happened. For Morris, the pain was gone.

But Vern Henderson had to know.

Tuffy Pleasant was silent, wondering where to begin—far more nervous about this statement than he had been when he spoke of Gabby Moore's death. He had already told Vern a great deal. It shouldn't be this hard to tell it all.

"Well," Vern said, "just tell us about before the night it happened—tell us a little bit prior to that."

"Well . . ." Tuffy finally spoke, rambling at first: "I'll just start. It was for a class. It was for a credit for this wrestling coaching class I was taking up there at Central Washington State College in Ellensburg. I needed to assist in a coaching class on a team, so I confronted my former head coach, Mr. Moore. So I saw him off and on there for a while. I was seeing him two or three times a week. And I noticed in this time the changes he was going through. We were tight, and like in my book he was Number One and I would do anything in the world for the man, you know, not to see him hurt—just not to see him hurt."

Henderson didn't doubt that Tuffy was telling him the truth about that.

"So he was talking about his wife most of the time. He was really upset over his wife, Jerilee. Jerilee this. Jerilee that. He was really caught up in her. And what really hurt him before their final divorce was when she moved back and started living with Morris again. That really broke him up. He couldn't see it. Because he didn't have that last chance, you know—that second chance he was always talking about."

Tuffy said that Gabby had begun to talk the way he did in coaching, about eliminating problems. "'You eliminate your problems,' he said, 'and then you take it from there.' So his problem was Morris, number one, because the second problem was Jerilee and she was *with* Morris. So therefore both problems were together so you eliminate one to get the other."

Tuffy laughed nervously, a harsh sound in the quiet room. He said that Gabby hadn't been himself for a long time. "Every time I saw him he was just losing it. *He was just losing it.* And we were so close, [I felt] like what he felt. He shed a tear—I shed a tear. . . .

"And so then he started talking about who could he find to eliminate Morris and how it was [to be] done—to waste him . . . about who could I find? First, he wanted to see if I could find a hit man for him and he asked for a couple of names, and I gave him one name: Max Phillips.' He asked me where he was, and I told him the last time I heard Max was in Wenatchee doing his thing, whatever it might have been at the time."

That had satisfied Moore for a while. He had a name of an alleged hitman, but he became restive when he couldn't get Tuffy to contact Max. Gabby had begun to talk about Stoney Morton and Joey Watkins—two of his former wrestlers—as possible hired killers. That was a ridiculous idea, and Tuffy said he had just kept stalling, waiting for Gabby to turn to some other harebrained scheme. But all the while, he was still feeling Gabby's agony. Even with the slight relief he achieved through alcohol, Gabby Moore was a walking, talking broken heart. Tuffy, who appreciated a good-looking female, was baffled that a man as strong as Gabby could be so humbled by the rejection of just one woman.

"Okay, so then that dies out. This man, this man, he's just tore up—he's just not himself. He's just bleeding inside and I could see it and I could feel it."

Vern believed him. Tuffy had loved Gabby. Gabby had been on him, Tuffy said, to find a gun. He delayed that too, as long as he could. "Time elapsed," Tuffy continued, "so much has been said I couldn't really say right now—not to the fact I don't want to—that I can't really remember it all word for word. . . .He said if I could find somebody, he would offer them seven hundred dollars, but five hundred dollars was all he could handle right at that time. Okay, so then he offers it to *me,* and I says, 'No five hundred dollars.' I couldn't take no life for that amount of money or any amount of money for that fact."

Tuffy said he was beginning to dread the visits with his old coach. He explained he had no choice but to go on seeing Gabby. He wanted to see him because he was worried about him, but he also was taking the coaching course and he needed the credit. More important, Gabby had simply allowed Tuffy to become the "head coach." Tuffy didn't feel competent to handle it all on his own, and even though he got no backup from Gabby, he still felt better talking with him. Sometimes in the first hour or so of their conversations—before Gabby was really intoxicated—they still talked about the sport they both loved.

"He never showed for the matches," Tuffy said. "I helped take out the mats. I'd even make the starting lineup. I had that much authority . . . and," he admitted, "I was digging it."

For a little while, Tuffy was living his dream—the dream that Gabby had promised him. If he got his college degree, Gabby had said, Tuffy *would* be the head coach. He *would* take Gabby's place one day.

Sitting in the interrogation room, Tuffy kept talking with little prompting, his words flowing out as if they had finally been released from tremendous pressure. Tuffy had held them in for a long time, and it seemed a relief to him to be telling it all. He told Brimmer and Henderson about getting the gun from his cousin, Loretta, and test-shooting it into a potato.

"I took it . . . and brought it back and took it to Mr. Moore. Then we tried it out. If you go up there to the house, you will see, between his bedroom and a divider and the living room, there is a hole right there in the rug. What we did was I went outside to listen for the shot, and he took a wastepaper basket full of water and set it right down there in that spot and shot it a couple of times. I was listening for the noise outside and he was seeing how fast and how deep it would go—how powerful the gun was altogether. Well, you couldn't hear it too good outside, just like a cap gun. And so we figured that would be the gun."

Suddenly, Tuffy Pleasant sighed deeply. *"And I just did it for the man. . . ."*

Vern Henderson managed to keep his voice steady as he asked, "Did you get any money for it?"

"No, I didn't get any money for it."

"You did it for him *as a favor?*"

"It was for him, *the man,*" Tuffy said. "He mentioned the fact of money, but he said I would never have to worry about money again."

"That he would give you things?"

"Yeah, whatever. Over a long-term situation."

They had not yet come to the moments just before Morris had died, and Vern knew he had to get there.

"Was a plan ever mentioned to you about perhaps sneaking up on Mr. Blankenbaker in the morning and shooting him while he was in the bathroom or someplace in his house, like it was a burglar or something like that?"

Tuffy said that Gabby Moore had thought up and then discarded several plans; he was always refining the method of his "problem's" death. He had suggested that Tuffy knock on Morris's door, and he thought that Tuesday would be a good day. Then he changed his mind again.

"Every Tuesday he [Morris] went to the 'Y,' and so it was when he went to the 'Y' that he wanted him to be hit. He had the time schedule down, see, and what it was. He wanted the hit in front of Rick [Morris's little boy]. . . . I was supposed to do it right there, and I was supposed to snatch his wallet and make it look like a robbery."

A brazen daylight robbery in downtown Yakima on a weekday was a remarkably stupid plan, and even Gabby Moore in his drunken scheming had realized that. He devised another scenario and then another.

"Who came up with the idea of waiting for him by the garage when he got off work at the Lion's Share?" Vern asked.

"He did. Everything was his idea."

"Mr. Moore had this plan laid out, right?"

"Yes, he had it all laid out. To the bone. *To the bone.*"

Vern Henderson moved to the Friday after Thanksgiving. "The night Mr. Blankenbaker was shot, okay now, in detail. Whatever time it was, were you actually with Joey Watkins?"

"Yeah, I was with Joey Watkins."

"From that point on, tell me in detail."

As Tuffy spoke, Vern could see Morris's house on North Sixth—the alley, the gate, the picture of Morris lying there in death, his eyes unseeing as the snow fell. Vern had stood where the shooter—had it *really* been Tuffy?—stood. Vern had walked to where the bullet casing landed. If Tuffy wasn't leveling with him, he would know it in an instant. He didn't *want* to hear the details, but he had to hear them.

"Well," Tuffy began again. "About nine-thirty, we took off—Joey Watkins and I, Angelo Pleasant—we took off to go girl chasing, but not to go girl chasing because we figured we looked good enough for them to chase us." Pleasant grinned as if this had been any other night, but his voice was taut. He had had two agendas that night.

"We hit the Lion's Share a little after nine-thirty. Joey went in for a few minutes and then he came out and said it was kind of slow. So we left there and went to the Red Lion for a while. We were there for about an hour or so. Then we parted company, and I was invited to this other table."

Tuffy said he had to back up a little. He had been at his girlfriend's house (the mother of his child, pregnant with his second baby) earlier in the evening. "He [Gabby] has the number to my girlfriend's house and he called earlier that night. He called about seven, and I was there. He was in the hospital—"

"Gabby called you?"

"Yeah, he called from the hospital. And he said, 'Well, if you are going to do it, tonight is the night'—while he was up there—for an alibi."

Of course. It was the perfect alibi. According to Dr. Myers, Gabby hadn't wanted to be hospitalized, and he'd gone in dragging his feet. But, once there, he must have realized that nobody could accuse him of murder if he could prove he was in the hospital.

Since Gabby hadn't called for someone to bring the phone to his room, Henderson figured he had strolled down the hall to the public phone.

Tuffy Pleasant had gone on out, obviously with his mind always focused on Gabby's orders. He and Joey Watkins had cruised around, looking for pretty women. Maybe Tuffy had even told himself that, if he got lucky, that would be a sign that he wasn't meant to carry out Gabby's plan.

And Tuffy *had* gotten lucky. A couple with an extra woman in tow had introduced themselves to him and pulled out a chair at their table. It could have been a reprieve for Tuffy—and for Morris. Vern tried not to think about that.

"So, okay," Tuffy continued. "I was invited to this table with these other people. This single lady, you know. I was there maybe about ten minutes, and I told them I would be back, to excuse me. [They were] unaware. They didn't know what I was going to do or where I was going. I went to my folks' house and got a little money from my mom, and I went back to the Red Lion and reunited with the people who invited me over to their table. We went from there to the Holiday Inn, and we went to the Thunderbird, and back to the Red Lion. Then we parted company just a little bit before two o'clock A.M."

Thinking about it years later, Vern Henderson commented, "He left because he had a job to do for Gabby. Any other night, I can't imagine he would walk away from a willing woman who was ready to stay the night with him. He must have been looking at his watch. He left the Red Lion a little before two o'clock A.M. He had something he had to do."

A little after 2:00 o'clock A.M. was when Morris was due to drive into his parking space off the alley after he had finished his Lion's Share job.

"You know, I wasn't going to do it if I didn't have time, because I was going to party," Tuffy said softly, perhaps regretting his final decision. "My intentions were that I had caught a lady for the night, and I was going to be with the lady the rest of the night, see, but we happened to part company before two . . . and I just went on over to Lincoln and waited until Morris came up the alley. As soon as he was coming up the alley and pulled in his yard, I ran up the alley and drew his attention. I drew and fired and ran back down the alley and took off. . . ."

Vern wasn't buying it, not the whole package. He believed now that Tuffy had shot Morris but he did not think for one moment he had heard the whole story. It was too simple, and Tuffy had glossed over it too quickly as if he were ashamed to linger over the deliberate deception that had thrown Morris so completely off guard. Vern knew that Morris had to have been completely relaxed. Otherwise, he would have tried to defend himself.

No, Tuffy had slid too rapidly over the actual murder. Vern had been there at Morris's autopsy, and he had made himself look at every bit of it. Now, he would make himself listen to every word about the last few moments of Morris's life.

Once again, he backed up a little. "Okay, now you and your friends parted down at the Red Lion shortly before two, and then you drove down and parked your car where? On Lincoln Avenue? Or Naches?"

"Lincoln."

"Lincoln Avenue—right up by the alleyway there?"

"Right by the alley."

"By the apartments—the redbrick apartments?"

"No, no—*Lincoln*. Okay," Tuffy corrected himself. "There *is* a little apartment there, yeah."

That was right, Vern thought. It wasn't the redbrick apartment next door to Morris's house that was on Lincoln; it was the little duplex where Mrs. Lenberg lived.

Tuffy denied that he had run into a garbage can as he ran down the alley, but Vern wondered if he would have even remembered in his state of panic, knowing what he was about to do.

"What kind of shoes were you wearing?"

"Platform type."

"Had a little bit of heel on them?"

"Yeah, a little bit of heel."

So far, Tuffy Pleasant's version of the night after Thanksgiving was meshing with Gerda Lenberg's statement. Most of the young guys wore platform shoes, Afros, flared plaid trousers, and leather jackets. Those shoes made a heck of a lot of noise.

"So you ran down the alley when you saw Morris's car come up the alley?"

"Yeah . . . like a trot."

"Okay, just a jog or whatever. And did you approach him from behind the garage?"

"No."

"You came right up behind his car?"

Vern could see it. He could see it in his mind, but he didn't dare look away. Maybe he could forget it . . . sometime.

"Yes." Tuffy nodded. "He was almost all the way up to the front of his house, and I called him back. I said, 'Morris! Morris!' you know."

"He walked back?"

Too late now to shout out a warning, but the impulse was there. *Morris, Morris, keep going—up the front steps. Shut the door behind you. Don't turn around. Don't go back. . . .*

Tuffy Pleasant shifted uncomfortably. "Yes, he walked back, and he had a bottle of beer in his hand, and the gate was open. And he walked back, and had just, you know, kind of closed the gate. And I said, 'My car stopped on me down the street,' you know. And he says, 'I can't hear you.' I says, *'My car stopped on me down the street.'* Just to wait until I got close enough. Then I got close enough and I unloaded on him."

Amazingly, impossibly, Vern heard his own voice speaking in a calm, professional manner. "Okay, so actually when you shot him, it was at most a matter of like you and I are sitting here across the table, just a matter of inches really?"

"Yes."

"And then he fell to the ground. Did you shoot him after he went down on the ground?"

177

"No." Tuffy said that he had just aimed at the big part of Morris's head.

He was lying. Vern knew that Morris had been shot once in the mouth to knock him down, and twice more behind the ear as he lay helpless on his stomach, dying. Vern didn't call Tuffy on the inaccuracies—not then.

". . . When he was standing up. Okay, now then, you ran back down the alley and got in your car, and then where did you go?"

"I went back to Ellensburg."

"What did you do with the gun?"

"I kept it."

"What happened to the clip?"

"I don't know. I lost it somewhere."

"And then you returned the gun to your cousin's place some days later?"

"Yes."

"The reason you did this, Angelo, is you talked to Gabby for a long time and you had these plans to shoot Morris. Is that right? You used one of his plans? Or did you think of this by yourself?"

"It was his. It was all his idea."

Tuffy said he had received no money at all. None of it had been about money.

"You did it for him as a *favor* because you liked him?"

"Yeah."

"You were going to help him out? Ease some of the pain he was going through about losing his wife?"

"Yeah."

Even knowing how close Gabby Moore had always been with his athletes, even having once *been* one of Gabby's athletes, it was almost impossible for Vern Henderson to imagine the control Gabby had obviously had over Tuffy.

"In other words," Vern asked again, "you felt he would have done you a favor in the years gone, and that you would do him this 'favor.'"

"Well, it really wasn't a favor. I don't look at it as a *favor.*"

"How do you feel?"

"I don't," Tuffy said stoically. "Because I really just did it for him."

"What else?"

"I was under the influence of him all the time, you know," Tuffy said wearily. "I was on *his* mind track. I wasn't on mine."

The confession was over. Two confessions really, one on Saturday and one on Sunday. This was the most unlikely killer either Sergeant Brimmer or Detective Henderson could have imagined. My God, Tuffy had been welcome in Morris's home. He had been over there only a week or so before he shot Morris. Morris had been a mentor to him too, showing him wrestling moves. Morris would have walked toward Tuffy with as much trust as he would have walked toward Vern himself. Tuffy Pleasant would have been the last person in the world that Morris would have expected to point a gun at him.

But it didn't matter. Morris was just as dead as if he had been shot by a complete stranger.

19

Angelo Pleasant's arrest was headlined in the *Yakima Herald-Republic*. It was the end of the dreams Coydell and Andrew Pleasant had held so long for their children. All of their years of work seemed in vain now. Andrew had asked Vern to find out the truth, but when the truth rose to the surface—just as Vern had feared—he didn't want to know it.

"Angelo and I always got along," Vern remembered, "but the family felt that I had tricked their son into a confession.

It brought such shame and hurt to them that I think they
needed to blame me—to feel I had used trickery. That was
the end of our friendship. I had always known that it would
be."

The Pleasants' shame was so unbearable they could not
believe that it could possibly get worse.

The article announcing that an arrest had been made in
the murders of Morris Blankenbaker and T. Glynn (Gabby)
Moore was maddening in its lack of details. It wasn't
reporter Duane Dozier's fault; the Prosecutor's Office and
the Yakima police were releasing very little information.

> Pleasant is charged in a Yakima County Superior
> Court warrant with aiding and abetting an unnamed
> person in first-degree murder.

What did *that* mean? And who was the unnamed person?
The article said that Angelo was being held under fifty
thousand dollars bail. In reality, that meant it would take
five thousand dollars and a promise of forty-five thousand
dollars more if he should not show up for hearings. That
was an awful lot of money to raise, and nobody close to
Tuffy came up with it. He remained behind bars.

His arraignment was set for March 1.

Every article about Tuffy's arrest reprised his glory days
as a champion wrestler, just as Jerilee was mentioned in
each retelling as having been married to both murdered
coaches. The scandal burned brightly in Yakima.

At Tuffy's arraignment, Yakima County Superior Court
Judge Howard Hettinger revised the charges against him; he
was now charged with two counts: first-degree murder in the
shooting of Morris Blankenbaker and second-degree murder in T. Glynn "Gabby" Moore's death. The first-degree
murder charge stemmed from the "premeditated" aspect of
Morris's death, whereas Gabby Moore was deemed to have
died while his killer was engaged in a felony, to wit: second-
degree assault. Hettinger also revoked Tuffy's bail and
appointed two attorneys to defend him: Wade Gano and
Chris Tait.

Angelo Pleasant's trial date was set for April 19, less than

two months away. Court watchers predicted that there
would be delays.

There were those who murmured that the man who was
ultimately to blame for the double murder was not the man
locked up in the Yakima County Jail. But that man could no
longer be made to answer for any misdeeds: Gabby Moore
was dead, and the kid who had listened to his every thought
and his every word so avidly now stared out through bars at
a world that no longer held any promise at all for him.

Angelo "Tuffy" Pleasant soon had three attorneys. Adam
Moore, arguably the best criminal defense attorney in
Yakima County, was appointed by Judge Hettinger as chief
defense counsel. He had more experience in murder trials
than either Gano or Tait, and Tuffy was going to need as
much legal help as he could get. Adam Moore and Jeff
Sullivan had once again switched places. Now Sullivan was
the prosecutor and Moore was the defense attorney.

As Jeff Sullivan explained, "Many of the players in our
county's trials are the same over the years—only the scripts
change." Sullivan viewed Adam Moore as a worthy adver-
sary; he always would, no matter how many times they met
on the legal playing field.

Loretta Scott had been granted immunity from prosecution on any charges stemming from her involvement with
the suspect Colt .22, which was still undergoing ballistics
tests.

It seemed that there would be no more surprises. Almost
routinely, Tuffy's attorneys asked that he be examined by a
psychiatrist to see if he was mentally competent to stand
trial. Dr. Frederick Montgomery asked Tuffy the usual
questions and gave him tests designed to point out any
aberrance that would indicate that he did not know the
difference between right and wrong at the time of the two
shootings or currently.

After Montgomery's evaluation, there was no further
mention of an insanity defense. It was possible that Tuffy
had been partially brainwashed, but he was not insane
under the law or clinically.

20

There was startling news about the Blankenbaker-Moore murders in the March 19 edition of the local papers. After listening to additional statements purportedly made by Tuffy Pleasant, Yakima detectives arrested his younger brother, Anthony Pleasant, nineteen. He too was booked into the Yakima County Jail, charged with first-degree murder in Morris Blankenbaker's death and held without bail.

Dick Nesary, the Yakima police's polygrapher, had run a number of lie detector tests on the men awaiting trial. Nesary, who had administered over eighteen hundred polygraphs, had reported that Tuffy Pleasant's first tests in January had been inconclusive. On March 18, Tuffy was put on the polygraph again and had implicated his own brother in Morris's murder. Adam Moore and Chris Tait thought another polygraph might verify that accusation; *this* test was done at the request of the defense team.

With Vern Henderson, Chris Tait, and Jeff Sullivan observing out of eye range, Nesary administered a Backster Zone Comparison Test to Tuffy—basically asking one question in two different ways, with control questions in between.

Nesary had never talked with Tuffy before the January 10 polygraphs, although he was aware of Tuffy's athletic fame. In January he had found Tuffy talkative and friendly. Now, two months later, he found himself talking to a different man.

"When I first started to run him on March 18," Nesary said, "he was a rather quiet, subdued type of person, and I had to pull things out of him to get him to talk in the pretest part."

Nesary listened as Tuffy told him who had shot Morris; it was a different story than he had told Vern Henderson. "He stated he was there and so was Anthony and Anthony was the one that had actually shot Morris Blankenbaker," Sergeant Nesary said.

Tuffy had worked hard in his life, and his hands were callused, not the best mediums for the Galvanic Skin Response test because they would not produce the classic "sweaty palms" reaction. Nesary also noted that Tuffy's breathing patterns were irregular. But he didn't think either condition would change the results of the polygraph significantly.

The results of the March 18 lie detector on Tuffy Pleasant surprised Nesary and caught the prosecution team off guard. Although Nesary was a Yakima police sergeant, he read the three charts he had taken on their own merit. Tuffy had told him that his brother Anthony shot Morris Blankenbaker, and Nesary said that his responses seemed to support that.

"In my opinion, he was truthful to the questions asked pertaining to the shooting situation. . . ."

Jeff Sullivan had had no choice but to order an arrest warrant for Anthony Pleasant, and on Thursday, March 18, Anthony was arrested. Later that day, Nesary got a call from Vern Henderson. "Come on down here," Vern said. "We want you to run Anthony."

Wanting to be absolutely certain that his reading was as accurate as it could be, Nesary ran six charts on Anthony Pleasant. Anthony too had "breathing problems," irregular respirations brought on perhaps by nervousness and the shock of having just been arrested.

In the end, Nesary's findings provided more shockers. "On the question, 'Did you shoot Morris Blankenbaker?' when the subject answered 'No,' it's my opinion that he was untruthful."

Vern Henderson, Bob Brimmer, and Jeff Sullivan were set

back on their heels. All of their investigation thus far had indicated that Tuffy—and not Anthony—was the shooter in both murder cases. Now one of the city police department's *own* sworn officers was telling them that his read of the polygraph tests indicated the reverse.

Nesary himself was startled; he had made mistakes in his readings of lie detector results only rarely, and that was because he had worded control questions incorrectly or because he had been given the facts wrong. Usually, he said, mistakes tended to favor defendants rather than hurt them.

Undoubtedly, the defense would attempt to enter the reversely weighted polygraphs into Tuffy Pleasant's trial. Just as surely, Prosecutor Sullivan would fight to keep them out. It would be impossible, however, for the results of lie detector tests to be admitted into evidence and presented to a jury, *unless* both sides stipulated to their admission.

On March 30, Tuffy Pleasant reneged on his confessions and pleaded not guilty to both charges during his pretrial hearing. Vern Henderson was nonplussed. He had heard Tuffy's confessions; Vern *knew* that Tuffy knew things that only the killer could have known. But it was more than that. There had been a despair in Tuffy's words as he told of shooting two men he had cared about, emotion that Vern didn't think could be manufactured. If Tuffy was scared and having second thoughts, that was understandable, but Vern didn't believe they had arrested the wrong man.

Among the defense motions entered that day was a request for a change of venue. Tuffy's attorneys argued that there had already been so much publicity about the cases that it would be impossible for him to get a fair trial in Yakima County.

Adam Moore said that radio, television, and newspaper reports had been "highly inflammatory" and that there was no way an impartial jury of twelve people could be picked. Mike Brown, an investigator for the public defender's office, said that he had taken an unofficial survey of community attitude toward the case, although Brown's techniques might not have been considered sophisticated in a large city. He said he had checked the pulse of opinion in Yakima. He had been to "three barbershops and three beauty parlors" within the city limits. His survey of employees showed a unanimous response that they had all heard rumors about the double murders. Brown said he had also interviewed twenty-eight people in The Mall and fourteen people in Sunnyside—twenty miles southeast of Yakima. Of those forty-two, only nine said they had not heard of the cases. Of those who did know of it, however, just three had formed opinions as to Tuffy's guilt or innocence.

According to Brown, they all thought Tuffy was guilty.

"This case stands like a Goliath over previous county murder cases," defense attorney Adam Moore told reporters as he explained his request for a change of venue. "Drugs, romance, and jealousy are the fabric upon which this motion is woven."

Prosecutor Jeff Sullivan demurred, citing other cases just as sensational which had been tried within Yakima County.

Judge Carl Loy ruled that he felt that Angelo Pleasant could get a fair trial in Yakima and that he would not move the trial to Seattle, Spokane, or some other city in Washington. "The publicity has been factual rather than evidential," Loy commented succinctly. He said he had seen no signs of prejudicial reporting and that media versions of the cases' progression had, in his opinion, "met bench-bar-press guidelines." Although Loy agreed that there had been a great deal of publicity in the Blankenbaker-Moore case, he attributed that to who the victims *were* and to the bizarre circumstances of the killings.

It was clearly not the kind of case that local reporters were going to bury on the back pages. However, given the gossip circulating through the Yakima Valley, the newspapers had been remarkably circumspect.

Still, reading the papers, Vern Henderson shook his head. Romance and jealousy . . . and now drugs. The whole case, as it appeared in the headlines, was beginning to sound like a regular soap opera.

The rumor mill ground on, fueled with no other ammunition than speculation, imagination, and half truths.

On April 8, there were more headlines and yet another suspect under arrest. Kenny Marino, Tuffy Pleasant's best friend and also a member of the 1972 championship wrestling team, was arraigned on charges of second-degree murder in Gabby Moore's death. While both Pleasant brothers were being held without bond, Marino's bail was set at fifty thousand dollars.

Prosecutor Sullivan would give no details but said only that the investigation was continuing. If things went on as they had, it seemed as if the murder case were going to tarnish every wrestler close to Gabby Moore.

Now two of Coydell and Andrew Pleasant's sons were charged with murder. Anthony was to go on trial May 3, two weeks after Angelo's trial was to begin. None of it made much sense to the public who could only speculate on their alleged motives for murder.

With the burgeoning list of murder defendants and arguments over when and where the trials would take place, little official attention was paid to an event that took place in that strange spring of 1976.

On April 18, Jerilee Blankenbaker Moore Blankenbaker quietly married for the third time. Where Gabby had been fourteen years older than she, and Morris three years older, Jerilee's new husband was seven years younger. He was Jim Littleton*, twenty-two. Littleton worked in the grocery business. A handsome young man, his lifestyle and interests bore little similarity to either Morris or Gabby, except that, like them, he was very protective of Jerilee. His ambition was to be a successful businessman. He had no interest in playing sports or coaching.

Olive was shocked to learn of Jerilee's marriage. So was Vern Henderson. He remembered that Littleton had been one of the pallbearers at Morris's funeral services, although Henderson had no idea who Jim Littleton was or what his connection to Morris and Jerilee had been.

It was not that Morris's family and friends didn't want Jerilee to go on with her life; it was just that it seemed too soon. Morris had only been dead five months and Gabby four when the woman who had been married to both of them appeared to have stepped completely out of the mess she had made of her life over the past few years. Of course, she would still have to testify in the trial—or *trials*—coming up.

People wondered if hers wasn't a rebound marriage. And maybe it was in the beginning. Jerilee had been searching for a secure family unit ever since her parents divorced when she was in high school. Now, even before the first daffodils bloomed on Morris's and Gabby's graves, Jerilee had a new husband and a new family. There were a few snide comments in Yakima about "the merry widow," and "I wonder how long *this* one is going to last?" but Jerilee and Jim kept such a low profile that the gossip and jokes soon died.

It wasn't just Jerilee who had been through hell. The double murders had left a number of women emotionally adrift. Olive Blankenbaker had withstood blows before and come back, and she now proved that she could do it again. She was back at work, back in the midst of life. She would not allow either her illness or the loss of her son to destroy her. She didn't care what the doctors had told her—she was going to survive.

Tuffy Pleasant's girlfriend, René, was six months pregnant and already raising a toddler. Although Tuffy had not been the most constant of lovers, she had always figured they would be together for good one day. Now René didn't know what was going to happen, but she feared she might be left all alone after Tuffy's trial.

And Coydell Pleasant was trying to adjust to the horror of having two sons in jail awaiting trials on murder charges.

The March polygraph test results and the subsequent arrests of Anthony Pleasant and Kenny Marino meant that Vern Henderson had to find more witnesses, enough so that they could *absolutely* account for both Tuffy's and his brother Anthony's movements on the nights of the murders. Tuffy had given them a reprise of his movements on November 21, but they needed someone who had seen him on his peregrinations that Friday night. And, with accusing fingers also pointing at Kenny Marino, there was yet a third suspect to backtrack on. The investigators devoutly hoped that there would be no more suspects in this increasingly convoluted investigation, but it was within the realm of possibility that Anthony Pleasant and Kenny Marino *had* been present just before—or even *during*—the murders of Morris Blankenbaker and Gabby Moore. However, the Yakima County investigators doubted it.

Prosecuting Attorney Jeff Sullivan and Yakima Police Detective Vern Henderson were about to become partners in a sense—if improbable ones.

Both Tuffy Pleasant and Joey Watkins had mentioned the name of one of the three people whose party Tuffy had joined at the Red Lion on the night of November 21. There had been two women and a man that Friday, and Tuffy said he had "caught a lady" that night.

Armed with the name of the man in the party, Sam Berber,* and the information that the trio had come from Pasco, Washington, Vern Henderson and Jeff Sullivan headed for the Tri-cities area, which had burst from the desert with the advent of the Hanford atomic power project during the Second World War. (Pasco, Kennewick, and Richland are rarely referred to separately by Washingtonians.)

Henderson's and Sullivan's investigation led them into a mostly black neighborhood in the Tri-cities, where the black detective and the blond Irish prosecuting attorney drew a lot of attention. "They used to take one look at us and say, 'Here comes Shaft and young Mr. Kennedy.'" Vern Henderson laughs. "They'd never seen a black detective before and Jeff *did* look just like John Kennedy. We made quite a pair."

They found Sam Berber, twenty-eight, in Pasco. He worked for Standard Oil and said he rarely had occasion to travel to Yakima, which was eighty miles away. However, on November 21, he had volunteered to drive a friend, Sally Nash,* to Yakima to see her brother who was in the Yakima County Jail. Sam, Sally, and her girlfriend, Melodie Isaacs,* arrived in Yakima about 8:15 that night, only to find they were too late for visiting hours at the jail. They left some money for Sally's brother at the booking desk and then ventured out on the town.

When Sullivan and Henderson asked Berber about Tuffy Pleasant, Sam said he did know the man, but not well; they had met way back in November. In fact, Sam could name the date easily. It was the day after Thanksgiving.

Berber explained that he and his two female passengers had been left with time on their hands after they missed visiting hours in the jail. They had looked for someplace in Yakima to have a few drinks and maybe dance. They went first to the Cosmopolitan Chinook Hotel and the Red Lion cocktail lounge there.

Berber said he and the ladies with him were interested in finding clubs that catered to blacks where they might find some music other than the standard hotel lounge canned music. They had noticed a young black man sitting at a table with another man.

"I approached him and asked him if there were some places we might be able to go . . . and he offered to show us around," Berber recalled. "He had asked if the lady with us was with someone, and I told him she wasn't and then he asked if he could come over and sit at the table with us."

Berber had then invited the man, who introduced himself as Angelo Pleasant, to join their party. The man who had been sitting with Pleasant left. They had sat there in the Red Lion until Pleasant told them to follow him; he would lead them to a place that might be livelier. It wasn't. "We just stayed long enough to have a drink and leave," Berber said, "because it was just as dead as the place we had just left." Henderson nodded. That would have been the Holiday Inn, according to what Tuffy had said in his confession.

Their new friend had then suggested that they go to the Thunderbird. They had stayed there until almost closing time, and Pleasant had asked if they were anxious to leave for Pasco, or if they would be interested in some after-hours parties.

"He took us past a couple of places," Berber said, "and there was nothing going on, so we just took him back to his car."

"Where was his car parked?" Brimmer asked.

"At the Chinook."

"And about what time did you get back to the Chinook?"

"I imagine it had to be just right around two A.M. because people were leaving . . . from the bar. That was about it. We invited him to Pasco and told him if he ever came around to give us a call or try to get in touch with us and we would try to return the evening."

Sam Berber wasn't sure if he could positively identify the man. But he had introduced himself as Angelo Pleasant and told them that he used to live in Pasco while he was attending Columbia Basin College.

Berber hadn't looked at the clocks in the bars they visited. He based his recall of when they dropped Pleasant off on his date's comment. "My young lady was in the front seat and she had fallen asleep and she had to get up and lean forward to let him out. We were right under a light, and she looked at her watch and said, 'It's two o'clock—we better head on back home.'"

Melodie Isaacs, who had been Tuffy Pleasant's date for the evening, remembered meeting him, a good-looking man in a black leather jacket. They had had three or four drinks and some dances between nine P.M. and a little before two and then they had let him out of the car at two A.M. She had given him her phone number in case he ever came to Pasco, but he hadn't called her.

Sullivan and Henderson knew that the Chinook was only a few blocks, a few *minutes*, from Morris Blankenbaker's house. Neither of them said what they were surely thinking. If the quartet *had* found an after-hours place open that night, would Tuffy have decided not to carry out Gabby's instructions? If it hadn't been that night, would it have been another night? Or would both Morris and Gabby still be alive?

While the Pasco witnesses had placed Tuffy only a few blocks from Morris's house a few minutes before Morris was killed, the investigators had to find witnesses who could either involve, or eliminate, Anthony from the shooting. One witness they found was ideal; the others they located were less desirable but made up in sheer number for their inherent lack of credibility. Eventually, they would find a plethora of witnesses who placed Tuffy's younger brother, Anthony, far away from the shooting scene and, moreover, in no condition to walk, much less commit murder.

Vern Henderson thumbed through the November 21–22 FIRs (Field Investigation Reports filled out by patrolmen for every incident on every shift). He was elated to find an officer who had had occasion to contact Anthony Pleasant that night. Patrol Officer Allen D. Bischoff of the Yakima Police Department was working C-Squad that Friday night from eight P.M. to four A.M. He told Brimmer that he had responded to an incident on La Salle Street—a "possible disturbance" shortly after ten P.M.

Bischoff and his partner found several young black men, a young white woman, and an older white female. The men were arguing. Bischoff said they had been a little wary about going to the call; there had been some threats against the lives of police officers, particularly in this area. Since it came in with an "anonymous" citizen reporting, they had wondered if it might be a setup, and Bischoff was actually rather relieved to find that he knew one of the young men. It was Anthony Pleasant, whom he did not consider a threat. Bischoff talked to Anthony, shined his flashlight in his face to check his eyes for signs of drinking (police officers know that there is an involuntary shifting of the pupils in the eyes of someone under the influence), and concluded that Anthony had, indeed, been drinking. The fight seemed to be over after Bischoff talked to Anthony and his partner talked to the other combatant.

"I told him to leave . . . and go directly home," Bischoff told Brimmer.

Anthony had gotten into a Chevrolet sedan and left the scene. As Bischoff went on the air to clear the complaint, it was approximately ten minutes to eleven. He assumed that Anthony had gone home as he directed, but he could not be certain of it.

However, Anthony did not go home, as Henderson found when he located a number of teenagers who told him about almost-weekly "floating" parties where the guest list was whoever showed up. The refreshments were beer and marijuana. Henderson might have wished to have witnesses whose memories were a bit more crystalline than those he found, but eventually, he did discover some party-goers who remembered the night of November 21 very well.

More importantly, they remembered exactly where Anthony Pleasant had been that night between the fight in the street and dawn. Most particularly, they remembered where he had been around two A.M.—the time when his big brother claimed Anthony had been shooting Morris Blankenbaker.

Although the party on the night after Thanksgiving had been full of drop-ins and drop-*outs,* there were a few people who remained in the home of the young woman who was the hostess that night. Everyone agreed that one couple had disappeared into a bedroom and stayed there. There was a girl who had had an argument with Anthony Pleasant, and there were several other people who had laughed to see Anthony passed out cold on a couch.

One of the best sources Henderson found was an eighteen-year-old girl named Casey Lynn Anderson. She was a recent graduate of Davis High School and was working as a cook and waitress at the Cosmopolitan Chinook Hotel. Casey and her sister, who also worked at the Chinook, went to the party-of-the-week on November 21. Casey said she had "babied a beer" all night, and she had had no marijuana at all.

She was upset with Anthony Pleasant because he had been in a fight with a friend of hers over a girl. (This was the "incident" that Bischoff had just investigated.) Anthony had returned to the party, and Casey said she had given him a good lecture about fighting. "I was trying to tell him that he was stupid," she recalled. "And then he told me I didn't know what I was talking about—that he had his reasons and he was man enough to take care of himself."

Casey said she found Anthony's arguments almost unintelligible because he was very, very drunk. "He was standing up—he was *trying* to stand up against the wall—and I remember telling him, 'Sit down before you fall down,' and he told me to shut up."

As far as Casey was concerned, her longtime friend Anthony was in no condition to remember anything about their argument that night. "He looked like he was ready to just say 'good night' to the world."

A number of people at the party confirmed that Anthony had fallen asleep on a large couch in the living room. A girl had vomited on the couch sometime earlier, but Anthony had been so out of it that he hadn't noticed. People watching had thought this was hilarious.

"What time?" Henderson asked again and again of those who had been at the Friday night party. "What time did you see Anthony Pleasant passed out on the couch?"

The consensus was that it was well before two A.M. Since two A.M. was the magic hour to buy beer and they were running low, a group left to buy more. When they left, Anthony had already been almost comatose and the subject of many giggles and guffaws.

One girl said that she had been there both when the beer-buyers left, and when they came back—without finding any stores open. She had stayed awake until three-thirty or four. When she and her friend finally did get tired enough to sleep, they had a problem.

"Okay," she explained, "we were laughing at him [Anthony] because he was on the couch and he was passed out. Me and a girlfriend were getting tired and we wanted to go to sleep, but he was on the double couch . . . and so we rolled him off the couch and he just fell right on the floor, and he was just *blah*. And we sat up for a while longer and kind of laughed at him, and then he crawled over to the chair and sat in that and fell asleep."

Under ordinary circumstances, Anthony Pleasant, nineteen, might have been chagrined that he had made such a fool of himself by getting passed-out drunk, and becoming "the main part of the night, because we were all laughing at him." However, the number of witnesses who recalled absolutely that he had not left the party between eleven and dawn would eventually save him from murder charges.

Vern Henderson reported to Jeff Sullivan that he now knew where Anthony had been at two A.M. on November 21, and where Tuffy had been.

They knew where Tuffy had been on Christmas Eve, but they still had to check on where Kenny Marino had been. Once more, it was the memory of teenaged girls that provided alibis. Kenny Marino had invited three girls to come to his parents' home that night for Tequila Sunrises, a curious Christmas libation. One of the girls told the detectives that she had to plead with her mother to go out, and only got permission when she promised to be home by midnight.

At midnight, while the others were raptly watching a horror film on television, the witness realized she wasn't going to make her deadline. In fact, it was 12:30 before she could convince Kenny Marino to drive her home. It was close to one when she got home, and her mother was waiting up for her. Kenny Marino and the other two girls returned to his house.

Over on Eighteenth Street, miles away, someone had just shot Gabby Moore. Figuring the times and the distances and the witnesses, there was no way Kenny Marino could have been the shooter.

Although Tuffy Pleasant would go into his trial still claiming to have been only an observer at the murders of Morris Blankenbaker and Gabby Moore, Jeff Sullivan had his witnesses in place, ready to show that Anthony Pleasant and Kenny Marino could not have been the killers.

Tuffy agreed to waive his right to a speedy trial (within sixty days of his arrest) and was given a new trial date in early June. Anthony Pleasant and Kenny Marino had their trials joined at the request of Marino's attorney. *Their* new trial date was now May 24.

With less than two weeks to go before their trial, Judge Howard Hettinger ordered that the Anthony Pleasant/Kenny Marino pretrial hearing be held in secret. No one in Yakima knew *what* was going on. Hettinger said that he would release a statement on the closed-door hearing as soon as a jury was sequestered. After defense attorneys argued that any reporting of the pretrial motions would "seriously jeopardize" their clients' right to a fair trial by an impartial jury, Hettinger issued an order excluding the press and public from the pretrial hearings.

Tuffy Pleasant's hearing, presided over by Judge Loy, had been open to the press although they agreed not to report on it—beyond change-of-venue arguments—until a jury was sequestered.

Interest in the trials was at fever pitch among Yakimans. Court Administrator Charlotte Phillips said that the trials themselves *would* be open to the public and that the press could expect special seating arrangements in the largest courtroom in the courthouse. The trials would run continuously, including weekends, partly because jurors would be sequestered.

Newspapers announced that security would be tight in the courtrooms. No one knew exactly why. No one beyond the principals involved and the police, attorneys, and prosecuting team knew the whole story, but everyone in town was curious.

And then, four days before Anthony Pleasant and Kenny Marino were to go on trial, Prosecutor Jeff Sullivan moved for dismissal of the charges against them. The defendants' jaws dropped; they hadn't been expecting this. Sullivan would have preferred to postpone their trial, rather than have it dropped, but, in the interests of justice, he said he did not have sufficient evidence to bring them to trial. (Sullivan said later that the dismissal of charges against Tuffy Pleasant's younger brother and his best friend not did not affect the case against Tuffy at all.)

Jeff Sullivan was between a rock and a hard place. He was not entirely convinced that Marino and Anthony didn't have some guilty knowledge, before or after the shootings, but he could not produce evidence linking them to the crimes. They each had witnesses who could prove that they were nowhere near the murder scenes at the time the shootings occurred. Although he did not want to reveal that information in this venue, Sullivan had asked for "dismissal without prejudice," meaning that he could refile the charges should the investigation come up with new evidence. Defense attorneys did not object.

Thirty minutes later, smiling broadly, Anthony Pleasant
and Kenny Marino walked out into the sunlight. Anthony
had been in jail for sixty-two days, and Kenny Marino for
forty.

"What's it like to be in jail?" a reporter called out.

"God, I can't say," Marino said. "You'd have to go
through it. I had nightmares and nightmares . . . every
night."

For them, at least, it was over. For Tuffy Pleasant, a trial
lay just ahead.

21

Despite everything, there was still a grudging respect
between Tuffy Pleasant and Vern Henderson. Vern didn't
exactly feel sorry for Tuffy. How could he when Vern knew
that Tuffy had shot his best friend and, for that matter,
Tuffy's best friend. But Vern sensed the waste, the tragedy,
the loss for so many people, all because Gabby Moore had
been ready to sacrifice anything and any*one* so that he could
regain what *he* had lost: *Jerilee.*

When Tuffy's girlfriend, René, gave birth to her second
daughter—to Tuffy's second daughter too—it was Vern
who took Tuffy from the Yakima jail up to the hospital so
that he could hold his new baby. It was a bittersweet
moment. Although Tuffy's murder trial had been continued
for a second time, until July 19, it loomed ahead like a dark
tunnel. If he should be convicted, Tuffy might not be around
to see either of his children grow up.

When Tuffy Pleasant had waived his right to a speedy

196

trial, he had allowed Jeff Sullivan the time he needed to bring the fragments of this peculiar case into some kind of order. Sullivan remarked that each "fact uncovered led to another." He wanted to be very sure that the person (or persons) who had shot Morris and Gabby was the one on trial. There were more witnesses to locate. It was becoming clear, however, that the state could never try the person who had instigated the shootings even though statute made that person just as guilty as the one whose finger pulled the trigger.

That person—Gabby Moore—was dead.

The public didn't know that, of course. Every facet of the case had been shrouded in secrecy. Adam Moore, Tuffy's attorney, had agreed to the continuance, saying inscrutably, "When the truth is finally known, a lot of questions will be answered."

Loretta Scott was a vital witness for the prosecution. Sullivan needed her testimony to show the transfers of the murder weapon from herself to Tuffy and back again. She would be granted immunity from prosecution on the weapons charges. It was possible that Kenny Marino and Anthony Pleasant, once suspects themselves, would end up being state witnesses too.

In late June, without fanfare, Prosecuting Attorney Jeff Sullivan and Defense Attorney Adam Moore flew to Germany. "We left Sunday morning," Sullivan recalled, "and although we went to Worms, Frankfort, and Heidelberg, we were back on Wednesday."

Although they were on opposite sides in this case, both attorneys had questions about the Colt .22 *and* about unconfirmed rumors that they needed answers for. Working on minimal sleep, Moore and Sullivan took depositions from David Pleasant, Loretta Scott's brother, who was serving in the army in Germany, and from Anthony Pleasant's girlfriend at the time of Morris Blankenbaker's murder. Her stepfather was also in the army in Germany. One of the most rampant rumors around Yakima was that she had been told the "real" truth about the double murder, and David was supposed to know where the gun had come from. As it turned out, Anthony's girlfriend knew nothing about the killings.

In his deposition given in Frankfort, Germany, on June 22, David Pleasant verified that he had once owned the .22, and that he had given it to his sister, Loretta, when he went into the army. He had gotten it from a friend who had gotten it from a friend. The gun had come from Vietnam, and it was virtually untraceable.

Had Loretta not panicked, the gun could never have been connected to her—and through her—to Tuffy Pleasant.

Jeff Sullivan had now found out everything he ever would about the death weapon, and about Anthony Pleasant's movements on November 21, 1975.

It was time to move ahead.

On July 8, Tuffy Pleasant's pretrial hearing was held in Yakima, and the possibility that Anthony and Kenny Marino would move to the state's side of the chess game that is the law became reality. It was not a good day for the defense camp. Shortly before the hearing began, Tuffy's attorneys learned that Jeff Sullivan was amending the charges against their client; instead of first-degree murder in Morris Blankenbaker's death, and second-degree murder in Gabby Moore's, the charge in Moore's death was also *first*-degree murder.

Appalled by what they termed "eleventh hour" tactics, Adam Moore and Chris Tait asked for more time. And they had other motions. They renewed their request for a change of venue, and for two *separate* trials. They told Judge Loy that Pleasant could not get a fair trial if the two murder charges were heard by the same jury. They argued that the alibi witnesses the state intended to call to corroborate the whereabouts of Anthony Pleasant and Kenny Marino at the moments of murder would "sandbag" a jury.

The philosophical question naturally arose: If a man is guilty of two murders, should a jury not hear the connection between those murders? And, then again, if a man is innocent of two murders, or of one of the murders, should the same jury hear about both crimes? Defense attorneys always choose to separate charges; prosecutors always prefer to let a jury see all the possible ramifications—the similar transactions—of conjoined crimes.

As it was, this trial promised to be one of the most expensive ever to hit the taxpayers of Yakima County. It would take an estimated three weeks, and jurors would be sequestered. That meant, of course, hotel costs and meals for the jurors on top of all of Tuffy's lawyers' fees and money for the defense's private investigator. It was true, as Adam Moore argued, that "There is no place on the scales of justice for dollar signs on one side and fairness on the other," but moving the trial to another city would be even more expensive than the projected fifty thousand dollars to hold it in Yakima. (Today fifty thousand dollars wouldn't pay for half a day of a headline big-city trial such as O.J. Simpson's or the Menendez brothers, but fifty thousand dollars would cut a huge chunk out of the Yakima County budget. As it was, legal fees for Anthony Pleasant and Kenny Marino had cost thirteen thousand dollars.)

In the end, Judge Carl Loy's rulings were split. He would grant the change of venue; he would not separate the two murder charges into two trials. The two murders had so many similar transaction aspects that Loy could not justify severing them.

Tuffy Pleasant smiled when he heard that there would be a change of venue, but Yakimans who had planned to attend every day of the sensational trial were disappointed. If they wanted to watch all the action, they would have to travel 140 miles west across the Cascade Mountains to Seattle. Some of them would; King County promised to provide an adequate courtroom.

Besides the family, friends, press, and gallery, there would be more than fifty witnesses traveling from eastern Washington for the trial in Seattle.

In the end, the question of sequestration of the jury would be moot. The murders in Yakima might well have happened 14,000 miles away rather than 140; Morris Blankenbaker, Gabby Moore, and Tuffy Pleasant were celebrities in their hometown, but very few residents of King County had heard of them or of the murders. Seattle and the county it sat in had its own homicides to think about. It was almost shocking to realize that out of the fifty-member jury pool of King County residents brought in for the Pleasant jury, only *one* had ever heard of the case, and that was because she had friends in Yakima. Bitter tragedy and shocking double murder in eastern Washington had not filtered through at all. Perhaps murder is an insular phenomenon, its impact diminished by distance and geography almost as if the looming Cascades that separated Yakima from Seattle had absorbed the shock and pain.

But the pain would come brilliantly alive again on August 16 and continue through the weeks of trial in Seattle. The case would be featured not only in the *Yakima Herald-Republic* but in the *Seattle Times* and the Seattle *Post-Intelligencer*. James Wallace, a *Herald-Republic* reporter, would file daily stories from the courthouse so that hometown people who could not make the trip could monitor the trial.

Olive Blankenbaker and her sister would attend every session of the trial. A long time later, when she remembered those weeks, she would sigh, "It was so hard—so hard."

Ned Blankenbaker, Morris's father, his face reddened with emotion and unshed tears, would sit nearby. Andrew Pleasant, Sr., Tuffy's father, and Tuffy's grandmother would be there, all of them at once linked and divided by the enormity of the crimes Tuffy stood accused of. Many family members were barred from the courtroom because they would be called as witnesses.

Tuffy Pleasant would be housed in the King County Jail, a two-story elevator ride to King County Superior Courtroom West 1019. He would be accompanied to court each day by Yakima police officers Dennis Meyers and Marion Baugher.

Seattle's media, caught up in the drama of this case, were prepared to be on hand. John Sandifer, anchorman for the nightly news of the ABC affiliate in Seattle, KOMO, marked off two weeks on his calendar, and photographers from the *Seattle Times* and the Seattle *Post-Intelligencer* did too.

Defendants and witnesses alike would walk the gauntlet from the elevators, through the marble-walled corridors, to the King County courtrooms.

Jeff Sullivan, Mike McGuigan, his deputy prosecutor in

this trial, Vern Henderson, Court Reporter Lonna Vachon, and the rest of the entourage from Yakima County had trouble simply finding a place to stay in Seattle; there was a huge convention in town that August. Eventually, they found enough rooms at the old Roosevelt Hotel, which was more than a mile north of the courthouse and had yet to be refurbished.

The sheer logistics of getting witnesses to Seattle to testify was a challenge. Jeff Sullivan was grateful for the transportation provided by the Yakima Police Department. "We had a number of teenage witnesses," he recalled. "We tried to bring them over in the morning and get them back home in the evening, so we didn't have to worry about their staying over in Seattle without adult supervision."

22

And so it began. This long-awaited trial that might reveal the seemingly inexplicable reasoning behind the deaths of two most unlikely murder victims.

Tuffy Pleasant invariably grinned at the cameras, as insouciant as a rock star passing through a crowd of fans. Female photographers got an extra-large smile. He spoke with the Yakima officers who escorted him as if they were old friends and they talked just as easily with him.

Were it not for his hands cuffed behind him, it would have been difficult to pick Tuffy out as the defendant. He looked like the young athlete he had been until his arrest for double murder. His shoulders were broad and thickly muscled, his waist trim, his ears were the "cauliflower ears" of a longtime wrestler. Despite his situation, he seemed optimistic and smiled easily for photographers.

Would he testify? Murder defendants usually don't, but Tuffy Pleasant had such an outgoing manner about him. He might make a good witness for himself, and then again, if he took the stand, he would risk opening himself up to Jeff Sullivan's fierce cross-examination. Time would tell.

Would Jerilee testify? And what about Anthony Pleasant and Kenny Marino? They were rumored to be potential witnesses for the state.

The players took their positions in the courtroom. Judge Carl Loy sat on an unfamiliar bench in Department 27 of King County. The six who would be present for the whole trial were seated at a long oak table. J. Adam Moore and Christopher Tait sat on either side of their client, Angelo Denny "Tuffy" Pleasant. Yakima County Prosecuting Attorney Jeffrey C. Sullivan sat at the far end of the table next to Vern Henderson who would be the "friend of the court," the detective responsible for bringing in evidence and being available for consultation on the investigative facts. Deputy Prosecutor Mike McGuigan sat to Henderson's right.

First, a jury had to be selected. Monday, August 16, passed and only eight jurors were chosen. It would be Tuesday at noon before a full jury was seated. Eight women and four men, and three alternates—two men and a woman. Potential jurors who had demurred had done so because they didn't want to be tied up for two weeks or possibly three, not because they had formed opinions on the case.

Adam Moore asked interesting questions of potential jurors. "If 'A' wants someone removed and he goes to 'B' and asks him to do the job, what kind of judgment would you make about 'A' and 'B'?' "

Moore asked one juror a question that spurred Sullivan to ask for a sidebar conference: "Have you ever known a man who became extremely jealous over a woman?"

After the sidebar with Judge Carl Loy, there were no more questions in that vein from the defense.

Moore also asked a potential juror, "Have you ever known anybody, who, out of loyalty, took the blame for something he did not do?"

Jeff Sullivan shifted uneasily at that line of questioning, but he did not object.

At 1:30 P.M. on August 17, Jeff Sullivan rose to begin his opening statements.

If ever opening statements were diametrically opposed regarding the facts of a case, those of Prosecutor Jeff Sullivan and defense lawyers Adam Moore and Chris Tait were. Sullivan's voice was disdainful as he paced in long strides in front of the jury box. He promised the jurors that the state would offer them proof that Angelo Pleasant was guilty of two murders, and that they would actually *hear* him confess to those murders on tape.

Sullivan told them that the defendant had killed Morris Blankenbaker "in cold blood" at the urging of his mentor and former coach. Then, Sullivan said, Pleasant had killed Moore himself because Moore "had a claw in him."

There was no one else involved, Sullivan said bitingly. Only Tuffy Pleasant. Jeff Sullivan was succinct as he gave the jurors two terrible scenarios of murder—the first of the night Morris was killed and the second of the Christmas Eve shooting of Gabby Moore. The prosecutor spoke for thirty-five minutes, as a hushed courtroom listened avidly.

It was the first time Olive Blankenbaker had really heard her son's death described. It was difficult to listen, but she could not *not* listen; this was what she had come to Seattle to do, to hear all the evidence and, hopefully, to see justice done.

Sullivan explained how Gabby Moore had told Tuffy Pleasant on November 21, "If you're going to do it, tonight's the night."

The prosecutor described Morris's arrival home after work, the familiar voice calling to him from the alley, and then the shot that hit him in the mouth, knocking out several teeth, before it lodged in his spine. The second bullet had struck him behind the left ear, and the third in the back of the head.

Sullivan said that on Christmas Eve, Gabby Moore had coerced Tuffy into retrieving that same gun by threatening to turn him in to the Yakima Police, his finger poised over

the final digit of the police number. Tuffy had gone back to
his cousin's, Sullivan said, retrieved the .22, and returned to
Moore's apartment later. According to Sullivan, he had
found his brother and Stoney Morton there, although they
didn't stay long. A short time later, Tuffy had shot Gabby
Moore from a distance of nine inches.

There should be no going back, the prosecutor stressed.
Tuffy Pleasant had confessed *twice*. Within days of Tuffy's
arrest, he had described both murders—and on tape.

More long-winded and perhaps a bit more histrionic,
Adam Moore and Chris Tait painted Tuffy Pleasant as an
innocent man, almost a saint, a family man who had
confessed to two murders only to protect his younger
brother and his best friend. For an hour and a half, the
defense team gave *their* version of the murders. Yes, they
readily acknowledged, Tuffy *had* known about Gabby's plan
to kill Morris, but he had absolutely refused to have any
part in it.

Chris Tait agreed with Jeff Sullivan's chronology of events
on November 21, but only up to a point. Tait said that when
Tuffy left the Red Lion, he was with his brother Anthony.
The Colt Woodsman .22 was under the front seat of Tuffy's
car. In this scenario, the two brothers drove around for a
while and then Anthony had said he wanted to go visit
Morris. Tuffy had obliged him and parked on Lincoln
Avenue, a half block away from Morris's house.

Yes, Tuffy had seen his younger brother take something
from beneath the seat, but he thought it was only a beer.
That's what Anthony had been drinking during the evening.
When they saw Morris's car pulling up, both brothers had
gotten out of their car.

Here, the script for murder changed radically as it played
out in the defense case. When they were a few feet apart, it
had been *Anthony* who told Morris he wanted to talk to him
about Jerilee. According to Chris Tait, Morris had said he
didn't care to discuss her and had walked menacingly
toward Anthony.

It was at that point, Tait said, that Anthony Pleasant had
pulled out the gun and shot Morris. Running away, the

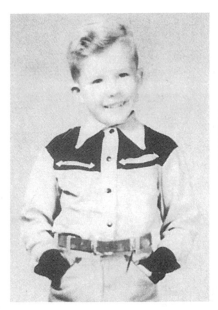

Morris Blankenbaker, about 6, shows off his new cowboy outfit. (Olive Blankenbaker collection)

Morris Blankenbaker at graduation from Davis High School. He won a number of athletic awards and a football scholarship to Washington State University. He dated, but there was no special girl–not then. (Olive Blankenbaker collection)

Morris celebrates a fish catch on the Yakima River. He and Gabby Moore often fished and boated. On one trip, Morris saved Gabby from drowning. (Olive Blankenbaker collection)

Morris trains in the desert with his Reserve unit. He and Jerilee were newly married and he hated leaving her for weeks every summer. (Olive Blankenbaker collection)

Morris Blankenbaker at his peak at Washington State University.
He had everything in the world to live for. (Olive Blankenbaker
collection)

Jerilee, Rick and Morris Blankenbaker in late 1969. Morris was trying to finish his college degree while working as a lineman for the telephone company. The couple had been married four years. (Olive Blankenbaker collection)

Jerilee, Amanda and Morris Blankenbaker. They were very happy in the early seventies in Yakima. (Olive Blankenbaker collection)

In the good years just before their breakup, Jerilee Blankenbaker rides on Morris's shoulders on a "whirligig" in a Yakima park with Amanda and Rick riding along. (Olive Blankenbaker collection)

Amanda and Rick Blankenbaker play outside their grandmother Olive's mobile home the spring before their father was murdered. (Olive Blankenbaker collection)

The winning wrestling squad from Davis High in 1972. Gabby Moore is on the far right. Tuffy Pleasant is third from left, back row. Everything worked for Gabby's wrestlers that year, culminating in the Washington State Championship and a trip to Japan and Hawaii for his top wrestlers.

Gabby Moore when he was a revered coach at Davis High–before his long decline over a lost love. *(Yakima Herald-Republic)*

Morris Blankenbaker in July 1975–four months before his murder. He had just come back from a trip to Hawaii. (Olive Blankenbaker collection)

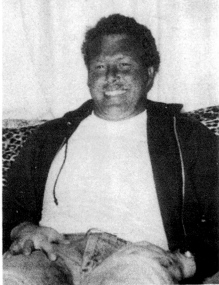

The front of the house on North 6th. Morris Blankenbaker parked his car in the back (visible in left center) and walked toward the gate beyond. Someone he trusted met him with a gun. (Court photo)

Morris and Jerilee lived in house at left. Witnesses Dale Soost and Rowland Seal lived in the apartment at the right. Vern Henderson found the vital .22 shell beneath the fence in the far center of the picture. (Ann Rule)

Morris had driven Jerilee's car on the night he died because they needed the bigger car to take their children out for pizza. Jerilee saw the car and thought he had come home … safe. (Court photo)

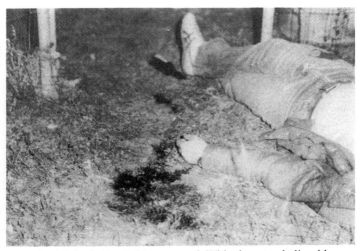

Morris's body lies in his own yard. With almost unbelievable strength born of desperation, Jerilee managed to turn him over and tried to save his life. It was too late. (Court photo)

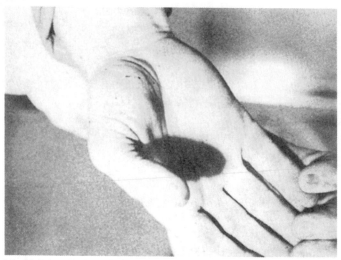

Morris's hand showed the blow-back of blood spatter from the wound in his mouth. Dr. Robert Muzzall said this proved he had had time only to fling his hand up in a hopeless gesture to stop a fatal bullet. (Court photo)

Gabby Moore's bedroom. He lay on the bed, listening to a song of impossible, lost love and pored over a photograph album on the floor next to the bed. Detectives found loaded guns beneath his bed. (Court photo)

Jeff Sullivan (left), 32, the new prosecuting attorney of Yakima County, is interviewed outside of the Blankenbaker/Moore trial by John Sandifer, anchorman for KOMO-ABC, Seattle, in the summer of 1976. (Leslie Rule)

Angelo "Tuffy" Pleasant grinned as he walked into the Blankenbaker/ Moore case trial in Seattle. (Leslie Rule)

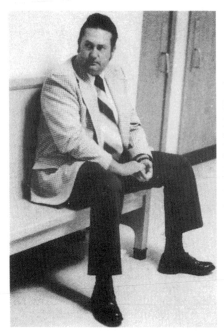

Yakima police sergeant Robert Brimmer, who processed both Morris's and Gabby's crime scenes and oversaw the investigations, awaits his turn to testify in the Seattle trial. (Leslie Rule)

Vern Henderson, 32, the young Yakima detective who vowed to find the person who had shot his best friend. (Leslie Rule)

Defense attorney Adam Moore (no relation to Gabby) represented his client well in the trial, which drew so much publicity that it had to be moved from Yakima to Seattle. *(Yakima Herald-Republic)*

Loretta Scott, Tuffy Pleasant's cousin, waits to testify. She would admit that she unwittingly provided the death gun to the person who killed the two Yakima athletic heroes. *(Yakima Herald-Republic)*

Yakima police officer Dennis Meyers (left) studies the witness list as Jerilee Blankenbaker Moore Littleton prepares to testify. *(Yakima Herald-Republic)*

Defense attorney Chris Tait stands behind his client as he fervently argues with the Court over an evidentiary ruling. *(Yakima Herald-Republic)*

Vern Henderson in 1996. After two decades he still works in law enforcement–as an investigator for the State Attorney General's Office. He will never forget the tragic solution to a pair of tragic murders, or the best friend he lost. (Ann Rule)

Yakima prosecuting attorney Jeff Sullivan in 1996. He has served an almost unprecedented six terms in office. The Blankenbaker/Moore case remains one of his most unforgettable. (Ann Rule)

Olive Blankenbaker in1996 at 85. (Ann Rule)

THE HIGHWAY ACCIDENT

When Marion County detectives developed film found in a camera in the victim's home, they found photographs of a happy couple. Within a few weeks, they would be separated forever. (Police file photo)

Bloodstained bedding found many miles from the duplex on Cedar Court matched sheets in Lori and Walt Buckley's home. (Police file photo)

When Detectives Jim Byrnes and Dave Kominek arrived at the fatal accident site along the Van Duzer Corridor between Salem, Oregon, and the Pacific coast, they were surprised to find there were no hesitation marks where the Buckleys' Vega left the road and crashed over a bank and into the forest. (Police file photo)

MURDER WITHOUT A BODY

District attorney Martin Sells successfully prosecuted the first murder case in Oregon in 73 years in which the victim's body was never found. (Courtesy of D.A. Martin Sells)

Herb McDonnell, blood spatter expert from the Laboratory of Forensic Science in Corning, New York, is one of the definitive experts in his field in the world. He was able to show that Vicki Brown had died of a gunshot wound, even though her body was never found. (Gill Photographics)

The victim's blood and hair were left on the walls of the bus barn, and that convicted her killer. (Police file photo)

Pretty Vicki Brown, whose body was never found, was school bus driver for the district. (Ann Rule collection)

From the magazine. "Dr." Anthony Fernandez raises a glass of champagne to toast his new bride, Ruth Logg. Their perfect love did not survive for long. (Ann Rule collection)

Roger Dunn, King County, Washington, homicide detective, worked with Detective Ted Forrester to prove that Ruth Logg had not died in a tragic driving accident. (Ann Rule)

Anthony Fernandez was so angry at Detective Ted Forrester for pursuing him on a murder charge that he sued Forrester for a million dollars. He did not collect. (Ann Rule)

Pierce County homicide detective Walt Stout looks into the black van owned by Larry Hendricks, a counselor in a sexual psychopath therapy program. Hendricks had outfitted the van as a traveling torture chamber. (Ann Rule collection)

Two of Larry Hendricks's guns. The young soldier he abducted turned the tables on Hendricks and shot him with his own guns. One of Hendricks's guns was later tied to two murders in the San Francisco area. (Ann Rule collection)

Niels Honegger, Hendricks's intended victim, was kidnapped and blinded with this black leather mask and gag. Pierce County detectives found this and other restraint devices in the killer's van. (Ann Rule collection)

MIRROR IMAGES

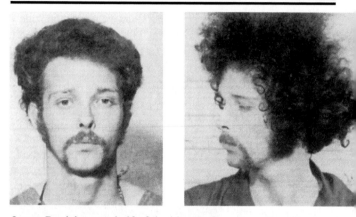

James Ruzicka, one half of the bizarre duo who referred to themselves as "Troy Asin." Ruzicka changed his appearance constantly. (Ann Rule collection)

Sex Crimes detective Joyce Johnson, Seattle Police Department. Johnson found the rape suspect she sought in a most unusual location. (Ann Rule collection)

MIRROR IMAGES

Carl Harp, known as the infamous "Bellevue Sniper" and the other half of the "Troy Asin" persona. Harp and Ruzicka had ironically similar backgrounds. (Chuck Wright collection)

Penny Haddenham, 14, was on her way home when she met a convicted sexual psychopath. Days later, detectives work in the woods where her body was found. They didn't believe she had committed suicide. (Police file photo)

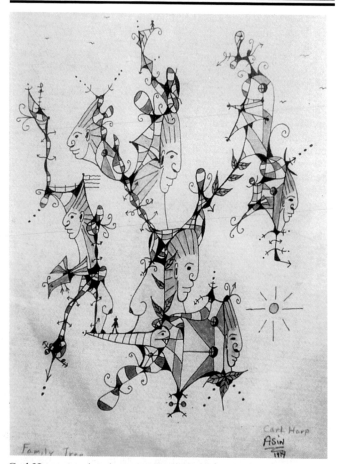

Carl Harp, convicted as a rapist and as the "Bellevue Sniper," drew this enigmatic "Family Tree" in 1974. He signed it with the alias he shared with James Ruzicka. Chuck Wright, of the Washington State Department of Corrections (8635 Evergreen Way, Everett, WA 98208), would like to hear readers' thoughts on Harp's vision of his "family." (Chuck Wright collection)

Pleasant brothers had driven off, promising never to tell anyone. They were "very close," Tait said.

Later, when Tuffy was arrested, he was "willing to take the rap." It was not until detectives bore down on him, saying they did not believe that he had acted alone that Tuffy had changed his story and admitted to them that Anthony had killed Morris. His first confession had not been the truth, only the words of a brother trying to save a younger brother.

Adam Moore rose to continue the defense's opening remarks. He explained how Gabby Moore had been killed. Moore listed four themes that sparked murder: jealousy, manipulation, loyalty . . . and irony. Gabby Moore had been living in a "fantasy world, consumed with the intent to get Jerilee back. It was more than he could hold up to . . . the loss of her . . ."

But, Moore said, Gabby's fantasy had "backfired." Jerilee had added up the facts and she suspected her ex-husband had had a hand in the murder of Morris, her once and future husband. Adam Moore gave Gabby grudging credit for being "clever in a bizarre way" when he planned his own shooting—to take the suspicion off himself. Yes, on Christmas Eve he *had* demanded that Tuffy go and get the same gun that had killed Morris and shoot him. But Tuffy had refused adamantly. Yes, Tuffy had stayed on talking with Gabby after Anthony and Stoney had left Gabby's apartment. Gabby had received a phone call and that call, said Adam Moore, was from Kenny Marino. Gabby had not wanted to discuss it with Tuffy, but Tuffy had said he was upset by the call.

Later in the evening, this rendition of the "facts" went on, Kenny Marino had come over to Gabby's. By this time, Adam Moore said that Tuffy had returned with the gun he had borrowed for the second time and he had given it to Gabby. When Kenny Marino came over, Tuffy had urged Gabby to take a walk in the backyard with him to clear his head and to help him forget his wild plan about wanting Tuffy to shoot him.

Apparently unconvinced, Gabby had walked into the

house, while Tuffy stayed outside, turning the situation over and over in his mind, trying to find some solution to Gabby's problems—and his own.

And then, according to Adam Moore, Tuffy had frozen in horror as a shot sounded inside. When he ran in, he had seen his best friend standing over their coach with the pistol in his hand. Gabby was lying on the kitchen floor with blood covering his T-shirt.

"Merry Christmas, everyone," Adam Moore said sarcastically, with a wave of his hand.

But Moore wasn't quite through. According to the defense attorney, Tuffy had promised Kenny Marino that he would take the rap for *him* too. Tuffy had said since he had no previous record, the court would go easy on him.

The jurors sat expressionless—as all jurors, everywhere, always do. What could they be thinking? The two versions of the murders were so disparate. Was it possible that the young man at the defense table was so good-hearted and generous of spirit that he would risk giving up years of his own life to keep his younger brother and best friend out of prison?

Or was it possible that he really had shot an old friend in cold blood and then turned on the coach he had once loved in a panic that he might be discovered?

The jurors had weeks of testimony to listen to. Maybe the truth would filter out like clear water from a silty stream.

Adam Moore had either misspoken in the last part of his dramatic opening remarks, or he was not aware of the details of the crime scene that Sergeant Bob Brimmer and Detective Howard Cyr had noted. Kenny Marino could not have been standing over a body dressed in a bloody T-shirt. There had been no blood on Gabby's T-shirt—not a speck of it—not until Brimmer and Cyr had lifted his body to turn it over.

Then it had gushed out, quarts of it.

But, by then, the killer—or killers—were long gone.

The prosecution began its case. Whenever possible, a good prosecution case begins with witnesses whose words can reconstruct the ambiance of the crime scene, using exhibits and evidence that will draw the jurors back in time to the moment of murder. It was the middle of an unusually hot summer in Seattle. To step from the marble halls of the King County Courthouse into the late afternoon heat was akin to walking into a sauna.

What Jeff Sullivan had to do was summon up the icy dawn the November before in Yakima, and then the snowy Christmas Eve that followed. He had to make the jurors shiver involuntarily, even as they perspired in fact. He needed to let them feel the shock Morris's apartment house neighbors had felt when they heard Jerilee scream. They had to "hear" the screams themselves.

Gerda Lenberg, Dale Soost, and Rowland Seal were only the first of dozens of witnesses who would make their way across the mountains to Seattle so that they could fill in their personal "segments" in a giant mosaic of murder.

Since the jurors were from the Seattle area and not familiar with the streets of Yakima, Jeff Sullivan provided an easel with a large sheet of white paper so that addresses, streets, and directions could be drawn in by witnesses. Gerda Lenberg picked up a crayon and made the first marks on the pristine white.

"Five-oh-six East Lincoln," she said, drawing in the location of her duplex. "That's Lincoln Avenue there and the alley runs north and south down here like this. (She drew a line south from her home to the other end of the alley, marking Lincoln Avenue where it ran east and west.) This would be 'B' Street here."

"Okay," the prosecutor nodded. "Would you draw the duplex in?"

"Right there on the corner . . . right on the alley." (She drew a rectangle where the alley connected with Lincoln Avenue.)

Gerda had heard the footsteps and the "firecrackers" between "five, six, seven minutes after two."

She had heard only one person running. She was sure of that.

Adam Moore rose to cross-examine, and the tone of the defense soon became evident. Tuffy Pleasant's attorneys would attempt to convince the jury that the police and prosecutors had unduly influenced witnesses. It is a standard and often effective technique. Any prosecutor, or defense attorney, will talk to his witnesses before trial, but nervous witnesses can be made to feel that they should not have spoken to anyone.

"In your statement," Moore asked, "on March second . . . you don't say how many people . . . were making footsteps, do you? Since then have you talked to Mr. Sullivan or any policeman about this?"

Mrs. Lenberg gave an odd non sequitur answer: "Just when I shut my eyes and looked back on the night, and I can hear the echo because of the close proximity of the buildings . . . and I just heard one echo."

"My question was: Did you talk to Mr. Sullivan or any of the policemen before getting on the stand about how many footsteps you thought there were?"

Gerda knew what she knew, and she said she had told that to one detective. Moore cut her off, asking about gravel and the interval between one foot and then the other hitting. It was not gravel, she said, but blacktop.

She was a good prosecution witness.

So was Dale Soost. He had heard three shots sometime between midnight and 4:15 A.M. He had not looked at the clock. He had heard the woman scream as he waited on the sidewalk around 5:00. He had not spoken to her or looked at the victim's body.

"No questions," Moore said.

Rowland Seal spoke rapidly but with infinite precision. "I'm an auto body and fender mechanic," he said in answer to Sullivan's initial question. "With a great many very busy hobbies. . . . I manage a couple of duck clubs. I am a professional roller skating instructor, I teach trapshooting, shotgun shooting . . . I have friends in the Game Department and I do photography work for them, and keep track of wildlife counts, big game, birds and such as that."

Sullivan had Seal draw the apartment house at 208 North Sixth on "State's Identification –2." (His and Soost's apartment house was on the opposite end of the alley from Gerda Lenberg's.)

"Were you awakened sometime during the night?"

Where Soost had been vague, Seal was right on the mark. "A few seconds before two-oh-five in the morning—"

"How did you know it was a few seconds before two-oh-five?"

"Well, I have a digital watch and digital clock next to my bed that I cross-checked the next morning . . . and I heard three shots—*bang, bang-bang,* and I and my wife both looked at the clock immediately, so I would say I was awakened a few seconds before—the length of time it takes you to come back down on the bed and turn over and look at the clock."

Seal had peered from his window, but he said he could not have seen Morris Blankenbaker lying dead in his side yard. The cones of lights from the porches and the alley all ended before they came to that part of the yard.

Rowland Seal had walked along the apartment house side of the wire fence and seen the dead man, and he had tried to talk with the screaming woman, who could not be comforted.

"She was very hysterical," he testified. "That's why I was rather blunt with her to kind of get her to do something and get her settled down. . . . She was in front of the house and I said, 'Get in there and call the police or I will.' And I said, 'Well, if you aren't going to do it, I will.' So I started into the house—started toward the steps—and the dog wouldn't let me in."

Rowland Seal was an excellent witness. His recall was obviously as set as Jell-O, and Chris Tait said quietly, "No questions."

The first three witnesses had described how it was in the wee hours of the Friday night/Saturday morning when Morris Blankenbaker died. Each had heard something slightly different, but their testimony meshed. Gerda Lenberg spoke of hearing the "firecrackers," and the sound of running feet with hollow-sounding heels in the alley just outside her bedroom window.

Dale Soost had heard shots and gone back to sleep. Rowland Seal, punctilious and precise, knew the number of shots, the exact time he had heard them.

Both men had seen the slender woman emerge from her

209

home and run through the snow, only to run back, screaming, "Morris! Morris!"

Despite the August heat, it *had* grown cold in the courtroom. Sullivan had been successful in turning back time and season.

Shortly before nine the next morning, Wednesday, August 18, the word that the woman at the center of the triangle was going to testify buzzed through the tenth floor.

"She's here. . . ." The murmuring passed along the oak benches outside the courtroom. Witnesses waited there. Family sometimes retreated to the benches when the testimony grew too graphic, while the reporters came and went. Today, they packed the press rows inside the courtroom and their cameramen waited outside for a glimpse of the woman who had bedazzled two men—one enough to forgive her for what many men would find unforgivable—and the other enough, allegedly, to both kill and die for her.

She *was* beautiful. There had been no exaggeration about that. Jerilee had a wonderful figure, slender and full breasted. She wore a tight-fitting striped shirt over a black turtleneck top and black bell-bottom slacks. Her hair was dark brown, parted in the middle, and fell to her shoulders. She had huge eyes under carefully arched brows. Her eyes were lined with kohl, which made them appear even bigger. Despite everything that she had been through, she seemed younger than twenty-nine.

Outside the courtroom, Jerilee posed willingly for the cameras and talked to reporters. Yes, she was nervous, but she was prepared to testify.

Only when Jerilee moved toward the witness chair to be sworn in, did her real anxiety show. She would now have to relive the most horrendous three years of her life. There was a quaver in her voice as she answered Jeff Sullivan's questions.

"First, Jerilee," he said, "I want you to sit up as close to the microphone as you can and speak loudly to all of the jurors, and so counsel can hear you. Would you please state your full name and spell it for the record?"

"Jerilee Littleton. J-e-r-i-l-e-e . . . L-i-t-t-l-e-t-o-n."

Vern Henderson stared at her from his spot at the prosecution table. Later, he commented somewhat sardonically, "Everybody was looking to see Mrs. *Blankenbaker* or Mrs. *Moore,* and neither of them showed up. Mrs. *Littleton* came to court. Most people were surprised to find that out."

The witness gave her address in Yakima, and said she was a loan interviewer at the Pacific National Bank. "Since October . . ."

"Jerilee, when were you married to Morris Blankenbaker?"

"August twenty-eight, 1965."

"Did you and Morris have any children?"

"Yes, we did—a boy, Rick—he's now seven, and a girl, Amanda, and she's five."

"Now, how long were you and Morris married?"

"It would have been nine years in August of seventy-four; we were divorced in June."

"After you divorced Morris, did you remarry?"

"Yes . . . Glynn Moore."

"Does Glynn Moore have a nickname?"

"Yes, it was 'Gabby.'"

"Now, when were you and Gabby Moore married?"

"September fourteenth, 1974."

"How long did you and Gabby Moore live together?"

"Till July of 1975."

"Less than a year?"

"Yes."

"From September to July, did you and he ever separate?"

"Yes, about three times."

"What was the longest separation?"

"I think about two weeks."

"Why did you and he separate during that period of time?"

"Well, he was a very unpredictable person. He would— he loved you a lot one minute and the next minute he just kicked you out of the house, and I was getting a little bit scared of him."

"Did he actually throw you out of the house on occasion?"

"Yes."

"What about his drinking habits during the time you were married to him?"

"He drank very heavily."

"When you say 'very heavily,' can you give me some idea of the amount?"

"Well, within a two- or three-hour period, he would drink a fifth of bourbon or whatever."

Jerilee testified that this level of drinking occurred three or four times a week, but she said she didn't think Gabby had used drugs.

"Not that you are aware of?"

"No."

"Now, were you separated in July?"

"Yes."

"When you left, where did you go?"

"I went back to my first husband, Morris Blankenbaker."

There was a slight murmur in the courtroom. What had been well-chewed gossip in Yakima was news to most of the spectators in this Seattle trial.

Jerilee kept her eyes on Jeff Sullivan. He was being gentle with her. She didn't know what kind of questions Adam Moore and Chris Tait might ask.

"When did you file for divorce from Glynn Moore?"

"In July."

"So when you moved out of Gabby's house, you moved back in with Morris? And where were you and Morris living in July of 1975?"

"At two-ten North Sixth Street in Yakima."

Jerilee answered questions about Gabby's obsession to have her back.

"Did you have any contact with Gabby Moore?"

"He would call daily and he stopped by a couple of times. He would call me at work and he would call me at home . . . he came out to the bank . . ."

"When he called, what was the general nature of his conversation?"

"He would just ask when I was coming back and wouldn't I give him another chance. He wasn't going to make it without me."

"Did he ever talk about Morris?"

"Not really that I recall."

"Did he ever threaten to do bodily harm to Morris?"

"No."

"Did he ever threaten to do bodily harm to himself?"

"Yes. . . . He would often say that he would like to commit suicide in front of me so that I would be on the fifth floor of Memorial—which is the psychiatric ward."

Jerilee testified that Gabby's children had all spoken to her on their father's behalf and begged her to give him another chance.

"Did you tell Glynn Moore that if Morris wasn't around that you would go back to him?"

"No, I *definitely* didn't."

"Did he ever ask you what you would do if Morris wasn't there?"

"I don't believe he did."

At the prosecution table, Vern Henderson listened and watched. He knew that Jerilee had met with Gabby Moore—he had seen them. From the distance at which he had observed them, he had no way of knowing if Jerilee had given Gabby any mixed signals. He wished that he had talked to her. Talked to Gabby. Done something. But he had kept out of it; he had followed his own rule not to mess in anyone else's relationship.

Jerilee told the jury about the night Gabby came into her house, and of how Morris and Joey Watkins had arrived to send him away.

"Do you remember where he [Morris] was teaching?"

"He was teaching physical education at the intermediate school—in Wapato."

"And sometime later in the fall, he took on another job; is that right?"

"Yes, he checked ID at the Lion's Share, at the door."

"And what is the Lion's Share?"

"It's a tavern, located on Second Street, I believe, in Yakima."

"How long had Morris been working at the Lion's Share?"

"He worked three days a week, and I believe this was his second week."

Jerilee's voice trembled more as she recalled the last night of Morris's life. They had had pizza with their children, and then he had gone off to work. She and a girlfriend had gone out to hear her friend's husband's band playing at the Country Cousin. They had stopped by to see Morris. The last time she had seen him alive was about a quarter to ten that night. Later, she had picked up Rick and Amanda from Olive's mobile home and taken them home where they'd all gone to bed. At two A.M., she had wakened, realized Morris would be home soon and she had moved the children from her bed into their own.

"Did you just wake up at two or did you have an alarm set?"

"I just woke up at two o'clock."

". . . How did you know it was two?"

"I have a clock by the bed. I took the children out of the bed and put them in their own beds. Then I went back to bed myself."

"Did Morris come in, come home?"

"He came home—just a few minutes after I put the children in bed."

"Tell us what happened then," Jeff Sullivan said.

"I heard our car drive in and I heard our car door shut. And then I thought that I heard two more car doors shut— and Morris didn't come in."

"What did you do when he didn't come in?"

"Well, at the time I didn't do anything because I had thought some fellows had asked him if he would like to go for a couple of drinks after work. So I thought the car doors that I heard later were the fellows picking him up, so I didn't do anything. I just remained in bed."

"Did you hear anything else, Jerilee, when the car doors closed?"

"I heard some voices . . . from the back of the house . . . toward the alley. . . . They sounded rather excited, kind of high-pitched."

"Did you recognize any of the voices?"

"No, I didn't."

"Could one of the voices have been Morris's?"

"Could have been, but I didn't recognize it at the time."

"How long did this conversation or these voices last?"

"Not long, maybe ten words."

Jerilee could not remember the sequence of the car doors slamming and the voices. She didn't know which had come first.

"Okay. How long did you stay in bed before you decided you better see what's going on?"

"About half an hour. Then I got up and went to the back window and looked out, and I saw that our car was there. So then I went outside and looked inside the car. Nobody was there so I went back in the house, went back to bed."

"How far was the car parked from where Morris's body was found the next day?"

"Maybe thirty feet, about."

"Is it dark out there?"

"Where Morris's body was . . . it was."

"Do you wear glasses?"

"I wear contact lenses."

"If you take your contact lenses out, how far can you see?"

"I can't see hardly at all."

Jerilee had taken her contacts out when she went to bed, and she had gone out to look in the car without them. She was nearsighted and had difficulty seeing at a distance. She had been able to see that both their cars were parked in their usual places, but not much more than that. She had gone back to bed, read for a while, and then slept fitfully until five A.M.

"You have a large dog, do you not, or did at that time?"

"Yes, we did—a black Lab."

"Where was he?"

"In my bedroom."

"Did he make any noise at two o'clock?"

"No, he didn't."

"Did he usually bark when there were strangers outside the house?"

"Oh, yes . . . he's very, very protective."

"To the point where you didn't have your mail delivered if he was outside? Is that right?"

"That's right."

"Did he bark when Morris came home—usually?"

"No, he pretty much could recognize the footsteps, I believe, because he never barked at anybody familiar."

At five A.M., Jerilee had called her brother-in-law Mike, who had offered to come over. He knew that Morris had had no plans to go anywhere after work.

"I said, 'Well, I think it will be okay,'" Jerilee testified. "'Rather than have you come down, I'll take Hike and we'll go around the house' . . . so I left Mike on the phone and took the dog and went out the front door. Before I did that, though, I put my contacts in this time. The dog ran ahead of me and started growling and barking at something on the ground. I couldn't tell right then what it was, but when I got there I saw that it was Morris."

Jerilee could no longer contain the tears that brimmed up in her eyes, trying as she obviously was to blink them back.

This was the worst part, but she kept answering Jeff Sullivan's questions.

"Was it dark?" he asked softly.

"Yes."

"How was Morris lying when you first walked over to him?"

"He was lying on his stomach, facedown—his feet pointing toward the alley—that would be west."

"And his head?"

"East toward Sixth Street."

"Where was his body, Jerilee, in relationship to your fence and the gate?"

"It was just inside the gate—just right inside the gate, and—" Her voice shook, thick with tears.

"What did you do then?"

"I rolled him over and tried to pull him toward me. I felt his face and I thought I felt something on his face which I thought was mud at that time. And he was really heavy. I mean he didn't help me at all. And I think I tried to hear a heartbeat. I don't remember exactly. . . . I took ahold of his jacket on his right side and rolled him toward the house, which would be north, and then I pulled him into a sitting position toward me with his jacket.

"And then I started screaming. . . ."

23

The summer morning in Seattle was lost to everyone in Judge Loy's courtroom. They were too caught up in listening to Jerilee Littleton recall a dark dawn in November. She explained to Prosecutor Sullivan how she had run to the phone where her husband's brother waited. "I just ran inside and picked up the phone and said, 'Mike, come quick. Morris has blood all over him!' And then I went back outside and I was screaming—and then two neighbor people came over and asked me if I had called the ambulance, and I said no, and they told me to do that—so I went in and called the ambulance. And by the time I went back outside, the police had arrived then and I went back inside and stayed."

There were photographs to be introduced into evidence. Sullivan began with the least upsetting. He handed Jerilee pictures of her car, the carport on North Sixth, the back of her house, of Morris's car, the side yard.

"The gate was always open," Jerilee said. "I don't know if the hinges weren't working right or—"

"Jerilee," Jeff Sullivan said gently, "I'm handing you what's been marked as Identification eight. Can you tell me what that is, please?"

Her breath caught, but she managed to answer, "The fence and Morris's body on his back."

"Does that picture fairly and accurately portray the position of Morris's body?"

"Yes."

Sullivan changed gears and asked Jerilee about her sister's conversation with Gabby Moore. "What did he talk to her about?"

"He would ask her to influence me or persuade me to go back to him."

"And, in that regard, Jerilee, was there ever a time after you left him in July that you indicated to him that you would come back to him?"

"No, I didn't."

"Did you encourage him in any way?"

"No," she said firmly.

"After Morris was killed, did you believe that Glynn Moore had something to do with it?"

"Yes, I did—from different things he said. He had told my sister that he knew people that would do anything for him. All he had to do was ask. I just felt that he felt that if Morris wasn't there, I would be back to him; he was very confident that I would be back with him."

This was a peculiar trial, indeed. Angelo "Tuffy" Pleasant was the defendant, certainly. But Talmadge Glynn "Gabby" Moore was also on trial. The prosecution had to show how Gabby had cajoled, pleaded, sobbed, and, finally, blackmailed Tuffy into killing Morris and wounding himself. The defense didn't really disagree with the portrayal of Gabby Moore, but they had to paint Tuffy as the self-sacrificing hero and lay the blame on Anthony and Larry.

The "ghost of Gabby Moore" was going to take a verbal beating in this courtroom, even if the man himself was beyond human reach.

Chris Tait cross-examined Jerilee. "After Morris's death and before Christmas, did you talk with Gabby about his possible involvement in Morris's death?"

"Yes, I talked to him once on the phone."

"Did you tell him you thought he was involved?"

"Yes, I did. . . . He said 'No way.' He couldn't have. He just couldn't have done it."

"Did you believe him?"

"No, I didn't."

"Did you tell him that you would never come back to him so long as you thought he was involved in Morris's death?"

"I told him I would never go back to him, no matter what."

"Regardless?"

"That's right."

And, Jerilee testified, Gabby had insisted he could prove to her that he was innocent of any complicity in Morris's murder. He told her he had ways, but he didn't go into details. She told him again she didn't care. Nothing would make her go back to him.

Nothing.

Tait elicited the dates of Jerilee's three marriages, and then turned away from her as she said she had married Jim Littleton on April 18.

"April of *this* year?"

"Yes."

"Thank you, Jerilee. I don't think I have any further questions."

Again, the courtroom was filled with a murmur of indistinguishable voices, whispers of shock that the witness should have married again so soon after her husbands' deaths.

Sullivan's redirect dealt mostly with having Jerilee draw a diagram of her house and yard for the jury. He could see that she was shaken and about to break into tears.

Just as Jerilee thought her ordeal on the stand might be over, Chris Tait rose with more questions. He wanted to know more about her marriages. How old was she when she married Morris?

"Eighteen."

"And how old are you now?"

"Twenty-nine."

219

"And how old were you when you married Gabby?"

"Twenty-seven."

"And how old was Gabby when you married him?"

"Forty-two, I believe."

"You had moved back with Morris. . . . Did Gabby threaten you in any way?"

"Not me, no."

"Okay. Did he threaten you the night he came to the house and got inside because there weren't any locks on the doors?"

"No."

"What did you mean," Tait pounced, "when you said that he told you that if you didn't unlock the door and come out of the bedroom into the living room that he was going to kick the door in and come in after you?"

"That's just what he said. I don't—"

"Was he threatening you when he said that, do you think?"

"I was scared, yes."

"I can imagine you were. What was Gabby's attitude about having you come back—did it seem important to him?"

"Yes—*very* important."

"Did you think it would be fair to say that it was probably the most important thing in his life?"

"He seemed to make it that way at that time, yes."

"Talking about his blood pressure and the nosebleeds and the medication—did you ever know him to quit taking his medication on purpose, so that he would *get* nosebleeds?"

"No, he didn't."

Tait had put that thought into the jurors' minds, however, to show how manipulative Gabby had been—to the point of hatching a convoluted murder plot.

Tait asked about the disintegration of Morris's relationship with Gabby: these two men who had hunted together, worked out at the YMCA together, and discussed coaching together, these men who had faced death on the river together. Jerilee recalled that Morris had become disenchanted with Gabby sometime after December 1973, when

Gay Moore had begun divorce proceedings. It had not been too long after Gabby had moved in with the Blankenbakers.

"After the divorce with Gay," Tait asked, " . . . the relationship between Morris and Gabby started to deteriorate? Did they see each other often after that—or not at all. How would you characterize it?"

"In January of 1974—" Jerilee's voice was too soft to be heard, and Judge Loy asked her to speak up.

"In January of '74, Glynn Moore moved in with Morris and myself for a couple of weeks while his wife and he were trying to settle problems, so he saw him very often, yes."

"So they were still friends, then?"

"Yes, to a point."

"But not as close as before?"

"That's right."

"Did this relationship deteriorate gradually or just come to an abrupt halt?"

"It pretty much came to an abrupt halt. Morris could just see a change in Glynn. . . . He took a gun up to his ex-wife's house and he made threats toward her, and Morris could just—he lost respect for him."

She answered queries about Gabby's prodigious drinking.

"Was it only when he was drinking," Tait asked, "that his behavior was unpredictable?"

"It was all the time actually. Glynn used whatever he felt could get an effect or something from his wrestlers. He had been in coaching so long that it just ran into his own life."

That was an answer Chris Tait savored. The manipulative coach pulling the strings of his wrestlers to get whatever effect he desired.

He asked Jerilee when Gabby Moore had begun to change.

"Well, after looking back, I would say that it began in December and just continued until his death."

"December of what year?"

"December of 1973."

"So we're talking about a period of approximately two years?"

"Yes."

"And would you say that things got worse—or better?"

"Worse."

As, indeed, they had. Gabby had lost two wives, his best friend, his job, his self-respect.

"What kind of difficulties did he have at school?"

"It was his temperament. He would yell—sometimes bodily shake people that went in the car when they were driving [in Drivers' Training] if they didn't do as he asked."

"Do you think that's the only reason he was asked to resign, or do you know?"

"I don't really know."

Jerilee was wary of Chris Tait. She didn't want to talk about her short-lived relationship with Gabby any more than she had to. She recalled that Gabby had blamed her for his losing his job.

"He told you that? He said, 'I'm losing my job because of you'?"

"Yes."

"I see. Do you think that he was trying to make you feel bad when he said that?"

"Yes."

"Was that a tool that he was using to try to get you to go back to him?"

"Yes, it was."

"Do you think," Chris Tait summed up, "that it would be fair to say that this idea of his to try to get you back sort of consumed his life?"

Jerilee looked down and then into Tait's eyes. "I would say so."

"No further questions."

Jerilee Karlstad Blankenbaker Moore Blankenbaker Littleton walked out of the courtroom free to go on with her life. She paused to speak with reporters and to pose, unsmiling, for a few more photographs. And then she disappeared down the hallway and into the elevators.

She would not be seen again at this trial. Even so, her testimony had made her the prime prosecution witness, but, in a strange way, also one of the best witnesses for the defense. She had described a man possessed of a power to control and exploit those who trusted him, an obsessive man who never surrendered. The Glynn she had fallen in love with had turned out to be Gabby, the master puppeteer, who dangled lives from unseen strings.

Jerilee was one of the few trophies that Gabby had grasped—and then lost. And one way or another, his losing Jerilee had killed Gabby.

And Morris too.

Olive Blankenbaker had listened to Jerilee testify and felt more pity for her than anything else. She was the mother of Olive's grandchildren, and Olive knew that Jerilee had loved Morris, perhaps more at the very end of his life than at any other time. They had both lost him.

Bitterness wouldn't help anyone now and Olive knew that cruel gossip would follow Jerilee for years. She wasn't going to contribute to it. Jerilee's mother and sister supported her emotionally. Only time would tell if her marriage to Jim Littleton had been a sound move or one made out of desperation and panic at being all alone.

A lot of Yakimans expected Jerilee and Jim to move away to Seattle or Spokane, but they had no plans to do that. The best way to deal with the rumors and disapproving stares was simply to stare back. After time had passed, maybe people would find something else to talk about.

24

The most avidly awaited witness had already testified, but the trial of Tuffy Pleasant had weeks to go, and there were surprises yet to come. The battle plans were clear now, and Adam Moore and Chris Tait would have an uphill battle if the jury was allowed to hear Tuffy's own voice confessing to murder.

In the meantime, Jeff Sullivan continued laying out the state's case in neat progression. Dennis Meyers, one of Tuffy's escort officers, was also one of the first Yakima police officers who had responded to the scene of Morris Blankenbaker's murder. He testified to what he personally had observed. He listed the other police personnel who were there: Officer Rosenberry, Sergeant Green, Sergeant Brimmer, Sergeant Beaushaw, and Lieutenant Kline.

Adam Moore cross-examined, asking questions designed to make the police crime scene investigation appear inept and bumbling. It was standard defense stuff, and he did nothing to shake Meyers. Moore wanted to know when the body had been photographed, when it had been covered with a sheet, how dark it was as they searched for the missing bullet casings.

Sullivan sat implacably, unruffled. He knew the crime scene probe had been properly executed.

"Did you take custody of any objects, any evidence?" Moore asked Meyers.

"Only the objects I took from the car."

"That was a bank statement and . . ."

"A set of keys."

"To the car?"

"Yes, sir."

"Were the keys in the ignition or were they in a more subtle place."

"They were laying on the floorboards on the driver's side."

"All right. Did you find any weapons? I assume you didn't?"

"No, sir," Meyers replied. "I did not."

The jury was relegated to their quarters for forty-five minutes after lunch while Adam Moore and Jeff Sullivan argued a point of law before Judge Loy. Loretta Scott, Tuffy's cousin who had loaned him the death weapon twice, was to be the next witness. Moore argued that Jeff Sullivan had overstepped his authority on February 27 when he had granted Loretta immunity from prosecution for disposing of the gun. He asked that Loretta be informed that she could be prosecuted at some future time by some future prosecutor because she had not *truly* had immunity when she gave a forty-page statement to the investigators in February.

Sullivan argued that giving Loretta Scott such a warning would undoubtedly frighten her and serve to make her a reluctant witness. He asked Judge Loy to compel her to testify, but at the same time, to grant her permanent immunity. She had not known about any of the murder plans beforehand, and she had come forward voluntarily to tell Sullivan and the Yakima detectives about the gun. Furthermore, she had had two attorneys with her to protect her rights at the time.

Without Loretta Scott, Sullivan pointed out, the state probably would never have been able to trace the gun to Tuffy Pleasant. He asked Judge Loy to grant her immunity to testify now and to restrain the defense attorneys from alarming her with scare tactics that would make her think she could go to jail at some time in the future because she attempted to dispose of a murder weapon.

Loretta Scott sat on one of the long oak benches in the hall, unaware of the argument inside the courtroom. In truth, she had no immunity from prosecution until the court granted it.

Judge Loy said that he would need time to rule on the motions.

Loretta's testimony was skipped over, and she was told she didn't have to wait in the hall that afternoon. But she would be back. It had been her visit to the prosecutor's office that had resulted in Tuffy Pleasant's arrest for murder several hours later. She was a *very* important witness. Good for the state. Potentially devastating for the defense.

Sullivan's prosecution plan was to connect Tuffy to the death weapon, and also to connect Tuffy to the murder sites by tracing his movements on the nights in question. The state's next witnesses were the trio from Pasco who had met a single guy in the Chinook Cosmopolitan's lounge on the day after Thanksgiving.

Sam Berber and his girlfriend, Sally Nash,* and Melodie Isaacs testified that they had met a man who introduced himself as "Angelo Pleasant" in the Chinook that night. To Sullivan's question about absolute identification, Berber said he could not honestly swear that the man at the defense table was the man he had met, but he remembered the name well.

Sally Nash couldn't be positive either.

Melodie Isaacs *was* positive; she had been Tuffy's date that night.

"So you recognize that man today?" Sullivan asked.

"Yes, I do," she said, and pointed to Tuffy Pleasant. Melodie was as positive as Sam was that it was right at two a.m. when Mary looked at her watch as they let Tuffy out of Sam's Cadillac at the Chinook Hotel.

"Yes, she [Sally] told me it was two o'clock and she better head back home."

"Did you have a baby-sitter at home too that you had told you would be home a little earlier than that?"

"Yes. I told my daughter—I have a fifteen-year-old daughter."

Adam Moore hit on the trio's drinking that evening, on Sam and Sally's failure to absolutely identify Tuffy, and he even managed to confuse Melodie.

"And there's no doubt in your mind that our man is Angelo Pleasant, the guy you met *nine months ago?*"

"I really don't know, but I'm saying it's him," Melodie vacillated suddenly. "I wouldn't know him, you know—"

"Does he look like the same man?"

"He don't to me. He had a little more hair."

"He had more hair then?"

"Yeah."

"Any other differences?"

"He looked like he gained a little weight—that's about it."

"*Could* this be the man? Is it possible?"

"Yes."

"You said he was the man when Mr. Sullivan was asking you."

"Yeah," Melodie, a nightmare of a witness, equivocated. "I'm sure it's him now since I seen him again."

Melodie was certain, however, that they had dropped her date off that night at two a.m. at his car at the Chinook.

Joey Watkins, Tuffy's former housemate and wrestling buddy, was the next witness. Joey might knit up the raveled mess of uncertainties the previous witnesses had left. That is the excitement of a trial. Players leave gaps, misinterpretations, outright lies, and prejudiced statements in the fabric of the case, and the attorneys must rush to present other players who will undo the damage, and maybe even push their side a few lengths ahead. Nothing is ever a given—nor should it be. Smug, overconfident trial lawyers can be humbled in an instant.

Joey Watkins, an extremely tall young man, took the stand. He recalled knowing Tuffy since grade school and living with him for six weeks in the fall of 1975. Tuffy, he said, was back and forth from college classes in Ellensburg, helping coach Gabby Moore's high school wrestlers.

"Did you know Morris Blankenbaker?"

"Yes. I knew of him when I was in school because he was like assistant coach to us."

"So you knew both Morris Blankenbaker and Gabby Moore; is that right?" Sullivan asked.

"Yes."

"Were you going up and assisting at the wrestling practices?"

"Angelo asked me to go up to get ahold of the heavyweights and teach them, because they were kind of slow in learning things. . . . I was helping him out."

"Angelo was up [at wrestling practice] all the time. Is that right?"

"Yeah, I believe he was."

Joey recalled going up to Morris's house the night Gabby broke in. Gabby was outside when they got there and he was "bamming" on the windows.

"What happened? Was there any kind of a fight or anything?"

"No." Joey shook his head. "Morris got out of the car and

went over there. He says, 'Man, Watkins, you know what? I would hit him' but he says it was his *coach*. . . . They just started talking and I guess Morris told him something and he just left."

Joey was the friend who had been with Tuffy in the Red Lion in the Chinook Hotel on the night Morris was murdered. He remembered it extremely well. "Me and Angelo were at the Lion's Share messing around. We went to the Red Lion. That's where he met these three people. We were sitting down drinking . . . Angelo looked over and saw these people sitting over there, so he went over and talked to them. So Angelo came back over to the table and told me that he was going to be with these people tonight—and so he took me home."

"Now, once you got home, do you remember what you did?"

"Well, I just stayed at the house and laid back on the couch. Then my woman came by and we just sat and talked."

"Did you ever leave home again that night?"

"No."

"How did you find out Morris Blankenbaker had been killed?"

"Well, Angelo's mother and father were going fishing to Moses Lake. . . . Me, Anthony, and Angelo were all out at his parents' house cleaning up the yard, and I just happened to see the newspaper and saw his picture in there."

"What day was that?"

Joey wasn't sure. He knew it was on the weekend, and thought it was probably on the Sunday—November 22.

Back to the Friday night/Saturday morning when Morris died—the witness said he had gone to sleep between twelve or one a.m. and he hadn't seen Tuffy-Angelo at all that night.

"Now, Joey." Sullivan's voice was strong. "Did *you* have anything to do with the death of Morris Blankenbaker? Were you there when he was shot?"

"No."

"Did you drive the car for Angelo?"

"No."

"You had *nothing* to do with it? You were nowhere near the scene?"

"No."

"Did you ever see Gabby Moore give Angelo money?"

"When we were wrestling, he probably gave him, say, about thirty-five, forty, fifty dollars."

Joey didn't know what the money was for, or exactly when Gabby gave it to Tuffy. "I imagine he gave it to Angelo for helping him out with the wrestling practice."

As for the Christmas Eve when Gabby was shot, Joey testified he was down at the home for handicapped children with his girlfriend—down in Harrah.

"Had you been down there before?"

"Yes."

"You worked for a while at another place that took care of mentally retarded children, didn't you?"

"Yes, the Yakima Valley School."

"Last year . . . and what did you do with these small kids?"

"I was a rec leader and what we did with the kids was have recreation planned like carnivals and games with them."

"And you worked in that capacity for six or eight months?"

Joey Watkins came across as a gentle giant and the least likely of the wrestling squad alumni to have committed two murders.

On cross, Chris Tait elicited answers from Joey Watkins that showed the last time he had seen Gabby Moore on Christmas Eve was in Kenny Marino's apartment.

Tait wanted to hear more about the change that had come over Gabby Moore in the months before he was killed.

"How long had you known him?"

"Since I was a sophomore in high school."

"You had known him for five years or so?"

"Yeah."

"Did you ever experience any change in Mr. Moore?"

"Well, the only time I really saw Mr. Moore was the first time when I was in the Lion's Share and he was wild—"

"Can you tell us what you mean by that?"

"He was—I mean—like he was just changed from the coach that I used to see—because he was strict on us."

"Are you saying he wasn't the same coach—you mean he wasn't the same kind of person?"

"He wasn't the *same* person."

"How was he different?"

"Well, for one thing his hair was longer and he just didn't dress like he used to."

Joey recalled a coach who had demanded strict adherence to training rules from his athletes.

"Do you know if Mr. Moore was the sort of person who drank quite a bit?"

"No. I never knew him to drink that much until I saw him in the Lion's Share."

Joey had been baffled by a long-haired, intoxicated coach who kept trying to grab his beer. He had been horrified to see Moore trying to break into Morris's wife's window, so drunk that he couldn't walk a straight line.

With one more witness denigrating Gabby Moore, Chris Tait moved on to show that Tuffy and Joey had known Morris too as a coach.

"How close were you to Morris Blankenbaker?"

"Not really close. I didn't really know him because he was like an assistant coach when I was a sophomore and he taught me little things—moves and stuff in wrestling."

"Was Morris older than you?"

"He was thirty-two."

"And you are twenty-two. So he was ten years older?"

"Yeah."

"You said that Morris was the assistant coach?"

"He just came in there to show us things."

"He wasn't formally the coach?"

"No."

"He just showed up at the practices and kind of taught you things? Was that when you were playing football or wrestling—or both?"

"Wrestling."

"Tell us, if you can, a little bit about the wrestling experiences that you had with Angelo."

"Well, Angelo was—to me—the best on the team."

"Did he win most of his matches?"

"Yeah."

"Do you remember going to tournaments together?"

"No, because I never made it to the tournaments."

Joey said that Angelo-Tuffy had, and that he usually took firsts. Tuffy Pleasant had been the best there was; Gabby Moore had coached him to be a champion.

Tait asked Joey about playing football. He said he had had bad experiences, losing experiences in that sport. He and Angelo had been the best players on the Davis squad.

"Were you the biggest?"

"Well, I *was* the biggest," Joey said, "but Angelo was the tough man for scrape lineback."

"No further questions."

Jeff Sullivan rose to ask some questions on redirect.

"When you say Angelo was tough, was he a good linebacker?"

"Yeah."

"He liked to hit people?"

"Yeah, he stuck people."

Sullivan half smiled. "If he's going to be a good linebacker, you have to stick people, don't you?"

"That's right."

There was a sense of regret in the courtroom as the afternoon lengthened. Tuffy had lived years of sports glory. He had almost always been first, and now he sat hunched over the defense table, his huge shoulders at their muscular peak. Like Morris before him, Tuffy was a perfect physical specimen. One could imagine him and Joey in the arena— the huge gentle witness—and the scrappy defendant.

No more.

Fifteen-year-old John Klingele and and his father, Wayne, were the last witnesses of the day. John told the jury how he had found the Colt Woodsman .22 in the Naches River under the Twin Bridges. His father testified that he had put it up on a shelf and told the Yakima Police Chief about it the next day.

Judge Loy dismissed the jury at 4:30 and reminded them not to watch television, read the papers, or discuss the case. The Seattle media had begun to report this murder trial in more depth with every day that passed. It had transcended a hometown story in Yakima, Washington.

25

At 9:30 the next morning, Judge Loy said he was prepared to rule on Jeff Sullivan's motion to grant immunity to Loretta Scott and her brother, Charles "Chucky" Pleasant, for their involvement with the murder gun. "The state's motion to grant immunity from prosecution to Loretta Scott and Charles Pleasant in return for their testimony in this case is granted."

It was a big boost for the state's case.

Loretta Scott, a beautiful woman, wore a white tunic dress, a wide-brimmed dark hat, and giant gold hoops in her ears for her day in court. She did not mind the cameras in the hallway and smiled for James Wallace, the *Herald-Tribune* reporter who was covering the trial and doubling as a news photographer.

Loretta's memory was excellent, and she was a compelling storyteller as she recalled her cousin Tuffy's two visits to her home to borrow the gun and her horror when she realized what it had been used for.

Her recall of the hysteria she and her brother, Chucky,

had felt as they tried to throw away a gun that kept bouncing back off the bridge made the Christmas Day event sound like a Keystone Kops episode.

Chris Tait asked her if Tuffy had ever told her what had happened, and she said he had told her about the death of Gabby Moore.

"Well, he told me a white boy did the shooting."

"Okay. What did he tell you happened?"

"I'm just trying to gather my thoughts. He told me that Mr. Moore and he had a plan that he was supposed to have been shot, but he wasn't supposed to be killed. He said that he was supposed to get five thousand dollars out of this—that he was just supposed to wound Mr. Moore, but he wasn't supposed to die and that the white boy did the shooting."

"Did he tell you where it happened at Mr. Moore's?"

"They were in the kitchen."

"Did he tell you about anybody else being involved in these two killings?"

"He mentioned a Joey Watkins and Kenny Marino."

"And what did he tell you about how they were involved?"

"He didn't actually say. He just said Blankenbaker, Moore, [somebody was] driving a car, and Joey Watkins and Marino. . . . He told me that Joey Watkins was on the list of suspicion for murder."

"Now, who was going to get this five thousand dollars? Was Angelo to get it or was Mr. Moore going to get it?"

"I don't know who all was supposed to get this money. He said they were supposed to receive five thousand after he was supposed to have been shot. He was supposed to sign a piece of paper and supposed to get five thousand dollars . . . When he died, everything went."

Tait sounded as mystified and confused as the gallery. "But when Mr. Moore died, it all went down the drain?"

"Right."

Loretta had a few skeletons in her own closet, facts that Chris Tait dragged out of her over her extended time on the stand. He wondered why Tuffy would think to go to her for a gun.

"Well, if you want to know the truth about it, when I lived in Seattle a long time ago, he used to come over and we were always having revolvers around the house."

"I'm sorry," Tait said, "I can't hear you."

"When I lived in Seattle, we always had revolvers around the house."

"Loretta, isn't it a fact that you used to *live* with a man who dealt in stolen guns?"

"Yes, I did."

Tait homed in on her drinking habits. "Do you drink often?"

"When I feel like I want to indulge, I will."

"How many drinks does it take before you start to feel the effects?"

"About three."

"Isn't it a fact that you had four drinks on Christmas Eve?"

"That was the beginning."

"How many was it in the end?"

"I wasn't counting."

"Were you intoxicated?"

"I was feeling nice."

Loretta said she had made a Christmas punch of McNaughtons and vodka.

"It must have been quite a punch," Tait said with a smile.

Loretta Scott was on the witness stand for a very long time, much of it while the defense attorneys and the prosecutors wrangled over what areas the defense could cover. Loretta had had a gun because she was afraid of an old boyfriend, but that had nothing to do with this murder trial. She was a colorful, often humorous, witness, but she was not swayed from the central testimony about her cousin Tuffy and the borrowed gun, or about throwing it in the Naches River when she learned it might well be a murder weapon.

On redirect, Sullivan asked Loretta once again the specific questions that mattered and only those. She was positive that:

- She gave the .22 to Tuffy in October 1975.
- That she took it back from him on the Saturday after Thanksgiving.
- That he came to borrow it again on December 24.
- That he told her she would read about this in the newspaper.
- That he brought the gun back to her late on Christmas Eve.
- That he came to her house on February 26, 1976, to ask what she had done with the gun.

Nothing else really mattered as far as the outcome of the trial.

Mike McGuigan questioned Chucky Pleasant, who was a last-minute participant in getting rid of the gun. Chucky proved to be the kind of witness who scarcely needs an attorney's questions to elicit information. He began by playing both roles.

"What did Loretta ask of you?"

"Well, she came in and she said, 'Chuck, I think I know who killed Mr. Moore.' And I said, 'You do! Who?' And she told me that it was Angelo. And I said, 'No, you are kidding.' I just couldn't believe it. And then she said, 'Yeah, it's true.' And I said, 'How do you know?' and she said, 'Because I gave him the gun.'"

Chucky Pleasant said he had been totally shocked. He testified that he had gone along with pitching the gun in the Naches, which proved to be more difficult than it looked. On the day before his cousin Tuffy was arrested, Tuffy had called him in his dorm in Ellensburg.

"He just said, 'Chuck, are you sure that you threw the gun in the river?' And I said, 'Yeah.' And he said, 'Did you have gloves on when you did it?' And I said, 'Yeah, I had some gloves.' And he had asked me, 'Don't you know you might get involved in all this stuff?'"

The plan that the state alleged Gabby Moore had forged had clearly spread its poison until it infiltrated the Pleasant family, a tightly connected extended clan. Even so, Loretta and Chucky's testimony was almost lighthearted in contrast to what the afternoon witnesses would say. Much of the rest of that day would be taken up with forensic pathology and toxicology, and the evidence found at the autopsies of the two dead coaches.

The participants in the Pleasant trial—the attorneys, law officers, witnesses, and the defendant himself—were in a strange city, in an unfamiliar courthouse, yet the halls were becoming familiar and so were the jurors' faces. The trial had taken on its own rhythm now, as all trials eventually do. The case had found its flow.

Olive Blankenbaker's sister lived in Seattle, so Olive had planned to stay with her, but the trip to downtown took so long in the morning and the rush-hour traffic going home was so bad that they rented a hotel room in the center of the city so they could walk to the courthouse. There was such a sense of urgency, a kind of anxiety that they might miss something, some bit of information, that could never be found and then there would never be any closure.

Although this was a trial marked with many sidebar arguments—one where the jurors were often banished to their chambers for an hour or more at a time—it moved along. Court started promptly each morning at 9:30, with a 10:15 midmorning recess, a noon to 1:30 lunch hour, an afternoon break, and then dismissal by 4:30 P.M. Because Judge Loy had noticed that the jurors often rode the same elevators as the gallery and were sometimes blocked by corridors thick with spectators, reporters, and family, he had ordered that the jurors were to arrive first and leave first.

Thursday afternoon began with Dr. Ted Loomis, who was the Washington State Toxicologist. Loomis testified that he had had occasion to analyze blood samples taken at the postmortem examinations of both Morris Blankenbaker and Gabby Moore. He said that Morris had had "essentially no alcohol" content in his blood. Gabby, on the other hand, had had .31.

Asked by Jeff Sullivan to comment on what impairment

this much alcohol in the bloodstream would cause, Loomis answered, "All people with a blood alcohol level of point thirty-one would have very significant impairment with respect to judgment and reasoning, with respect to vision, with respect to hearing. They would have some impairment with respect to speech, but it might not be particularly noticeable. Some people, but not *all* people, would be impaired significantly with respect to their gross body muscle activity; that's walking, turning, standing, or sitting. Some people are so affected at .31 that they are actually out of contact with reality—they are in a comatose state."

"But it is possible that somebody in that condition would be able to speak . . . and somebody else not feel that they were intoxicated? Is that correct?"

"Possible for them to speak fairly well."

"Some other people's speech would be slurred?"

"Yes, and some people would be out cold."

Dr. Richard Muzzall, the Yakima County Coroner, testified next. His voice was matter-of-fact as he explained the terrible damage done by the old .22.

"Mr. Blankenbaker suffered three small-caliber wounds to the head—one passing through the upper lip and embedding itself against the base of the spine just below the skull, the other two entering behind the left ear, transversing the brain and lodging within the skull. Death, of course, was caused by extensive brain injury hemorrhage. I think it's more likely that death was caused by the two behind the ear."

Because of the gunbarrel "tattooing," Muzzall estimated that all three of the wounds were the result of a gun held at almost point-blank range, and one was a contact wound.

Olive kept her face expressionless, although she felt like screaming. Ned Blankenbaker's normally ruddy face was bright red with pain. Each of them had loved their boy so much. It still didn't seem possible that it was Morris that Muzzall was talking about.

The coroner moved on to the complete autopsy he had performed on the body of Gabby Moore. Gabby has asked

Dr. Myers where it was safe to take a bullet, but the shot to the ribs under his left arm had gone chaotically awry, and he had drowned in his own blood.

"Somebody who had sustained that kind of wound," Sullivan asked, "would it be possible to save him surgically?"

"No, I think it would be extremely unlikely, even if it happened right in the hospital."

On cross-examination, Adam Moore wondered what kind of wound Gabby would have had if the .22 bullet had not deflected and tumbled.

"If it had continued at forty-five degrees after penetrating the rib," Muzzall answered, "it would have gone through the part of the left lung, would, in all likelihood, have missed the heart and come out somewhere in the anterior [front] chest."

"I see. Uh-huh. You thought that if it hadn't been deflected by the rib, it would have been a nonfatal wound?"

"The chances it were nonfatal would be much higher."

Dr. Muzzall said he had not noticed any powder tattooing on Gabby's T-shirt, and he knew there was none on the skin itself.

Adam Moore asked Muzzall to talk about the specks of dried blood found on Morris's hand. "Your inference is that the hand was raised in a defensive—"

"It would be the only explanation . . . to explain the blood on the hand. . . . In other words, the hand had to be somewhere in front of his head where blood could get on it. . . . Blood would shoot out of the wound . . . in the direction of a cone, just as any spray from a spray can."

"In your opinion, was the gun closer to the circular wound by the ear with the dense powder patterns or the lip wound?"

"Of the two wounds, the one in the mouth would be the farthest away."

This did not seem to be information that a defense attorney would want to bring out. All of it seemed to bear out the state's theory that Morris had been lured toward someone he trusted, shot in the lip and then twice in the 'back of the head—at near contact range—by someone who must have wanted to be sure he was dead. He had thrown up his hand in a vain attempt to stop the first slug.

Eight photographs of the shooting site, Morris's body, and the blood flecked hand were entered into evidence over the objections of the defense who called them "inflammatory." Every defense attorney, *everywhere,* every time, objects to pictures of the victims as "inflammatory and of no probative value." Some get in. Some don't. For the average juror, unused to the sight of *any* dead human being, the photographs they must view are often the most jarring part of a murder trial.

But what had happened had happened, and the jurors would need to *see* the crime scenes in order to make their decisions about the guilt or innocence of Angelo "Tuffy" Pleasant.

26

Well into the first week of Tuffy Pleasant's trial, Jeff Sullivan called John Anderson, the Director of the Washington State Patrol Crime Laboratory in Spokane. Anderson had testified in more than nine hundred trials; he was a brilliant criminalist and an expert in firearms examination. Sergeant Bob Brimmer had sent the bullets and casings retrieved from the victims and the crime scenes in the Blankenbaker-Moore murders to Anderson. He had performed his forensic alchemy and connected that evidence to the Colt .22 found in the river.

Anderson gave the jury a quick lesson in the way guns propel bullets. "Except for shotguns, which are essentially smoother bore weapons, if you look down the barrel, you will see a series of circular patterns. These are caused by indentations made by the cutting implement making the barrel. The land and groove is a high point and a low point . . . and gives the direction of twist. When a cartridge is fired and the bullet is forced down the barrel, the direction of twist and the land and groove impart a spin to the bullet, putting it on a truer course."

He pointed out that the lands and grooves in a gun barrel are designed to prevent a bullet from emerging and "flip-flopping," going off course when it hits the friction of the air.

The soft metal of a bullet is marked by these high and low swirls in the gun barrel, leaving striae. These are highly individual markings. The same tool making a half-dozen gun barrels will itself be worn down imperceptibly so that no two barrels are ever exactly alike, and the bullets propelled from each barrel will have slightly different striae.

Bullets are compared in two ways: for *class* characteristics and for *individual* characteristics. Some are so battered that they meet the former criteria but not the latter. In this case, the bullet taken from Morris's head and that from Gabby's body were alike in class characteristics—each with six lands and grooves striae and with the same dimensions. Anderson, however, testified he could not say absolutely that they had come from the same gun.

However, when he compared the shell casings—the one Vern Henderson had found at the edge of Morris's yard, and the one found on Gabby's kitchen floor—he *had* been able to match them conclusively in *both* class and individual characteristics. "When a round is chambered in the barrel," Anderson said, "the *extractor* is a piece of metal that wraps around the cartridge case itself. As it is fired, the extractor will pull the empty shell case from the breech. Another piece of stationary metal hits the shell case—that is the ejectory and that will force the empty shell case out of the weapon."

Each of these actions leaves its mark on the base of the

casing. Sullivan asked Anderson how he had concluded that the same gun had fired both bullets.

"I found an ejectory mark at 'eight o'clock,' holding the firing pin impression at 'twelve o'clock,'" he said. "At 'three o'clock,' there was an extractor mark."

These marks were identical on both bullet casings—from each murder. Combined with the same firing pin mark stamped on the bottom of each shell, this left no doubt at all that the same gun had been used to kill both Morris and Gabby. And that was the gun found in the river. Everything dovetailed perfectly.

Vern Henderson had not been exaggerating when he told Tuffy how much evidence can be detected when a crime lab has both a gun and bullets for comparison.

Further, John Anderson testified that his test firings indicated that the person who shot Gabby Moore had been *nine inches or, at the most, twelve inches away.*

That warred with Tuffy's taped confession to Vern Henderson where he said he had been *six or seven feet* away from Gabby when Gabby had ordered him to shoot him. In reality, Tuffy had been very, very close to Gabby when he fired. Gabby's bloodied T-shirt with a bullet hole just beneath the left armpit was entered into evidence.

It was Friday, August 20, 1976. For the casual observer and the media too, trials are fascinating to watch. For the families of those involved—both victims and defendants— a trial is an ordeal to be gotten through, a reminder of horror and loss.

Derek Moore took the witness stand to testify about how he found his father dead before dawn on Christmas morning. His girlfriend, Janet Whitman, followed him on the stand, and then his sister, Kate, and his grandfather, Dr. A. J. Myers.

All of them related their memories of the final night of Gabby Moore's life, remembering the last time they had ever talked to someone whom they had truly cared about, but someone they could not save from his own obsessions.

Everyone in Judge Loy's courtroom was caught in those hours between sunset and the first glimmers of light on

Christmas Day, trapped, somehow, in the tiny apartment on Eighteenth Avenue, along with the dead man.

And then Jeff Sullivan skillfully elicited testimony which summed up more of the weeks and months of investigation into the two murders. The jury had heard from all the police personnel who were present at the scene of Morris Blankenbaker's murder, and now they heard about the scene at Gabby Moore's apartment—right from the call: "Unattended death."

Adam Moore and Chris Tait knew that the time when Sullivan would introduce the tapes of Tuffy Pleasant confessing to the two murders was approaching. They could not stop the tapes from being heard, but they sensed that Jeff Sullivan was about to wind up the state's case, and they were adamant that they did not want the jurors to adjourn for the weekend with those confessions ringing in their ears.

If they expected an argument from the prosecutor, Sullivan surprised them. He was not finished with his case, he said, and he had no objection to the tapes being played on Monday rather than Friday.

The day was far from over. Adam Moore made a motion for mistrial, arguing that the state had made promises to Tuffy Pleasant that they would not use a portion of the statements he had made against him if he should ever be tried for murder. In Brimmer's testimony, he had mentioned that two other people (unnamed) had been arrested and charged with murder before being released. The defense insisted Brimmer had breached their agreement and demanded a mistrial.

The motion was denied, although Loy ordered the jury to disregard Brimmer's statement.

"You cannot unring a bell," Moore said ominously.

As an offer of proof, Jeff Sullivan prepared to call Stoney Morton, one of the coterie of young wrestlers who had made up Gabby Moore's social circle. Chris Tait objected on the grounds of hearsay and irrelevancy. Morton's testimony would not be a happy thing for the defense. He had accompanied Gabby Moore on a visit to Tuffy in Ellensburg the previous October. At some point, Gabby and Tuffy had told Stoney to go out and "start the car." He had done so, but as the two had come out of the dorm, Stoney had overheard a conversation.

"I got out of the car," Stoney had told investigators, "and I heard Tuffy say, 'But they will *know* it was a black man.'"

"No," Gabby had said, "not if you wear a full-faced ski mask."

The defense prevailed, at least for the moment, and Stoney Morton was sent back to Yakima, to testify, perhaps, on another day.

Although the jury was unaware of decisions being made over the weekend of August 21-22, those days marked the most agonizing part of the whole trial for Prosecuting Attorney Jeff Sullivan. And it all concerned lie detector tests.

At the time, only three states in America allowed polygraph results into a trial without stipulation (agreement) by both the prosecution and the defense. Several lie detector tests had been given to both Tuffy and his brother by Dick Nesary, the Yakima police polygrapher. And, ironically, the tests tended to suggest that Tuffy was telling the truth and Anthony was not.

The defense team wanted Sullivan to agree to a stipulated polygraph, one whose results could be presented to the jury—no matter what the outcome was. They were prepared to call in an out-of-state polygraph expert, Dr. Stanley Abrams, to administer the test to Tuffy. Adam Moore and Chris Tait were obviously confident that Tuffy would pass this *fourth* and *stipulated* polygraph test, confident enough to offer the results to the jury.

Jeff Sullivan's first impulse was to say no to the stipulated polygraph. His case was flowing well, each witness building on the foundation laid down by the witness before. Unless Sullivan agreed to allow the fourth polygraph in, there would be no mention of any of the lie detector tests. A prosecutor's political reputation is built on his win-loss record, and this was a huge case, particularly for a thirty-two-year-old newly elected prosecuting attorney.

But, for Jeff Sullivan, there were other factors more compelling than winning for the sake of winning.

"I was in the middle of a trial," Sullivan recalled, "and I knew I could lose it all. But, morally, I could not risk convicting an innocent man."

After wrestling with the dilemma all weekend, Sullivan agreed to the stipulated polygraph. Everything in him agreed with Vern Henderson that Tuffy's taped confessions *were* the real truth and that the polygraph by someone totally unconnected with the case or the Yakima Police Department would substantiate that. And yet, if Tuffy should *pass* the lie detector test, Sullivan's case would be dead in the water.

It was an awesome risk. But not as awesome as the prospect of convicting an innocent man without giving him every opportunity to prove his innocence.

Jeff Sullivan's decision proved to be the correct one. Dr. Abrams, a defense witness, was impressive. It was Abrams who had given a lie detector test to Patty Hearst (although the results were not allowed into her trial). His credentials were impeccable.

Abrams had examined the lie detector test results that Dick Nesary had administered to Tuffy and Anthony Pleasant. He had found that the first two tests given to Tuffy were "inconclusive" and he thought the third was leaning "slightly toward the truth." Like Nesary, Abrams found Anthony's test more untruthful.

It was all moot. The jury never heard Abrams testify. They lingered all of Monday morning in the jurors' room, curious about what was going on in the courtroom.

Dr. Abrams was to have administered a fourth—and definitive—polygraph examination to Tuffy Pleasant that morning. However, after the pretest conversation with Abrams, Tuffy asked for some time to think. After fifteen minutes, he spoke to his attorneys. He had decided he didn't want to take the polygraph from Abrams, after all.

The defense team, who had been so anxious to have Prosecutor Jeff Sullivan stipulate to this polygraph, now backpedaled. They went back into the courtroom and told Judge Loy that *they* would not now—or ever—stipulate to a new polygraph test.

"We will not agree to it," Adam Moore said.

The jury never heard a word about polygraph tests. Sullivan heaved a discreet sigh of relief. He had gambled on the side of his conscience and it had been the right way to go.

27

The state's case was drawing to a close. Vern Henderson testified just before the two taped confessions were played. Adam Moore and Chris Tait cross-examined Vern fiercely, suggesting that the witness had tricked Tuffy into confessing.

It didn't fly. Vern Henderson was perfectly willing to discuss his friendship with Morris Blankenbaker. There had been no vendetta on his part. All he ever wanted was the truth. He told of finding the casing ten feet from where Morris lay dying.

Chris Tait questioned why Tuffy had been put in a private cell the night of his arrest, and why he had given his confessions on two separate days. He suggested that Vern and Bob Brimmer had told Tuffy they were going to "pretend they were in court" and that a jury was listening to the story Tuffy was telling about the murders.

"Yes, sir," Vern said quietly. "He did say that to him." Vern did not remember every word of the conversation between Brimmer and Tuffy before the tape was turned on.

"Isn't it a fact that Sergeant Brimmer told him they would never buy his story, and that he didn't believe him?"

"Yes, he did say that."

"What did Angelo say about this game of 'pretend'?"

"What do you mean what did he say, sir?"

"How did he react to it?"

"He was telling him what happened—that's how. . . . He told a story and Sergeant Brimmer told him that there weren't any facts to back it up. . . . He couldn't tell us where he was between two o'clock A.M. and three o'clock A.M." [the night of Morris Blankenbaker's murder].

"And you told him 'There aren't any facts to back up your story'?"

"We told him to *give* us some facts to back up the story."

Chris Tait had a slight touch of sarcasm in his voice as he questioned Vern Henderson, but he didn't shake the young detective. Vern had a cleanness in his testimony that no amount of cross-examination could sully.

Yes, Tuffy had trusted him, but Vern had promised nothing, ever. He had bought Tuffy a hamburger and a Coke, but Tuffy had repaid him.

"Did you loan him more money?"

"Bought him a Coke out of the pop machine. . . . Loaned him a quarter."

"Why was it that you didn't participate in this pretending session that Sergeant Brimmer was the jury and Angelo was telling his story?"

"Because *he* was talking to him, sir. He was the chief investigator. He didn't need both of us talking to him at the same time."

"You didn't take any part in that at all. You were just kind of along for the ride, sir?" Tait mimicked Henderson.

"I wasn't along for the ride, sir. I was sitting there listening."

"Did you call *Angelo* 'sir' every time he answered a question the way you are to me this afternoon?"

"I really doubt that, sir."

The gallery laughed, and Judge Loy rapped for order. There had been so little to laugh about in this trial.

Tait kept trying to box Vern Henderson into a corner, to get him to say that Tuffy had been tricked—promising him that he could continue his education in prison. "Tell us about that conversation," Tait directed.

"He was concerned about he was going to have to go to jail and lose out on all of the things that he really wanted in life—that he was working hard for his school and stuff."

"Did you tell him that you would help him with his education?"

"He was told by Sergeant Brimmer that there were programs he might get into . . . we would try to make a request . . . if it was possible. That's all."

Scornful, Tait asked, "Did you tell him to trust you?"

"No. I didn't use the words 'Trust me.' *He* used the word that he trusted me."

The tapes that Tuffy Pleasant and his attorneys now wished to recant played to a hushed courtroom. This was powerful direct evidence, the sound of Tuffy's voice speaking of the coach he had once revered. "We were tight. In my book, he was Number One. . . . I would do anything for the man, just not to see him hurt."

Tuffy's voice detailed the last moments of Morris Blankenbaker, and then the last moments of the man who had planned both murders. These tapes that had long since become familiar to the attorneys and the detectives were riveting and horrifying to the gallery. The jurors' faces remained unreadable.

"Everything was his idea." Tuffy Pleasant's voice cracked.

"Mr. Moore had this plan laid out, right?" Vern Henderson asked.

"Yes, he had it all laid out. To the bone. *To the bone.*"

"How do you feel?" Vern Henderson's voice asked, as the second tape came to an end.

"I don't," Tuffy said stoically. "Because I really just did it for him."

"What else?"

"I was under the influence of him all the time, you know," Tuffy said wearily. "I was on *his* mind track. I wasn't on mine."

As a defense, would it have flown? Murder by brainwashing? Mind control? Perhaps. Perhaps not. But it might be too late now. Adam Moore and Chris Tait had gone with a straight "Our client is innocent" defense.

Now, Adam Moore leaped to his feet and asked for a dismissal of the murder charges in the death of Gabby Moore,—or, at the very least, a reduction to manslaughter.

"The facts before the court clearly proclaim the involvement of Gabby Moore as the prime mover behind this whole sordid mess, this whole sickening sequence. He's the grand artificer about everything that we've heard in court. He brought it all about. There isn't a scintilla of evidence that Angelo Pleasant intended the death of that man, not a bit, not a scrap, not a tidbit, nothing."

Chris Tait argued that Gabby Moore had never intended to die, and that the defense believed that Tuffy never intended to administer a fatal wound.

"He was supposed to *live*. That's why the telephone was off the hook, so that Mr. Moore could crawl across the floor with the bullet wound in his shoulder and call for help. We know that he wanted to live because it was with the bullet wound, the attack on his person, that he hoped to convince Jerilee that he was innocent of his prior involvement. . . . He was *supposed to live*. He wanted very much to live. He wanted to get Jerilee back. . . . [Even] taking it in the light most favorable to the state, it's got to be by some magical, mysterious process that we turn it into evidence of premeditation. It isn't by any logical process that any of us are normally acquainted with. It's by some other process that I will never understand as long as I live. That's not premeditation."

Ahh, but it was.

And Jeff Sullivan had the evidence in the defendant's own words. Tuffy Pleasant had been afraid of the power Gabby Moore held over him.

"It seems to me," Sullivan began, "there are a number of logical inferences from the evidence that indicate that Glynn Moore was killed premeditatively and Angelo Pleasant intended his death. . . . Glynn Moore contacted Angelo on Christmas Eve. Angelo came up there and he threatened him. *He threatened him.* He said, 'Angelo, go get that gun and shoot me or I'm going to turn you in for the death of

Morris Blankenbaker.' So he went and got that gun. I think his exact words were, 'I will put your neck on the chopping block if you don't do what I say.'"

Sullivan pointed out that the defendant was supposed to shoot Moore high in the left shoulder. "He also told the police that the shot came from six or seven feet away. I submit, Your Honor, that Exhibit fourteen shows the bullet hole of entry in the body of Glynn Moore not high on the left shoulder but seven or eight inches *below* the left shoulder. The testimony of Dr. Muzzall is clear—from twelve inches or less."

VERN HENDERSON: Well, this is the plan?

TUFFY: Well, it wasn't a plan. I just did it.

VERN HENDERSON: Now, you did this because he had you up against the wall, or did you do this because this was mainly a plan he had?

TUFFY: I really did it because he had me up against a wall. I really believed he had me.

"Angelo realized," Sullivan said firmly, "that if he didn't eliminate Mr. Moore he was going to be able to use this threat of exposing him for the death of Morris Blankenbaker, and he would keep it over him for the rest of his life. And he adopted some of Mr. Moore's philosophy: *'If you got a problem, eliminate the problem,'* and he eliminated him. As soon as he shot him, did he try and help this man that he loved so much? No, he didn't help him. He ran."

Jeff Sullivan submitted that the evidence of premeditation was in place to support the first-degree murder charges.

The prosecution rested.

At nine the next morning, Judge Loy ruled that he would not reduce the charge against the defendant in Gabby Moore's death.

Coydell Pleasant began the defense case. She was in an untenable position. If she stood up for her son Angelo (Tuffy), she endangered Anthony. And vice versa. She testified that Anthony had only visited Angelo once in jail, and he said he was "nervous" after Angelo was arrested.

She said she and other family members had encouraged Angelo to tell the police everything.

In tears, Coydell Pleasant said that Angelo had told her about Anthony during one of her visits to the Yakima County Jail. "He told me, 'Mom, it's going to hurt you, but Daddy raised us up to tell the truth.'"

It was almost as if Coydell believed that if *two* of her sons shared the guilt of the murders, each would pay only half the penalty. Her testimony was clearly a desperate—and heartbreaking—attempt to protect both Tuffy and Anthony. In the end, her words had little impact.

It was Tuffy Pleasant who would be the main defense witness. Handsome, with a broad grin that seemed completely without guile, Tuffy proved at times to be a garrulous, even charming witness, as he recalled his rise to fame under Gabby Moore's tutelage and his glory days. Despite the fact that he had been in jail for six months, he was still in peak condition. If he had been brought down by the long months of waiting for trial, he did not betray it. It was almost as if Tuffy Pleasant believed he were going to walk away from the courtroom a free man.

To do so, of course, he would have to implicate his own brother and his own best friend.

Adam Moore clearly wanted the jurors to get to know his client as a person, rather than as the defendant in a double murder case. Tuffy obliged by recalling the high points of his life. "My senior year I took second in state. Coming up my sophomore year and my junior year, I was a two-time state champion in freestyle wrestling."

"In what weight class, Angelo?"

"My sophomore year, it was one hundred thirty eight and two pounds on would be one hundred forty. As a senior, I wrestled at one hundred fifty eight pounds."

"Would you say that the height of your athletic career [was] going to Japan?"

"Japan and Hawaii, yes."

"And you fellows competed for the honor of being on that team to represent Washington?"

"Yes—the best in the state."

After Tuffy had established his commitment to sports,

Moore asked him about Gabby. "Now, how did your relationship with Talmadge Glynn Moore develop during your high school years? You have said that he recruited you as a small boy from junior high school and he developed you into a wrestler good enough to go to Hawaii and Tokyo. How did your relationship with the man grow—*if* it did grow during this time?"

"I feel that it was a tight relationship."

"'Tight'? Was that the word? What do you mean by that?"

"By 'tight' I mean that it went a little further than just teacher and student or coach and student. I could visit him and we visited as friends."

Tuffy likened Gabby to a father—a *strict* father figure who demanded that his athletes, including Tuffy, stuck to spartan training rules. He said that Gabby had continued to oversee his wrestling progress even when he went off to Columbia Basin College.

Moore asked about Tuffy's children with René Sandon.

"We have two." Tuffy smiled.

"Names and ages?"

"Reneshia Naomi Pleasant* is four years old . . . Melenae Tonyia Pleasant* is two months old."

The dark shadow of two murders lingered at the edge of the courtroom as Moore asked questions that were easy to answer. Slowly, he moved into Tuffy's relationship with his brother Anthony. This too Tuffy characterized as "tight." He could not say how his younger brother felt about him.

The logic of Moore's question was emerging. Tuffy was the older, self-sacrificing brother. Anthony was heedless and greedy.

"We went out together quite a few times. But whenever he needed a car, he would always come and ask for mine, or else my older brother—but usually it would be mine. I would let him have it."

"You would let him use your car?"

"Yes, I would cancel my night just so he could have fun on his night because I felt there's always time for me to do my thing, so he can go on and do his thing."

"Did you ever talk to him the way Mr. Moore was talking

to you about direction in life and motivation and that kind
of stuff?"

"Yes. *Yes.* I always tried to steer him forward and I felt he
could be better than me and his older brother and our
cousins, you see, because I felt that he had a lot better
potential."

"Did you ever talk to Mr. Moore about Anthony in this
vein?"

"Yes, and we felt the same, that he could be the best of all
of us if he just put his mind to it, and really strive for it and
work for it."

"If he just put his mind to it?"

"If he just put his mind to it."

"But he didn't stay in the program, did he?"

"No, he didn't."

"He strayed from the path that you followed, didn't he?"

"Yes, he did."

"Did he keep the training rules?"

"No, he didn't. . . . I just tried to help him out. I said
that's not really the way to do it, and I tried to give him
explanations why not. . . . I never held nothing against
him."

Was it possible that Adam Moore had gone a bit too far?
Some gallery watchers rolled their eyes, as if a chorus of
Salvation Army singers were about to emerge and say
"Amen, brother." Tuffy was being painted with a very, very
broad brush of goodness.

Kenny Marino, Tuffy's longtime best friend, whom he
had also fingered as a murderer, was the next subject
discussed by the witness. Moore asked about how close
Tuffy and Kenny had been after they were in college.

"Were you tight then? Were you close?"

"Yes, I would say we were very close. I took him in as
another brother; I loved him just as much."

"You had accepted Mr. Moore as kind of a second father
and Mr. Marino as a substitute brother?"

"As *another* brother," Tuffy corrected.

But Moore elicited testimony that Kenny Marino had
dropped out of school and seemed to Tuffy to have no goals
in life.

Once Anthony's and Kenny's characters were found lacking by Tuffy as he sat on the stand, Moore moved on to the disintegration of Gabby Moore's ethics and values. There was no question at all of the defense strategy. They were attempting to let all blame slide off Tuffy Pleasant's broad shoulders.

It was a plan, but was the defense underestimating the jurors' intelligence? Jeff Sullivan had been mightily impressed with this jury. He studied them, wondering as always what they were thinking, and realizing as always that he would not have a definitive answer to that until they came back with a verdict.

Tuffy was telling them now about his shock at finding Gabby Moore "on the skids" in the autumn of 1975, of how he had tried to help him by putting in a driveway for him and helping to coach the high school wrestling team. This testimony sounded sincere. There seemed to be little question that Tuffy Pleasant had cared about Gabby Moore, that he had been slowly drawn into Gabby's madness.

"He was telling me that they [he and Jerilee] had gotten a divorce. He started telling me about the good times they had, and that she had left him and went back to stay with her former husband—that he had hoped she would make up her mind pretty soon. Maybe in a couple of weeks, she would make up her mind and she would be back with him."

"Was he optimistic that she might come back to him?"

"Yes."

"But he was planning to sell the house?"

"Yes."

"Because she left him?"

"Yes."

"Would it be a fair statement that he was unsure whether she was going to come back or not?"

"I don't know. I don't feel I could answer that."

"You don't know what was in the man's head at that time?"

"No, I don't."

"Did you notice a change in him between Labor Day and Thanksgiving?"

"Yes. He was changed. He wasn't like Mr. Moore, the one

I used to know, and I could hardly ever talk to him unless he was drinking. Usually what was on his mind was Jerilee, and he always would talk about Jerilee. . . ."

This jury of Seattlites had never heard of either Gabby Moore or Morris Blankenbaker before the trial. Skillfully, Adam Moore sketched in all the connections between Gabby and Morris and Tuffy and Morris and Gabby. Tuffy said he had met Morris years before when Morris was the lifeguard at the Washington Pool. He had talked to him there and known him through the years at wrestling practice. Tuffy acknowledged that relations between Morris and Gabby had not been good.

"Mainly it was Moore toward him [Morris], wasn't it?"

"I felt it was, yes."

"Now, Moore started talking about Blankenbaker being in the way and that sort of thing. Did he talk about actually killing him?"

"Well, he talked about a problem, see, and that Morris was presenting a problem to him at the time. And so then he started talking about eliminating the problem."

Apparently, Tuffy had forgotten that Jeff Sullivan had used that "eliminating the problem" quote from his taped confession the day before when the prosecutor was successful in keeping first-degree murder charges in force against Tuffy.

"Did you know what he meant by that?" Adam Moore asked, unruffled.

"No," Tuffy answered. "Not until later. I was still trying to understand where he was coming from as a matter of speech."

"You didn't understand he meant having him killed?"

"Eventually, that's what he meant."

"What was your position on that?"

"Well, my position was I felt that he should forget about it—because he was an older man. . . . Eventually he could forget about the situation and latch on to another lady, form another relationship with another party."

"Did you tell him that?"

"Yes, I did. He said all he wanted was Jerilee. That's all that was on his mind."

Tuffy described the impasse he and his former coach had come to in late October. Gabby drank and talked about Jerilee. "He had him a few glasses down and he started talking about Jerilee. And I told him he should just try to forget about the woman—like I was repeating myself also. And then he started getting down. He would break out his pictures—"

"Pictures?"

"Yes."

"Was this the album Sergeant Brimmer was talking about? There were two albums found in the bedroom there. Is that what he meant by pictures?"

"Yes, and then he would play some music that he would say he and Jerilee had a good time to. It stood out in his memory and he played the music over and over."

"What else happened this particular night?"

"Then he started talking about Morris. Then he came out and he finally told me—he was finally to that point to have Morris eliminated."

The facts had not changed from the statement Tuffy had given to Vern Henderson, the facts the jury had heard on the tape. It was up to Adam Moore now to work his rhetorical magic and turn his client, the defendant, into the hero of this American tragedy instead of the shooter.

It would be a gargantuan task even for the best criminal defense lawyer in Yakima County.

But that would wait until the morning. It was five P.M., and Judge Loy was strict about letting the jurors go home at a reasonable time. The trial was in high gear though, and he announced that he would begin court a half hour earlier in the morning.

Tuffy Pleasant was back on the stand the next day. Adam Moore asked him to relate the events of one Sunday in the first part of November—a few weeks before Morris Blankenbaker's murder.

"How long were you at his [Moore's] house that day?"

"About a couple of hours—two hours."

"Okay. Just tell the jury about everything that you remember about that two hours, will you?"

"I got there and Mr. Moore was drinking. He asked me when I stepped through the door, 'Why don't you go ahead and pour yourself a drink?' So I went ahead and poured myself a shot or two. Then he watched TV and he turned the TV down and then he started talking.

"And he started talking about Jerilee again. And I was just listening, you know. I wasn't going to tell him too much. I was already trying to talk to him. I was just waiting until he finished because he just continually kept talking and then you kind of interrupt him. I noticed at the time I interrupted him he would get mad and jump right back at me and say, 'Well, I'm talking. Just wait until I'm through talking and then you can give me your response.' But then he kept carrying on and he finally said, 'Well, I can't find nobody to do it.' And then he asked me if I would do it. I told him, 'No,' I wouldn't do it. I wouldn't even think about doing it. I felt that he was a grown man, and I said, 'You are a grown man and you are asking me to do this for you. Now, I would do a lot for you but shooting somebody—that's something else.' "

Gabby had gotten angry, Tuffy testified, and he had tried to calm him by giving him the name of someone who might do it, just to stall.

"I felt I was trying to talk him out of it."

In this new recanted version of events, Tuffy said that Gabby had said he would try to get in touch with this man—another former wrestler of his, but a few years older than Tuffy. Then he had suggested that Joey Watkins might do the shooting.

"He was talking about having a professional hit man come in and do the job, and I says, 'No, you are really getting carried away with this.' "

Tuffy testified he left, only to return a week later to find Gabby more obsessed with his plan to kill Morris. "I said 'No—and don't ask me again,' and he didn't ask me again."

"Okay. Up until which time?"

"Up until the night Morris got shot."

On that Friday night, Tuffy's revisionist version was that he had come home from college, met Joey Watkins and agreed to a blind date with Joey's girlfriend's friend. He then went back to his fiancée's house. (Tuffy apparently saw nothing wrong with having a pregnant fiancée, and a daughter—*and* a blind date with another woman.)

While he was at René's house, he *had* received a call from Gabby who was in the hospital. "He wouldn't tell me what was wrong with him. I asked him three or four different times. He said, 'I'm in the hospital and tonight would be a good night to shoot Morris—if you know what I mean.'

"I says, 'Well, I have got other things planned for tonight. I'm going out tonight for myself and you are just going to have to take care of yourself, and I'll see you later.' And I hung up on him."

Tuffy testified that he had asked his fiancée to find out which hospital Gabby was in so he could go up and visit him. Then he had kissed his fiancée and left for his blind date. But even though he had met Joey Watkins, he said they had only spent ten minutes talking to the two women. Later, after several trips to Watkins's house, the Red Lion, the Lion's Share, and around Yakima in general, Tuffy testified he had met the trio from Pasco and joined their party.

Joey Watkins had said, "Well, man, things are pretty slow tonight so you might have you a catch over there—so why don't you just go on. I can take care of myself."

There were refinements to Tuffy's recall of Friday, November 21. Now, he testified that when he had gone home sometime in the evening to borrow some money from his mother, he had met up with his brother Anthony for the second time that night. He said that he told Anthony about Gabby's phone call instructing him to shoot Morris, and Anthony had agreed with him that it was "odd."

Back with the Pasco group now, Tuffy testified they had all gone to the Thunderbird to dance. "We were dancing and I met some people—schoolteachers. Mr. Pryse and another schoolteacher—Mrs. Pryse. She used to be Mrs. Moore."

"Anything significant between you and Gay Pryse at this time?" Adam Moore asked, trying to keep this peripatetic story in some kind of order. "Just some small talk, wasn't it?"

"Small talk, yes."

"You didn't communicate to her how her husband was acting—or ex-husband, I mean?"

"No."

The quartet had returned to the Red Lion, Tuffy said, and he had finally parted from them after looking for an after-hours place. He had then gone back to Joey Watkins's house. He was packing his clothes to return to Ellensburg when his brother Anthony came to Joey's.

"I saw he had about four cans of beer, and he asked me what I was doing and I told him I was figuring to leave and go up to Ellensburg to a party. And, well, he asked me, 'Why don't you—Let's go riding for a bit and let's go have a drink.' . . . I said, 'Okay, I will go riding; I will drink a beer with you.'"

Adam Moore suddenly backed up. He had not asked Tuffy Pleasant about the gun! Now, he did. Tuffy nodded and agreed that he had gotten a gun from his cousin Loretta. But his version of that transaction was vastly different from her statement *and* from his taped confession. Tuffy testified that he had gone to see Loretta, bought her some groceries, spent the night, and been awakened by—ironically—"firecrackers going off in the back."

"I went to the backyard and she was there looking at the garage door. I saw a couple of holes she was looking at. I don't know if they came from the gun or not. I saw some potato peelings on the ground and I saw some smashed on her face. Then I asked her whatever she was doing, and she said she was just shooting the gun. . . . I looked at the gun, and says, 'Well, I will buy it from you' because earlier in the night she told me she was in debt. . . . She needed money pretty bad to pay some of her debts."

"Did you buy it?" Moore asked.

"No, I didn't. I just took it from her and I told her I would pay her later. I thought I would make some money in Yakima, you know, make a few extra dollars."

"Sell it?"

"Yes."

Tuffy said that he had slipped the gun under the front seat of his car. Under the driver's side.

"Did your brother know that?"

"Well, he knew I had the gun. Earlier when I was down at my girlfriend's house, I had showed it to him and asked him if he knew anybody that was interested and he said yes, he did."

Tuffy specified that Anthony had seen the Colt .22 under the bucket seat of his car a week earlier.

Adam Moore had brought it all together. The gun, The car. The two brothers. And now, Tuffy explained how he had suddenly become aware that they were "apparently" driving up to Morris Blankenbaker's house.

"Why do you say 'apparently'?"

"Because my brother asked me to slow down. Eventually, as time went on, I found out it was his house.

"He asked me to slow down. He says he wanted to see if Morris was home. I says, " 'This time of the morning, you know, nobody is going to be up. You don't go visiting at this time in the morning.' "

But Tuffy said Anthony said he and Morris were "pretty tight" and that he would get up.

"He saw that the car was missing, and that 'Morris isn't home, so apparently he's at work.' "

"What happened next?" Adam Moore asked.

Tuffy gave a long answer about his younger brother's concern with Gabby and Jerilee—saying that Anthony wanted to talk to Morris about it. He had just assumed that Anthony knew Morris better than he himself did. They had driven by the Lion's Share and saw Morris come out to his car. And then, at Anthony's insistence, they had returned to North Sixth Street.

"We went down the alley and . . . I saw Morris going through the gate. We were walking a little bit faster, a lighter trot. We were coming around the back of his garage and I had seen Morris just about up to the front of his house and I had called him. I called him, and apparently—"

Adam Moore cut in quickly. Tuffy Pleasant had unconsciously slipped into the first person.

"*Okay*. You called Morris then—or you *had* called him?"

"I called him then."

Tuffy's attorney let it go; it was better than drawing attention to the slip. "What did you say?"

"I said, 'Morris—'"

"And what happened next?"

"Apparently I took it he didn't hear me, and my brother hollered at him. He said, 'Morris! Morris!' . . . Morris turned around and he saw us and he came back. He said, 'How are you guys doing?' And I said, 'I'm doing all right. How are you doing?' He said, 'I'm doing pretty good.' And I didn't hear my brother say anything, and then he asked Anthony, 'How are you doing, Anthony?' He said, 'I'm doing all right.'"

The courtroom was very quiet. Everyone listening knew what was going to come next, and no one wanted to hear it. Whoever had been there, whoever had pulled the trigger, the ending was going to be the same.

"And then," Tuffy went on testifying, "there was just a little light conversation. Morris had kind of relaxed himself on the gate and Anthony said, 'Well, it's about Jerilee.' And then Morris kind of stiffened up and told him, 'Well, I don't want to hear nothing from you or nobody else about Jerilee, and if I hear anything from you or anybody else about Jerilee, I will see to it they don't say nothing else.' And then he kind of stiffened up and took a step toward us."

"Did he have anything in his hand?"

"He had a beer bottle in his hand."

"And then what happened, Angelo?"

"Well, when he took the step, next thing I know it, I heard the shot. I saw some fire, and I saw him turn, I saw his head turn."

"Who was holding the gun?"

"My brother Anthony . . .

"I don't know if I saw the second shot or not, but I saw some fire and I took off running . . . down the alley, headed north toward my car."

"Where was your brother?"

"He was right behind me. Well, probably not *right* behind me but I heard his footsteps."

Tuffy's voice was full of emotion as he described how

shaken he had been. "I didn't turn on my car lights. . . . I was scared and I just took off from there and went on down First Street. And I was telling my brother, I said, 'Look, I don't know what happened back there. Just don't tell me nothing,' and I took the gun from him and I told him, 'Just don't tell me nothing, but I'm not going to be able to vouch for you tonight. If you say anything to anybody that I saw you tonight about this time I'm not going to be able to tell them nothing.'"

"Did you say anything to him about taking the blame?"

"Yes, I did. I told him if it came down to it, and if my name came up first that I would take it."

"Take what?"

"The blame."

Jeff Sullivan had written steadily on the long yellow legal pad in front of him as Tuffy testified. He had seen slight flaws and then widening tears and finally huge gaps in Tuffy's latest version of the death of Morris Blankenbaker. If Tuffy had been so anxious to protect his younger brother and his best friend, why was he telling it all now, placing the blame squarely on their shoulders?

Sullivan was anxious for the time to come for cross-examination.

28

Before Jeff Sullivan could cross-examine Tuffy Pleasant about this new scenario on the death of Morris Blankenbaker, he had to sit through a new script about the shooting of Gabby Moore on Christmas Eve. Tuffy said he had still visited Gabby and heard the same obsessive discussion about how Gabby would win back Jerilee, the conversation becoming increasingly maudlin as his coach drank bourbon mixed with Pepsi or Kool-Aid—or straight, if he had nothing else. The more he drank, Tuffy testified, the more hostile Gabby became. Interestingly, Tuffy himself seemed to have become hostile too—hounded as he was by Gabby.

"Angelo, how would you characterize Gabby Moore's demeanor when he would discuss with you his situation with Jerilee?"

"I would say it wasn't working out too good. . . . You couldn't say nothing to him. He would just get upset or holler at you."

"Did he cry?"

"I saw him cry one time—one time earlier. And then the night that he was shot."

"Okay, let's talk about Christmas Eve. Let's start in the morning."

Tuffy moved through his day, going into agonizing detail about all of his visits with René, his family, his cousins. He finally arrived at the evening hours when he was at a party at Stoney Morton's house.

"Who was there?"

"Stoney, his lady friend, my brother Anthony, Stoney's younger brother . . . I was there. . . . We were sitting down and looking at a game on TV and drinking a little bit. There was this knock at the door . . . and it was Kenny Marino."

"Then what happened?"

"He came in. He didn't say 'Hi' or nothing. He just said, 'Angelo, Mr. Moore would like to see you up at his house as soon as possible.' And I told him, I says, 'Look, now don't be ordering me like that. I'm out here trying to visit people and I'm just not going to up and run and go visit somebody else just because they ask somebody to come see where I'm at.' And he said, 'Mr. Moore would like to see you as soon as possible.' And I said, 'Well, I see him when I get around to seeing him. . . . I'm not going to rush for nobody.' "

He testified that Kenny had left after "cussing him out." Tuffy said that Mr. Moore had called him at René's house, saying, "Tonight's the night if you know what I mean."

"I said I didn't know, and he says, 'Why don't you come up and find out?' I was getting ready to take my lady friend out, but it was eating away at me, so I talked with my lady and then I left and went on up to Mr. Moore's house."

"What time did you get there, Angelo?"

"Between eight-thirty and nine."

Gabby had been dressed nicely, Tuffy testified, and he had kicked off his shoes and told Tuffy to pour himself a drink. Tuffy testified that Moore had said that he couldn't wait any longer, that this was the night he wanted *himself* shot.

"He asked me if I would do it. . . . I told him, no, I'm not going to do it. And he says, 'Yes, you are. You're going to do it.'"

"How did he want himself shot?"

"High in the shoulder, left shoulder. He wanted an attempt to be made on his life. He figured that was the only thing—if it was made on his life like it was made on Morris, he figured he could get Jerilee back in a couple of weeks or even before the first of January."

Although Tuffy had insisted he would not shoot Gabby, he testified that Gabby said, 'Well, I'll see to it that you get the blame for Morris Blankenbaker's shooting.' And I didn't tell him I didn't do it. I didn't want nobody else to know [about Anthony] not even him—*nobody*. . . . And he says, 'Well, I will see to it that your neck is on the chopping block for Morris's death.' And I says—well, I don't know what I really said. I was kind of quiet. He asked me if I knew where the gun was—was it close, and I said it was nowhere around here. And he said I was lying. . . . I said, 'I don't know where the gun is—it's gone. It's a long ways from here. . . .'"

Gabby had said he would gas up his car, Tuffy testified. "I said, 'It's a long way from here and it's buried.'" That, he said, didn't stop Gabby, who said they could take a shovel. When Tuffy still refused, he said Gabby had picked up the phone book and showed him the police number.

"He dialed the digits down to the last one. He asked me if I was going to do it. . . . I said, 'I'm not going to do it,' and he dialed the last digit and so I says, 'Okay, I will do it.'"

Tuffy said he still thought he could talk Gabby out of it until he dialed that last digit, and then he realized his old coach "wasn't playing."

Vern Henderson had heard this before. He wondered what spin Tuffy was going to put on it this time. So far, it was almost verbatim with that was on the tapes. Yes, Gabby was going to "put down" a lot of whiskey while Tuffy went for the gun—just as it had been in the first confession.

"I told him," Tuffy was saying, " 'You can't take the shot, because I don't think even I could,' and I felt I was a little bit stronger than he—just on street strength-wise. But he was a bigger man than I was and I told him, 'I don't think you could take the shot.' I was trying my best to talk him out of it. And he said, 'No, this is what I want and this is the only way to get Jerilee back.' "

Gabby had accused Tuffy of stalling for time. Gabby had ordered him, "Go get the gun."

"Did you go get the gun?"

"Yes, but I told him that he was talking crazy, completely crazy."

Now, as Jeff Sullivan and Vern Henderson listened for the slightest straying from the tapes, they heard Tuffy veer off.

"What happened then?"

"I had parked in front of another car, and I was waiting, talking to myself. I says, 'Well, I'm not going to do it no matter what, but I will take the gun in and show it to him anyway, just to see if it would calm him down—and see if I can talk to him a little bit more.' "

But while he was waiting, Tuffy said he honked twice, and he had seen his brother Anthony and a friend drive by. Then they went in Moore's house.

"Did you go in the house?"

"Yes."

In this version, Tuffy said that he had tried to get his brother and his friend to help him get Gabby out of the house, to go visiting or to a tavern. But it didn't work. Gabby was "as drunk as I've ever seen him. He was swaying back and forth. He could hardly stand."

After the others had left, Gabby took off his shirt, his shoes, and started talking about Jerilee. He broke out his

photo albums. He was single-minded about what he wanted
done.

Emotions washed across Tuffy Pleasant's face as he testified. There was little question that he was remembering a
desperate night. There *was* a question about whether he was
confabulating—taking a real event and rewriting it so that
it emerged in a manner favorable to him. He could not have
been making this monologue up; he didn't seem that
sophisticated. But it was quite possible he was weaving self-
serving "memories" into what had really happened at
Gabby Moore's apartment on Christmas Eve.

The phone rang twice, but Gabby wouldn't say who it
was. Tuffy said that Kenny Marino had appeared a short
time later. But Kenny had stayed in the house while Tuffy
was walking Gabby around the backyard. Tuffy testified
that he'd managed to get his coach out in the backyard for
air only to have Gabby order him to shoot him there. Tuffy
said he refused and Gabby stumbled back into the house.

"Where was the gun?" Adam Moore asked.

"In the house—on the right side of the daveno on the
floor. I was kind of upset because he [Gabby] saw where I
put the gun because he was looking right at me when I put it
down there. I don't know if he was in a daze or looking past
me."

Tuffy said he was thinking then of "bookin'" (leaving)
and letting his friend Kenny deal with their old coach. But
then he had remembered the gun was in the house. "I can't
leave without the gun. My keys are in the house, my coat
was in the house, so I says, I'm going to go back in there. I'm
going to talk to this man one more time and if he doesn't
come around, I'm leaving."

"And so," Tuffy continued, his voice taut, "as I went
stepping through the door—I just opened the door—there
was a shot. Mr. Moore was on the floor and Kenny was just
lowering the gun."

In hours and hours of testimony, Tuffy had explained
away all of the blood on his hands. His brother Anthony had
killed Morris; his best friend Kenny had killed Gabby. He
himself had just happened to be in close proximity to both
murders.

Pleasant's attorneys called for the noon break, and Judge Loy agreed but cautioned the spectators in the gallery to sit in their seats and say nothing until the jury filed out.

When the jury room door was shut tight, Adam Moore and Chris Tait voiced their concern about the way Jeff Sullivan would present testimony on the defendant's recanting of his original confessions. Without the jury present, Tuffy took the stand again and said he felt that Vern Henderson and Jeff Sullivan had been dishonest with him by pretending to believe him when he implicated Anthony and Kenny as the guilty ones. Now, he felt he had been tricked.

Sullivan reminded Tuffy he had always told him that—if he was not telling them the truth—Tuffy would be tried for the murders. The defendant's attorneys had been present and aware of every step of the case. Faced with Sullivan's questions, Tuffy backed up, admitting that he had been warned what would happen if he was lying to the detectives and the prosecuting attorney.

In truth, Jeff Sullivan and Vern Henderson *had* believed Tuffy's recanting, enough so that Anthony Pleasant and Kenny Marino had been arrested. But, as witnesses and forensic evidence failed to validate Tuffy's version and did nothing to connect the other two suspects, they had changed their minds.

Tuffy Pleasant's direct testimony continued for hours. Adam Moore ended it on a poignant, dramatic note. He asked Tuffy to tell the jury about Gabby Moore's trophy case.

"[He had] wrestling trophies, trophies he had received from different teams that were sentimental to him as a coach, pictures of his different teams, pictures of his different companions throughout the years that he was coaching there at Davis High School. Pictures of his son, the baseball team he played on and their national team that they had last summer."

"What did Gabby tell you Christmas Eve about the trophy case?"

"He said, 'Some people live and strive for what I have

here'—and he pointed to his trophy case—'to have a lot of trophies to really make something out of themselves, but I have a whole trophy case full and I have what I wanted in that department and in my other department I would like Jerilee.' What he wanted was Jerilee; that was his biggest goal."

"How old were you at the time?"

"I was twenty-one."

"How old was he?"

"Approximately forty-four."

"Did you shoot Morris Blankenbaker?"

"No, I did not."

"Did you at any time intend for him to die?"

"No, not at any time in my mind did I intend for Morris Blankenbaker to die."

"Did you know that your brother was going to kill him?"

"Not at no time did I know that my brother, Anthony Pleasant, was going to shoot Morris Blankenbaker."

"Did you shoot Talmadge Glynn Moore?"

"No, at no time did I shoot Mr. Moore."

"Did you want Mr. Moore to be dead?"

"No, I did not."

Angelo Pleasant and his attorneys had taken a calculated risk when he decided to testify. Now, the danger was at hand. Jeff Sullivan rose to cross-examine Tuffy.

There were so many lies and half truths to cut out of the defendant's direct testimony and hold up for the jury to see. Within the first few minutes of Sullivan's cross-examination, the first lie popped up. Tuffy admitted that he had lied to police about the time he had left Gabby Moore's house on Christmas Eve.

"Actually," Sullivan moved in, "the first three or four or five contacts that you had with the police you admitted whatever you thought they already knew. Is that right?"

"Yes."

Regarding the February 27 and 28 taped confessions, the prosecutor asked, "Anybody beat you or force you to make those statements?"

"Didn't nobody beat me."

"Did they force you to make the statements?"

"No force."

Grudgingly, Tuffy answered questions about Gabby Moore's plans for murder.

"He talked to you about those plans, didn't he?"

"He talked *at* me."

"But you listened, didn't you?"

"I was there in his house."

"He had a plan to kill Morris Blankenbaker when he came home from work, didn't he? . . . How many other plans did he have?"

"Two other plans. Every Tuesday, Morris went to the "Y" with his son—and to have him shot in front of his son, Rick, but if Rick wasn't with him to just shoot him going to the "Y" and to take out his wallet and make it look like a robbery. And another one that I remember was that Jerilee and Morris went to work about five minutes apart in the morning. After Jerilee went, [I was] to park off of Naches and to walk up to the house . . . and knock on the door."

"And actually shoot him at the front door?"

"Or step into his house . . ."

The final plan had been the one that transpired. Only Tuffy denied that he had been the shooter. He was certainly familiar with all the details. "He suggested to me that *whoever* did it—that he would like him shot once by the heart and once—if he fell, then to walk up to him and put one in the back of his head."

"And you shot him in the head?"

"No."

"He *was* shot in the head?"

"Yes."

"I mean he was shot just like that plan, wasn't he?"

"He wasn't shot in the heart," Tuffy blurted, "so I feel that's not exactly like what he was talking to me about."

"I see," Sullivan said sarcastically. "Just three times in the head. Is that right?"

Sullivan's cross-examination was adroit; at the first sign of an opening, he pounced. The defendant was so busy straining at gnats that he forgot to show "appropriate" emotion where he should have. The gallery could see that, and surely the jurors could.

And the lies and semi-lies. There were so many.

Tuffy admitted he could have easily reached Morris's house from the Chinook Hotel in five minutes. He knew there had been three shots in Morris's murder, but he could not remember how he knew. He gave three or four scenarios, weakening his impact with each new reason. He couldn't remember what he had said in his taped confession. In retelling, he confused the order of his own statements.

Jeff Sullivan was like a boxer looking for an opening. When he found one, he jabbed. He caught every hesitation, every contradiction. Tuffy Pleasant was on the ropes, confused and wobbling.

"You are trying to tell me that he [Gabby] didn't have it planned very well?"

"I felt he didn't—I'm right here this very day on charges."

"Oh, I see. I see. Your conception of the plan is that it is very good if you don't get caught?"

"No. I did not do it."

"He told you where he wanted the man shot . . . and he told you where you could park your car. . . . And he told you the layout of the back of that house? Right?"

"Yes."

"But he didn't tell you *where* the house was. Is that right?"

"Well . . . he *mentioned* where it was."

"Why did you testify here today . . . that you didn't know where he lived? That it wasn't until Anthony told you that you found out where Morris lived?"

"I did not exactly know which house he lived in."

Suddenly, it was five o'clock. Sullivan would have happily continued all night, but Judge Loy would not. The rhythm was broken, but the prosecutor would pick it up in the morning.

29

And so he did. If Angelo Pleasant had been engaged in a wrestling match, he could have detected where his opponent was going to move next. But he was not a debater and he seemed to have no inkling of when Jeff Sullivan was about to catch him up in yet another inconsistency in his testimony. Time and again, Sullivan winnowed out a lie.

Adam Moore finally stood up and complained that he didn't want Sullivan reading from Tuffy's earlier statements and then pointing out that his client was lying. Judge Loy asked Sullivan to rephrase his questions.

It didn't matter. With each slip, Sullivan repeated what Tuffy had said—and repeated it incredulously, or derisively, or with amusement—and sometimes with a question mark. The carefully reconstructed events of Tuffy's testimony began to buckle. It could be only a matter of time before the whole construction imploded and fell back on Tuffy.

From time to time, Sullivan had Tuffy read his earlier confession silently to himself. Sweat beaded on the defendant's forehead. There was no way to mesh what he had once said with what he was now claiming.

"Angelo," Sullivan said, "are you saying that this statement was not true?"

"Yes, I'm saying that."

"Even though you were telling your lawyers and telling me that this was the truth?"

"Some of it."

"Some of it. Some of what you told us after you were arrested then was not true; is that what you are saying?"

"Well, I was still on my own, Mr. Sullivan, wasn't nobody looking out for me but myself."

"So you chose to tell us something that wasn't true?"

"Well, I don't know what my thinking was at the time."

Sullivan had elicited testimony that seemed to suggest that Tuffy had felt nothing about Morris Blankenbaker's death but fear that he would be caught. But Gabby was another matter entirely. His coach had been so much a part of the defendant's life for so long. Sullivan needed to focus on a heedlessness, a failure to grieve, on Tuffy's part as Gabby lay dying.

"Angelo," he began, "at that time Glynn Moore was lying on the kitchen floor, you didn't know whether he was dead or alive. You indicated to us he was one of your best friends, and you were no *more concerned* than just to go to a party. Is that right?"

"Yes, I was concerned."

"But you *went* to a party?"

"Later on, yes."

"Angelo, as you saw Mr. Moore lying there after 'Kenny shot him,' why didn't you try and help him?"

"Mr. Sullivan, I was scared and I didn't want to be caught in the house; I had the gun in my hand."

"But you didn't shoot him, did you?"

"No, I didn't, but I had the gun in my hand."

"You didn't call an ambulance for him?"

"No."

". . . Now, Mr. Moore's plan was that he would be wounded with that same gun, but he was supposed to get to a doctor soon, wasn't he? So that he wouldn't get injured seriously?"

"He was going to call one of his lady friends—or he felt that he was strong enough to take the shot and go across the street and talk to the lady who owned the house—"

"That was Jerilee's sister?"

"Yes . . . I was telling him, 'You can't do it.' "

"He's laying there on the floor—not moving. Didn't you say that you heard him groan or something?"

"When I was leaving."

"When you were *leaving?*"

"I heard a noise."

"Did you look back to see what was happening?"

"No, I was trying to get out of there."

Stubbornly, despite being confronted with his oft-repeated statement that Gabby Moore had "his neck on the chopping block," Tuffy denied that he had thought about the danger of Gabby exposing him as a killer. "I did not shoot Mr. Glynn Moore," he insisted.

"You intended to kill him, didn't you, Angelo?"

"I did not kill Glynn Moore. And it hurts me just to sit up here and to listen to you, Mr. Sullivan—with all due respect to you—and keep accusing me and accusing me and I didn't do it. I really loved that man. But at the time when I did leave, when Kenny did shoot him, I was scared and confused and I just thought of leaving and not being caught on the premises."

When Jeff Sullivan turned away at last from Tuffy Pleasant, he had effectively revealed the truth. Tuffy had shot Morris and he had shot Gabby. But had he shot Gabby, intending to kill him? Or had he merely been following Gabby's orders? It was still impossible to tell. But he had left. That much was clear. Perhaps Tuffy could not look that fact straight in the face. Perhaps he could not allow himself to recall stepping over Gabby's body, hearing his last gasps for life, and walking away.

In the end, Tuffy *had* deserted "The Man," his mentor, his hero, his friend, his role model. In a sense, Gabby had deserted Tuffy too. Together, they had made wrestling championships their only goals. But Gabby had no longer cared about the glory of winning.

On recross, Adam Moore asked Tuffy again about Gabby's complete defection from all they had believed in.

"Well, he was talking about the trophy case," Tuffy answered. "Some young men—also some young ladies— [he said] who are pretty good in sports and have pretty good ability to achieve, all they had to do was try hard. He said he was forty-four years old and that he felt he was over the hill. That trophies didn't mean nothing anymore—his biggest goal and trophy in life was Jerilee . . . and that I was pretty young and I didn't know what he meant, but when I was older, and time went on, I would realize what he meant."

Tuffy Pleasant had been on the witness stand for three days. He had clung to his position that his brother and best friend were the true killers, but their testimony and the rebuttal testimony of more than a dozen witnesses would place both Kenny Marino and Anthony Pleasant well away from both crime scenes. Jeff Sullivan knew that, and he was not concerned.

When Tuffy had stepped down from the stand, the trial began to wind down rapidly.

On Saturday, August 28, Adam Moore and Chris Tait and Jeff Sullivan made their final arguments. Two weeks before, they had promised the jury that they would give them certain facts. And they had all stayed close to their opening statements.

Prosecutor Jeff Sullivan's voice boomed through the small courtroom and bounced off the walls as he reconstructed the entire trial, the evidence that had, he said, pointed to only one man. Sullivan focused on Tuffy's taped confessions. "He learned from Glynn Moore that when you get a problem," Sullivan said, "you *eliminate* the problem." The prosecutor called Morris Blankenbaker's murder a "contract killing."

"Gabby Moore was killed to shut him up."

Despite Tuffy Pleasant's open and affable appearance, Jeff Sullivan said he was cold. "A man who could shoot two people and then go to a party . . . that's callousness. That's why he could come into this courtroom and say what he did. This man would have us believe that he missed [hitting Gabby high up in the shoulder] from twelve inches away. He shot him . . . and then where did he go? He picked up his girlfriend and went to a Christmas party."

Adam Moore for the defense said he had "utter contempt" for Gabby Moore for drawing Anthony and Angelo Pleasant and Kenny Marino "into the sewer."

Moore's face and words were full of rage as he characterized Gabby as "vile and despicable." Everyone in the

273

courtroom jumped as Tuffy's chief lawyer bellowed, "GOD! The worst tragedy of this is that he isn't sitting here today. I blame him for the whole mess."

Adam Moore literally vibrated with anger. "I have for two weeks seen the prosecutor stand before you and tell you to convict this man on two counts of first-degree murder. . . . I could puke," Moore said as he slammed his fist on the table in front of him.

The gallery jumped again.

Adam Moore, an attorney with a courtroom demeanor that long predated the antics of a Johnny Cochran, grew suddenly calm. He walked to Tuffy Pleasant and placed his hands on his client's shoulders. "I apologize for the emotion, but it's real," he said with his voice cracking. "It's the way I feel."

As he asked for an acquittal on both counts, Moore pleaded, "Let it be done with. Let Gabby Moore's end be his just reward."

It was over for the gallery, for the regulars who had shown up for the trial every day. Many of them would probably not have enough forewarning of the verdict to get to the courtroom in downtown Seattle in time to hear it read.

Fourth Avenue, just outside the King County Courthouse, was quiet. It was a Saturday, and Saturday trial sessions were a rarity. Few cars headed north up the one-way street. There were no pedestrians. The courthouse was closed except for the trial just ended. It was still hot but the sun was blocked by the courthouse, and its warmth came up only from the sidewalks where it had baked all day while the lawyers inside talked on and on of death and blood and guilt.

It didn't seem possible that two weeks had gone by. All trials are engrossing, but this one had been more compelling than most, and the gallery straggled out, reluctant to have it over. All the players had been unknown entities when the trial started. Now, they were almost as exposed as family members sometimes are. So many secrets told.

At the corner of Fourth and James Street, the sun blasted

through the gap in the buildings built along James up from Eliott Bay, but the air suddenly felt sweet and cool.

High up in his cell in the jail, Tuffy Pleasant waited to hear what his future would be. He thought of "time."

The eight-woman, four-man jury retired that Saturday evening and deliberated for close to five hours before stopping for the night. Judge Loy had instructed them that they had several options. They could consider first-degree *and* second-degree murder in the murder of Morris Blankenbaker. In Gabby Moore's killing, they could choose between first-degree and second-degree murder, *and* manslaughter.

Unless they came back with the two acquittals that Adam Moore had asked for, Tuffy would, indeed, be doing heavy "time."

The jurors were sequestered in a hotel that Saturday night. They began deliberation again on Sunday. They had an awesome task, and they knew that whatever their verdicts, no one would win. They deliberated all day Sunday and, shortly before six in the evening, they signaled that they had finally reached a verdict.

It was obvious that several of the jurors had been crying. Not a good sign for the defense. And it was not. Jury Foreman Earl Willey read the verdicts. The jurors had found Tuffy Pleasant guilty of first-degree murder in the death of Morris Blankenbaker and guilty of manslaughter in Gabby Moore's shooting.

Tuffy was impassive when the verdicts were read, but his mother and his fiancée burst into tears as did many of the jurors. He would not be sentenced on this night, but he faced a maximum sentence of life imprisonment on the murder charge and twenty years for manslaughter. He was returned immediately to his jail cell on the tenth floor of the courthouse.

Jurors, waiting for the elevator, hugged Coydell Pleasant. "This was the hardest day of my life," one juror said, and another sobbed, "I'm sorry . . . I'm so sorry," as she put her arms around Tuffy's mother.

ANN RULE

"Just as long as you were honest," Coydell Pleasant said, "Just as long as you were honest, that's all I can ask."

One juror, an airline flight attendant, leaned against the marble wall and cried uncontrollably. Another, who also had tears streaming down her face, told a reporter, "It was the law. We had to do it. It was the law. It was the god-damned law."

Other jurors led the woman away, and a bus took them all back to the hotel where they had stayed the night before. They had come to trial knowing nothing about Tuffy Pleasant or Morris Blankenbaker or Gabby Moore. Now, they would never forget them.

Sentencing was set for Friday, September 10, 1976, in Judge Carl Loy's Yakima County Superior Courtroom. Under Washington statute, Loy could, technically, still grant Tuffy probation, or he could sentence him to the maximum. For first-degree murder, the maximum would be twenty years with one-third off for good behavior, meaning that Tuffy would have to serve thirteen years and four months before he would be eligible for parole. The maximum for manslaughter (while armed with a deadly weapon) was also twenty years. Jeff Sullivan said that he would ask that the sentences be served consecutively, rather than at the same time.

After hearing arguments, Judge Loy sentenced Angelo "Tuffy" Pleasant to the maximum on each count, but acceded to the defense's request that the sentences run concurrently. In the best of all worlds for Tuffy, he could be released by late 1989.

On September 17, Tuffy was taken from the Yakima County Jail in chains and delivered to a prison bus which would take him to the Washington State Prison facility in Shelton. He flashed his familiar grin to newsmen as he left the jail.

Afterword

Since books on criminal cases usually follow hard on the heels of a conviction, readers seldom find out what happened "later." One advantage of my lack of confidence in my ability to write a "whole book" back in 1976 is that I came to know the rest of the story—or "stories"—over the intervening years. Life *does* go on, even after the most horrendous tragedies, even after so much heartbreak. When Talmadge Glynn "Gabby" Moore fastened his obsessive eye on Jerilee Blankenbaker, his hell-bent manipulations ultimately changed the course of many lives. Nothing was ever the same again, but people went on, following the new paths that loss and grief had cut out for them.

Vern Henderson continued working for the Yakima Police Department. He regretted that Tuffy's father, Andrew, Sr., blamed him for everything, but he was not surprised. He had known it would be this way, but he had had no choice.

One of the cases assigned to Henderson in the late seventies involved a robbery ring. He solved that case and saw the perpetrators convicted. They swore they would get revenge. And they did. Vern's house was firebombed and reduced to rubble. He didn't care about the furniture and other replaceable items, but he lost a lot of photographs and sentimental possessions. It was too much. Just as his house had burned, Vern had "burnout."

In 1978 Vern Henderson resigned from the police department and accepted a job working security on the Alaska Pipeline. He spent eighteen months in the vastness of Alaska. It proved to be a healing time for him. He dealt, finally, with losing Morris and with having his world blown up both literally and figuratively.

In 1980 Vern came back to Yakima where he would spend the next decade as an investigator for the Public Defender's Office. Since the early 1990s, Vern Henderson has worked for the Attorney General's Office in both Washington State and, currently, in a southwestern state. At present, he is assigned to fraud cases, white-collar crime, and internal investigations.

The little kid from Shreveport, Louisiana, has carved out a remarkable career and is a credit to law enforcement. He is in his early fifties—as Morris would be, had he lived.

Sergeant Bob Brimmer is retired from the Yakima Police Department and, at last, has time to go fishing whenever he wants.

Yakima County Prosecuting Attorney Jeff Sullivan has held that office for six terms. He is a past president of the Washington Association of Prosecuting Attorneys as well as being one of the most reelected prosecutors in the state of Washington. Yakima County has burgeoned and Sullivan now supervises thirty attorneys and seventy civilian employees. Somehow he found time along the way to help his wife raise four children, to coach AAU basketball teams—both boys and girls—Grid Kids Football, and to be a lector in his church. His thick blond hair is now thick white hair and he is a grandfather. His oldest son is an accountant; his youngest an army lieutenant. One daughter is a successful television producer and the other a civil attorney.

Although Sullivan has tried many, many cases since the Pleasant trial, it remains "one of the top ten of all the cases I've handled in over twenty years. It stands out as a highlight of my career. There was so much involved," he comments. "A good blend of scientific investigation, good detective work, interesting legal aspects—particularly the polygraph question." Sullivan acknowledges that the local celebrity of the principals and the "love triangle" helped to make the case unforgettable. "This has always been one that you remember. I've tried to explain this case to people and they just stare at me. They can't believe it really happened. But then truth *is* stranger than fiction. In the end, the reason we were able to solve it was because 'People don't keep secrets.' You can count on that."

Sullivan's deputy prosecutor, Mike McGuigan, practices law in Hawaii.

Adam Moore is still one of the best criminal defense attorneys in the state of Washington, and he and Sullivan cross swords regularly. As this is written, they are preparing to meet in court once again. Neither could tell you how many trials this will make. Adam Moore is also a longtime friend of Vern Henderson's. At the time of the Tuffy Pleasant investigation and trial, no one knew it, but Adam and Vern ran together every noon. By tacit agreement, they did not discuss the case they were each immersed in.

Despite gossips' smug predictions that Jerilee's marriage to Jim Littleton would never last, they have been happily married for more than twenty years. They lived in Yakima for many years after they were married. Jerilee became a successful stockbroker while Jim built a huge wholesale produce business. Eventually, the Littletons moved over to "the coast." In Seattle, Jim's enterprises expanded even more.

It wasn't really surprising to me that Jerilee was reluctant about an interview to talk of the tragic events of the midseventies. Finally, we did meet briefly, and I saw that she had changed from the vulnerable, shocked young woman I had watched testify at Tuffy's trial. She was still beautiful, but it was a sophisticated, mature beauty. She stood straighter and she seemed taller, with her shining dark hair drawn into a French roll atop her head. She had clearly become a woman in control of her life, a world away from the teenager who had walked into a bank in Tacoma in 1965 and asked for a job.

Jim Littleton accompanied Jerilee to our meeting. He had grown handsomer as he reached forty and he was obviously very much in love with Jerilee. He was not eager, however,

ANN RULE

to have his wife recall bad days of long ago. Although they had never had children together, they had raised Jerilee and Morris's children, Rick and Amanda. Rick, taller than Morris by six inches and as attractive as a movie star, had gone into business with Jim. Amanda was going to college in Seattle, studying to become a teacher. Both of the children had grown up to be happy, well-adjusted adults.

I did not blame Jerilee for demurring when I asked about her feelings after the murders of Morris and Gabby. Those days were all in the past for her and whatever regrets she might have had, she chose to keep private. She said that she might want to talk to me in depth one day. I never heard from her again, however.

Amanda and Rick remained close to Olive Blankenbaker, their paternal grandmother. Married and living once again in Yakima, Amanda gave birth in February 1996. The baby would have been Morris's first grandchild.

Mike Blankenbaker, Morris's half brother, joined the Yakima Police Department. Although there were no blood ties between Mike and Olive, he gradually became her son too. He understood how much she missed Morris, and tried to be there for Olive.

René Sandon, Tuffy Pleasant's fiancée and the mother of his two daughters, gradually distanced herself from the lover who had never been entirely faithful to her. With new confidence, she went to college, earned her master's degree, and became a school counselor. Tuffy's daughters grew up to be fine young women.

Joey Watkins, the huge but gentle wrestler who had been so much help to Vern Henderson in the investigation, also went to college and is now a teacher.

Kenny Marino, Tuffy's best friend *once,* has vanished from Yakima. No one can say where he is or what he is doing today.

Coydell and Andrew Pleasant, Sr., held their heads up proudly in Yakima, but nothing was ever the same for them. Their son Anthony lives in the house next door. Their other children finished college and prospered. A few years ago, Andrew, Sr., nearing seventy, put a ladder against his store so he could climb up and fix the roof. While he was working, the ladder fell. Always a robust man who was used to working hard and being in good shape, Pleasant didn't call for help. Instead, he attempted to jump from the roof onto the bed of his truck. He fell short and was badly injured. He died in the hospital without ever seeing his middle son again as a free man.

Angelo "Tuffy" Pleasant, who had dreamed of being a teacher and a coach, did not get out of prison in 1989. He served six years more, spending almost twenty years in prison. Given the choice, one wonders if he would not have traded his few moments in the sun as a state champion for a normal life—a free life. Gabby Moore had filled his head first with ambition and hope, and then with paranoid plots. When Gabby fell to earth, so had Tuffy.

Two decades ago, Gabby had told Tuffy, "You don't understand what I'm feeling now, but when you are middle-aged—over the hill—you may." And now, Tuffy Pleasant is forty-two years old, one year younger than Gabby Moore was when he declared that Jerilee was the only trophy that mattered to him. *Does* Tuffy understand? Perhaps. Perhaps not. No one would blame him for being bitter toward his old mentor. Gabby, at least, had a life, a wife—*two* wives—children, a magnificent coaching career. Tuffy, who "hurt" when Gabby "hurt," has had twenty years behind bars. How many times must he have realized that "The Man" cared nothing at all about *his* future or *his* dreams?

Out of prison, but on probation, Tuffy scarcely resembles the perfectly muscled young athlete he once was. Twenty years of prison food and confinement have piled on untold pounds. No one looking at his newspaper photographs in 1976 could recognize Tuffy Pleasant today. Probation authorities have noted Tuffy as "a good candidate for rehabilitation," and have recommended schools and programs.

Olive Blankenbaker lived to see her son's killer sentenced to life in prison. She had not asked for any more time than that. In trying to convince me to write this book, she gave me a number of her precious photographs of Morris. I accepted them, but I told her I didn't think I would be able to sell a book to a publisher as I had no track record. She said she understood.

I didn't hear from Olive over the next few years, and I concluded, sadly, that she had succumbed to lung cancer; I knew she had accepted her "terminal" diagnosis. Ten years later, I was giving a lecture at Yakima Valley Community College. By that time, I had published six books and I spoke often on topics such as serial murder and high-profile offenders. Afterward, I was signing books in the school library when I glanced up to see a woman who looked quite familiar. I stared at her, thinking, "No, it can't be. She looks so much like Olive Blankenbaker."

As the woman came up to the table, she smiled at me and said, "Yes, it's me. I didn't die after all."

Olive had one request beyond a signature; she still wanted me to write the story of her son. I promised that I would try. Over the last ten years, I have visited with her often in her mobile home in Yakima. She still grows flowers and she pampers a family of cats. Olive and Jerilee have long since made their peace with one another. Jerilee, Rick, and Amanda are in close contact, worrying about her and helping out when they can. When Amanda moved back to Yakima, she became her grandmother's strongest support.

Mike Blankenbaker still drops by often to see Olive, and pictures of Mike in his Yakima police uniform sit on Olive's piano next to wedding pictures of Olive and Ned, childhood photos of Morris, and photographs of Olive's grandchildren.

Nevertheless, Olive never forgot her pleas to me to write "Morris's story."

And so, at last, I have kept my promise. After twenty years, it wasn't easy to track down people who once lived in Yakima, Washington, some scattered to the four winds. For this book is not just Morris's story—it is the story of many others as well.

Yakima's houses, buildings, and streets are all still in place—some a little shabbier—some freshly painted. Only last week, I walked down the alley behind the big frame house on North Sixth, walked south from where Tuffy

Pleasant parked his car on Lincoln, past the window where Gerda Lenberg heard the hollow heels of a running man, and into the backyard where Morris Blankenbaker died in the snowstorm. The wire fence where Vern Henderson found the vital bullet casing is, amazingly, still there.

I could almost hear a voice calling, "Morris! Morris . . ."

Olive Blankenbaker is eighty-five years old. I am grateful to her for waiting for me. This is for you, Olive.

The Highway Accident

There is such a thing as a perfect murder. Any detective will admit that some homicides are never recognized for what they are. All of the popular sayings such as "Murder will out" and "There's no such thing as a perfect crime" are the stuff of fictional mysteries. Although the advent of the space age of forensic science is shifting the odds to the side of law enforcement, there will always be murderers who are never caught. And there will always be murders that are written off as something else.

The rule of thumb followed by an experienced homicide detective investigating an unexplained death is that he must look skeptically at what may very well be a crime scene. First, he must suspect murder, and next suicide, and then accidental death. Only when he has exhausted all other eventualities should he decide he is looking at a natural death.

Even so, some cases of murder do slide through savvy investigators' tightly woven nets of suspicion. The case that follows, one of Oregon's most memorable investigations, might never have come to the attention of homicide detectives if sharp-eyed state policemen and apprehensive neighbors had not raised questions. The incredible story that evolved shed harsh light on a marriage that seemed happy despite the fact that its very fabric was riddled with lies and betrayal.

The sounds coming through the bedroom wall in the duplex apartment in suburban Salem, Oregon, were too loud and too disturbing for anyone to sleep through. It was very early in the morning on February 25, 1976, when both Marilee* and Doug Blaine* had the same dream, or rather, the same nightmare. Wrenched from deep sleep in the dark winter night, they sat up in bed. Doug fumbled for a light.

They could hear a woman screaming over and over, "No! No! Don't!" Then there was only silence, which was followed by a softer sound that was almost like a moan. That was suddenly cut short.

Blaine looked at the clock beside their bed and saw it was three A.M. He and his wife discussed what they should do. Although they had never heard the couple in the adjoining duplex fight before, they agreed that they were probably overhearing a domestic squabble. They hated to interfere in something that was none of their business. What should they do—go knock on the door in the next unit and ask, "What seems to be the problem?" Maybe pound on the wall? They couldn't phone because they didn't even know the last name of the people next door, much less their telephone number.

There were no more screams, now. They tried to get back to sleep, but Doug Blaine was troubled and he tossed and turned, watching bare tree limbs bend grotesquely over the streetlight outside as the wind pushed them.

287

After awhile, he thought he heard someone open the front door of the adjacent duplex. Blaine got out of bed and, without turning on any lights, crept to his living room. Feeling somewhat like a busybody, he eased out of his front door silently and stood in the frigid dark where he knew he was hidden by his car. Everything seemed perfectly normal. Both of the neighbors' cars were parked in the driveway: a Volkswagen bug and a Chevy Vega. Far off, a dog barked and the trees creaked in the wind, but there was no other sound.

Back inside, Blaine heard nothing but the ticking of clocks and the furnace blower. He crawled back in bed and he and his wife tried to go back to sleep.

It was quiet for about twenty minutes, but then they heard drawers being opened and shut next door, closet doors squeaking, and bedsprings settling. Beginning to feel like a fool, Blaine looked out his front window once more. This time, the man next door was carrying what looked like laundry or bedding to the Vega. He made several trips back and forth to the car. Then he got in and started it up. Without pausing to let the engine warm up, he backed out, accelerating as he disappeared down Cedar Court.

Wide-awake, the Blaines discussed what they should do. It looked as if their neighbors had had a spat and the husband had left to cool off. They didn't know the couple except to nod and say "Hi" when they happened to meet. The wife was always friendly, but her husband seemed aloof. If they didn't even know the couple's names, they certainly hadn't the faintest idea about the state of their marriage. The only times they had heard any loud noise from the other side of the wall was when the couple had parties, and that had not happened very often.

It was after 4:30 A.M. when the Blaines finally decided they should notify the police; they couldn't forget the screams they had heard. If the girl next door was all right they would feel a little foolish, but feeling foolish was worth peace of mind.

Their call came into the Marion County Sheriff's radio

room at 4:47 A.M. Corporal Tim Taylor and Deputy Ralph Nicholson were dispatched to Cedar Court. They knocked on the door of the neat duplex, but there was no response. Since the Blaines didn't know their neighbors' last name, Taylor gave the radio operator the license plate number on the Volkswagen parked there and asked for a check on the registered owner. The owners came back as Lori Susan* and Walter Louis Buckley.* Taylor asked the operator to look up the Buckleys' phone number and telephone the residence. Soon, he heard the lonely sound of a phone ringing again and again in the empty apartment.

It there was anyone inside, they either would not—or could not—answer the phone.

The Blaines were positive that the woman who lived next door had not left with her husband in the Vega. They pointed out that her car, the Volkswagen, was still parked there. Tim Taylor contacted the man who owned the duplexes. Even though it was still very early in the morning, he said he would be right over with a key to open the door for the deputies.

The door to the Buckleys' duplex swung open and the deputies stepped in. They saw that the place was immaculate. Tentatively, the two sheriff's officers peered into each room, calling out the Buckleys' names. No one answered. There wasn't that much to look at; there was a living-dining area, a kitchen, and two bedrooms. The southeast bedroom looked as if it were being used for storage. A drawer had been left pulled out in one chest. Oddly, there was a pile of walnuts on the floor in front of it.

The master bedroom—the southwest bedroom—was the room that shared a common wall with the Blaines' bedroom. It was as neat as the rest of the house. The queen-sized bed had been stripped of sheets, and clean sheets rested atop the mattress as if someone had begun to change the bed linen.

There were no visible signs of violence. The missing bedding was something of a puzzle, but then Doug Blaine had said it looked as if Buckley had been carrying laundry to the car. Well, that's why twenty-four-hour Laundromats stayed in business. People did their laundry at all times of the day and night.

Even though he hadn't found anything suspicious inside the empty duplex, Tim Taylor radioed in that he felt there should be a recheck of the premises in daylight. "The occupants will probably be back by then," he said.

Taylor left his business card on the dining room table with a note asking the Buckleys to call the sheriff's office on their return. Then they could write the complaint off in a simple FIR (Field Investigation Report).

But there were no calls from the Buckley duplex. Six hours later, Deputy Bernie Papenfus returned to the Cedar Court address and knocked on the door. There still was no response. But now in daylight, Papenfus noticed a faint red spot on the front step. It looked very much like dried blood. Once again, the landlord, who had also felt strangely troubled since he had opened the door for the deputies at five that morning, produced a key.

Their voices hushed, Papenfus and the landlord entered the duplex. It was bright and airy; the sun was shining through the windows. The home had been decorated with charm and good taste, with paintings, plants, and a wine rack with bottles of homemade wine bearing the Buckleys' names. Wicker lamps and end tables complemented the furniture. There was nothing out of place in the living room—not even a magazine or newspaper.

They moved to the master bedroom. Papenfus's trained eye noted another reddish stain that was barely visible on the rust carpet in the bedroom. Still the room looked normal enough.

But cops see things that other people don't. Papenfus's throat tightened a little as he saw that the blue-flowered mattress was not sitting square on the springs. He raised it. The underside was a mass of bloody stains. Blood had soaked into the surface and it was still damp.

Hurrying now, Papenfus looked for more signs that something violent had taken place in this little duplex unit. He didn't have to look far. There were more dried scarlet streaks on the towel cupboard and on the entryway into the kitchen. The stains on the carpet were blurred, as if someone had tried to rub them out.

Deputy Bernie Papenfus had seen enough; something terrible had happened here during the night. Careful not to use the phone in the Buckleys' duplex, he radioed Sheriff Jim Heenan's office and asked that detectives respond to what could now only be considered a "possible homicide."

Lieutenant Kilburn McCoy and Sergeant Will Hingston left their offices in Salem and headed for the address on Cedar Court. Lieutenant James Byrnes, chief of detectives, and Detective Dave Kominek had left Salem very early to attend a narcotics conference in Portland. Enroute, McCoy radioed Byrnes to stand by because the circumstances at the Buckley home were most suspicious.

Byrnes would not be going to Portland, after all.

Kilburn McCoy learned that Lori Buckley, who was twenty-six, was employed as a sixth grade teacher at the Highland Elementary School in Salem. It was possible that she was in her classroom, teaching. That would explain why she was not in the apartment at eleven A.M. on a Wednesday morning. He called the school and learned that Lori Buckley was not there. However, she had arranged to have a substitute because she had a dental appointment scheduled for Wednesday morning. She was not due at school until the afternoon sessions. The school office staff didn't know her dentist's name. They gave the detectives the phone numbers for Lori Buckley's relatives, suggesting that they might know her dentist.

While they waited to hear from Lori Buckley's family, the Marion County detectives moved around her home. They found more and more bloodstains marring the otherwise immaculate apartment.

Whatever had happened here, the scene had to be protected. Hingston and Papenfus strung heavy rope, cordoning off the entire property from the sidewalk back, and posted a sign that read, POLICE LINE: DO NOT ENTER. They half expected Lori and Walt Buckley to come driving up and ask them what in the world they were doing. But no one came by except curious drivers who gawked at the rope and the sign.

Finally armed with the name of Lori Buckley's dentist, McCoy called his office, only to find that Lori had not shown up for her appointment. It was to have been a preliminary session for a long-term teeth-straightening procedure. Lori's dentist was concerned when she didn't keep her appointment or even call. He said she was always thoughtful about calling to cancel if she could not make an appointment.

Lori Buckley's family arrived at her duplex, worried and completely mystified. They talked with detectives outside, since no one but police personnel could go in until the place had been processed. Her family said that Lori and Walt had been happily married for four years. Lori had been teaching since her graduation from Oregon College of Education. Walt was attending Oregon State University in Corvallis. He was about to graduate with a degree in accounting. Lori's folks commented that Walt had recently applied to become an FBI agent. He had told them about the fifteen-page form he had to fill out, laughing about what specific details the Bureau wanted to know about every facet of his background.

Asked if it was possible that Lori and Walt had gotten into a brawl, her family was aghast. They could not imagine such a thing. That just wasn't possible. Lori and Walt just didn't have that kind of a marriage. They had never known them to have *any* kind of physical confrontation.

The Marion County detectives wondered if it was possible that someone had entered the Buckleys' duplex during the night. Doug Blaine had admitted he didn't know the neighbors that well. He had seen a man going out to his neighbors' car and he thought it had been the man who lived next door, but he admitted he could have been mistaken. Could the Buckleys have been abducted by someone who had injured one—or both—of them?

Doug Blaine said he hadn't seen Lori Buckley at all. Just her husband with his arms full of laundry.

In whatever manner Lori had left her duplex, she wasn't

there now. A thorough search of the apartment proved that. She wasn't in the closets or in the crawl spaces. She and her husband were both missing.

The Oregon State Police Crime Lab and ID Bureau in Portland responded by sending criminalists to the scene. Sergeant William Zeller and Troopers Sherie Kindler, Cliff Daimler, and George Matsuda set out at once to help. Chief of Detectives Jim Byrnes and Detective Dave Kominek were already on their way back from Portland.

It was apparent that someone had been gravely injured in this apartment. The bloodstains on the underside of the blue mattress measured between four and ten inches in diameter. That much blood could not have come from a minor cut.

Doug Blaine described again for the detectives what he had heard. "I've never heard a scream like that before. It was kind of a moaning scream like someone was being hurt, not like someone had just knocked the coffeepot off."

The sheriff's office sent out a teletype on the missing couple to all police agencies in the area. They were described as Walter L. "Walt" Buckley, twenty-six years old, 5'9" tall. He weighed 180 pounds and had light brown hair and a mustache. Lori Buckley was 5'5", weighed 130 pounds and had long brown hair. Their missing car was a light green Chevrolet Vega bearing Oregon plates: DRY-255.

Detectives canvassed the neighborhood along Cedar Court looking for someone else who might have seen or heard anything unusual during the early morning hours. But no one had.

A complete crime scene search of the duplex and its carefully tended yard disclosed more unusual or misplaced items. There was a Tab bottle cap on the kitchen counter, and bits of a Tab label and pieces of bottle glass under the sewing machine in the master bedroom. There were fragments of bloodstained glass behind the dresser on the north wall. There was evidence of blood residue in the bathtub and on the drain plug.

The clean, folded flower-patterned sheets that rested on the blue mattress were flecked with blood. A man's large-sized T-shirt and a knit shirt taken from a clothing basket in the bedroom were slightly stained with some red material. All of the bloodstains were tested and proved to be Type A.

An amazing response to the sheriff's teletype came from the Oregon State Police office in Lincoln City, a resort town on the Oregon coast. The state police reported that a Lori Buckley had been *killed* that morning in a traffic accident along the Van Duzer Corridor. The corridor is a winding highway between the Pacific Ocean coast towns and inland cities. The fatal accident in which Lori Buckley had been killed was almost fifty miles from the duplex where she lived.

The detectives shook their heads. How could that be? How could the Blaines have heard screams on the other side of their bedroom wall at three A.M. when Lori was in an accident so far away? If they had been men who believed in ghosts, which *very* few detectives are, they might have come up with some otherworldly scenarios.

It took the Marion County detectives a number of phone calls before they established that Walt Buckley was alive but had been injured in the accident that killed his wife. The Oregon State Police said he had been taken to a hospital in Lincoln City in Lincoln County.

The next report that seemed connected to the increasingly peculiar case was a call from Sergeant Lee Miller of the Polk County Sheriff's Office. Polk County lies between Marion County and Lincoln County and the Buckleys would have had to pass through it to get to Lincoln City. Miller said a hiker had found a pile of bloody bedding—sheets, blankets, a bedspread, and a mattress pad—among the forest undergrowth along Mill Creek Road in Polk County. Jim Byrnes checked the description of the bed linen against that of the list of the bedding found in the Buckleys' duplex. He found many similarities.

Byrnes and Dave Kominek left Salem and headed over to the coast. Crime lab technicians went to Polk County to pick up and bag the blood-soaked bedding found along a narrow dirt logging road.

When Jim Byrnes and Dave Kominek arrived at the scene of the fatal traffic accident, the Buckleys' Vega had already been towed away. They parked at Mile Post 14 on Highway 18 at 4:20 P.M., aware that there was precious little daylight left. But they could see where the Vega had gone off the shoulder of the road. It had crushed vegetation when it went over the bank and then dropped about twelve feet through a thick stand of fir trees. The two Marion County investigators commented to each other that there were no skid marks or torn-up areas on the shoulder of the highway; there were only parallel tracks in the soft dirt and grass.

Oregon State Troopers Michael Luka and Wayne Price had been the first to respond to the report of the accident. A log truck driver had called for help over his CB radio. The trucker told the troopers that he had seen a man lying beside the road shortly after eight that morning. He had managed to call for an ambulance by relaying his emergency request through two other CB-ers.

"Then I got out of my rig and ran to help the guy in the road."

"Did he say anything?" Luka had asked.

The trucker had shaken his head. "He kept repeating, 'Lori. Lori.' Then I looked down through the trees and spotted the green car down in there."

Luka and Price told the Marion County detectives that they found Lori Buckley lying outside the Vega. Her feet had been partially under the right door, and her head was resting on a pillow. Someone had covered her with coats. But Lori Buckley had been dead for a long time when the troopers got to her.

They had photographed her body where it lay in the fir forest, and then released it to a mortuary. Her husband, Walt Buckley, had been rushed to Lincoln City for treatment.

There was no question that the Walt and Lori Buckley who had been in the accident along the Van Duzer Corridor were the same Walt and Lori Buckley who lived on Cedar Court. But Jim Byrnes and Dave Kominek were still trying to figure out just *how* they ended up miles away, almost at the Pacific Ocean.

Walt Buckley had given statements about the accident to Trooper Price—both at the scene and at the hospital.

According to Price, he had explained that he and his wife had left Salem the afternoon before. They had planned to drive to the coast for dinner. They had eaten at the popular Pixie Kitchen in Lincoln City. He said they had decided to drive south a short way to have an after-dinner drink at the lounge in the plush Salishan Lodge. Buckley told Price he and his wife had left for Salem about midnight. They were on their way home when the accident occurred.

Buckley said they had lain in the ditch beside the highway all night waiting for help. He had done what he could to make his wife comfortable and to keep her warm.

The ambulance attendant who had transported Walt Buckley told the detectives that Buckley had been very tense—so tense that he had held his arms tight against his chest. Both of his fists were tightly clenched and full of dirt and grass. He had kept his eyes closed and mumbled incoherently as the EMT checked him for injuries. Although he had appeared to be seriously hurt, his injuries had proved to be only superficial.

It had looked like a normal, if tragic, accident. At her husband's request, Lori Buckley's body was scheduled to be embalmed as soon as possible. However, the mortician who removed her body from the accident scene had been busy that Wednesday afternoon and several hours passed before he began the embalming procedure. He had just made the first cut—an incision into the femoral artery of the thigh—when the phone rang and Dave Kominek told him to stop immediately. *Nothing* was to be done to the body until the accident investigation was complete.

Kominek went to the mortuary and viewed the corpse of Lori Buckley. He noted immediately that she had suffered many, many deep cuts around her face and shoulders. It would take a complete postmortem examination to establish the cause of death, but her injuries seemed far too severe to have been sustained in a car wreck in which the vehicle was damaged as slightly as the Vega had been. There had been only minimal damage to the right front fender and grill. The windshield on the right, where Lori had reportedly been sitting, was shattered in a wide "spiderweb," but it had not been broken clean through. It was safety glass with no sharp edges that might have cut her face and upper body. Odd.

Kominek received the clothing that Lori Buckley had worn when she was found. He looked at the blood-soaked blue-and-white checked blouse and the jeans. There were no cuts or tears in the clothing.

Marion County detectives questioned even what seemed obvious. They interviewed personnel at both the Pixie Kitchen and the Salishan Lodge about the evening of February 24 to see if anyone remembered serving the Buckleys. The Pixie Kitchen, which was usually jammed with lines of people waiting to get in, had been rather quiet on Tuesday night, but none of the waitresses remembered serving the couple. One waitress said she would have remembered Lori particularly because she had been saving to get braces for her daughter and she noticed anyone with a similar dental problem. The Pixie Kitchen cashier said there had been no out-of-town checks or credit cards used by customers on Tuesday night.

The cocktail waitresses and the bartender at Salishan Lodge were positive they had not served drinks to the Buckleys.

It would be days before the widespread investigation could be coordinated and evaluated. Lieutenant Jim Byrnes wanted to talk to Walt Buckley. Maybe Buckley would have some explanation as to why the edges of his story didn't come together cleanly.

Byrnes talked first with the emergency room nurses at the Lincoln City Hospital. They had treated Walt Buckley at nine A.M. when the ambulance brought him in. One nurse said that his arms were stiff and shaking and that he had appeared to be in shock. He had cried out the same phrases over and over: "Lori—where is she? I couldn't stop. Lori yelled. I couldn't stop the bleeding," and "It's my fault."

"If he was acting, he sure was a good actor," the nurse commented. She said that Buckley had stared into space and cried intermittently as he was being treated.

One thing had been a little odd. Walt Buckley's feet had been very cold, as they would expect in someone who had lain out in the cold of a February night for hours. But his *body* was warm—so warm that his temperature was up one degree above normal. The staff had thought it was strange that he hadn't shown signs of hypothermia.

They had sedated Walt Buckley and he had grown a little calmer. He had talked of how he and Lori had gone out to have a nice dinner. He told them he was a college student, majoring in accounting. He had explained that Lori was supposed to be in Salem that morning so she could have braces put on her teeth. But when the nurses asked, "Was Lori your wife?" he had started to cry again.

Jim Byrnes had to wait until almost six before he was allowed to talk with Walt Buckley. A local physician checked Buckley to be sure that he was well enough to talk to Byrnes. As the doctor left Walt's room, he nodded his consent and said, "He wants to talk to you and is very alert."

Jim Byrnes had a fairly good idea what had happened to Lori Buckley. He didn't believe that Lori had been alive when the accident occurred; he felt she had either been dead or very badly injured when the Vega had pulled away from the duplex on Cedar Court at 4:30 in the morning.

Now, as Dave Kominek stood by, Byrnes read Walt Buckley his rights under the Miranda ruling, and the widower signed the MIR card as Byrnes questioned him casually about subjects unconnected to the accident. He wanted to be sure that Buckley was alert enough to be questioned about his wife's death. Byrnes was surprised to find him as stable as the doctor had indicated.

Asked what he remembered about the night before, Walt Buckley first repeated a version of the evening's events that, in essence, corresponded with what he had told troopers earlier. He said Lori had been very tired when she came home from school the day before. He had suggested that they go out to dinner so that she wouldn't have to cook. Lori had agreed happily to that, so they had driven over to the coast, leaving about six. He estimated that they had eaten dinner about eight at the Pixie Kitchen in Lincoln City.

"What did you order?" Byrnes asked casually.

"I had the salad bar plate, and Lori had the combination plate."

Then, Buckley said, they had gone to Salishan Lodge where they had after-dinner drinks and walked on the beach. Oregon beaches are wonderfully smooth and wide when the tide is out, and tourists walk on them all the time. But Byrnes wondered how many people might have wanted to be out there after ten at night with a cold February wind blowing.

He said nothing about his thoughts.

It had been very late, Buckley said, when they started home. Much too late, really. He hadn't realized how exhausted he was. He sighed heavily as he said that he had fallen asleep at the wheel.

"The last thing I remembered was Lori yelling 'Walt!' and then the car ran off the road."

Walt Buckley had tears in his eyes as he recalled how he had tried to help his wife. He had covered Lori up the best he could and tried to talk to her, but she hadn't responded at all. Finally, he had crawled up the bank to get to the road. He had hoped a car would come by and he could signal for help. But they had lain there for hours before the log truck stopped.

Jim Byrnes let silence fill the hospital room. Neither he nor Kominek said anything as Buckley stared down at his own hands. And then Byrnes told Walt Buckley that the sheriff's office had sent deputies to his home early that morning—and what they had found there. He asked Buckley if he and his wife had been lying next to the wreckage of their car after midnight, who was it who had been screaming and moaning in their duplex at three A.M.? Whose blood had stained their mattress and left telltale spatters around their house?

Jim Byrnes, whose flinty blue eyes had intimidated scores of suspects, watched Buckley's reaction. Despite the sedation, Buckley was nervous. Sweat dotted his forehead and he sighed deeply. Even so, while Walt Buckley began to modify his version of his wife's death in the accident—attempting to make his recall fit the facts he now realized the detectives knew—he refused to give a complete statement.

Instead, he talked *around* what had happened, coming close to something terrible and then veering off into extraneous detail. He admitted a great deal without really admitting anything. He said that he hadn't meant to hurt Lori. He talked about putting her in the back of the car, but then he mentioned that he thought he had heard her moan once as he drove through Salem.

The *back* of the car? *Salem?* Buckley had finally changed his story from that of the highway accident fifty miles from Salem, and Byrnes realized that he was talking about what had happened on Cedar Court.

"I drove to a doctor's office by the freeway but the lights were out," Buckley said weakly.

As Jim Byrnes and Dave Kominek stared at him, Walt Buckley repeated over and over again, "I was going home."

What did he mean by that? Had Buckley actually driven to the Oregon coast with his dead or dying wife and then changed his mind and headed toward his home? That was possible.

Walt Buckley was scared, worried about what would happen to him if he told the whole truth.

Byrnes asked him if he knew District Attorney Gary Gortmaker. (Gortmaker had arrived at the hospital a short while before. Gortmaker went to the scenes of homicides and worked side by side with detectives.)

"I don't know him but I've heard of him," Buckley said.

"Do you want to talk to him?"

Buckley nodded, and Byrnes and Kŏminek left the room.

Gortmaker pulled a chair up to Walt Buckley's bedside and answered his questions about the legal ramifications of the situation. After they had talked quietly for several minutes, Gortmaker stepped into the corridor. He told Jim Byrnes and Dave Kominek that Walt was ready now to tell them what had really happened to Lori Buckley.

The story that Walt Buckley told proved once again that no one can really know what goes on behind the closed doors of a neighbor's home. The most serene facade can hide turmoil beyond our most wild imaginings. What appears to be an ideal marriage can be, in reality, a bomb waiting to explode. As Walt Buckley spoke, the detectives quickly perceived that the neat and tastefully decorated duplex on Cedar Court had not been a real home at all, but only a stage where a massive deception was played out.

Walt Buckley admitted there were things in his marriage that even Lori had never known. He said he had managed to live two lives, not for weeks or months—but for years.

Their families, their friends, and Lori's school associates had been under the impression that they had had a perfect marriage. The Marion County detectives had already learned that in their preliminary interviews. Everyone they had talked to when they were searching for the missing Buckleys had described them as a loving couple.

Lori Buckley had always seemed happy at school and was a well-liked and competent teacher. She often talked about Walt's upcoming graduation from college. Although she loved her job, Lori had been eager for Walt to begin *his* career so she could resign from teaching and start having a family. Still, she had never seemed to resent the fact that she was the sole breadwinner in the marriage. She had not only paid the bills with her teacher's salary, but she was putting Walt through college.

And she had never mentioned any quarrels—not to her family, her friends, or other teachers.

As Walt Buckley began to talk about his *real* life, the detectives listening remembered that his and Lori's friends had described them as "a beautiful couple." They had both loved to play tennis, and several friends had recalled that Lori and Walt often did things on the spur of the moment, including drives to the coast. They had taken carefully planned vacations too; during the summer of 1975, they had gone off on a junket to Europe.

Everyone they had interviewed had told the investigators that Lori had been as cheerful as always on her last day at school. She would have been tired—just as Walt said in his first statement—because she had stayed late working on a chili dinner for the school. Detectives knew that she had left for home around 4:20.

No one—*no one*—had described Walt Buckley as a man with a temper or as an abusive husband.

However, as he spoke now, it became rapidly apparent he had kept many secrets from Lori. Yes, she had been paying his tuition and supporting him. She had believed that he was about to get his bachelor's degree in accounting. She had been so proud of him, and thrilled that he might become a special agent with the FBI.

But it had all been an incredibly intricate sham. In reality, Buckley had been dropped from Oregon State University in 1974—an academic suspension. He had then enrolled in Linn-Benton Community College, but anyone who checked his records would see that he hadn't completed any courses. He hadn't even paid his tuition. He had left home each morning with his briefcase as if he were going to school, but he didn't go to college classes. And he hadn't had schoolbooks in his briefcase; he had carried copies of *Playboy* and *Penthouse*. He spent his days as he liked, returning home at the right time had he been going to college in Corvallis which Lori believed.

There was more to Buckley's machinations than Detective Kominek already knew. In looking through papers in the Buckleys' duplex, seeking some clue as to where the couple might have gone, Kominek had discovered that Walt Buckley had been playing games with Lori's bookkeeping and their household accounts. It was apparent that each month, after Lori had written checks for the proper amount of the bills, she had given them to Walt to mail. But he hadn't mailed them; instead he had made out *new* checks for smaller amounts. This had left most of their bills only partially paid, with a growing accumulation of debt. Kominek had found many overdue accounts, and he had also seen where someone had altered the bills that came in so that this wouldn't be apparent.

It looked as if Walt Buckley had been "skimming" money from their joint bank account, but that was puzzling too, because he hadn't removed the money from the bank; he'd only written duplicate checks for lesser amounts. There was no explanation for that double-ledger bookkeeping, although he might have been planning to withdraw a very large sum at some future time.

Walt Buckley *had* filled out a fifteen-page application to the FBI, just as he had told everyone, and it was dated February 19, six days before he killed Lori. But he had never submitted it.

Of course Walt Buckley knew that the FBI wouldn't hire him. He had no college degree in accounting. He hadn't been going to college for two years.

Buckley continued his confession, describing the house of cards that had just grown higher and higher until it was bound to tumble. It may have been on the last night of her life that Lori Buckley finally discovered Walt had dropped out of school. There would be no degree for Walt, she would not be able to stop teaching, and there would be no babies. Worst of all, she discovered that the man she trusted implicitly had been lying to her for *years*.

Buckley said Lori had been angry at him that Tuesday night when she walked into the living room and found him "wasting his time watching television."

That's how it had started, at least in Walt Buckley's memory. The argument had been over television. He had fallen asleep on the couch watching the set, and she had turned it off and called him a "rotten whore." When he had fallen asleep, Lori had been sewing. He wasn't sure what made her so angry.

How long she had known the truth was debatable. It must have been a sickening shock for her to discover that all her plans had evaporated. They were behind in their bills and she wondered where all the money had gone. She had bragged to everyone about how well Walt was doing in college; she had even been planning a party for his graduation.

Walt said that Lori had been furious with him—angry enough to threaten to leave their home at three in the morning and go to her mother's house. When he walked into their bedroom, she had been slipping on her shirt. "When she told me she was going to her mom's house, I picked up the quart bottle and hit her until it broke."

"What kind of bottle?" Byrnes asked.

"I hit her with a Tab or Safeway Diet Coke bottle."

He wasn't sure just what kind of bottle it was. He said he recalled only that it was a clear quart bottle. "I don't remember if the bottle broke the first time I hit her or not."

He did remember that Lori had been sitting on the bed, and the bottle had been on the dresser.

"She was mad and wanted me to stop watching TV and go back to school. I didn't want to disappoint her. I got mad and hit her. I put pillows over her to stop the bleeding. Blood was everywhere."

Buckley said he had carried Lori and the stained bedclothes out to the car and headed out of town. But he was sure he heard her moan when they were driving on Cherry Avenue. He said he stopped in a parking lot, but when he checked her, she was dead. He knew he couldn't go home, so he had headed toward the forest in Polk County. He had planned to leave both Lori's body and the bedding deep among the fir trees.

"I couldn't leave her there," he said regretfully. Instead, he said he had dumped all the bedding and some bags with the broken bottles near Buell, Oregon. But he couldn't bring himself to leave his wife's body there or in the river.

Buckley said he couldn't face what he'd done and that he had taken a bottle and tried to kill himself. But he didn't have the nerve. And so he had driven farther and staged an automobile accident, deliberately driving his car off the road and over the embankment.

The windshield had not broken in the accident, so Buckley said he had broken it himself. Then he had lifted his wife's body and positioned it near the car. After that, he had crawled up to the road. He admitted he had told the troopers that he had fallen asleep at the wheel.

"Had you been drinking—taking drugs?" Jim Byrnes asked.

Buckley shook his head. "I only had one drink all day. I've never taken speed or barbiturates."

He had no excuse for killing his wife, not really. He said he had no medical problems, and he had never suffered from blackouts—he just knew there had been an argument.

Jim Byrnes arrested Buckley at 8:25 P.M.; a guard was

placed outside his hospital room for the night until he could be returned to the Marion County Jail.

Part of the puzzle was solved. Lori Buckley's killer was under arrest, but the investigation wasn't over. The question of why Walt Buckley had struck out at Lori so violently bothered the detectives.

Dave Kominek attended Lori's autopsy. State Medical Examiner Dr. William Brady and Dr. Joseph Much, the Marion County Medical Examiner, performed the postmortem exam. Lori Buckley had suffered a number of deep, gouging wounds to her scalp, forehead, neck, nose, and shoulders and left upper back. There were no wounds below her breasts except for defense wounds on her hands and arms where she had tried valiantly to fend off the cutting edges of the broken bottle.

Lori would have been left terribly scarred from these wounds and she would have lost a great deal of blood, but, according to Dr. Brady, she would not have died. None of the bottle wounds were fatal. Death had come from suffocation or asphyxiation, but not from manual strangulation. The hyoid bone at the very back of her throat was not cracked and there were no finger or ligature marks on her throat. It was more likely that Lori's killer had held a pillow over her face. Her lungs were fully expanded and discolored, which indicated trapped air. Perhaps Walt Buckley had been trying to stop her screams.

Walt Buckley came very, very close to getting away with murder. If no one had heard Lori's two screams, if the neighbors had not been at home, there might not have been such a careful investigation of the automobile accident. Lori Buckley would have been embalmed and buried, and her widower would have been the object of concern and pity. He would have had plenty of time to return to their apartment and destroy the blood-soaked mattress, throw away the bits of broken bottle and wipe up the bloodstains. Since everyone, even their closest friends and relatives, thought their marriage was so loving, questions might never have been raised.

But questions *were* raised, and a thorough investigation followed. The Vega probably would not have been checked had the state police not been forewarned. When the car *was* processed, it held many clues that warred with the theory of an accident. Technicians found that the passenger side of the windshield *had* been broken from the inside, but the force had not come from a round, yielding object like a human head. Instead, some sharp, hard instrument had been used, centering the focal point of force in a small area.

The backseat was folded down and there was Type A blood in the far rear inside floor as well as in the wheel well. A gold rug in the back was stained with blood. Lori had not ridden in the front seat on her last ride; she had been in the back, already dead.

Her blue sneakers and a broken Tab bottle were on the floor in the front, along with a bloody hand towel.

When it was coordinated with what was already known, the cache of bedding found in the forest in Polk County was very important. Alone, without being linked to all the other information detectives and criminalists had unearthed, it would have been almost impossible to identify and might never have been connected to a fatal "accident in another county." As it was, the flowered sheets were found to be identical to bedding back in the Buckley duplex. The bloody bits of a broken bottle were stained with Type A blood, Lori's type. A dishcloth wrapped around a chunk of broken bottle matched Lori's dishcloths. In all, twenty-two items had been taken from the woods and tagged into evidence.

Walt Buckley was returned to Salem by Sheriff Heenan and Undersheriff Prinslow and arraigned on murder charges.

Lori Buckley was buried on Monday, March 1. Lori had been an outdoor education enthusiast and she had frequently organized trips for sixth graders to Camp Cascade. A memorial fund was set up with contributions to the "Camp Cascade Memorial Fund in Honor of Lori Buckley."

When detectives developed a roll of film they had found in the Buckley duplex, they found prints of a happy family gathering, obviously a celebration honoring Lori and Walt. There were a number of pictures of the couple. Walt was handsome with a luxuriant dark mustache; Lori was winsomely pretty. In one shot, Walt held his arm protectively around his smiling wife; in another, the two held a basket of flowers and champagne.

Lori didn't live to see those pictures.

Walt Buckley had been living a lie for a long time. Perhaps he was afraid Lori would leave him. Perhaps he truly loved her, in his own way. Maybe he only thought of losing the cushy life he had led. He may have panicked, or he may have been maniacally angry when she impugned his masculinity and scorned him for letting her carry all the responsibilities while he did nothing.

Walt Buckley pleaded guilty to murder charges during the first week in April 1976, and was sentenced to life imprisonment.

Sheriff Jim Heenan commented on the case: "One thing I know. I don't think any of us who worked on this investigation will ever look at an automobile accident again without having second thoughts."

In prison, Walt Buckley was depressed and morose for weeks. In time, he became a model prisoner. After a little more than a decade, he was released on parole. He remarried, had a family, and found a job with the State of Oregon. Ironically, he now lives the life that Lori dreamed of.

Murder Without a Body

Despite its frequent misuse by mystery novelists, the term "corpus delicti" does not mean the corpse itself; rather, it means the "body of the crime," the physical evidence, the tangible proof that a crime has been committed. A defendant can be convicted of a murder without the discovery of his victim's body, but only if there is enough of this tangible evidence to prove that a murder has been committed. And then the detectives and prosecutor must be able to connect the suspect to the victim at the time the crime occurred. However, there are few prosecutors in America who have the temerity to go into a courtroom with a murder charge when they have no body and no autopsy report to show to the jury.

Oregon's last murder conviction in which the body was never found was in 1904. It would be seventy-two years before a young district attorney in Columbia County prepared to attempt such a feat again despite advice from more cautious legal heads who doubted he—or anyone—could carry it off.

The victim was a lovely young woman who thought she could judge human nature. She trusted the man who followed her and longed for her because she thought she was the one who controlled their relationship. Her own flawed judgment betrayed her.

309

Marty **Sells** is the District Attorney of Columbia County, Oregon. It would seem to be one of the least likely spots in America where the solution to a murder would be a textbook case of forensic science. Columbia County extends northwesterly so far above the rest of Oregon that it almost seems as if it is a piece of Washington that broke off as the Columbia River coursed through it. It isn't a big county, 744 square miles, thirty-one thousand total population. Sells is a former teacher who fulfilled his dream of becoming a lawyer the hard way. He went to law school nights and supported his young family during the day. Sells, whose sense of humor belies his profession, would be the district attorney in Columbia County for more than two decades and serve as president of the Oregon District Attorneys' Association.

In the second week of February 1976, Marty Sells was faced with his greatest challenge.

Rainier, Oregon, is a little town with fewer than two thousand residents. It sits at the edge of the Columbia River amid forested countryside, some twenty miles north of the county seat at St. Helens. A deceptively fragile-looking bridge connects Rainier to Kelso-Longview on the Washington side of the great river. Until the events of February 9, Rainier was seldom in the news; it was like any small town, with its share of gossip and secrets, where everyone knew one another.

311

Hilda Victoria "Vicki" Brown lived in Rainier. She was a tall striking blonde whose Finnish origins were evident in her bright blue eyes and high cheekbones. At 5'9½" and 140 pounds, Vicki was not the helpless type; she was slender but strong and could work beside any man. And she had to work. She was only twenty-five, but Vicki had a nine-year-old daughter to support. Her teenage marriage had failed years before. Vicki worked as a school bus driver, wrestling the huge yellow vehicles around the winding back roads near Rainier.

Vicki was buying a house in Rainier, where her mother, to whom she was emotionally close, also lived.

Vicki Brown didn't lack for male companionship. Her vibrant good looks and sensual nature attracted men easily. She wrote her dating experiences down in a black diary, something that might have given some of her suitors pause had they known of her penchant for keeping records. But she was a good mother, and never left her daughter alone. If she planned to go out, she either left her child with her mother or with the family of Myron Wicks,* who, with his twin brother, Byron,* oversaw the bus barn for the school district. Byron was the boss, and Myron the chief mechanic.

On Monday, February 9, 1976, Vicki left her little girl at Myron's house while she drove the after-school activity bus. It was the last school bus of the day and she transported high school students who stayed late for after-school sports and other extracurricular activities. The run lasted from five to six-thirty, and the Wickses expected Vicki to pick her daughter up shortly after that.

When seven, and then eight o'clock, came and went, they decided that Vicki must have had an unexpected date. They took her daughter over to Vicki's mother's house for the night. Vicki's mother was vaguely worried; it just wasn't like her daughter to go off without making special preparations or leaving word with someone. But then, Vicki knew that the youngster was safe at the Wickses and that they would take her to her grandmother's house if they couldn't care for her.

When Vicki did not show up for work on Tuesday morning, it was a different matter entirely. Vicki Brown *always* arrived at school on time for her bus routes. Her bus was there—parked in its place in the six-stall bus barn just behind the high school. But where was Vicki?

A highly reliable senior at the high school recalled that he had seen Vicki bring the bus in the night before around 6:30. He was sure it was Vicki. He had even waved at her, and she waved back. He had ridden with her often enough so that he recognized her, even from a distance. Asked if he had seen her leave the barn after she parked the bus, he shook his head. "I walked into school after I waved to her, so I didn't see her leave."

Vicki's worried relatives and friends checked her house, hoping against hope they would find her. But she wasn't there. Inside, everything seemed completely normal, as if she had stepped away for just a short time. There was a brown-paper package of almost thawed frozen steak on the counter. Vicki had obviously left it there because she had planned to be home to fix supper the night before. But they found no indication that she had been been home at all after she finished her late bus run. Her mother could locate no one who had seen Vicki *leave* the bus barn after she parked her bus in stall 21.

Vicki's family notified the Rainier police as soon as they left her house. The Columbia County Sheriff's Office and the Oregon State Police were also alerted. It would take twenty-four hours before Vicki, an adult, could officially be considered a missing person. It was still possible that Vicki had found someone whom she really wanted to spend a few days with, someone who had swept her off her feet so completely that her normal predictable patterns were tossed aside. Possible, but not very likely.

It became even less likely later on February 10 when one of the mechanics saw a peculiar stain on the inside wall of the bus barn. The barn was dim inside and badly lighted. When the work crew came to work that morning, they had found it was even dimmer; the main light was out. Someone had unplugged its extension cord at the wall.

Dexter Bryson,* another mechanic, looked at the smears on the wall and scoffed, "Oh, that's just oil."

It was later in the afternoon when someone noticed a pool of some liquid right outside the doors to the mechanics' office on the far end of the barn. The ground was graveled there, and the sticky, mahogany-colored substance looked suspiciously like blood. But then, everyone was spooked by Vicki's disappearance and they soon realized that it might only be transmission fluid.

Determined to find out, the mechanics did a comparison test. They poured transmission fluid over the gravel. It spread out immediately and practically disappeared into the gravel. It didn't seem to have the same properties as the thick clotting stuff they had found and it was a different color.

They found Vicki's green Mazda parked in front of the high school wood shop just next to the barn. The hood wasn't warm; it had been parked there a long, long time, probably since the night before.

As the search for Vicki continued, police noted all the cars around the bus barn. Dexter Bryson's vehicle, a gray-green '51 Chevy pickup, sat parked just outside the double doors on the other side of the mechanics' office.

When Rainier police were notified of the pool of red fluid and the smears inside the bus barn, they asked for help from the Oregon State Police. (In Oregon, the state police work felony investigations as well as traffic accidents.) Captain V. L. Kezar assigned Lieutenant George Winterfeld and Criminal Investigator Dean Renfrow to assist in the search for Vicki.

Columbia County Sheriff Tom Tennant put his chief investigator, Captain Bruce Oester, at the disposal of the investigative crew. D.A. Marty Sells felt that Oester could aid most in deploying the search of the area, while Winterfeld and Renfrow would handle the scene at the bus barn and interview any witnesses who might turn up.

Criminalists from the Oregon State Police Crime Lab in Portland would test the fluid found in the bus barn to see if it was, indeed, blood, and, if it was, to determine if it was animal or human.

As night fell, Vicki had been missing more than twenty-four hours; her fellow bus drivers and employees of the bus barn were baffled. They searched the area around the barn, the high school, and the athletic field and found nothing.

Dexter Bryson volunteered to walk up into the fir and alder sapling forest behind the barn. He was back in only minutes, holding what looked like a woman's water-soaked purse at the end of a stick.

"It's Vicki's. I poked the stick in just enough to see her wallet with her name in it," he said. "I found it floating in a little pond back there."

The twenty-three-year-old mechanic hadn't found anything else that belonged to Vicki in the woods. Still it didn't look promising. The fact that her car and her purse were both located so close to the bus barn made investigators feel that Vicki had not left the area of her own accord.

If Vicki Brown had been injured, she had to be found quickly. Daylight ended early and February nights were cold. She would surely die of exposure—if not from wounds she had suffered—if she wasn't found soon. Explorer Search and Rescue Scouts, Coast Guard helicopters, the National Guard, the Civil Air Patrol, search dogs flown down from Seattle and Tacoma, the Argonauts (a diving group), and local groups with picturesque names like "The Stump Humpers" and the "Over-the-Hill-Gang" from Mount Hood joined every lawman in the area who could be spared from other duties.

But there were so many places to look: forests, caves, wells, ravines; even the tumultuous Columbia River was searched, at least to the degree that it *could* be searched. The Oregon State Police team concentrated first on the bus barn. With every discovery they made, hope diminished for Vicki Brown.

Using powerful floodlights, the troopers could see that something—or some*one*—had been dragged or carried along the front wall of the barn, leaving great splotches of dried blood on the rough wood. The attack, and surely there had been an attack of awful ferocity, appeared to have begun in stall 21. That was where Vicki Brown had parked her bus. It looked as though she had either been dragged or had run into the end stall, Number 20. The bus parked in that spot was encrusted with dried blood.

There was blood on a fender over the tire, and there were a few strands of long blond hair caught in it. In the corner of that stall, they found a huge puddle of blood at the bottom of a two-by-six beam. Farther up, they noted a spray pattern of blood flecks. One investigator said softly, "It's just as if someone had sprayed it with an aerosol can."

The physical evidence left behind gave investigators the basis to form a tentative scenario. It looked as if Vicki had been assaulted by someone waiting for her as she drove her bus into the barn around 6:30 on Tuesday night. But how could that be? The bus barn was not an isolated building; it was right in the middle of the high school complex. The wood shop teacher held night classes right next door, although, admittedly, the noise of sawing and hammering might well have drowned out screams.

But then again, there had been a play practice for the senior play in the high school. Students and teachers were wandering all over. Before the investigation was finished, every student in the school would be questioned. However, while this was being done, the detectives were finding more and more evidence, and it was grim. They discovered a partial dental bridge caught under the door of stall 21.

No woman would run away with a lover without her teeth. If the bridge belonged to Vicki Brown, as they feared it did, her dentist would be able to give them a definitive answer.

District Attorney Marty Sells coordinated the entire case with his chief investigator, Phil Jackson, who had retired after many years in the Homicide Unit of the Portland Police Department. Neither man had ever had a case like this one.

State police detectives Dean Renfrow and George Winterfeld interviewed students and teachers at Rainier High School. They talked to the senior boy who had waved at Vicki Brown at 6:30 on the night of the ninth. They found a girl student who had been waiting for play practice to start. It had been a little before seven when she stepped out on a rear balcony to sneak a cigarette. From that vantage point, she had had a clear view of the bus barn behind the school. She had seen nothing unusual, but she had *heard* something—sounds of scuffling or fighting coming from the barn. It hadn't lasted long, and she had not been alarmed enough to report it to anyone at the time.

One of the female teachers had pulled her car into the circular driveway between the barn and the school five minutes later. She parked next to gas pumps there and headed into play practice. She remembered seeing the girl smoking on the balcony. "I called out, 'Snuff that cigarette!'"

And then the teacher had heard a dissonant sound. She recalled that it had been a sharp report like a gunshot. She had stood listening for perhaps fifteen seconds, but there was nothing more. She had finally decided it must have been a car backfiring. She was sure of the time: 6:55 P.M. She had glanced at her watch.

Things were beginning to fall together. A male student said he had driven into the driveway a little after seven. He parked his van behind a pickup near the bus barn. "I knew I wouldn't be blocking it because I recognized it as the school's pickup, and they wouldn't need to get out until morning."

It had been a green-gray 1951 Chevrolet, and it *had* been the school's property until a few weeks before. One of the mechanics, Dexter Bryson, had bought it from the school, but the student didn't know that.

The boy had then walked into the school; he said he had heard nothing and seen nothing unusual. Minutes later, one of his friends had walked out of the high school. As he neared the bus barn, he saw his friend's van, lights out, coasting down the driveway. He looked inside, expecting to see his friend driving. Instead, he saw a stranger—a man wearing a black stocking cap and a dark jacket. He had a droopy Fu Manchu mustache and long sideburns. The boy ran inside the school to tell his friend that someone was trying to steal his van. When they came out the van was there, but the pickup was gone.

The boy who owned the van told detectives he was still angry. He had his van back, but someone had broken his wing window to get in. There had been blood on the window, on the steering wheel, and the gear shift. He had assumed the car thief had cut his hand on the window. He had used a paper towel to wipe the blood off. Fortunately, he was able to show the state police investigators where he'd thrown the towel, and lab tests proved it was human blood.

The description of the man seen coasting the van matched Dexter Bryson exactly. And Bryson had been one of the prime searchers for Vicki. Every time they looked around he had been there helping out. It was he, of course, who had found her purse, after he walked almost unerringly into the woods to the pond where it was floating.

When they went to talk with him, the detectives noticed that Bryson seemed upset. There could be at least two reasons for that. He might simply be truly concerned about Vicki's disappearance. And then again, he might have a more malevolent reason for being so jumpy. Experience has taught detectives that some killers—and arsonists—get a thrill out of putting themselves in the center of an investigation, of playing games with the very men and women who are trying to solve the crime.

Dexter Bryson became decidedly nervous, however, when the investigators asked him to sign a consent to search his truck. He told them he didn't see what good that would do, and they explained casually that since his truck had been parked near the bus barn when Vicki vanished, the killer might have touched it or thrown some bit of evidence in the truck bed. Bryson finally gave his permission for them to search his truck, albeit somewhat reluctantly.

There were some plywood sheets, wood chips, a tire, and a steel cable in the bed of Bryson's truck. Some dark stains were visible along the bottom edges of the plywood, and they noted that some of the wood chips were discolored too. There was another dark splotch in the center of the bench seat in the cab. Oregon State Police Criminalists Bonnie Garthus and Ray Grimsbo processed the truck. The stains were human blood. They found a human hair caught in the tailgate and another on the rear bumper.

It suddenly became important to know more about Dexter Bryson's movements on February 9 and detectives asked him to give them a statement. If he had been seen by other witnesses working in the mechanic's office at the time Vicki disappeared, someone else could have used his truck to stash her body temporarily.

According to his statement, however, Bryson had left work before five on the day Vicki vanished. He said he had gone to see his mother at Alston's Corners five miles away. She had offered to split a load of Presto Logs with him. He said he had picked up his half and his brother had helped him load them into the pickup. Just then, it had begun to rain. He said he had rushed to get home before the sawdust logs disintegrated. He lived, he said, in a mobile home parked on a Christmas tree farm.

Dexter Bryson had a remarkably precise memory of his movements on the night Vicki Brown disappeared. About six, he continued, he had stopped at a little grocery store to get gas and a six-pack of beer. Then he had driven his pickup to a shed next to his trailer, stacked the logs, and washed out the truck bed to get rid of any wood chips.

Bryson said that he was married and living with his wife, but they worked different shifts. She worked the swing shift at a grocery store across the bridge in Longview, Washington, so he had reheated some chili for his supper.

"What did you do after that?" a detective asked.

"I watched television and shaved. Then I saw that my clock had stopped, and I called my mother to ask the time. It was seven thirty exactly." Bryson had also asked what his share of the cost of the Presto Logs was. At *"exactly* eight fifteen," he had called his mother again. He said he was concerned because a white Chevrolet truck had pulled in in back of his trailer and someone had jiggled his doorknob. He said he had been alarmed because he had been "hassled" before. He lived in a very isolated area and there was no one nearby to help in case of trouble.

He asked that his brother come over to back him up. His brother had come over, but the truck was gone by the time he got there. Then the two had driven into Rainier to call on Bryson's best friend, Rex Simcox.* It was about nine then, Bryson said, and his friend wasn't home.

Then, as it happened, they had driven by the bus barn. Bryson said he had been concerned because he noticed that the double doors into the mechanics' office were not securely closed. He had gone in and looked around for any sign of vandalism. He said he had called his boss, Myron Wicks, to tell him about the open doors. Wicks had told him not to worry—just to lock everything up. Bryson had checked for signs that anyone had been inside and found nothing amiss, so he said he had locked the doors securely and left.

"I told my brother then," Bryson said, "that I thought I'd seen Vicki's green Mazda still parked there."

Bryson said he had thought something was funny. He and his brother had driven back to Simcox's house and found him home this time. He asked Rex if *he* had seen the open door to the shop, and Rex said he hadn't. Nor had he noticed that Vicki's car was still there.

Dexter Bryson was either a most conscientious employee or he was a little paranoid. He said he had brought a gun—a .44 Magnum—to work with him the day after Vicki vanished. He was nervous because Vicki had disappeared, the double doors had been open, and because someone in a white truck had tried to get into his mobile home.

"Why do you think you need protection?" he was asked, and he shrugged. It wasn't because he had any information about Vicki's disappearance, he insisted, it was just that so many unexplainable things had happened on Tuesday night.

Bryson was released from questioning after he gave his consent to have his mobile home on Fern Hill Road searched. The Oregon state police investigators and criminalists headed for the mobile home on the Christmas tree farm. Bonnie Garthus noticed that Bryson had what appeared to be fresh blood on his thumb, but when she asked him about it, he said it was from his own bloody nose. She took scrapings from his fingernails. They were dirty but that would be expected on a bus mechanic's hands.

If the state investigators had hoped to find Vicki Brown in Bryson's trailer, they were disappointed. However, they noted things that only increased their suspicions. In the bedroom Dexter Bryson and his wife shared, they found dress boots with splatters of blood on them. In the spare bedroom, they found a black vinyl motorcycle jacket. (It had been recently washed, yet lab tests would show that it had been soaked inside and out with human blood.)

While the search went on, the state police saw that Bryson was attempting to push something out of sight in his bedroom. When they checked, they found a pair of black leather gloves soaked inside with blood and with a hair similar to the one they had found on his truck. Bryson looked at the gloves and said he had never seen them before. He said that he always marked his gloves inside and these had no marks.

Bonnie Garthus had found a holster in the bedroom and asked where the gun was that fit it. Bryson walked over to a plastic box that sat on the kitchen counter near the sink and pulled out a .22 Ruger. Investigator Winterfeld stepped forward quickly and took it from him. There appeared to be blood on the exterior muzzle. The Ruger would join a growing cache of possible evidence slated for crime lab tests.

Dexter Bryson had become a prime suspect—but in what crime? *Kidnapping? Assault with intent to do bodily harm? Murder?* There was no victim. Someone's blood had stained Bryson's clothes and his truck—but whose? The case was not as simple legally as common sense made it appear.

All the authorities could do was place Bryson under constant surveillance while they continued their investigation on many different levels. The search team still worked against time to find Vicki Brown. No one said what they all were thinking. They were looking for a body now.

Regular duty hours meant nothing. Officers from every department in Columbia County donated unpaid overtime. They searched 127 square miles of forests, fields, water, and land in Columbia County and used 7,023 manhours.

Detectives weighed the variables they had to work with.

Only three people had had keys to the bus barn. One was Dexter Bryson, and the other two were the twin brothers: Byron and Myron Wicks. Myron Wicks was a middle-aged man with a family and it had been Myron who took Vicki Brown's daughter to her grandmother the night Vicki vanished. As a matter of course, both twin brothers were asked about their whereabouts on the night in question. Each of them had a sound alibi; many people had seen them elsewhere at the critical time.

Myron Wicks, however, admitted ruefully that he was one of the men in Vicki's black book. He said they had had a brief affair. His wife knew about it and had already forgiven him. With astounding frankness, he said he had only had sex with Vicki once. He had tried twice more, he said.

"What do you mean you tried?"

"I couldn't get it up," he confessed with a shrug.

The investigators looked at each other. The man had to be telling the truth; no man is going to lie and say he is impotent. It would have been more realistic if he had lied in the other direction. This man wasn't boasting—he was being honest.

Yes, Myron Wicks said he would testify to the "affair" in court if it came to that, although he hoped it wouldn't.

Vicki Brown's close confidantes said that she had one man whom she really wanted, but he was far away from Rainier. He was in Alaska. The rest of Vicki's suitors had merely filled her time while she waited for him. Reportedly, none of the men she dated expected anything more. Detectives didn't uncover even one rumor that any of Vicki's casual dates had been jealous.

There *had,* however, been a disturbing incident the previous November. One evening while Vicki was out, someone had broken into her house. The intruder, who was never caught, had entered through a broken window. Once inside, he (they *assumed* it was a "he") had pawed through Vicki's negligees, bras, and panties. He had also snooped through her personal diary and papers. Nothing was missing except two bras and a pair of panties. A bottle of beer had been taken from her refrigerator, emptied, and thrown into the toilet bowl.

Odd. Frightening? An underwear thief is usually a man with some sexual aberration, a step beyond the window peeper. Laymen consider voyeurs, exposers, and those who collect undergarments—fetishists—among the most harmless of sexual offenders. Experts in sexual deviation know these offenders often escalate their fantasies to a point where they include rape—and even murder.

To prove probable cause to bring charges against Dexter Bryson, District Attorney Marty Sells had to first establish that the person injured in the bus barn had been Vicki Brown. It seemed obvious, but it had to be proven absolutely. Although the Oregon State Police crime lab had found enough blood to type for a dozen victims, there was a problem. When the investigators checked, they could not find Vicki Brown's blood type on file anywhere. The doctor who had delivered her daughter had noted only that her blood was RH negative but had neglected to jot down the type. For some reason, none of the medical procedures she had undergone had required blood-typing.

Dexter Bryson had Type O blood, RH positive. The blood in the bus barn, his pickup, his jacket, his gloves, and on a shovel found in a search of Bryson's property, was all Type O.

District Attorney Sells feared that the blood found at the crime scene and on Bryson's clothing would be useless if extensive tests were not done at once and so he asked that the crime lab proceed with the tests.

The O blood was broken down to its enzyme components. It had DCc and E factors. The small "c" factor indicated that the person who had lost that blood was RH negative—just as Vicki Brown had been.

Dexter Bryson's blood broke down to DC, with no small "c" or big "E" factors. None of the blood found could have come from *his* body.

The next step in proving who had been attacked in the bus barn was to retrieve some hair from Vicki's brush and rollers and compare it microscopically with the hairs found matted in blood on the bus fender, the tailgate of Bryson's truck, and inside the bloody gloves in his trailer. The crime lab technicians found thirty points of microscopic similarity in class and characteristics with the comparison hairs. Although hair cannot be considered as individual as a fingerprint, or DNA matches (not yet in use at the time), thirty points of similarity made it very likely that the hair found stuck in dried blood was Vicki Brown's.

Vicki's dentist examined the bridge found in her bus stall. "It's Vicki's," he said firmly. "It's what we call a cantilevered bridge. Until she came in, I hadn't seen one in ten years. They aren't done anymore because they put too much strain on adjacent teeth. That's why she came in. I had to modify it with a drill and affix tabs to make it fit better. There were all kinds of x rays. I still have them."

The dentist's drill fit perfectly into the holes in the bridge.

There were no fingerprints to check. They had found only smudged marks along the inside of the bus barn. Criminalist Bonnie Garthus said they had been left by someone wearing blood-soaked gloves.

The investigators looked into Dexter Bryson's background. He had no criminal record at all. He had graduated from high school and then served in the Marines. He was 5'10" tall and weighed 170 pounds. Vicki at almost the same height, even thirty pounds lighter, would probably have given him a good fight if he had tried to grab her in the bus barn.

Although Bryson was married, he had not confined his attentions to his wife. The investigators learned that he had had a couple of girlfriends. One was rumored to have married and moved away. The other was still in town.

Witnesses described Dexter Bryson's demeanor at his job the day after Vicki vanished as out of character. He had shown up very early, long before he was due to check in. When someone asked him why he was there so early, he had answered, "Oh, one of the drivers might not come in. I might have to fill in for them. . . ."

His thumb had been black-and-blue. He had explained

that away by saying a "giant Presto log" had fallen on it. He was in so much pain from it that he couldn't pull the hand brake on a bus or change a tire.

Packing his .44 Magnum for protection, Bryson had later tried to convince fellow workers that Vicki had been kidnapped, saying with conviction, "She was snatched."

One of the other women bus drivers, who was initially suspicious that Vicki had simply taken off on a fling, had said to Bryson, "Wouldn't it be nice to live like that—a free life?"

Bryson had snapped, "No!" curtly to her comment, startling the woman with his vehemence.

Like all small towns, Rainier, Oregon, was rife with rumors and Dexter Bryson's name was at the top of the murder suspect list for some residents. Others were convinced a homicidal maniac was loose. Special guards were posted at the bus barn and on the school buses to allay the fears of worried parents.

Someone who believed that the bus mechanic was responsible for Vicki Brown's disappearance painted "Bryson's a Killer" on the street in front of the school. Bryson himself painted it out. Then he spray painted a whole wall of the bus barn where there had been bloodstains.

His efforts did not impede the investigation. The vital sections of the wall had already been cut out and sent to one of the leading criminalists in America—one of the foremost authorities on the patterns that blood can make *after* it leaves the body. He was Herbert L. McDonnell, adjunct professor in criminalistics at Elmira College and Corning Community College in New York State. McDonnell is the director of the Lab of Forensic Sciences and has an MS degree in chemistry. Over the years, among the hundreds of cases he worked on were the Dr. Sam Sheppard case and the assassinations of Bobby Kennedy and Martin Luther King. (One day, he would testify in the O.J. Simpson trial.)

Both the barn beam with the blood spray pattern on it and the Ruger found in Bryson's kitchen had been sent to McDonnell and he was analyzing them as the investigation continued three thousand miles away.

Dexter Bryson had no idea of how closely he was being watched. If he had begun to feel that he was home free, he had not reckoned with the combined forces of the Oregon State Police, the Columbia County Sheriff's office, and District Attorney Marty Sells. The organized search for Vicki was suspended after a month, but the hidden investigation continued unabated.

One of the most interesting pieces of information detectives discovered was that Dexter Bryson had been obsessed with Vicki Brown. There had been nothing he wouldn't do to gain her approval. He had fixed her stove and made repairs on her house—all for free. On the very day she disappeared, he had fixed her car. For all of his efforts, he had received nothing more than a smile and a thank you.

Marty Sells figured that Bryson must have been disappointed and frustrated, perhaps even angry that Vicki had no interest in sleeping with him. Sells had confirmation of his suppositions when the probe led to one of Bryson's former lovers, a girl who had married and moved away to Mississippi, and was now the nineteen-year-old wife of an airman. She gave a statement to police that it had been Dexter Bryson who had broken into Vicki's house in November. She said he had found her diary and read about the other men who had enjoyed Vicki's favors. Bryson, who had done so much for her, had always been rejected. He had been enraged to find he had been such a patsy.

"He gave me two bras and a pair of panties he took from her house," the girl said. "I still have them. He said he broke in because he wanted her to suffer. He was angry because he'd fixed things for her and she rejected him."

Detectives found it hard to contain their elation. Here was the motivation the investigators had looked for all along. Dexter Bryson's ex-girlfriend agreed to mail Vicki's stolen lingerie to Oregon.

When Vicki's small daughter viewed the bikini panties mailed from the East Coast, she cried, "Oh, you've found my mom."

She identified the panties by the strawberry pattern on them. "They're my mom's," she said, nodding vigorously.

"Hers are pink and her friend has the same kind, only the strawberries are orange on hers."

It all fit. Dexter Bryson had probably been seething over his latest rejection. Now, the investigators knew that he had fixed Vicki's car on the afternoon of the ninth. He had probably decided to take what he considered his right. If Vicki had not submitted willingly, and they doubted that she would have, then Bryson must have attempted to force her.

It was easy to imagine him as he waited in the darkened bus barn. He would have known Vicki was due in from her run at 6:30. All the other drivers would have come and gone by that time. When Vicki alighted from her bus, unaware, Bryson would have had the upper hand. Or maybe he had expected it would be easier to subdue her than it was. She might well have put up more of a fight than he had foreseen. Struggling and kicking, the pair must have scuffled through the empty barn. That would account for the sounds the girl smoking on the balcony had heard.

And the one gunshot—the sound heard by the teacher a few minutes later—would have ended the fight. And then Vicki Brown, dead, would have had to be disposed of as rapidly as possible.

The bloody smudges on the wall could be explained. Vicki's killer would have had to drag her inert body, or lift her in a fireman's carry over his shoulder. They believed that someone had moved her body along the length of the barn, swabbing the walls with streaks of blood as he went. In his panic to avoid detection, it wasn't likely that he would have noticed that Vicki's dental bridge had fallen out.

If Dexter Bryson had planned to put Vicki in his pickup truck, he must have been appalled when he had found it blocked in by the student's van. He had had to break the wing window and release the brake. He must have cut himself—that would account for all the blood in the van, and maybe his bruised thumb. Then Bryson would have had to get into the van and steer it while it coasted far enough so that he could move his truck. Had he realized that someone saw him in the van? Probably not. In his panic to hide the body of his victim, he had undoubtedly been totally focused on getting away from the high school.

Reconstructing the scenario of the crime, the investigating team could almost hear Bryson's ragged breath and smell the fear in his sweat. He would have been terrified that he would be discovered on the high school campus with Vicki Brown's body in the bed of his pickup truck. He had to get her away, and he had to cover his own trail.

Police were convinced that Bryson *had* picked up the Presto Logs from his mother—just as he had called her at precise times, making sure that he commented on the time so that she could, albeit unaware of the truth, substantiate an alibi he was constructing.

The Oregon State Police investigators, the sheriff's detectives, and the district attorney's staff believed they now knew what had happened to Vicki Brown, but they were no closer to finding her than they had been the first night. Perhaps Bryson had left her body somewhere while he went about his errands and his coverups. He might well have returned later to dispose of it. But, in the meantime, he had been busy. He contacted his brother, his best friend, his boss—all to set up his red herring story about the mysterious white truck behind his mobile home, the open doors at the bus barn. He had even made a casual comment that Vicki's car was still parked near the barn.

It would have been feasible for Bryson to hide Vicki's corpse in the dark woods behind the bus barn. That would allow him to return at his leisure to bury it or hide it somewhere where it would never be found.

The question of whether he had enough to charge Dexter Bryson still sat heavily on D.A. Marty Sells's mind. "Can you charge a man with murder when you have no body?" If he went ahead, Sells knew he would be fighting heavy odds. He had checked the law books and he knew that there had been no successful prosecutions in similar cases in Oregon in seventy-two years. The defense would be sure to suggest that Vicki Brown had had her own reasons to disappear.

Still, Sells was morally certain he had his man, and so

were Renfrow, Winterfeld, Oester, and Phil Jackson. If Sells didn't risk losing in court, he would be betraying every lawman in the county who had worked so long and so hard gathering information.

With all the negatives he was facing, Sells nevertheless had an ace in the hole: He had Herb McDonnell as a prosecution witness. Sells was convinced that McDonnell's testimony would blast any defense case right out of the water.

When Sells called in the investigative crew and handed out the arrest warrant, there were satisfied grins all around. The time had come to jar Bryson's self-confidence. He was shocked when he was arrested on April 6, 1976. Vicki Brown had been missing for eight weeks and three days and no one expected that her remains would ever be found. Even so, her suspected killer was going to go on trial.

Dexter Bryson's trial began on September 8 in Judge Donald L. Kalberer's courtroom in St. Helens, Oregon. As expected, the courtroom was jammed with spectators. Bryson had been given a choice of facing a jury or letting Judge Kalberer decide his fate. He waived the jury. Judge Kalberer would make the final decision.

District Attorney Marty Sells had scores of potential witnesses, but he chose only thirty local ones, the most convincing, to build his case: the students who had been on the school grounds on February 9, the teacher who heard the shot, the state police criminal investigators, and, finally, Vicki Brown's own little daughter, who made a good, strong, credible—if tragic—witness.

Herbert McDonnell, the criminalist from Elmira, New York, was the key witness even though he had never been in Columbia County, Oregon, before, even though McDonnell had never seen Vicki Brown in life, and had certainly never had occasion to see her body. McDonnell's special expertise allowed him to describe what had happened seven months before in the high school bus barn as accurately as if he had been hiding in the shadows and watching. It was eerie to comprehend the true meaning of "Blood will tell."

Professor McDonnell first held a pointer to blown-up photographs of the distinctive spray pattern of blood on the corner of the bus barn. This was the blood that looked as if someone had aimed an aerosol can full of red paint at the wood. McDonnell said that the diffuse specks indicated that they were "high velocity impact blood." This blood could only have resulted from a gunshot wound. He estimated that the gun had probably been held less than three inches and probably closer to one inch from the victim. The bullet had probably penetrated the victim's head.

McDonnell explained that if the blood had been the result of bludgeoning, it would have left an entirely different kind of pattern. A club or hammer would have "cast off" blood in much larger drops with "tails" that showed the direction of force. Cast-off blood is nothing like the pin-points of sprayed blood. There was no question in McDonnell's mind that whoever had been injured in the bus barn had been shot.

McDonnell then addressed himself to the .22 caliber Ruger gun found in Bryson's trailer. There had been blood on the exterior of the gun when it was found. The surface of the weapon had been "tacky" with it. Blood had also been found inside the muzzle and the cylinder wall. This, McDonnell explained, was entirely in keeping with his findings after examining the two-by-six beam. High-velocity blood is drawn back into the cylinder of the gun. The terrific energy released from the gun breaks the blood down and it speckles the surrounding area. Herb McDonnell said that the high-velocity blood hit the beam and the interior of the muzzle at the same time. As the hot gases from firing the gun begin to cool almost instantly, the victim's blood was pulled back into the barrel of the gun. The blood *inside* the gun was what led McDonnell to deduce that the gun had been held less than three inches away from the victim.

Dexter Bryson shifted uncomfortably in his chair at the defense table. He had had no idea that his victim had connected him and his weapon to her murder, even as she died. *She had marked his gun with her blood!*

Through Herb McDonnell's expertise, the method of murder was exposed. By itself, the testimony of the teacher who heard the loud report would not have been enough to prove absolutely that a gun had been fired in the bus barn, had hit a human being, and that that human being had been severely injured—perhaps killed.

The sheer amount of blood at the crime scene had been measured and a careful comparison with its percentage of Vicki Brown's entire blood supply had told the investigators that she could not have survived long.

Herb McDonnell's testimony was electrifying. Anyone listening could almost see the awful struggle in the darkened barn. As Dexter Bryson realized that he could not overcome Vicki with his strength and that rape was out of the question, he also must have realized that she would report him. He had turned to the gun he carried—just in case. Vicki Brown had been trapped in the corner with nowhere left to run when he held the gun against her head and fired. Then she had slid down the wall, either dead or dying. From there, the defendant had carried or dragged her body along that wall.

The inexorable parade of physical evidence continued: Vicki's hair samples and the hair found on Bryson's truck, her blood type, her dental bridge, Bryson's bloodied clothing, Vicki's stolen strawberry panties, Bryson's bloody shovel.

And then Marty Sells pointed out the many disparities in Bryson's story. The clock in Bryson's trailer was not broken; it was an efficiently working pendulum type clock, which incidentally, Bryson could have seen from his phone. No one other than the defendant had seen the "phantom white truck" whose occupants had allegedly tried to break into his trailer. Another woman bus driver had seen Bryson in town at nine P.M., the time he said he had been at Rex Simcox's house. Finally, Rex Simcox himself testified that he had called Bryson back after *he* had checked the bus barn that night. And Bryson had *not* been at his mobile home. No one knew where he had been on the night Vicki Brown vanished.

Marty Sells presented other possible "suspects" before the defense could bring them up. Myron Wicks fulfilled his promise to testify to his brief affair with Vicki and, predictably, the gallery gasped at his frank testimony about his impotency. No defense attorney was going to touch that.

Vicki's former husband was mentioned as a suspect in her disappearance, but Marty Sells quashed that. Vicki's ex could not have murdered her, even if he had had a motive. He had been in a hospital miles away from Rainier on the night of February 9.

Investigator Renfrow testified that he had been discussing Vicki Brown's disappearance with Dexter Bryson and his wife when Bryson suggested that whatever had happened to Vicki "had to have been an accident." How could he possibly have known that, if he himself had not been there when she died?

There was more than enough testimony to titillate the courtroom watchers. In an effort to show that Vicki Brown had vanished of her own volition, the defense tried to show that Vicki was lonesome for her boyfriend in Alaska, that she had disliked her job, and that she had been unpopular with the other female bus drivers. They even brought in an interesting witness, one "Skip Tracy," the alias of a private detective who said he was an expert witness on people who simply chose to run out on their responsibilities for their own reasons.

Tracy cut a rather bizarre figure as he entered the courtroom, dressed immaculately in suit, tie, and high-top tennis shoes. He regaled listeners with tales of adults who simply took off, stepping out of one life and into another where no one knew them. He recalled that he had located one woman whose apartment was found soaked with blood. "She wasn't dead at all," he finished firmly. "We found her in Las Vegas."

When Marty Sells cross-examined Skip Tracy, he asked, "Have you read *this* case? Do you know anything at all about Vicki Brown? Do you know if she is dead or alive?"

"No, sir, I do not," Skip Tracy admitted.

It was a long trial, seventeen days. On September 25, Sells rose to make his final arguments. "Mr. Bryson—" he began. "When he went out there that night, he took away from Vicki Brown the most important thing that any human being can possess, the most important *right* that any human being can possess, and that is the right to be, the right to exist, to live. He took that away from her and he did it intentionally, and he did it unlawfully, and we ask the court to find him guilty."

Judge Kalberer did not deliberate long. When he returned to confront Dexter Bryson, he explained that he had three factors to consider in his decision. "I must decide if Vicki Brown is dead, if she has been murdered, and if you did it. I am satisfied beyond any doubt, Mr. Bryson—beyond all possible doubt—that she is dead, (that) she was murdered, and that *you did it.*"

Dexter Bryson stared back at Judge Kalberer. His expression did not change, his posture was erect, and he did not tremble. It was almost as if he hadn't heard at all.

Bryson was sentenced to life in prison. He appealed his life sentence and lost. Under Oregon law at the time, he was technically eligible to ask for a parole hearing after serving six months in prison. He served more than six months, of course, but he did not serve life. "Life in prison" is a deceptive term. In most states, it means anywhere from ten years to eighteen years—unless the sentence is *mandatory.* Even then, new administrations, new governors, and new laws can mitigate the length of what seemed at the time to be endless years in prison.

Dexter Bryson has been a free man for some years now. Vicki Brown has never been found and quite possibly Bryson is the only one who knows where she is. And he will not say.

Perhaps one day a camper will find a skeleton or a fisherman in the Columbia River will discover some small fragment of bone or clothing. It is no longer likely that that will happen. But time reveals all things in one way or another.

Vicki Brown's murderer was convicted even though her body was never found. And there is a kind of poetic as well as legal justice in that. Vicki was a good mother, good daughter, dependable on her job, and she had every reason to look forward to many years ahead. That ended for her in a darkened bus barn when a rejected would-be lover's frustration and rage exploded.

As Marty Sells pointed out in his final argument, Dexter Bryson had made one clumsy mistake after another when he murdered Vicki. "The only clever thing he did was to hide the body."

And because of the silent testimony of Vicki Brown's own blood, that just wasn't enough.

I'll Love You Forever

I learned about this story of ultimate betrayal long after
it was too late to save the victim. Ruth Logg's daughters and
other relatives could not save her either, but they prevailed
and saw a certain kind of justice done in a landmark court
decision.

This is the kind of nightmare case that haunts every
woman on her own. Each of us can identify with Ruth Logg.
Each of us would like to think that we would never fall for the
blandishments of a man like Ruth's "Tony." And yet, inside,
I think we must admit that any woman who hopes to find
permanent love risks meeting the perfect liar instead of the
perfect lover.

When I researched this case many years ago, I found Ruth
Logg's "perfect lover" so sinister that I actually changed my
usual pen name to a completely different pseudonym so that
he wouldn't be able to find me.

I think you will see why as the story of the man who
promised to love Ruth "forever" unfolds.

When her life was viewed in terms of worldly goods, Ruth Logg had everything. The lovely blond widow had been well provided for by her late husband, Les. She lived alone for several years after Les's death in her sprawling house in Auburn, Washington. The grounds were impeccably maintained and there was even a huge swimming pool. Ruth's home was valued in the early seventies at $85,000. Today, it would be worth well over a million dollars. Les Logg's business holdings had amounted to something over a quarter of a million dollars at the time of his death. Again, that $250,000 would be worth ten times as much in the economy of the nineties. Ruth herself had a good business head. She had moved smoothly into her new place as owner of a business.

Unlike many women who are suddenly widowed, Ruth Logg was able to manage. Her two pretty teenage daughters, Kathleen and Susan, lived with her and she loved them devotedly. But Ruth was only in her early forties, and she sometimes dreamed of finding a man to share her life. She was lonely and the years ahead often seemed to stretch out bleakly.

Ruth knew that her girls would soon be moving away to start their own lives, and that was as it should be. She accepted that. But she couldn't bear the thought of rattling around her huge house alone once Kathleen and Susan were gone. In March of 1971, she put the house on the market. Perhaps she would buy a condominium or take an apartment where she wouldn't have to worry about yard work. Her personal safety was on her mind too. A woman in a house alone wasn't as safe as one who lived close to other people in a security building.

Most single women hold on to a romantic dream that a special man will come along one day and change their lives. Ruth Logg was no exception. She was far too young to give up on love, even though her prospects looked slim. She hated the idea of dating services or Parents Without Partners, or blind dates set up by well-meaning friends. She sometimes wondered why it had to be so difficult to meet someone.

And then Ruth Logg *did* meet someone in such an unexpected way. It was a blustery March afternoon when she first encountered the man who would suddenly launch her world in exciting new directions. A sleek luxury car pulled up in front of her home and a compactly muscled, impeccably dressed man emerged and knocked at her door. He had a great voice. He introduced himself as "Dr. Anthony Fernandez."

No one would have described Dr. Fernandez as handsome, and yet he had an undeniably charismatic quality. He had wide shoulders and thickly muscled arms and wrists, and he looked at Ruth with warm dark eyes under thick brows. Ruth could sense that he was gentle. His manners were wonderful; he was almost apologetic for interrupting her schedule, but he did want to see her home. Ruth assured him that she would be delighted to show him through the house.

Dr. Fernandez explained that he was forty-eight years old and divorced. He said he had just opened a family counseling clinic in the Tacoma area and that he was hoping to buy a house within easy commuting distance to his business.

Ruth Logg was quite taken with Dr. Fernandez, who urged her to call him "Tony." They talked as she led him through her home and he seemed impressed with the floor plan, the way she had decorated the rooms, and with the lawn and gardens. It wasn't long before they stopped talking about the house; they discovered that they shared many interests. Dr. Anthony Fernandez asked Ruth Logg if she would join him for dinner and she accepted, a little surprised at herself for agreeing to a date with someone she really didn't know.

Tony and Ruth had such a good time on their first evening that they both knew they would see more of each other. More dates followed and Ruth suddenly found herself caught up in a whirlwind courtship. After so many years at the edge of other people's lives, she found it incredibly exciting to have this fascinating man pursuing her. And Tony Fernandez *was* pursuing her. At first, Ruth questioned her great good fortune, but then she accepted it. She was, after all, a good-looking woman with a lush figure and a pretty face. She had forgotten that in her years as a widow. Now, Ruth became even prettier with her newfound happiness.

It never occurred to Ruth that Tony might be interested in her because she was wealthy. In fact, she believed that what she had was chicken feed compared to what he owned; Tony had told her that he was a man with substantial assets. He spoke of timber holdings and real estate, and, of course, he had his counseling practice. He didn't *need* her money.

Ruth didn't know that the plush car Tony drove was rented, nor did she know much about his life before they met. None of that mattered. Ruth Logg was totally in love with Anthony Fernandez.

Ruth's family and friends were not as enthusiastic about Tony. They wanted her to be happy, of course, because she had devoted so many years helping other people, but they were worried. They had checked into Tony's background, and they soon heard rumors that "Dr." Fernandez had spent time in prison for fraud. They doubted that Ruth would believe the rumors, so they pleaded with her to check into Fernandez's background before she considered marriage.

Ruth only smiled and reassured them that she knew all about Tony. He had told her that he had had a little bit of trouble in the past. He had been honest with her, she said, and his past didn't matter to her. Ruth's philosophy was that everyone deserves a second chance. Why should she dredge up unhappy memories? Ruth's sister was particularly persistent in trying to coax Ruth off her rosy cloud.

When Tony Fernandez discovered that, he told Ruth's sister that if she didn't like his plans with Ruth, then she could just consider herself excluded from their social circle and future family gatherings. Amazingly, Ruth went along with Tony's decision.

No one is blinder than someone in the first stages of romance, and Ruth refused to listen to one detrimental word about Tony. By September of 1971, Ruth and Tony were engaged. She gave up all thoughts of selling her house; she and Tony would need it to live in. At his suggestion, Ruth and Tony drew up new wills. Although the will Ruth had drawn up three years earlier had left everything she owned—$250,000 plus her home—to her daughters, her new will left it all to Tony. She was confident that if anything should happen to her, Tony would provide for her girls. In turn, Tony left everything he owned to Ruth in his will.

What Anthony Fernandez actually owned was debatable. Despite his grandiose boasting to his fiancée, Tony's assets were negligible. When he met Ruth, he had seventy-five hundred dollars in the bank, a thousand-dollar bond, and some mining claims and real property that would one day sell at a tax sale for less than four thousand dollars. Beyond that, Tony had substantial judgments filed against him. His financial statement would have been written entirely in red ink.

Despite objections and pleadings from the people who truly loved Ruth Logg, she and Dr. Tony Fernandez flew to Puerto Rico on January 5, 1972, where they were married. She had only known him ten months, but it seemed as if they were meant to be together. They toasted their new life with champagne, and Ruth was blissfully happy. Her honeymoon with her new husband was everything she had hoped. She was confident that, in time, her family would come to see Tony for the wonderful man he was.

While she had left Tony everything in her will, she didn't plan on dying for at least four more decades. She had too much to live for now. When Tony casually mentioned that it would be easier for him to help her manage her affairs if he had her Power of Attorney, Ruth didn't hesitate. They went at once to a notary and Ruth gave her husband the power to sell her property or do any other business in her name.

In retrospect, it is easy to see that Ruth Logg Fernandez knew pitifully little about this man who was her husband. Even her worried family had no idea.

It would not have been difficult for Ruth to have found out about Tony's recent and remote past. Reams of newspaper copy had been published about Tony Fernandez's checkered career. In his home territory, he had been at first famous—and later *infamous*.

In the early 1950s, Tony Fernandez had been an important player in the timber industry of Washington and Oregon. When he was in his twenties, he had made a killing in the logging business. He operated mainly out of Longview, a city of twenty thousand in southwestern Washington. The Longview *Daily News* frequently carried reports of Fernandez's new and massive timber buys. Some of his deals involved millions of dollars worth of virgin timber.

Tony Fernandez was listed as a partner in many companies, and he was considered one of the more solid citizens in Longview. He was headline material: "Fernandez Buys Timber at Dam Site in Oregon" (this was on July 19, 1954, when Tony had purchased 40 million board feet at thirty-two dollars per thousand feet); "Chinook Region Logging Planned" (this was on October 4, 1954, when he had bought eight million board feet); "Fernandez Buys Pacific Timber" (on March 9, 1956, when Tony Fernandez estimated his newest contract would eventually cost $300,000).

At the time Tony Fernandez was only thirty-one, but he was on a roll and he didn't stop at timber. On March 22, 1955, the Longview *Daily News* told of a new mining company being incorporated in Cowlitz County, Washington. Tony Fernandez was its president. The purpose of the company would be "to mine, mill, concentrate, convert, smelt, treat and sell gold, silver, copper, lead, zinc, brass, iron and steel." The new company also expected to obtain oil rights. Stock valued at $100,000 had been authorized.

Tony Fernandez maintained a high profile. He drove new Cadillacs. As an honorary deputy sheriff, he was allowed to install a siren in his car. He lived in a big house on the hill above Longview with his wife and four children. He was a Boy Scout leader and a Longview city councilman.

In April of 1957, Fernandez announced that he was branching out into Canada and that he had purchased a *billion* board feet of timber—an early land grant by the British Royal family—near Nelson, British Columbia for $1,500,000. He said he was considering setting up a branch office near the Canadian border.

In reality, Tony's business empire seemed to have been built on shifting sands. Several huge timber companies brought suit against him, saying that he had logged off areas long after his contracts had expired. He was also accused of selling sections of timber by misrepresentation; he had identified the wrong sections of trees to prospective buyers. They thought they were buying acreage thick with timber when in reality Tony had simply shown them property that he didn't own. They had signed purchase agreements without checking legal descriptions.

It wasn't only the big corporations who were after Tony Fernandez. Several elderly landowners claimed they had been cajoled into signing their names to blank contracts, only to find to their regret that they had signed quit-claim deeds to their timberland.

Tony Fernandez couldn't juggle his books forever. By July 1958 the IRS began to look at him with a jaundiced eye. The Internal Revenue Service filed notice of a tax lien of $95,246.31 against him for taxes that he hadn't paid in 1951, 1952, and 1953. The IRS filed what was known as a "jeopardy assessment" against Fernandez's assets. This amounted to a lien against all his property. It followed two Superior Court memorandums saying that the wheeler-dealer logger had to pay two logging firms over half a million dollars as the result of civil suits.

Still, Tony Fernandez drove his Cadillacs, lived in his nice house, and kept up the facade of a highly successful businessman and a pillar in Longview.

Individuals who had done business with Fernandez were nothing if not confused. An Oregon man, Bill Belcher, was foggy about a trip he had made to Nelson, British Columbia, with Fernandez in March of 1958. Tony had offered to "fly over" his timber holdings there so Belcher could have a look. But the clouds had been so thick that Belcher couldn't tell whether he was looking at fir, pine, spruce, hemlock . . . or tumbleweed. When they attempted to reach the woods later by Jeep, they were forced back by deep snowdrifts.

While they pondered their predicament, Belcher stepped behind the Jeep to light a cigarette. The next conscious memory he had was of lying beside a railroad track; his head felt as though a train had run over it. He was found by railroad workers who called for medics. Belcher was hospitalized with severe head injuries for ten days.

Later, he learned that Tony Fernandez had returned to the guest cabin where the two men had been staying. He had told the managers that Belcher had decided to stay up in the woods in a miner's cabin.

The Royal Canadian Mounted Police notified Bill Belcher's family that he had been critically injured. His wife left at once for Canada. After assuring herself that he would survive, she followed Belcher's instructions to retrieve his briefcase in which he had carried important papers and money. She found the briefcase but Belcher could not explain a logging contract that had been tucked inside. There was also a receipt for $40,000 in payment for some land.

Bill Belcher had no memory whatsoever of what happened to him after he stepped out of Tony Fernandez's vehicle to have a cigarette alongside a snowy road. However, he was adamant that he would never have bought timber he had not even seen, and he would not have given someone $40,000 for trees hidden in fog.

While Belcher had lain unconscious, a bank officer in Grants Pass, Oregon, where Belcher had an account, received several phone calls from a man who identified himself as Bill Belcher. The caller directed the banker to transfer $40,000 to a Gresham, Oregon, bank to the account of the "Fernandez-Belcher deal."

Belcher, who had never suffered blackouts, fainting spells, or anything akin to them before his mysterious "attack" behind the Jeep in the snowy Canadian timberland, eventually recovered thirty-six thousand from Tony Fernandez's company in an out-of-court settlement.

In 1959 Tony Fernandez faced charges of another kind. He was arrested in March of that year and charged with three counts of carnal knowledge and indecent liberties after a teenage girl alleged that he had forced sex on her two years earlier. After many delays and a change of venue to Clark County, Washington, Fernandez was acquitted of the charges.

Tony Fernandez continued to remain active in timber commodities. In the latter part of April 1961, another bizarre incident took place when John Casteel, an elderly Cresswell, Oregon, lumberman, flew over the Canadian timberland with Fernandez. It was almost a replay of what had happened with Bill Belcher. Casteel couldn't see well enough to judge the quality or kind of timber far beneath him. All the while, Fernandez kept talking, mentioning that the syndicate he represented had recently purchased 1,800 acres in Wasco County, Oregon, for two million dollars. Casteel craned his neck to try to see the trees that Fernandez wanted to sell him, but the plane was much too high and the weather didn't cooperate.

After the abortive flight, Fernandez and Casteel stayed in a Spokane hotel and Tony said it would take about $100,000 to protect the rights to the Canadian timber. Casteel said he didn't have that kind of money to invest in timber at the moment and wasn't interested. Tony knew, however, that the elderly man had plenty of money; earlier, Casteel had given Tony a three-day option at a price of three million dollars on some timberland Casteel owned.

When the two returned to Longview, Fernandez invited the old man to look at a tract of timber twenty miles east of Longview. After they had looked at one stand of trees, Tony suggested they check out another forest which grew at the end of a logging road.

They viewed the trees and Casteel wasn't very impressed. On the way out of the deep woods, Tony Fernandez had suddenly shouted that he had lost control of the Jeep.

"When I looked up, I saw Fernandez bailing out," said Casteel, who proved to be more resilient than Tony had figured. "He was still hanging on to the steering wheel."

Casteel himself had had no choice but to ride the out-of-control Jeep to the bottom of a sixty-foot grade, "bouncing like a rubber ball" inside the closed cab. To his amazement, he was still alive when the Jeep finally stopped against a tree trunk. He had clambered out of the wrecked Jeep and made his way painfully up the slope.

Fernandez was waiting at the top, towering over him as he climbed hand over hand. Casteel wasn't sure if he was in trouble, but Tony had snorted and said only, "You're a tough old devil—I couldn't kill you with a club."

Casteel hoped Fernandez wasn't about to try.

The two hitched a ride into town on a logging truck and Casteel drove himself two hundred miles to his home, where a doctor found he'd survived the crash with only some torn ligaments.

Later, when John Casteel opened his suitcase to show a friend a map of the Canadian timberland, he found copies of a memorandum of agreement between himself and one of Fernandez's companies. He had never seen it before, yet it was a deed conveying Casteel's timberland to Fernandez in consideration of an option on Tony's Wasco County property, *and* an assignment of the Canadian timber asserting that Casteel had offered $400,000 for it.

John Casteel was a sharp businessman and he immediately set about clouding the title to his three-million-dollar stand of timber so that Fernandez could not take it over. He eventually paid Tony fifteen hundred dollars to release all claims and considered himself lucky to have lost only that much.

It would take a book-length volume to describe the intricacies of Tony Fernandez's timber dealings. One would suspect that he had some successful incidents where would-be buyers "signed" papers without being aware that they had. There may even have been other "accidents" in the woods that were never reported.

Fernandez's financial world blew up finally in April of 1962 when he was indicted by a federal grand jury on charges of engaging in a multimillion-dollar timber swindle. It was the culmination of a four-year investigation into Fernandez's business machinations. The incidents involving Belcher and Casteel were cited in the charges along with many others.

Tony Fernandez was convicted of seven counts of interstate fraud and one of conspiracy in Judge William G. East's Federal District Courtroom in Portland, Oregon, in December 1962. Two months later, he was sentenced to eleven years and eleven months in prison. That April, his remaining property was sold to satisfy judgments against him. Despite appeals, Tony Fernandez remained in the McNeill Island Federal Prison until his parole on January 15, 1970.

Tony was far from idle during his years on the bleak prison island in Puget Sound. In 1968, claiming status as a taxpayer in the state of Washington, he sued Washington's Secretary of State Lud Kramer and U.S. Representative Julia Butler Hansen for a hundred thousand dollars on the grounds that Ms. Hansen was not qualified to serve in Congress because she was a woman. The suit was capricious, not to mention chauvinistic, and it got nowhere. However, it netted Tony Fernandez more headlines and he liked that.

Six months after he was paroled, Fernandez was awarded a degree from Tacoma Community College's extension program. He became the first convict in the State of Washington to earn a college degree through an innovative program that allowed prisoners to take courses while they were in the penitentiary.

And so, in 1970, Anthony Fernandez was free—both from prison and from his twenty-three-year marriage. His wife had divorced him in 1965 while he was in prison. Surprisingly, she said she had no ill feelings toward Tony. He had always been a good provider and never mean or abusive. She did mention his wandering eye, however. She just hadn't wanted to be lied to any longer. It had been a most civilized divorce. *So* civilized, in fact, that when Tony was paroled, he often brought his new girlfriends to visit his ex-wife.

Scattered accounts of Tony Fernandez's postprison activities boggle the mind. He reported to hometown friends that he was a senior at Pacific Lutheran University in Tacoma, majoring in psychology and ecology. This wasn't long after his release from prison. As part of his studies, he joined a student tour to Arizona and New Mexico to study Navajo Indian history, culture, and economy. In an article in the Longview *Daily News,* it was also noted that Tony was enrolled simultaneously in an MA and Ph.D. program in a Florida university. (As it happened, all this "college" required its students to do to get a "diploma" was to write a thesis of unspecified length.)

Tony Fernandez's doctorate had been awarded simply because he had submitted a paper entitled "The Innovated Navajo." And *voilà!* Tony Fernandez became Dr. Anthony Fernandez.

When he was heard from next, *Dr.* Fernandez reported he was attending the North American College of Acupuncture in Vancouver, British Columbia. Tony is quoted as saying he attended classes in Vancouver three times a week and would be spending fifteen weeks in Hong Kong and sixty days in Peking as part of his training.

It wasn't that Fernandez believed that acupuncture, was particularly important in the Western world. "It is," he pontificated, "at best, a fad. But I'm going into this with the point of view that it is most likely a psychological tool. And even if I never use it, the experience and knowledge will be a benefit."

On March 30, 1971—the same month he met Ruth Logg—a small item appeared in the Longview *Daily News.* "Anthony Fernandez, formerly of Longview and a recent Pacific Lutheran University graduate, will open a counseling office complex next month at 8815 S. Tacoma Way. He is also negotiating for property in Kelso on which to construct a family counseling clinic."

Dr. Fernandez promised to provide a twenty-four-hour answering service and said he had contracted to evaluate welfare recipients for the Tacoma office of the Department of Public Assistance.

On June 10, 1971, "Dr." Fernandez's picture appeared in the Wenatchee, Washington, *Daily World* beside an article about his plans to establish a "rehabilitation center" for drug addicts and alcoholics on eighty acres he owned in the rural town of Alstown. He promised that he would build a modern clinic but retain the flavor of the historic old cabins on the eastern Washington property. He assured nearby residents that his patients would not be "turned loose" in the community. He did not mention, of course, that he himself was a parolee from a federal prison.

None of Fernandez's new endeavors ever got off the ground. He didn't need them. He had Ruth Logg and the fortune her late husband had left her.

This was the man with whom Ruth fell madly in love. This was her soft-eyed, warm-voiced hero who was going to make the second half of her life a wonderful time of love and companionship. She had never known anyone with no conscience at all; she was naive about the world of the con man. Les had loved her and protected her.

Once married to Ruth, Tony Fernandez was kept busy overseeing her business interests and fortune. He encouraged Kathleen, her older daughter, to move out almost immediately after his marriage to her mother. He told Ruth it would be good for Kathleen to have an apartment of her own. Ruth's younger daughter, Susan, lived with them but was involved with her own friends.

At first, the Fernandez marriage seemed idyllic. If Ruth's former friends and relatives didn't call often, she didn't notice—she was so caught up in loving Tony.

The marriage turned bitter and disappointing far too soon. While Tony's first wife had turned a deaf ear to rumors of his infidelities, Ruth could not. She suspected he was seeing other women. It tore her apart.

In May of 1974, when she had been married to Tony for just over two years, Ruth took a trip to Texas—alone. Tony remarked to one of her daughter's boyfriends, "When she comes back, she'll have to shape up or ship out."

While Ruth was gone, Fernandez used Ruth's Power of Attorney and sold some of her property without her knowledge for $100,000—far less than its actual value.

Only six months before, Ruth and Tony had vacationed at a plush resort in Mazatlan, Mexico, where they had impressed other couples as an "ideal couple." But that had evidently been the last try on Ruth's part to make the marriage work. One reason for the end of the perfect romance—and a good reason at that—was the fact that Tony reportedly had another woman he was seriously involved with. She lived in Centralia, Washington. Although Ruth didn't realize it, he had used *her* money to give the other woman an expensive fur coat and a diamond solitaire. He told the woman that they would be married soon.

While Ruth Fernandez was on her lonely trip in May, Tony also took care of some other pressing business. He took out a $100,000 accidental death insurance policy on Ruth through Mutual of Omaha. There was never any concrete evidence that Ruth signed the application for that policy.

To her everlasting misfortune, Ruth still loved Tony. She still believed she could win back his love and that he would be faithful to her. During the third week of July 1974, she was excited about a camping trip they were going to take together. It would be like another honeymoon. They had rented a fully equipped Winnebago Brave motor home from a local dealer, and also took a four-wheel drive vehicle with them.

On Sunday afternoon, July 26, Ruth and Tony Fernandez stopped at the Mount Si Golf Course restaurant in North Bend, Washington, for cocktails and lunch. They lingered in the picturesque spot for a long time.

Just beyond North Bend, the I-90 freeway and back roads head east swiftly up toward the summit of Snoqualmie Pass. The land drops away steeply at the edges of the byroads.

The Fernandez's campsite was eight miles up the mountain from North Bend.

According to witnesses, both Ruth and Tony had seemed somewhat affected by the drinks they had with lunch. They left, saying they were headed for their campsite. At 4:15 that July afternoon, the Fernandezes visited the Snoqualmie office of the Weyerhauser Lumber Company on a business errand. Employees there recalled that Ruth seemed to be unhappy and a little querulous, while Tony was reflective and quiet. Neither of them, however, seemed to be intoxicated. When they left, they said they were going on up toward Snoqualmie Pass to the place where they were camping.

The first hint that something might be wrong came at 8:30 that Sunday evening. Tony called the waitress at the Mount Si restaurant to ask if she had seen Ruth. She had not. Next, he called the Little Chalet Café in North Bend, asking the staff there if they had seen Ruth. They knew her, but they hadn't seen her that evening.

At 8:36 P.M. Tony called the Washington State Patrol station in North Bend, expressing his concern for Ruth's safety. When the trooper on duty asked him why he was worried, Tony said first that Ruth had left the campsite for a walk in the woods alone and she had not returned. But then he changed his story. He said she had driven in the Winnebago, and he thought she had been heading for their home in Auburn.

"I followed her twenty minutes to half an hour later in my four-wheel drive Scout," he said. "But I couldn't find any sign of her."

Coincidentally, Susan Logg and her fiancé, Don Stafford, had headed up the Granite Creek Road toward the campsite between 8:30 and 9:30 P.M. that Sunday night. They had passed neither Ruth nor Tony along the way. When they got back to the big house in Auburn at 10:40 P.M., they encountered Tony, who had just emerged from taking a shower. He told them he had no idea where Ruth had gone off to. He figured she would come driving up any time, and there was no use to go looking for her. It was too dark.

The long night passed with no word at all from Ruth. The

next morning, Don Stafford and Tony Fernandez drove back to North Bend and officially reported Ruth as a missing person to the State Patrol. Then they drove up the Martha Lake Road to the Granite Creek Road along the route to the vacated campsite. There was no sign of the Winnebago along the roadway. Suddenly, Stafford spotted some tracks in the dirt shoulder next to the Granite Creek Road. The tracks appeared to disappear over the cliff's edge. When Stafford pointed them out, Tony Fernandez asked him, "Do you think I should look here?"

Stafford volunteered to look. He walked to the edge of the precipitous cliff where rock had been blasted out, making it an almost sheer drop. Bracing himself, he looked down. Far, far below, he saw the crumpled mass of metal that had been the Winnebago.

Before he turned back to give Tony the bad news, Don Stafford forced himself to look along the cliff side between the wrecked camper and the top. About halfway down, he saw a body and he knew it was Ruth Fernandez.

In a very short time, the sunny mountain road was alive with King County Police and Washington State Patrol troopers. The wreckage was three hundred feet below. The investigators were able to approach it only obliquely by using a logging road farther down the grade. When they finally got to Ruth Fernandez, they confirmed that she was dead, and that she had been for many hours. Rigor mortis was almost complete. She appeared to have suffered massive head injuries. Oddly, her clothing was remarkably untorn for someone who had ridden the hurtling camper off the embankment and then one hundred fifty feet down the hill before she had fallen out.

Tony Fernandez complained about the hours the police were spending at the scene. It was perfectly obvious what had happened. He muttered to Don Stafford, "They are just creating red tape." Tony asked Stafford to leave with him. He didn't want to stay around there any longer, watching from above as the cops worked over his dead wife.

There were aspects of the accident that puzzled and bothered the investigators. Trooper Don Caughell of the

Washington State Patrol's Fatality Investigative Unit looked with his discerning eye first at the road and then at the shattered motor home. The road had no defects that would make control of a vehicle difficult; there was no breaking away of the shoulder area where the rig had gone over. This indicated to him that the Winnebago had been moving slowly and that no one had stomped on the brakes in a desperate attempt to keep from plunging over. "Why?" he wondered. Why hadn't Ruth Fernandez tried to save herself?

Although the motor home itself was thoroughly crumpled, there was no sign inside it to indicate that a body had bounced around during the terrible drop. No blood, no torn flesh, no hair. Ruth Fernandez had been wearing a loosely woven blouse which would have been likely to catch on *something* during the terrible bucketing down the steep hill. But her blouse had no tears or snags at all.

Ruth Fernandez's body was lifted with the use of a carefully balanced litter, from the side of the cliff and taken to the King County Medical Examiner's Office in Seattle to await autopsy.

The postmortem examination showed that she had suffered two severe injuries, neither of which was typical of a victim who had ridden a vehicle down a slope for almost two hundred feet. The first wound was caused by some kind of blunt object striking her omentum—the fatty, apronlike membrane that hangs from the stomach and transverse colon in the abdominal cavity. The omentum is rich in blood vessels. Ruth's second wound—and the fatal wound—was a fractured skull. She had died sometime between 11:30 A.M. on the 26 and 11:30 A.M. on the 27. The best clue to time of death is when the victim has last been seen. As Ruth was known to be alive at 4:30 P.M. on the Sunday she disappeared, the time-of-death period could be cut to nineteen hours.

According to autopsy findings, she could have lived a maximum of six hours without treatment and a minimum of one hour. Blood alcohol tests indicated that Ruth had been legally intoxicated at the time of her death, that is, she had at least .10 of alcohol in her bloodstream.

Tony Fernandez was Ruth's sole heir, and he applied almost immediately for her insurance benefits. Mutual of Omaha declined to cut him a check, however, because there was an ongoing investigation into her death. Indeed, King County Police homicide detectives Ted Forrester and Roger Dunn would spend months in their initial probe of the strange circumstance of Ruth Logg Fernandez's death. Those months would stretch into years.

Circumstantial evidence indicated that some outside force had caused Ruth's Winnebago to plunge over the cliff. Forester and Dunn suspected Tony Fernandez of killing his wife, but they could not prove it.

What did happen between 4:30 and 8:30 P.M. on July 26, 1974? No one but Tony saw Ruth during that time, and he insisted that she first took a walk in the woods and then decided to drive home alone from their campsite.

He liked to imply that Ruth had been out of control, hysterical, irrational—a woman who should not have been driving the big Winnebago rig. Tony even suggested obliquely that Ruth might have been suicidal. But was it consistent with human psychology that a healthy, forty-four-year-old woman, slightly intoxicated, perhaps upset at her failing marriage, would deliberately drive herself off a cliff? She had two daughters who needed her, family, friends, a considerable fortune. If she was so angry at Tony that she wanted to die, would she have done this knowing that it was Tony and Tony alone who would inherit everything she owned?

Probably not.

The case dragged on. No criminal charges were filed against Tony Fernandez. Fernandez himself pooh-poohed the theory that he might have killed his wife. He remained in the family home and gave frequent interviews to the media, appearing often on the nightly news television programs. He appeared affable and confident.

Tony Fernandez was *so* confident, in fact, that he began to date publicly. He was a grieving widower, yes, but a man got lonely.

In February of 1976, a year and a half after Ruth Logg Fernandez died, her daughters, Mrs. Kathleen Logg Lea, twenty-two, and Susan Logg, nineteen, brought civil suit against Tony Fernandez, charging that he was not eligible to inherit any of Ruth's fortune. Under the Slayer's Act, no one shall inherit benefits resulting from the death of someone whose death they have caused.

Ruth's daughters were so frustrated to see Tony Fernandez going blithely on with his life that they felt they had to do something. Ted Forrester and Roger Dunn had explained that they had not yet come up with enough physical evidence to take to the King County Prosecutor's Office so that criminal charges could be brought. Criminally, guilt must be proved beyond the shadow of a doubt. *Civilly,* however, a judgment can be made on the "preponderance of evidence." Testimony on "prior bad acts" (of which Tony Fernandez had plenty) could be introduced.

Ruth's daughters decided to go for it.

Enraged, Tony Fernandez brought a million-dollar lawsuit against Ted Forrester.

It was a marathon four-week trial and received more press coverage than most criminal trials. Superior Court Judge George Revelle's courtroom became a kind of microcosm of the lives of Tony Fernandez and Ruth Logg Fernandez. Ghosts of Fernandez's past reappeared. John Casteel, the man who had bounced in a Jeep sixty feet down a cliff after Fernandez bailed out, was there. So was William Belcher, who wound up with a head wound in the snowy wilds of Canada. Neither man came right out and accused Tony of violence—they merely related what had happened to them.

Tony's ex-wife testified—for the defense—saying he was faithful "in his own way" and that he had never thrown his other women in her face during their marriage. She smiled at him as she testified.

After the background of the couple's meeting, romance, and marriage was presented, both sides called experts in forensic pathology to the stand.

Dr. F. Warren Lovell, Chief Pathologist of Northwest Hospital, testified for Fernandez's defense. Lovell, who specialized in the study of fatal accidents and designed the autopsy program for the NASA flight project, said that it was likely that, when the Winnebago went over the cliff, Ruth Fernandez's body became an essentially weightless object, thrown against the motor, which would have yielded on impact. This, Lovell testified would explain why Ruth's injuries were not more extensive. He also said it was not unusual that her clothing was untorn.

On cross-examination, however, Dr. Lovell conceded that the fatal skull fracture could have been caused by a man taking her by the hair and striking her head on a rock. "But it would be very hard to do," he added.

Dr. Lovell did not agree with the plaintiffs that the injury to the abdomen was consistent with a blow from a fist. He said that it could have been caused by Ruth's belly hitting the steering wheel.

Detective Roger Dunn, however, testified that he had examined the steering wheel of the Winnebago and found no damage consistent with a great force pushing against it.

Dr. Gale Wilson, who had been the King County Medical Examiner for forty years before his retirement and who had done over seventeen thousand autopsies, testified that, in his educated opinion, Ruth was not in the motor home when it left the road. He was convinced, rather, that she had died from a blunt instrument applied with great force to her head. Dr. Donald Reay, the current medical examiner, testified that Ruth had died of a skull fracture and that it was possible—but not very likely—that she was in the motor home when it left the road.

The options open to the deciding judge were essentially this:

1. Ruth Fernandez, distraught and a little intoxicated, drove accidentally off the cliff without even applying the brakes of the motor home. Her body fell out halfway down.
2. Ruth Fernandez drove deliberately off the cliff and her body was thrown out halfway down.

3. Someone bludgeoned and beat Ruth Fernandez, pushed the motor home off the cliff and flung Ruth down after it. *Or* someone carried her body halfway down to make it look as if she had been in an accident.

4. Someone pushed the Winnebago over and persuaded Ruth to go down to it to help retrieve valuables. That someone then killed her where she was found.

Tony Fernandez himself did not testify in the trial.

Arthur Piehler, the attorney for the Logg sisters, summed up the plaintiff's case dramatically: "Tony Fernandez *did* fall in love when he met Ruth in 1971. He fell in love with her house, her five acres, her swimming pool, her stocks, her bonds, and other assets."

Piehler recalled that medical experts had testified that Ruth would have had broken bones, multiple cuts, lacerations, foreign objects in wounds, and torn clothing had she been in the Winnebago when it crashed. He theorized that Fernandez had somehow crashed the motor home and then persuaded Ruth to walk down the mountainside with him to recover items in it. It would have been easy for him to hit her on the head and in the stomach, and leave her there to die alone.

Piehler contended that Fernandez had forged Ruth's signature on the one-hundred-thousand-dollar accidental death policy two months and six days before she died. He said Tony had probably become concerned that his wife was considering a divorce. "He could see all his lovely property drifting away from him." Piehler told the court about the other woman Tony was seeing, the woman who had received the diamonds and furs.

John C. Hoover, Fernandez's attorney, argued that the couple had been happy and that they had taken a week's camping trip together. The Winnebago had crashed, he said, only because Ruth had had too much to drink. Hoover insisted that Ruth had been completely content with all the property agreements between herself and her husband. If

she had not been satisfied with their arrangement, she had
had plenty of time to change it.

In March 1976, Tony Fernandez's fortune evaporated
when Judge Revelle read his oral decision to a packed
courtroom, a decision in which he found the defendant
without credibility. "I do not believe anything he says,"
Revelle began succinctly.

Revelle read his thirty-one-page decision and concluded,
"I have examined many possibilities and numerous high
probabilities of the cause and method of her death. Each
such probability requires the participation of the only
person I know who was with her; that's Anthony Fernandez.
One of those methods or probabilities is a method suggested
by Mr. Piehler, but I can't say that's it. I just know that
under the burden of proof here—even stronger than necessary to be found—Anthony Fernandez, I conclude, participated as a principal in the willful and unlawful killing of
Ruth Fernandez."

In his conclusions of law, Judge Revelle said, "Anthony
Fernandez, as the slayer of Ruth Fernandez, shall not
acquire, in any way, property or receive any benefit as the
result of the death of Ruth Fernandez. Anthony Fernandez
is deemed to have predeceased the decedent (under the
Slayer's Act) Ruth Fernandez. All property which would
have passed to or for the benefit of the defendant, Anthony
Fernandez, by the terms of the Will of Ruth Fernandez, or
any agreement of the defendant and Ruth Fernandez, under
the provisions of RCW 21.16.120 shall be distributed as if
the defendant had predeceased Ruth Fernandez."

With that, Tony lost the financial ball game. But he did
not lose his freedom. He had only lost a civil case.

It took another court order to get Fernandez to vacate the
home in Auburn. He had lived there since July of 1974
when Ruth died. Tony was ordered not to attempt to
remove furniture, appliances, or anything of value that
would be part of the estate. Judge Revelle also restrained
Fernandez from using credit cards drawn on the estate.

Counsel for Sue and Kathy said, "Fernandez has been dissipating everything he can get his hands upon and has spent about $155,000 that was part of the estate." Even as the trial had progressed, Tony was said to have been involved in a $200,000 land purchase.

Finally, Tony moved from the home that now belonged to Ruth's daughters. But, in the end, there was little of the estate left for the two orphaned young women. After lawyers' fees and Tony's free spending, they obtained less than 10 percent of the money their parents had put aside for their futures.

On June 3, 1976, Fernandez was charged in Lane County, Oregon, with forgery and theft by sale of timber valued at nearly $75,000 and was arrested on a federal parole violation warrant. He was not inside long. Yet another woman besotted with Tony Fernandez put up his bail.

On August 12, 1977, Fernandez was charged with seven felony counts in Thurston County, Washington—second-degree theft, two counts of unlawful issuance of bank checks, and four counts of first-degree theft alleging unlawful sale of timber rights that he claimed were his to a third party. These violations were said to have occurred in Thurston County in the winter of 1976–77. Convicted on all these counts, consecutive sentences could net him fifty-five years in prison.

On September 1, 1977, the charge for which Ruth's daughters and loved ones had waited so long was made. The King County Prosecutor's Office charged Anthony Fernandez with first-degree murder in the death of Ruth Fernandez. His trial, scheduled for January 9, 1978—almost four years after Ruth died on the lonely mountainside—was one where the evidence was mostly circumstantial, one of the most difficult cases for a prosecutor to press. It was lengthy, and full of surprises. Tony Fernandez's mistress, wearing her fur coat, was present at his trial every day.

Tony Fernandez was convicted of Ruth Logg Fernandez's murder in February 1978, and sentenced to life in prison. And that was exactly what he served.

On Christmas Day 1995, Anthony Fernandez, seventy-three, enjoyed a hearty holiday meal in prison. And then he dropped dead of a massive heart attack.

Who was the real Tony Fernandez? Was he a timber baron, a doctor of psychology, an acupuncturist, a historian of Navajo culture, a master of city government? A lover—a studied conman—or a methodical killer?

It doesn't matter anymore to Ruth Logg Fernandez. The man who promised to love her forever betrayed her. She lost her hopes for the perfect romance in the darkness on the steep mountainside along Granite Creek Road. She will never see her grandchildren and never know her daughters as mature women.

Perhaps she knows, however, that those daughters saw their quest through to the end and gave her the only gift they could: justice.

Black Leather

The cases that follow next—"Black Leather" and "Mirror Images"—are companion pieces, a close look at the injustice that resulted when those who should have been paying attention looked the other way.

The first case, which allows a rare insider's look at the crimes of a sexually aberrant criminal, is ugly; it may be offensive to some readers. Still, it demonstrates more than any other I have written how ridiculously dangerous misplaced trust in a sexual psychopath can be. This case will lead you into the next in the natural order of unnatural behavior—if such a thing is possible.

Larry Hendricks, the murderer in "Black Leather," was a sexual psychopath. So are the two killers in the case following this one. They shared one identity between them; Larry Hendricks was two people all by himself, a man with a respectable facade and a secret life so dark and so sick that his crimes left even experienced Pierce County, Washington, detectives, who have seen their share of grisly murders, shaking their heads.

This killer was trusted far beyond limits that anyone might imagine, trusted by the system that released him into society, and he betrayed that trust in a series of unspeakable crimes.

It was a little after eight A.M. on Monday, the first of May, 1979, when Sam Brand, a farmer who lives in an isolated, wooded rural area near Roy, Washington, heard someone pounding frantically on his front door. Drop-in visitors at Brand's farm were a rarity and he was a little ill at ease when he heard the insistent beating on his door.

He was more alarmed when he opened the door and saw a young man, apparently badly beaten and drenched in blood—some of it dried, some freshly glistening. The man was shouting almost incoherently. In New York City or Detroit or Chicago—and probably even in downtown Seattle—Brand would probably have slammed his door and called police. But this was the country where neighbors helped neighbors and even strangers.

"Hey, I need some help!" the youth cried.

Sam Brand opened the door wider, beckoning the boy in. "Yeah . . . it sort of looks like you do."

"A guy took me out in the woods, and he beat me. And there was another body there already," the youth blurted. "I shot him. I *had* to. He was going to kill me too."

Brand didn't doubt that the young man had been beaten. His fair hair was scarlet with blood, one arm dangled awkwardly, and he winced as if every movement caused him pain.

"He kidnaped me," the man babbled on. "I was finally

363

able to overpower him and I shot him with all the guns. They're back there. I just drove until I found someone."

Still not convinced that the injured man wasn't under the influence of hallucinatory drugs, Brand moved to the phone and called to ask that the Pierce County Sheriff's Department and an aide car respond. He offered the stranger something to eat, some coffee, but all he would accept was water.

The location of the Brand farm was so obscure that only deputies who worked the region were familiar with it. It was deep in the southern end of the county about eight miles east of the crossroads town of McKenna. Deputy Greg Riehl and Rescue Squad Number 15 arrived simultaneously at 8:51 A.M.

Sam Brand had set a mattress on the ground outside his garage so that the injured man could lie down while three emergency medical technicians worked over him. Riehl noted that fresh blood continued to seep from a wound at the back of the man's head.

The victim quickly identified himself as Private Niels Honegger,* twenty-one, and said he was stationed at Fort Lewis. He produced a military ID card with his picture on it.

Honegger talked so rapidly that the deputy could barely understand him; he repeated over and over that he had had no choice but to shoot. Gently, Riehl asked the young soldier to start from the beginning and try to slow down.

Honegger said that he had been waiting for a taxi back to the base at about 3:40 that morning when a man driving a black van stopped. At first he had beckoned to Honegger to come over to the van, and then the stranger had pulled a gun and ordered him into the back. The rest of his story was so terrifying that it sounded like it had happened in a nightmare.

"He put some kind of black leather hood over my head and drove around for hours," Honegger said. "Then he drove out to some logging road, made me take off all my clothes, and then he handcuffed me and put leg irons on me. He forced me back in the woods. That's when I saw the body. He said the same thing was going to happen to me."

He said the man had been dressed entirely in black leather. Once Honegger was handcuffed, his captor beat him with a billy club. Realizing that he was in the hands of a sadomasochistic crazy man, who was probably planning to subject him to a sexual assault, Honegger said he had feigned unconsciousness while he tried to think of a way out of his predicament.

The young soldier said he had waited for his chance. When the man in black had bent over to unhook his leg irons, he had been able to break free. The man had several guns.

"I shot him," Honegger said. "I shot him with all the guns. Then I beat him with the gun barrel until I was sure he was dead."

The paramedics and Riehl stared at the wild-eyed young soldier. Could this be true, or was he in the grip of some delusion?

Honegger said he had thrown on his clothes, and then he had driven the stranger's black van until he found a house. "I was so scared I drove right through the gate. Then I found I couldn't find a road in so I parked the van and walked down. This man let me in."

Riehl advised Niels Honegger of his rights. He had just admitted to shooting a man to death, and it was procedure that he should be read his rights under Miranda. Honegger shook his head impatiently and said he understood all of that and waived his right to counsel. He repeated his story again, and it was exactly as he had told it before.

More deputies arrived and looked for the area where Honegger said he had left two bodies—one his captor's, and another that had been there when they drove in at dawn. The woods were so thick on the property, which was owned by the Weyerhauser Lumber Company, that they doubted they could find the location of the attack without help from Honegger.

"I marked it when I left," the soldier told them. "I took an empty six-pack out of the van and put it by the road so I could find it again."

The medics nodded when asked if Honegger's condition was stable enough for him to give assistance in searching the area. They drove over the narrow roads in Deputy Riehl's patrol car until Honegger spotted the six-pack marker he had left.

"They're in there," he said quietly.

Deputies went over a deadfall fir tree that blocked access to a dirt road that wound up and then disappeared into the woods. When they returned a few minutes later, they looked sick.

"He's right," one said. "There are two bodies back there. I've never seen anything like it."

Detectives Walt Stout and Mark French were notified at sheriff's headquarters in Tacoma and they left at once for the site. They arrived at the Brand farm as Niels Honegger was being loaded into an ambulance for the trip to Madigan Army Hospital. A full statement would have to wait; the young soldier was clearly going into shock.

Briefed by Riehl, Stout and French accompanied him and the other deputies deep into the woods and the body site. The area was thick with new-growth timber and criss-crossed with logging roads. Each one looked much like the last, and it seemed a miracle that Honegger had been able to find his way out and to the Brand farm.

It was a brilliantly sunny spring morning—May Day, in fact—and birds sang in the grove of fir trees, an ironic contrast to the grotesque scene the investigators found.

Detective Walt Stout came upon the first body which lay sprawled in the undergrowth of Oregon grape, sword ferns, and salal. The body was that of an extremely short white male; he was so chubby that he looked oddly like an overgrown infant. But there was nothing childlike about the man's outfit. He was dressed entirely in black leather: a motorcycle jacket, pants, pull-on boots, gloves. Even a billed cap of black leather lay near the body's head. A black turtleneck sweater completed his grotesque outfit.

Although he was clothed from head to foot in leather, the dead man's genitals were exposed. His tight pants had a square of black leather which could be unsnapped at the crotch, not unlike the codpieces worn by men in the fifteenth and sixteenth centuries. The Pierce County detectives had heard of this kind of gear, but they had never actually seen it before. The body's penis and testicles had a kind of "penis ring" or "penis harness" looped around them, a strange rig of black leather thongs.

The man had been shot many, many times in the head and body and had apparently had his skull cracked by blows from a blunt instrument.

The investigators found a second body twelve feet away from the first. It was that of an extremely tall and lanky man who was completely nude. His general physique was all they could tell about him. Most of his face and head had been obliterated, probably blown away by a large caliber weapon. The dead man had a second wound to the left groin area which had torn away much flesh from his genitals and his thigh.

The second body had obviously been in the grove of trees for several days.

The detectives gazed at an assortment of macabre equipment that lay scattered in the undergrowth. This was gear that could only have been intended for bondage and torture: handcuffs, leg irons, several dogs' choke chains on black leather leads, a billy club. Walt Stout and Mark French had no trouble now believing the strange story that Niels Honegger had told.

This quiet woods had been turned into a torture chamber for someone whose sexual fantasies were apparently fulfilled through sadomasochistic rituals.

After measuring the scene, the investigators began to pick up and bag items into evidence. There were enough weapons scattered around for a small revolution: a Winchester double-barreled shotgun, a Colt Python .357 revolver, a Smith & Wesson Airweight 9mm revolver, a Smith & Wesson .44 Magnum revolver, another Smith & Wesson .44 Magnum, and a Browning .25 caliber automatic. The body in black leather still wore two gun belts, two holsters, and a handcuff case and ring for the nightstick that dangled from one belt.

Almost all of the torture gear was bloodstained; the nightstick bore bits of hair and blood, and one of the dogs' choke chains appeared to have been tightened around the neck of someone who was bleeding profusely.

Stout and French found a pair of silver-colored opaque sunglasses lying near the leg irons, all of the items blood-flecked and resting under a sword fern.

As the detectives worked, they didn't talk much. Sado-masochism was something they had learned about in training classes on abnormal psychology, but they could never recall actually *seeing* anything as grotesque as this. They marveled that the stocky young soldier had ever emerged from this thicket of torture alive.

When Pierce County Deputy Coroner Casey Stengel arrived, a closer examination was made of the two bodies. The squat, little man in the black leather suit had a smashed nose, bullet wounds to the left ear and temple, and there were also numerous bullet holes in the leather jacket.

The second victim lay on his back, his legs straight and together, his arms behind his back as if he had been handcuffed when he died. Marks around his ankles indicated that his legs had been shackled for some time.

After the bodies were removed to await autopsy, Deputy John McDonald arrived with his K-9 dog, Duke, and worked the entire area to see if there might be more physical evidence hidden in the woods, but nothing more was found.

Detectives Stout and French left to look at the black 1978 Dodge van that Niels Honegger had driven in his desperate escape. It was still parked on a hill overlooking the Brand residence. Identification Officer Hilding Johnson processed it as the detectives looked on.

They found a registration slip which showed the vehicle was being leased by a Larry Hendricks at an address on North G. in Tacoma. Johnson photographed the rig inside and out and dusted for latent prints before the trio moved in to check for more evidence.

Inside the van, Stout and French found a brown leather bag jammed full of ammunition, some live and some spent cartridges. There was also a black leather hood much like the kind that executioners wore in days of old. The hood had snaps on the front where covers for the eyes and mouth could be attached. The blinder attachment and the mouth-piece were nearby. The mouthpiece had a hard rubber protuberance designed to effectively gag the person who wore the hood.

The hood, which had a label from "The Trading Post" in San Francisco, could be laced tightly up the back and secured at the neck.

The traveling torture chamber also held a black dildo and a black crotchpiece, probably from the leather pants the short dead man wore.

There were some "normal" things too, that seemed out of place: empty beer bottles, cigarette butts, cigar butts.

ID Officer Johnson moved along with Detectives French and Stout, filming every step of the processing. Then he went to the morgue to fingerprint the near-headless corpse in an attempt to identify the man.

Detective John Clark was dispatched to Madigan Army Hospital where he would wait until medics gave the okay for him to take a complete statement from Private Niels Honegger.

In the meantime, Stout and French drove to the apartment house on North G. where the man named Larry Hendricks had lived. They were sure now that Hendricks was the man in the black leather suit. When his clothing was removed in the coroner's office, his driver's license was there, and the picture on it matched. The round, almost childish face was the same. Hendricks was thirty-two years old.

If they had been expecting to walk into quarters designed by the Marquis de Sade, they were to be surprised. Using keys they found on a ring in the van, they entered an immaculate apartment furnished entirely in exquisite antiques. There was nothing at all that might indicate that the apartment's occupant was into kinky sex. Rather, it looked like the home of a wealthy interior decorator. There were pieces of perfectly restored furniture, tapestries, paintings, silk rugs, vases, and lamps. The place might well have come right off a page in *House Beautiful*.

They looked further, however. There was a black vinyl case on a desk in the two-room apartment. Inside, they found nine one-hundred-dollar bills. And, when they opened a closet door, they found a number of items that suggested they had the right man. Either Larry Hendricks had unusual sexual hang-ups or he owned several dogs. There were three black leather dog collars on choke chains in the closet, but no dog dishes, no dog hair on the plush furniture, nor any other sign that Hendricks had pets.

The detectives also found a vinyl shoulder weapon case that would fit the Winchester shotgun found at the scene, and a box of .38 caliber ammunition. There were no kinky magazines in the apartment, but there were two issues of *Soldier of Fortune,* a somewhat militant paramilitary publication for avid gun collectors.

Tenants had storage lockers in the basement of the building, and Larry Hendricks had kept some of his possessions there. Walt Stout and Mark French found several holsters for handguns—both hip and shoulder type, another billy club, and a box of 16-gauge shotgun shells.

What a paradox—a man living in delicate luxury in an antique collector's paradise—but also a man who collected guns and ammunition as if he expected a civil war.

At Madigan Hospital, Detective John Clark was finally allowed to enter the emergency room where Niels Honegger was being treated for his extensive wounds. The youth's broken right arm was splinted and in a sling, and the thick turban of bandages around his head was stained with still-seeping blood. His back was covered with ugly red welts from a beating and burn marks, round and vicious looking, dotted his skin. Honegger's ankles and wrists had abrasions where the handcuffs and leg irons had cut into the skin.

While a military policeman stood by, Niels Honegger agreed to a tape recording of his statement.

He told John Clark that he had gone into Tacoma the previous evening—Sunday night—to see friends, but he hadn't found them at home. He had had one or two beers and then gone to an all-night grocery store where he called a cab to take him back to Fort Lewis.

"I was standing out front, waiting, when this black van pulls up and the driver says, 'Well, what are you doing?'"

As Honegger had peered into the van, he said the driver had pulled a gun and ordered him inside.

"He made me lie down in the back and he put handcuffs on me. I wasn't about to argue with him. He had the gun. He drove for a while and stopped someplace and he put some manacles on my ankles, and then this black leather hood over my head. He tried to put that mouthpiece thing on, but I fought him."

Honegger said that the gun the man had pointed at him in the kidnaping had been one of the .44s.

"My arms were cuffed behind me. I tried to work out of the cuffs, but they were too tight. The manacles had about eighteen inches of chain between them so you could walk, but then he had this little bar with hooks on it and he fastened that on and you couldn't move your legs more than six inches apart."

Honegger said that his captor had driven him around for a long time, until he could see daylight through the eyeholes of his mask. He couldn't be sure but he thought it had been about 5:30 A.M. when they arrived on the lonely logging road. He had heard the stranger moving his guns around, and then the sound of him uncapping a beer bottle.

Next, the man in the black leather suit had come back into the van and demanded that Honegger strip, all the while holding a gun on him.

"He unlocked the manacles on my feet, took off my shoes and socks, and then pulled my pants off. Then he locked those manacles back up, unlocked my handcuffs, and held the gun to my head, telling me to take my shirt off. Then he handcuffed me again."

The man in black leather had then loosened the leg irons so that Honegger could walk and forced him out of the van. He had placed the dog choke chain around his neck, pulling it tight, and prodded Honegger deep into the woods, all the time holding the shotgun to the back of his head.

"He made me say 'sir' all the time—'Yes, sir,' and 'No, sir.' He told me where to go and I guess we walked about twenty-five meters back into the woods. We ended up right by the other body. I thought it was a dog at first, and then I

371

realized it was a man. He wanted to shock me. I was scared as hell, and shivering from the cold. He told me I was going to die and he kept calling me 'Punk.' "

Honegger said that his captor had begun to beat him with the nightstick and that he had been helpless to resist because he was still handcuffed and shackled. Even though he was much bigger and had had combat training, he had been caught and bound up by the little man in black leather before he was aware of what was happening.

"I thought my arm was broken," Honegger said. "He hit me on the head too. He hit me a couple of times in the stomach but I've been trained how to take a stomach punch and I breathed out when I saw it coming so it didn't hurt."

Honegger said that he had tried to make his captor believe he had passed out from the pain, but that had only infuriated the man in leather.

"I lay there and he started burning me with cigarettes and cigars. He put them out on my back and on my nipples. I just couldn't take the pain so I had to get up."

During all this time, Honegger hadn't really seen the other man's face. The black leather cap was pulled down over his eyes and he had worn dark sunglasses that were like mirrors. Honegger, who was a solidly built 5'5" tall, said he had thought his abductor was taller when he had been picked up. He realized now that the man had been much shorter than he was. "I guess the guns made him seem taller," he said, somewhat ruefully.

Hendricks had demanded that his captive perform fellatio on him, but the plucky youth decided that he would rather die than submit to that. "He hit me a couple more times with the nightstick when I refused."

Honegger had reconciled himself to the fact that he was going to die. He told Clark that he had been an atheist up until that point, but he found himself praying and the face of his grandmother kept flashing through his mind. He was shivering from cold and shock, and he was getting dizzy from loss of blood. At that time, Hendricks had told him he was about to die.

"He unlocked my arms first," Honegger recalled. "And then he bent over to unlock the leg irons. I was sitting there watching him and wondered if I ought to do something. He didn't have any of his guns out. After he unlocked my right leg, I leaned back and kicked him as hard as I could. I tried to aim for his face, but I can't remember if I hit it. He fell over backward and I jumped on top of him. I hit him with my right arm—and it hurt me pretty bad—but I kept on hitting him until I saw his nose flatten out and start bleeding."

Honegger's combat training and instinct for survival had given him superhuman strength despite his injuries. Hendricks had tried to pull a gun from the holster he wore and it had gone off twice in the struggle. One bullet had come so close to Honegger's hand that the gunpowder burned it.

"I hit him first, and then I started shooting him." Niels Honegger's eyes closed; he was clearly back once again fighting for his life. "I couldn't tell if I'd hit him or not. He was still moving. When I got done with the first gun, I picked up another one. I shot every single round into him."

Almost hysterical with terror and pain by then, Honegger said he had picked up another weapon and emptied that into his tormentor. He recalled that the man in the black leather suit had assured him quite calmly, "Hey, man, you've *killed* me." But he had kept on firing almost automatically.

For a sadomasochist, receiving pain is almost as pleasurable as inflicting pain, but Larry Hendricks had finally gotten more than he had bargained for. When he stopped moving, Niels Honegger said he had scrambled to the van, thrown his clothes on, and headed for help. But first, afraid he would never find the path to the carnage in the woods, he had stopped to leave the six-pack marker so that he could lead police back to the scene.

Completely unfamiliar with the lonely area, Honegger had driven quite a while before he had seen Brand's farm and barreled the van through the gate in an effort to get help.

"Finally I parked the car at the top of the hill and walked down to the house. And the guy—a real nice guy—looks at me, sees I'm all covered with blood, and he let me into the house."

It was a chilling account, but Detective Clark had no doubt that the soldier was telling him the absolute truth.

Honegger had survived, and Hendricks was dead, but the case was far from over. At headquarters, Walt Stout and Mark French met with Chief Criminal Deputy Henry Suprunowski and ID Officer Johnson concerning the identity of the second victim at the scene. Johnson said that he had a tentative identification from fingerprints he'd taken off the body.

"He only had a minor arrest on a traffic warrant in Port Angeles, but it was enough to get his prints on file. His name is Michael Bertram Zahnle, born June twelfth, 1956. Six feet two, one hundred sixty pounds, red hair, green eyes. His last address is in Tacoma, but they don't know anything about him there."

They agreed that they would give Zahnle's description to the news media in the hope that someone would have more information about him.

Walt Stout received a phone call from a retired firefighter who said that he knew Larry Hendricks. "I deal in antiques and that's how I met him. He has a business he called 'The Merchant Prince' and he does—*did*—quite an antique business. I saw him last night about a quarter to one when he came by my place to talk business."

"How was he dressed?" Stout asked.

"Casual . . . a shirt and slacks, I think."

Hendricks had apparently gone home and dressed in his prowling outfit of black leather before encountering his victim in front of the all-night grocery.

The Pierce County investigative team immediately placed the information on the incident on teletype wires to the eleven western states. They doubted that Larry Hendricks had just begun his bizarre prowlings; the labels on his kinky gear indicated they had been purchased in San Francisco.

But there was a lot more they didn't know about Hendricks. If the case was not already shocking enough, the further revelations into his background would prove almost incomprehensible to the detectives working the case.

They were not particularly surprised to find that Hendricks had been arrested for robbery, assault, and sodomy by the Seattle Police Department in 1969 and sent to the Sexual Offender's program at Western State Hospital. A man who had refined his prowling to a fine art had not done it overnight. He had the van equipped to take prisoners and was well supplied with bondage gear.

What absolutely stunned the case-weary detective veterans was that Larry Hendricks had "graduated" from the Western State Sexual Offender's program after two years—only to be *hired* as a therapy supervisor by the same institution.

There was no question that Larry Hendricks was brilliant. He had graduated with a degree in English literature from the University of Washington, and his friends described him to the detectives and the press as personable and articulate. He had evidently been adept at keeping his straight life separate from his secret world of stalking and sexual aberration.

Larry Hendricks had passed an extensive battery of psychological tests and had been deemed "completely reliable" during his six months work-release period from the mental hospital before he was given the job as counselor.

As a counselor rather than a patient, Hendricks had been promoted steadily until he reached a position where, as a therapy supervisor, he was responsible for a group of twelve to fifteen patients. He monitored their progress, sat in on group therapy sessions, and was responsible for recommending patients' promotions from one stage to the next.

According to hospital spokesman Sidney Acuff, Larry Hendricks's patients were rapists, child molesters, and voyeurs. Embarrassed, the hospital's administrators stressed to the press in a rather obvious statement that Hendricks would never have been employed at Western State for six and a half years if they had known of his bizarre activities.

"Of course, you never know about the private lives of individuals," Acuff said. "But there was never any indication of anything like that."

However, there were those who claimed that there was,

indeed, evidence that Larry Hendricks was absolutely unsuited to be a counselor. Even though he had reorganized the hospital's drug treatment program and become director of the new unit he had established, Larry Hendricks behaved inappropriately both at his job and in his private life.

Several residents of the drug program signed sworn affidavits that were released to the media on May 2 when the news of Hendrick's suspected crimes hit the press. One eighteen-year-old patient, who had been transferred to Western State after being raped several times in Alabama State Prison, stated that Hendricks had read about his background in his file. "As soon as he saw the data on the rapes, he started rubbing my leg. Once, he started feeling me all over. I got upset and Larry said if I did that one more time, I would be sent back to prison."

A twenty-two-year-old patient said Hendricks had made a pass at him, telling him he had dreamed of putting his arms around him.

One outspoken critic said, "I threatened to quit if (administrators) didn't deal with Hendrick's rapacious verbal attacks on other staff members." He claimed that instead Hendricks was given even more power and responsibility. Two months later, the employee who had complained about Larry Hendricks resigned in disgust.

Larry Hendricks wasn't particularly unique in his "qualifications" to work as a therapist. At least five members of the paid drug unit at the hospital were reported to have been graduates of the sexual psychopath program.

Larry Hendricks had left his job at the hospital of his own accord in September of 1977 when the drug unit was transferred out of Western State. He had gotten married, but it hadn't lasted. In March of 1978, he returned to his former position of Therapy Specialist III and worked as a ward attendant until the end of July when he started his antique store, "The Merchant Prince."

The Pierce County Sheriff's detectives didn't have to wait long to hear from detectives in other areas. On May 2, they received calls from Captain Bill Cashdollar of the Tehama County Sheriff's Office in California and Sergeant John

Robertson of Napa County. They had two unsolved homicides that fit the pattern.

One California victim had been Tom Gloster, a comptroller of the California School of Professional Psychology in San Francisco. His nude body had been found on February 9 in a remote area of Tehama County. Witnesses said they had seen a black van speeding from the scene. Gloster had been shot many times with either a Colt .38 or a .357 Magnum.

The second victim was Larry Harland Niemeier, thirty-two, who had disappeared on February 5 and been found in Napa County. He had been shot with the same gun as Gloster, although the exact caliber and make would have to be determined by microscopic ballistics tests. He too was found naked. A piece of orange carpeting and a cigarette butt were found at the scene. The latter was the same brand found at the scene where Hendricks attacked Niels Honegger.

A thorough search of Larry Hendricks's apartment had turned up credit card slips indicating that he was in the San Francisco area at the time of these slayings, his van had orange carpeting, and he smoked the same brand of cigarettes. Several packs of that brand were found in the apartment wastebaskets. Oddly, each pack was thrown away with a single cigarette remaining—apparently a compulsion with the man.

Mark French contacted an auto body shop whose business card had been found among Hendrick's belongings. The shop confirmed that Hendricks had had the van in the shop from April 16 to April 19 to have bullet holes repaired. Bullets had been fired into the left front door post, the left rear double door, the left side of the van, and the left side of the driver's door.

"He had covered them with black electrical tape," the owner said. "He told us he got into a beef in a parking lot of a bar in San Francisco."

On May 4, Captain Cashdollar and Sergeant Robertson arrived from California to discuss their cases. Both of their victims had last been traced to a bar in San Francisco—

"The Brig," an S-and-M–oriented bar—and both men had been dressed in "leathers" similar to Hendricks's outfit when last seen.

Larry Hendricks had apparently suffered a grazing bullet wound sometime before the first of May. Detectives had found eight used bandages in his apartment. And, on autopsy, a similar bandage was found on his body. Dr. J. Cordova said a bullet had grazed the suspect's back on the right side.

It left a question. Had the bullet holes in the van occurred during the killings of Gloster and Niemeier or had there been another victim yet unaccounted for?

On May 6, the results came back from ballistics. Hendricks's Colt Python .357 matched the bullets used in the California killings. He was now linked absolutely to three murders and one attempted murder.

The saddest of all was the murder of Michael Zahnle. On May 3, Detective Art Anderson had received several calls from relatives of Zahnle. They said his parents lived in California and that he had come up to live in Washington about two years earlier. Zahnle was married, and his relatives knew he lived in the Tacoma area but they didn't have his present address.

At 6:15 P.M., after Zahnle's driver's license picture had been shown on the evening news, Anderson received a call from his wife's sister. She said that Michael Zahnle had been missing since April 27, and her sister had moved in with her while waiting for word of his whereabouts.

On May 4, Zahnle's widow came in to talk with Detective John Clark. The grief-stricken woman had had to bear more tragedy in a short time than any young woman should. On April 20, the Zahnles had lost their baby son, who was only eleven days old when he died. The grieving parents had been coaxed to go out with relatives on Friday, April 27, to try to forget for a while. But a few drinks had made Michael Zahnle more morose than ever. In tears, he had left the restaurant in Puyallup, Washington, on foot. Zahnle, a carpenter, had been unemployed. The young couple had no car of their own.

"He hitchhiked a lot, but he was very good at martial arts," his wife said. "And he always got himself out of any situation he got into."

She said her husband had been wearing a yellow pullover, a shirt with "California" on it, blue corduroy pants, and black zip-up boots when he left the restaurant. He had a ninety-two-dollar income tax refund check with him, and a key ring with a picture of their baby on it.

She was adamant that her husband had never shown any homosexual tendencies at all. Moreover, he had been scornful of anyone who was "into weird sex." If Michael Zahnle had gotten into Larry Hendricks's van, it would have been because he needed a ride home. He might not have been as alert as usual because he was upset about the loss of the baby.

The Pierce County detectives talked to others who had known Larry Hendricks, or who *thought* they knew him. The woman who had bought out his interest in "The Merchant Prince" said he was very knowledgeable about antiques but was somewhat strange. "Two or three weeks ago, I went to his apartment on a Saturday," she said thoughtfully. "When he opened the door, I saw two spots of blood on his forehead that had run down from his scalp. His face was flushed and his eyes were glazed. He said he'd been looking at an apartment to buy and he'd struck his head on some nails in the basement. I didn't believe him. I suspected he was into some kind of sexual deviancy, but I let it drop."

A relative of the man who had been addicted to sadomasochism tried to explain what might have caused Larry Hendricks's lifestyle. He knew that Hendricks was gay and said his marriage had lasted only two months. Hendricks had served in Vietnam, but not as a combatant—he was a courier for the military police.

As a child, Hendricks had been very gentle and had never shown the least sign of sadism. When he was seven or eight, he had suffered severe head injuries after being struck with a chunk of concrete. He had had to have brain surgery, and the relative thought this might have caused some of his later deviant behavior.

Larry Hendricks had had a peculiar childhood, dysfunctional in every sense of the word. His mother had dressed Larry in baby clothes until he was well past six. If her baby did not grow older, perhaps she thought that she too would remain young.

When Hendricks was ten, his parents separated and later divorced. Larry had hated his father, blaming him for the divorce. In later years, he was able to forgive his father, but, apparently, the traumas of his youth had scarred him.

Hendricks was an extremely small man. His gun collection, his macho clothes, all the sadistic gear he secreted in his fantasy world might have been part of his almost-psychotic obsession to be a big man.

In an ironic twist, Private Niels Honegger was awarded a $2,500 reward collected by a gay tavern association and "leather" motorcycle clubs in the San Francisco area for information leading to the arrest of the killer of Tom Gloster. A spokesman for a San Francisco gay group said, "We intend to pay Private Honegger the $2,500 for acting as judge, jury, and executioner. We admire his courage and stamina."

Honegger, on leave, had no comment.

A $1,000 reward collected for information leading to the killer of Richard Niemeier was not sent to Honegger but went instead to establish a memorial reward fund to be used in future killings involving homosexuals.

The backlash to the program that let prisoner-patients free to wander was sharp and biting. At least three King County Superior Court judges and local probation and parole officers said that their primary concern with any sex offender program is security.

Superior Court Judge Barbara Durham (now a Washington State Supreme Court Judge) said, "The potential for danger is so great that security has to be the first concern and treatment second. However, I have a feeling that the program is too amateurish—anyone who gets too difficult is bounced out. In California, there is a sexual psychopath unit separate from the hospital that has fantastic security. It has the highest rate of success in the country."

The laissez-faire program at Western State did not survive the scandals, and its policies tightened up. Two decades later, sadistic sexual predators are housed in a new prison where they have no freedom to roam Washington or any other state. They have no parole dates and some may never get out of prison.

Private Niels Honegger never considered himself a hero. He is a victim like all the others—albeit a victim who survived. What he endured in his fight for life is a memory that no young man should have to carry. And he *does* carry that nightmare for the rest of his days.

Mirror Images

Everything is cyclical—even the death penalty. In most states capital punishment is on the ballots every decade or so. It often takes horrendous crimes to wake up a complacent public. On November 2, 1976, only one referendum passed overwhelmingly in the Washington State elections. Voters, outraged and sickened by a wave of brutal murders, voted to restore the death penalty by a margin of two-to-one, and the governor of Washington signed the death penalty into law in June 1977. It was the backlash of a public surfeited with stories of coddled offenders—particularly sexual psychopaths—who had been paroled, furloughed, and work-released until they could virtually come and go at will. Many ex-convicts reverted to type when they found no walls around them and no eyes watching. Too many innocents died. It seemed that the inmates were running the asylum.

While some argued for mercy for convicted killers, particularly since Washington executions harkened back to the days of the Old West and murderers would be hanged, one mother of a teenage murder victim faced television cameras and said quietly: "Has anyone thought that the deaths our children died were easy . . . or pleasant to think about?"

And so for the next two decades murderers feared the gallows in Washington State. Hanging is not an easy death, not something that the average man on the street cares to contemplate for very long. In the end, Washington hung only *two killers: Charles Rodman Campbell and Westly Alan Dodd.* Although both were sexual offenders who had tortured their victims, the public nonetheless blanched at the details of their last moments. There will be no more hangings in Washington State. In the future, executions will be administered by lethal injection.*

---

*Charles Campbell killed a young mother, her nine-year-old daughter, and their neighbor to wreak revenge on the women for testifying against him in an earlier rape trial. (See Ann Rule's Crime Files: Vol. 1.) Westly Alan Dodd, an admitted sadistic pedophile, tortured and killed three small boys.

James Ruzicka and Carl Harp were convicted killers of the 1970s—and rapists too—several times over, but they never faced the hangman's noose. Both their crimes and convictions occurred in time to get them in under the wire. Since the death penalty cannot be invoked retroactively, they were home safe. In the preceding case—that of Larry Hendricks—justice was done without the help of the authorities.

The fact that Ruzicka and Harp should in all likelihood have been executed is not why I chose their stories for this book. Rather, they are remarkable in the way that their formative years were almost mirror images of one another. Their eventual destinies were bleakly similar. When they met, they recognized the commonalities that bound them together. At one point, they actually used the same pseudonym: "Troy Asin." These men were basically loners who shared their bizarre fantasies for a time.

When "Troy Asin" was cut in two, however, and James Ruzicka and Carl Harp parted, each of them continued his personal rampage of rape and murder. Neither should have ever been released to prey once more upon society. Each of them had the capacity to be as charming as any Don Juan and as harmless-appearing as a lost puppy. Behind their masks, they were full of betrayal and black purpose.

Their story is one of the strangest I have ever encountered.

Carl Lowell Harp was born in Vancouver, Washington, on March 8, 1949; James Edward Ruzicka was born almost exactly a year later on March 24, 1950, in Port Angeles, Washington. Were one to set out to find early case histories that would almost guarantee that the subjects were headed for trouble, Harp and Ruzicka would make "ideal" focal points.

There is an awful fascination in reading such case histories, akin to watching an out-of-control train barreling down the tracks. We can see what is going to happen, but there is no way in the world to stop it.

Public records describe Carl Harp's father as "a young, emotionally unstable carnival roustabout," his mother was only sixteen years old. By the time Carl was a year old, his parents were divorced. His mother remarried at least once and then moved on to a half-dozen common-law relationships. The child, Carl, could not count on any permanent father figure. When he was not committed to one or another mental institution, Carl's natural father had to live with *his* parents, his mental illness forcing him to be dependent.

Carl trailed after his mother, a small, thin boy with blue eyes and blond hair that would later turn brown. He and his mother lived on welfare in California, Arizona, New Mexico, Texas, Oklahoma, Alaska, Oregon, and Washington. In time, his mother descended into alcoholism, and Carl lived in such terrible conditions that authorities moved in and took him from her custody. He was placed first with a maternal uncle and aunt.

Carl Harp left a home where promiscuity and drinking were the norm and was suddenly plunged into one that was as staid as a church picnic. His uncle's affiliation with the Salvation Army barred booze, sex, swearing—and rowdiness of any kind. Carl would recall later that he was mistreated and punished severely. He was expected to attend religious services, and when he balked, his uncle forced him to go.

Not surprisingly, Carl Harp didn't last long in his uncle's house. He moved on to live with one of his former stepfathers. There, he finally found someone to love and connect with—his half sister. She was an epileptic and he was very protective of her. But by the time he was twelve Carl was a handful. He had committed uncountable curfew violations, petty thefts, burglaries, and even one car theft.

When Carl Harp was about fourteen, he was hit in the head while playing basketball. Another player struck him so hard with his elbow that Harp's temple bone was actually fractured. After that, his behavior changed markedly; he suffered excruciating headaches and blackouts. During one blackout, Carl choked his beloved half sister and almost killed her before someone pulled him off. Later, he would have no memory of the incident.

When he was fifteen, he was admitted to the Napa State Hospital in California in June of 1964, for a ninety-day observation. When the three months were up, he was voluntarily committed to the hospital. His diagnosis at that time was that of a "borderline psychotic," and the staff psychiatrists' impression was that he suffered from "schizophrenic reaction—chronic undifferentiated type." It was an ominous diagnosis.

All in all, Carl was considered amenable to treatment during the ten months he spent at Napa State. Although he did walk away one night, he returned the next morning. He was released on April 15, 1965.

Carl Harp completed the ninth grade at Castro Valley High School and entered Mount Whitney High in Visalia. He didn't finish high school, however. Indeed, it would be years later before he got his GED degree while in prison. Despite his unstable genetic heritage, Carl Harp was intelligent and quite artistic. He drew strange but intricate pen-and-ink pictures and wrote poems.

In January 1966, Harp was arrested for car theft and burglary and committed to the Preston School of Industry in Ione, California, where he stayed for a little over a year.

Two states away, there was another teenager whose life history had been almost a mirror image of Carl Harp's.

James Edward Ruzicka was born 228 miles from Carl Harp's birthplace. Ruzicka's mother, Myrtle, would type a summary of the births of her children for authorities one day, a sad little list of tragedy upon tragedy. She had been only seventeen when she had her first child. Thereafter, she gave birth every year—save one—until she had borne ten babies. She knew the precise details of each pregnancy and delivery. She wrote:

1. John Ruzicka, born 5/16/48—deceased 5/16/48. Cause of death was placenta came first and also a 5½-month pregnancy.
2. Stanley Edward Ruzicka, Jr., born 3/2/49—deceased 3/17/49. Seven-month pregnancy and child born with pancriest [sic] which caused death.
3. James Edward Ruzicka, born 3/24/50 . . .

James Ruzicka was the first of his mother's children to survive and she was amazed when he lived a week, two weeks, a *month*—and then continued to thrive. However, Myrtle's next child—her fourth—was born with a congenital heart defect on November 19, 1951; Linda Marie died in July 1957, three days after surgery to correct a flawed pulmonary artery.

Myrtle's fifth child was born on October 20, 1952. He was healthy enough, but she noted that he was in prison by the time he was in his early twenties. "On the honor farm," she added, almost proudly. The list continued:

6. Basil Arthur, born 9/4/53—deceased January 1954. The doctor and the autopsy diagnosed it as a combination of drowning and strangulation. A curd of milk lodged in his throat during the night, forcing the fluid down into his lungs. The doctor said he did not have a chance to utter a whisper or cry.
7. Wayne Allen, born 7/27/54.
8. Myrtle Elaine, born 8/7/55.

9. Christine Louise, born 10/20/56—deceased 10/27/56. Cause of death was pancriest [sic].
10. Morris Lee, born 7/16/58.

Myrtle Ruzicka had lost five of her ten children to premature death, a series of losses almost unheard of in the 1950s in America.

Who can say if her troubles with her son James caused her more pain than the deaths of five of his siblings. Myrtle was a woman who did her best to gloss over problems. "In all honesty," she wrote, "my children got along better than some families."

Perhaps. Just as Carl Harp's father disappeared from *his* life through divorce when he was a year old, Myrtle Ruzicka recalled that she divorced Jimmy's father when the child was one. Stanley Ruzicka was a longshoreman, and he continued to visit until Myrtle remarried. When he stopped coming, Jimmy was bereft. He complained to his mother that his daddy didn't love him. Although she tried to explain that he did, Jimmy said that wasn't true. If his father loved him, he would take him to his house or come and see him.

It is questionable if Ruzicka was, indeed, Jimmy's father. He would one day completely disown him in a letter to Jim's parole officer, suggesting a chronology that supported his argument. "James Ruzicka is not my son. I gave him my name only. Was married to his mother at one time. He was born thirteen months after she left me. Know nothing of his childhood days. You'll have to get in touch with his mother."

One thing was certain. Jimmy Ruzicka never had much in the way of paternal approval. Myrtle's second husband, Sam, used him as his whipping boy when he wanted to get back at Myrtle about something. He would either ignore him or spank him or slap him. Since Jimmy was the only child who survived Myrtle's first marriage and all the others were Sam's children, he resented the boy. Jimmy Ruzicka tried to make his stepfather love him, even after he'd been beaten. "As soon as he quit crying," Myrtle wrote, "Jimmy would crawl up on the easy chair or daveno and put his arms around his neck and say, 'Daddy, I love you.'" But Sam really didn't care for his stepson. He told him he was stupid and that he didn't know "a damn thing."

Myrtle remembers Jimmy as "kind, affectionate, and good-hearted . . . a hard worker, friendly and outgoing to everyone—including strangers."

The Ruzicka family barely made it financially; Myrtle was the sole support of her five children much of the time, working as a clerk for $1.25 an hour. "We had necessities," she explained, "and that was it. No Saturday matinees, ice-cream or candy money. No weekly allowance or bikes or trikes like the other playmates."

Of necessity, she was away from the family home much of the time. Jimmy had been especially close to his sister Linda and was inconsolable when she died at the age of five. "He was only seven or eight," Myrtle recalled, "and he would comment that she was an angel in Heaven with God, and he picked the brightest star a couple of times and said, 'There's Linda.'"

Although James Ruzicka's mother remembered his good qualities, she was also aware that something was wrong with him. He had chronic tonsillitis from the age of one to three when his tonsils were removed. When he was two, he had convulsions and had to be hospitalized. A year or so later, he had convulsions again and there was no definitive diagnosis as to their cause. "He was rigid and completely out," his mother said. Jimmy Ruzicka was delirious for three days with chicken pox. He had weak eyes and wore thick, magnifying glasses from the time he was about five.

As late as 1972, when he was in his early twenties, he fell to the floor, turned blue, and stopped breathing. His brother had to smack him hard in the back to get him breathing. (This latter attack could have been a drug reaction, however.)

But it was not his physical problems that alarmed his mother the most. Rather, it was his premature and obsessive interest in sex play. He molested his younger brother and even his sister, Linda, when he himself was only six or seven. Myrtle thought perhaps it was her fault; she had taken hormones during her pregnancy for James to ensure that she would carry him to term. She wondered if they were responsible for his unhealthy interest in sex.

She took him to a series of doctors. They all found him very restless, but they disagreed on what was wrong with him. One doctor told her Jimmy had brain damage; another found no brain dysfunction.

James Ruzicka was a hyperactive child, and probably would have been diagnosed today as having ADHD (Attention Deficit Hyperactive Disorder). He could not sit still to watch television and had to be doing *something* all the time. Sometimes his activities were constructive. (He could make tepees of gunny sacks and sticks when he was four or five and amuse his younger siblings.) Sometimes they were not.

"As Jim got older," his mother wrote, "he masturbated in his sister's slips and panties from the dirty laundry hamper. On different occasions, he asked his sister to let him look at her genitals. . . . At the age of nineteen or twenty, he tried to get his sister, Myrtle, to have sex with him. When she told me, he became almost wild—denying it, screaming, yelling, and accusing me of calling him a liar. His eyes were odd and the look on his face, I must admit, scared me, even though I didn't let on."

As an adult, James Ruzicka recalled a home life that was not nearly as idyllic as his mother remembered. He described a constant marathon of divorce, remarriage, divorce, ad nauseam. "There were always fights . . . it was all one big turmoil."

He said his weak eyes were discovered early and he had glasses before he was five. He remembered that he ran into a tree limb and knocked them off a few days after getting them and that he lost them. He recalls that his mother beat him severely for that.

When James Ruzicka was nine, he stole bicycles to ride. When he was finished with them, he either hid them or destroyed them. Later, he began to shoplift. Sex—aberrant sex—had become a part of his life at an age when most young boys were only concerned with baseball and marbles.

Besides his sexual interest in his own half sisters, he had also begun molesting little girls his own age when he was ten. During that period, he experimented with having sexual relations with animals.

James Ruzicka was thirteen when he went "into the system" for stealing and was sent to the Washington State juvenile center at Fort Worden in Port Townsend. He spent his time there trying to run away—and learning about marijuana. Before he was eighteen, James Ruzicka would try LSD, mescaline, cocaine, heroin, speed, and alcohol. On one authorized home visit, he became so violently angry at his brother over a minor incident that he choked him hard enough to leave fiery red marks on his throat. His mother had him returned to Fort Worden.

When he was sixteen, Ruzicka was paroled from Fort Worden. He stayed free for six months and eventually was sent to a youth camp in Mason County after a burglary conviction. Still, he tried to run away, and after a year, was transferred to the Green Hill State School for Boys in Chehalis.

The runner still ran. During one of his escapes, he was involved in three burglaries. They were penny-ante stuff; he stole $160 from a Texaco station, $400 from a dry cleaners, and broke into a drugstore—but fled before he could take anything. He pleaded guilty to one charge and the other two charges were dropped. In July 1968 he was sentenced to fifteen years at the state reformatory at Monroe.

A month later, Carl Harp was arrested and sentenced to the Monroe facility. Harp's path through his teenage years had not been that different from Ruzicka's. Neither had had secure home lives, and they had both been involved in drugs and thefts. Harp resented women and referred to them in obscene terms. He felt the world had treated him badly— which, indeed, it had—and he cared about no one.

Harp's first adult arrest was on December 30, 1967, in San Luis Obispo, California, when he was charged with possession of stolen property. He was eighteen years old. On August 11, 1968, he was arrested by Seattle police after he robbed a grocery store in the south end of the city. He had held a .22 caliber starter's pistol to the head of a small boy while he ordered the clerk to "Give me the bills, or I'll blow his head off."

Carl Harp, who also used the aliases "Troy Asin" and "Carroll Lowell Trimble," was sentenced to the Monroe Reformatory despite his plea that he was a drug addict and had needed money for a fix.

And so it was that, in the winter of 1968–69, James Ruzicka and Carl Harp met—two men of almost the same age and of remarkably similar backgrounds. Each was a smoldering cauldron of rage that transcended anything we might imagine. They came to prison on robbery and burglary charges, but any forensic psychiatrist who reviewed their case files could have warned that their potential was for violent sexual crimes.

Although the two convicts both wore thick glasses, that was the only physical similarity they shared. James Ruzicka was 6'1" tall and weighed 155 pounds. Carl Harp, who was only 5'8", weighed 162 pounds. Ruzicka *looked* like a poet with his finely hewn features, while Harp's face was flat and bland. But it was Harp who *was* the poet. He was probably the smarter of the two; Ruzicka had tested at 100 to 109 on the Otis IQ scale, which put him squarely at "average." Both men were cunning and manipulative.

In the worst possible sense of the term, Ruzicka and Harp were kindred spirits. No one but the men themselves can know what they talked about in their moments in the yard or when they worked on the kitchen crew, but at some point Harp shared his prized alias with Ruzicka. From that point forward, they agreed that if they should get free and if they were stopped by the law, they would each give the name "Troy Asin." That would be their private joke and it would certainly confuse the damned cops.

There is little question, though, that the two men spoke of rape and of the pleasures inherent in controlling women absolutely through fear and intimidation. The little boys who had followed their mothers through a series of marriages and who had been buffeted about from one home to another had grown up resentful of females and obsessed with sex.

* * *

James Ruzicka and Carl Harp had a plan to be free. All they needed was an opportunity. Ruzicka recalled that opportunity for prison authorities sometime later.

"I escaped from the Honor Farm. Harp and I left together. I would guess it was about seven-thirty P.M. on November twentieth [1970], when we took off. I didn't really plan it, but I had thought about it several times when I was on the farm. I had heard earlier that evening that several guys were going to jump me and beat me up because I had been flushing the toilet all hours of the night and this had upset them. I guess it kept them awake. I had found some Pruno [prison liquor made from fermented potatoes or fruit and yeast and hidden from the guards] out in back of the kitchen, and after I had some of it, I suddenly decided I just had to get out of there. I guess Harp had been thinking about taking off too, so when he saw I was going to escape, he came with me. We cut across the field behind the kitchen, then crossed the railroad tracks and on into the brush. We spent the first night near the fairgrounds, right outside the town of Monroe. The next day, we found an old abandoned house and sort of holed up in it. Harp and I separated at that time and we met again, later, in Seattle.

"I finally got to Seattle late that night and went directly to the University District. I stayed in the district for about three weeks. I slept where I could—at whatever 'crash pad' I could get into."

While he was free, he met a pregnant woman who had a little girl. He considered her his fiancée. She was one of the few women he ever felt compassion for. "One day I took my fiancée and my little daughter [not his child, but the daughter of the woman] to Bremerton to see my stepdad because I wanted his permission so I could marry my fiancée. The woman my stepdad was married to excused herself from the house and left. A few minutes later, the police were at the front door. I heard them ask if I was there so I ran to a back bedroom. The police came in the house so I jumped out the window, and they pounced on me."

Ruzicka had been gone two months before he was arrested. After he was caught and returned to prison, he married the woman and felt proud to give her unborn baby his name. Their marriage lasted just a year. The breakup of this marriage only served to substantiate Ruzicka's belief that emotional involvement with a woman was an open-sesame to getting hurt. "You get to know each other and then the bottom drops out," he said. "That's why I don't want to get emotionally involved with anyone for fear of getting hurt."

Despite his escape, James Ruzicka was paroled from Monroe on November 4, 1971. He was con-wise, and a decade of perverse sexual behavior had blossomed into a need for violent sex. Carl Harp, also recaptured, was paroled from Monroe two weeks after his friend. Essentially lone wolves, they went their separate ways, but, in a sense, they followed the same trail.

"Troy Asin" was loose.

It was January 18, 1973 when Nina Temple*, a twenty-one-year-old department store clerk, left her job in downtown Seattle around 4:30 and headed to the bus stop where she would catch the bus to her Capitol Hill apartment. She was tired, her feet hurt, and she thought longingly of getting home. While she waited, a tall, bushy-haired man asked her for directions and she pointed out the bus he should take. It happened to be the Number 9 bus she was taking. "You can catch it here," she told him.

When Nina exited through the rear doors of the bus, she didn't notice that the man got off too. She bent her head against the north wind that was blowing rain against her face. It was only five in the afternoon, but it was already dark and she hurried as she walked away from the lighted storefronts of the Broadway District. Huge homes, once single-family dwellings, had long since become apartments and boarding houses, their gardens gone to weeds except for stubborn laurel hedges and a few rosebushes.

Nina Temple was unaware of the man who kept pace with her as he walked on the opposite side of the street. She didn't see him at all until she opened the door to her apartment house and stepped in out of the driving rain. Suddenly, there he was—right in the lobby with her. He murmured something about knowing someone in the building, but he didn't seem to know where his friend's apartment was.

Before she could even move, he pinioned her with a strong arm around her waist and pressed the sharp edge of a four-inch knife against her neck. Then he wrestled her down the dark stairs to the basement.

In the black abyss beneath the stairs, he held her close as he told her that the "pigs" had shot his brother. "He's bleeding to death," he panted. "He sent me to get a girl to help."

"But why?" she blurted. "Why me? I don't know anything about first aid."

The bushy-haired man said that his brother was on parole and that he couldn't risk calling a doctor, and he shoved his knife harder against her flesh to coerce her to come with him.

There was nothing she could do. She was afraid to scream and she let him lead her back up the stairs, across a street completely empty of traffic, to another rooming house. It was a large, turreted house with leaded glass windows, a "Peace" symbol drawn on cardboard was tacked on the door's frame. Hopeless, she saw that the lobby of this house was empty too. The man pointed to stairs leading to the basement. "My brother's in there."

As he dragged her down the steps, she looked where he gestured. There was nothing but padlocked storage bins made of wood slats, designed to hold tenants' belongings. There was no brother. She was alone in the basement with the man and his knife. Nina prayed that she might hear the voices of someone coming, but there was no sound at all but her captor's heavy breathing.

"I'll have to tie you up, of course," he said. He bound her wrists with rope until it cut into her flesh. And then he carefully crossed one of her feet over the other and tied her ankles. He took off his T-shirt and gagged her with it. She could smell his perspiration and fought to keep from vomiting. While she lay there helpless, he urinated in a corner of the basement.

Returning to Nina, the stranger yanked her slacks and panties to her ankles and pulled her bra up to her shoulders, exposing her breasts. Then he stared at her as she lay helpless, naked, and trembling. He straddled her body but he was unable to achieve an erection; his impotency sent him into a violent rage.

Nina managed to choke out some words past the gag, taunting him. "Why don't you just kill me?"

"Don't worry," he answered. "I *will.*"

And then he set about trying to do just that. Again and again, more than a dozen times, his closed fists thudded against Nina Temple's jaw. She could feel her head bounce off the concrete floor and then slam into it again. The pain in her jaw was so intense that she almost lost consciousness.

When he stopped hitting her, she felt his strong fingers close around her throat as he began to choke her. Pinpoints of light exploded behind the darkness in her eyes. She went limp and pretended to be dead.

Oddly now, Nina's would-be killer became concerned; he patted her cheeks gently and talked to her, urging her to live. But as soon as she responded, he became violent again. She realized that he was actually *kneeling* on her neck, using his entire weight to suffocate her.

Nina decided she had nothing left to lose. She wasn't going to let him kill her without a fight. Although her hands and legs were still bound, she managed to raise her feet high enough to kick some metal bedsprings that leaned against one wall. The springs clattered and clanged, distracting the man who was intent on raping her. Using her teeth and her tongue, she loosened the gag enough so that she could scream—and she did—over and over.

The sound of running feet thundered overhead and the bushy-haired man suddenly leaped off her. When she opened her eyes, he was gone.

Nina Temple saw the flash of a match above her head, and then heard a different male voice gasp, "Oh, my God." Gentler arms picked her up and carried her from the basement. An ambulance rushed Nina to nearby Harborview Hospital. ER doctors found that she had suffered a broken jaw and severe contusions all over her face, a badly cut lip, and rope burns on her wrists and ankles. Her face was so swollen that she was unrecognizable.

While Seattle Police Sex Crimes Detective Joyce Johnson waited for Nina Temple to emerge from deep shock, the young man who had rescued her said that he had passed a man running up the basement steps as he ran down. "I drew a sketch of him right after the ambulance took the girl away. Would that help?"

Johnson assured him that it would, and he handed her a pen-and-ink sketch of a thin-faced man with thick curling hair and a drooping mustache.

Once Nina Temple was able to talk, she was a good witness. She described the tall, thin man with the deceptively gentle face and thick glasses. She too remembered his distinctive mustache. He had told her his name was Jim.

When she left the hospital, Nina viewed a dozen mug-shot books of sex offenders' photographs, but she didn't find "Jim." Joyce Johnson was worried. The man who had attacked Nina Temple seemed to harbor tremendous rage against women, far more than most rapists. She was afraid they were going to hear more from him.

She was right. Only a month later—on Valentine's Day— the man with the mustache surfaced again. This time his victim was a nineteen-year-old girl—Tannie Fletcher.* Tannie and her husband, Jon*, hadn't been married long, but with him, she finally felt safe after a childhood marked by continual upheaval. They had found temporary living quarters with a friend in the University District of Seattle, but they both hoped to get jobs so they could have their own place.

Tannie soon found that local papers required payment in advance for "Work Wanted" ads, so she printed up several cards and tacked them on bulletin boards in coffeehouses and supermarkets around the district. She said she was seeking work as a housekeeper/nanny. Only one person responded. The man who called her explained that his house was difficult to find by the address alone. She agreed, therefore, to meet him on a corner of N.E. Fiftieth and Fifteenth Avenue N.E., near where she lived, at eight P.M. on Valentine's night.

Tannie waited nervously. She had assumed that he lived in a house on one of the nearby corners, so she knocked on the door of one of the houses and asked if someone there needed a housekeeper.

"Right on," a woman said with a laugh. "But we can't afford one. You've probably got the wrong address."

Tannie nodded and went back to the corner. She began to feel as if she were the target of a practical joke when, suddenly, she saw a man just beyond the streetlight's circle of yellow. He was tall and thin and wore a ski jacket.

"Tannie Fletcher?" he asked in a pleasant voice.

"Yes," she said with relief. "I thought we'd missed connections."

As he moved into the light, she thought he looked very young to require a housekeeper, but she needed a job badly, so she agreed to follow him down an alley that he told her led to his home. He said he had a very large house and he needed a full-time housekeeper. She darted a look at him and wondered if he was telling the truth; he wasn't dressed very well.

The alley opened onto another and then another. After about eight blocks, Tannie realized that she had been duped. There was no house. There was only a cold knife held now against her side. Tannie didn't know it, but she was hearing the same story Nina Temple had heard a month before, "My brother's hurt bad in the park. The pigs shot him and you have to help me stop the bleeding."

The petite girl was forced deep into Cowan Park at knifepoint. Tannie kept protesting that the sight of blood sickened her and that she couldn't possibly help her captor's wounded brother. Finally, he looked at her with an odd smile and said, "If you ball me, I won't make you look at my brother."

She wanted to stay alive. Thinking rapidly, she asked, "If I say yes, will you throw the knife away?" The man responded by flinging the knife into the bushes, but he said coldly, "Be nice. I still have a razor."

Fighting her revulsion, Tannie Fletcher submitted to rape. When the man had climaxed, he let her put her clothes back on. Perversely gallant now, he walked her back to within a block of her home. She thought he must be crazy. He talked to her as if they were truly lovers, as if she had made love with him willingly. "I want to be with you again," he said in a soft voice.

Tannie kept walking, nodding as if she agreed with him. He told her he had been in the Monroe Reformatory from 1968 until 1971, and that he had been married but was divorced. She lied, telling him she had once been in a girl's training school.

Expansive, taking Tannie Fletcher's conversation as approval, he became even more talkative. He bragged about his extraordinary job. He told her he was part of a research project at the University of Washington—one where he was given massive doses of vitamins every day and received seventy dollars a week just to let them study him. "It's some research deal, ten dollars a day for doing nothing but swallowing pills." He showed her a card with some medical phrases on it. It was too dark for her to read much of it, but she saw the name "Jim R."

Tannie felt a hysterical giggle rise in her throat. Was her abductor so revved up on vitamins that they had turned him into a rapist? Had she just gone through the worst ordeal of her life because the scientists at the university had given him too much Vitamin C or something?

She said nothing when the man told her he would call her the next day, but she couldn't control a shudder as he removed a pendant from his neck and placed it around hers as a memento of their meeting. All that mattered now was that she believed he was going to let her go. She wanted to get home alive.

Terrified that he would come after her, Tannie Fletcher made herself walk normally as she headed away from him. If she ran, he would know she was frightened.

Tannie's husband found her crying hysterically, covered with mud from head to foot. At the University Hospital, physicians verified that she had been raped.

While Tannie and her husband were at the hospital, two phone calls came in from a man who said he wanted to "apologize" to Tannie. He told the people who owned the home Tannie and her husband were sharing temporarily to tell her that "Jim Otto" had called.

Detective Joyce Johnson studied the almost identical MOs used in the two attacks, reading first one victim statement and then the other. This "Jim" had to be the same man who had attacked Nina Temple. Everything fit. Johnson suspected that the "vitamin guinea pig" story was as false as his ruse about his brother being shot by "the pigs," but it was all she had to go on. The pendant the rapist had given Tannie Fletcher was a disappointing piece of evidence; it proved to be a mass-produced bit of jewelry that could never be traced.

Joyce Johnson telephoned the University Hospital and, to her surprise, she found that there was indeed such a vitamin research program. In fact, the next massive vitamin administration was to be given that very afternoon at one P.M. Johnson alerted University of Washington police and asked them to stand by when the test subjects reported.

Sure enough, the officers spotted a tall, slim man with bushy reddish brown hair, thick glasses, and a drooping mustache. His name was Jim. However, it wasn't Jim Otto; it was James Edward Ruzicka. And he had had his last massive dose of vitamins.

Ruzicka was charged with one count of attempted rape while armed with a deadly weapon, one count of second-degree assault, and a second count of rape. He gave a five-page statement to Joyce Johnson. Yes, he agreed, he had met Tannie Fletcher when he asked her for a cigarette. Then she had asked him to have sex with her, and, according to Ruzicka, he had obliged and accompanied her to a nearby alley.

But Tannie had said "Jim" had forced her into a muddy park. And detectives found footprints in the ground there that *exactly* matched the bottom of Tannie's "waffle-stomper" shoes.

Although both rape victims identified Ruzicka as their attacker, he finally admitted only to the rape of Tannie Fletcher. He was subsequently convicted and certified as a sexual psychopath. His ten-year sentence was suspended on the condition that he take part in the sexual psychopath program at Western State Hospital.

This sexual offenders program may well have been one of the reasons that Washington voters restored the death penalty. It was a program that allowed its participants incredible freedom. The premise was that locked doors suggested that the hospital staff did not trust the sexual psychopaths. Counselors argued that unless the inmates felt affirmation and trust from their captors, they would never get well. The program featured frequent passes on the grounds and then into Steilacoom where the hospital was located, and finally into other Washington cities. Of course, the patients had to "prove themselves" before they were given more freedom.

Viewed in retrospect, this philosophy of the midseventies was an almost Utopian "feel-good" therapy approach, in tune with the times where everyone did their "own thing."

James Ruzicka stayed nine months at Western State. After some months inside where he attended group therapy faithfully and participated in a appropriate manner, he was granted a number of leaves.

On January 31, 1974, he failed to return to the hospital after an unsupervised twelve-hour pass.

On Friday, February 15, sixteen-year-old Nancy King-hammer stormed out of her West Seattle home shortly after six in the evening. She and one of her sisters had disagreed over which television show to watch. It was a relatively minor sibling disagreement, but Nancy was angry. Her family assumed she had walked down the block to visit friends and would be back in a few hours.

But Nancy did not come home. By three-twenty the next afternoon, her worried father had called all her friends and even contacted West Seattle High School administrators where she was a junior. No one had seen her. Her father was convinced she had not run away; she had taken neither extra clothes nor money with her when she left.

The tall, brunette teenager was simply gone.

It was even less likely that fourteen-year-old Penny Marie Haddenham should vanish from *her* home several blocks from the Kinghammer residence six days later. The red-haired, freckled youngster hadn't even had a tiff with anyone. In fact, she had been laughing the last time her father had seen her. That had been at 6:30 in the evening of February 21 in a West Seattle restaurant. Penny had needed twenty dollars to buy material for a pantsuit she was making in home economics at Madison Junior High School.

Penny was a strong "B" student at Madison and her father had been glad to give her the money. The last time he saw her she was headed toward the fabric store a few blocks away. A friend's mother saw her about 8:30 that evening. Nancy had stopped in to see the friend, who lived only four blocks from her own home and had been told she'd already gone to bed. Penny had been in good spirits then. She had said she was going home.

But, like Nancy, Penny had not gone home. And there was no way in the world her parents would believe she'd run away. She was too happy at home, too dependable, too concerned with her friends and schoolwork.

For the next three weeks, police, family, and friends looked for Penny and Nancy in vain. Seattle police detectives wondered if there could be any connection between Penny's disappearance and Nancy's. The only link they could find was the proximity of the girls' homes. They had not known each other, they went to different schools, and they traveled in different crowds. Now, they were linked only by terrible speculation.

Penny was found first. On March 12, a newsboy cut through a woods edging the Fauntleroy Expressway in West Seattle. The woods was made up of deciduous maple trees with only a few clusters of evergreens, and the ground was covered by a deep carpet of brown leaves. Although the freeway was close by and there were several houses at the edge of the woods, the wooded area itself was as isolated as the center of a forest.

The boy stopped in his tracks, transfixed with horror at the sight in front of him. A girl hung from a tree, her neck bent sharply to the side. It was so quiet that the boy's own involuntary cry and the pounding of his heart seemed to echo and reecho through the trees.

Police patrol units soon responded to the boy's phone

call. The officers looked at the body of the red-haired girl hanging from the bare limb; it was obvious she had been dead for some time—days at least. They made no effort to approach closely, but called for homicide detectives.

Seattle homicide detectives Roy Moran and Bernie Miller noted that the girl's feet were almost touching the ground, her body leaning back against a slight embankment angling down from the tree. She was not bound; there was just the rope around her neck attached to the limb. The petite girl was dressed in jeans, a yellow nylon jacket (whose right pocket was turned inside out), and platform boots. Her purse was nearby and some items spilled from it were not far away in the leaves. A thorough search of the area turned up a pantsuit pattern envelope and some gray wool and gray silk yardage.

Could it be a suicide? If this was Penny Haddenham, and her description matched that of the body in the woods so closely, it seemed impossible that she would have taken her own life. She had been such a happy girl. But it isn't unheard of for teenagers to take life's small problems very, very seriously. Teenagers think they will live forever, and sometimes they make dramatic gestures and find that they cannot turn back.

As darkness descended, the body was carefully cut from the tree—not at the noose—but farther along the rope so that the direction of the fray marks could be studied. If the girl had committed suicide by hanging, the fraying would point upward; if someone had killed her first and then *hoisted* her up over the tree limb, the fraying would slant downward.

Uniformed officers guarded the scene all night. With the first light of day, there would be a further search. There was no doubt now that the body hanging from the tree was Penny Haddenham; the state of decomposition indicated she had been there for a week or more. The question was *how* she had gotten there. How could a smiling, joking fourteen-year-old girl end up a suicide? Or, more likely, how had some sadist enticed her away from her own neighborhood and forced her into the woods to die this lonely death?

The postmortem examination on the 5'2", 110-pound girl quickly eliminated any possibility that Penny had killed herself. She had died from hanging—asphyxiation—but she had been raped before she died. Her underclothing and jeans were soaked with semen. Her killer had obviously redressed her after the attack and then hanged her to make it look like suicide.

Once again, detectives went over the scene where Penny had been hanged, where she had waited for ten days for someone to come and find her. It was not an easy scene to search with the thick leaf carpeting obscuring the ground, but they found some interesting items. The most damning was a fishing knife, its point honed to a fine edge. It lay half under a cover of leaves, its tan taped handle blending in with the leaves. The killer had probably dropped it and been unable to find it in the dark. It had not been out in the elements long, no longer than Penny's body had hung there.

Penny should have had seven or eight dollars left in her purse when she headed home after purchasing the material (and two forbidden packs of cigarettes, according to her best friend), but her purse had had no money at all in it when she was found. The cigarettes had been found, sodden with rain, on the ground beneath her feet.

When Penny Haddenham's body was found, the fear that Nancy Kinghammer was dead—murdered too—was exacerbated. On Saturday, March 16, detectives, patrol officers, and sixty Explorer Search and Rescue Scouts scoured the neighborhood where Nancy had vanished. They searched through empty houses, woods, vacant lots—anyplace where a body could have been secreted. Penny had not been far from home; detectives didn't feel that Nancy was either.

Police helicopters took aerial photographs on the chance that a body with bright enough clothing might show up from that vantage point. Throughout the day, the search proved fruitless. It was almost five and growing dark when one detective returned to a vacant lot at the corner of Andover and Avalon. The lot had become a very convenient, if unofficial, dumpsite for the community.

Unerringly, almost as if he had some kind of psychic clue,

Detective George Cuthill walked through the blackberry brambles and garbage until he came to a pile of boards, cardboard, and junked furniture. "I think she may be under here," he muttered.

Bit by bit, as the pile of junk diminished, the remains of a human being were exposed to the fading sunlight. It had been five weeks, and the nearly nude corpse was much deteriorated, the only seemingly alive part of it the long brown hair and the bright rings still glittering on the fingers. A green scarf was tied around the neck of the body, which had been wrapped in white drapery material and towels, fabric that seemed too new to have been part of the debris dumped in the lot.

Dental charts, the rings, and a watch gave absolute proof that the body was Nancy Kinghammer's. There was no way now to find *what* had killed her; the method vanished with her flesh. But a sexual motive was apparent because Nancy was found naked.

Two girls had been raped and murdered in less than a week in a quiet family neighborhood. Residents asked what kind of prowling animal was loose in West Seattle? Detectives had a knife, a towel, and a strip of white drapery to tie the killer to the bodies, but where could they start looking? There was nothing in either girl's background that indicated they might have known their killer. He had probably been a stranger who waited on a dark street until they were alone.

An arrest in Beaverton, Oregon—almost two hundred miles south of Seattle—brought some answers, but more questions. Washington County, Oregon, detectives called the Seattle Police Department with a request for information on a man named Troy Asin.

The man in the Washington County Jail was tall, slim, and had dark red, bushy hair.

The Oregon offense which had landed "Troy Asin" in jail sounded familiar to Detective Joyce Johnson. A thirteen-year-old girl had phoned the Washington County Sheriff's office to report that she had been raped. She and a girlfriend had met her bushy-haired, mustachioed man and his friend near a penny arcade in Portland. After talking with the junior high school girls for a while, the men said they had decided to ride the bus out to Beaverton, a suburb of Portland, with the teenagers. Once in Beaverton, they had all gone to a pool hall restaurant for something to eat. The man with the mustache, the one who said his name was "Troy," had offered to walk one girl home.

She didn't get home; instead she was raped at knifepoint in a churchyard and when "Troy" finally let her go, she had stumbled out sobbing to call the sheriff. "Troy" was apprehended almost immediately as he walked near the pool hall; his thirteen-year-old victim pointed him out to a Beaverton patrolman.

In the Washington County jail, he gave his name as Troy Asin. The Oregon officers were slightly suspicious of his identity as he had no papers in his wallet that listed that name. "Troy Asin" had given a home address in the West Seattle area of Seattle, however, and a routine request to verify Asin's identity had reached Seattle detectives shortly after Nancy Kinghammer's body was found.

When Beaverton detectives questioned Asin about the rape, he maintained an attitude of calm disbelief. He insisted that the thirteen-year-old girl had been completely willing—even *grateful*—for the act of intercourse in the churchyard. In fact, he said that she had told him she was glad she wasn't a virgin anymore because her friends had been calling her a prude. "When I asked her if she wanted to ball, she didn't say yes or no so I figured she wouldn't mind," he said easily. Asin seemed to be puzzled that the girl had called the police.

The name "Troy Asin" baffled Seattle detectives at first. "Moniker files" brought up the name all right, but it was one used by a parolee from the Monroe Reformatory named Carl Harp. He had used that alias, or variations of it, for years. But Harp's physical description was nothing like that of the man in custody in Oregon—not unless he'd grown a half a foot and dyed and permed his hair. "Troy Asin" wasn't exactly "John Smith." There couldn't be two men who had accidentally picked such an unusual pseudonym.

The mystery of the identity of the man charged with rape in Oregon was solved when Seattle detectives checked the address "Asin" had given. The home, occupied by a married couple and two other women, was only a block from the lot where Nancy Kinghammer's body had just been found. The woman who lived there said that the man in Oregon sounded like her ex-husband: James Edward Ruzicka.

In a remarkable show of civility, her new husband had allowed Ruzicka to stay with them after he had walked away from the sexual psychopath program at Western State Hospital. "He was here from February first to February twenty-fifth," she said.

When the detectives asked Ruzicka's ex-wife if anything was missing from her home, her answer was one of the biggest jackpots of information any homicide detective ever hit. Yes, she answered, she *had* found that some towels, some white drapes, and a fishing knife were missing. She added that Ruzicka had asked her to leave the back door unlocked on March 3, and when she returned home, she found $37.95 in cash missing. Ruzicka had not returned after that, and she hadn't heard from him since.

The ex–Mrs. Ruzicka was asked about any memory she might have of the night of February 21, the night Penny Haddenham vanished. She recalled that night well, because "Jim" had left at 6:30 absolutely broke. When he returned after 10:30 P.M., his coat had been covered with mud. He had had seven or eight dollars when he came home (exactly what Penny Haddenham's change from the twenty-dollar bill her father gave her would have been after she bought material and two packs of cigarettes).

"He told me that a man had given him the money for helping him change a tire," Ruzicka's former wife said. "That was how his clothes got all muddy."

She identified the knife found at the scene of Penny Haddenham's hanging site as the one missing from her house.

It looked as though James Ruzicka, "The Guinea Pig Rapist," had cut a leisurely swath of terror since he'd left the grounds of Western State Hospital. His alibi in Beaverton, Oregon, about merely obliging a willing girl sounded familiar to Detective Joyce Johnson. "Jim Otto James Ruzicka" had also claimed that Tannie Fletcher had propositioned him. He either suffered from some delusion that women found him sexually irresistible, or he chose to gloss over the fact that he had actually forced himself on his victims.

James Ruzicka's trail, from Western State Hospital to West Seattle to Oregon, was traced as closely as possible. He apparently had made at least two trips south into Oregon. In Eugene, a hundred miles south of Beaverton, a forty-eight-year-old housewife told police that she remembered him all too well. The mother of eight children, she had quit her job so she could take care of her husband who was terminally ill.

A tall man with wildly curly hair had come to her door and asked for a ride into Eugene. "He called himself 'Jack,'" she recalled, "and when I told him I couldn't take him anywhere, he held a knife to my throat, tied me to my bed . . . and raped me."

Then "Jack" had stolen money from her children's rooms and, still holding the knife to the woman's neck, demanded that she drive him to downtown Eugene. "Along the way, he told me a story about some friend of his leaving a knapsack beside the road for him. I knew it was just an excuse to get me into the woods so he could rape me again."

She had had no choice but to let him lead her into the woods. All she wanted to do was survive and her mind raced feverishly as she submitted to a second sexual attack. "Then I told him I had lost my car keys on the ground," she told police. "I guess he believed me because he went back to the road and started hitchhiking. I had my keys all along, and I ran to my car and headed in the other direction. He told me if I called the police, he would come back and kill me and my family."

* * *

409

Few would question that James Ruzicka's diagnosis as a sexual psychopath had been accurate. Now, all circumstantial and physical evidence pointed to the conclusion that he was also a merciless killer. Detectives believed that he had murdered Nancy Kinghammer exactly one year and one day from Nina Temple's rape in the basement of the Capital Hill rooming house.

While James Ruzicka was locked up, awaiting trial, the first "Troy Asin" was still free.

Carl Harp had left the Monroe Reformatory a few weeks after his friend James Ruzicka. He presented a bland, cooperative facade to his parole officer and was given a "conditional discharge from supervision" on April 2, 1973. By this time, his "other half" had raped two women—at the very least.

Harp had a good job working as a shoemaker and repairman at the Bon Marché department store in South Center, a huge mall in south King County. Like his "twin," Harp had had unsatisfactory experiences with women, finding them untrustworthy. His first marriage ended when he discovered his wife was working in a body painting studio in Seattle, and that she had been arrested for prostitution while he was in prison. His second wife simply left.

Carl Harp lost his job in the shoe department when a female employee complained that he was writing her obscene letters. He feigned amazement; he had only been trying to "create a relationship" with her.

While James Ruzicka was out of circulation and temporarily out of the headlines, Washington State was jolted by a terrifying sniper attack along one of its freeways.

May 14, 1973, was a Monday, a wonderfully sunny spring day in Bellevue, Washington; drivers could finally roll their windows down without fear of being blasted in the face with rain.

Interstate 405 freeway runs along the east side of Lake Washington from Renton on the south to Mountlake Terrace beyond its north shore. It has always been a tremendously busy freeway, day or night; workers in the Renton

Boeing plant clog 405 during morning and afternoon rush hours.

But at three in the afternoon as he headed back to his office, Abraham Saltzman, fifty-four, who sold houses for a living, was enjoying relatively light traffic. He had gone out as a favor to give another realtor a jump start when his battery went dead. Abe, a short man with a bald head and a heart of gold, had a wife, daughter, a sister, and brother who loved him, and he had a list of former clients who swore by him. He was the kind of realtor who would rather let a commission go by than sell the wrong house to the right people.

Now, the middle-aged realtor drove his dark Plymouth Fury skillfully beneath the 520 overpass. As his sedan emerged into the bright sun, Abe Saltzman's world exploded. A bullet he neither saw nor heard ended his life. He died at once, his hands on the wheel; his car veered sharply to the left, across traffic lanes, into a ditch and then hit the grassy embankment.

At the same time, John Mott, another motorist, was driving with his left elbow on the doorjamb of his car. He heard nothing—just felt a flash of white-hot pain. His head whipped to the left and his mind numbed with shock as he saw that his elbow was virtually gone. Somehow, he managed to get his car stopped.

Other motorists heard *ping-ping-ping*s against their cars. Only luck saved them from taking the bullets.

Someone was standing high up on the hill that looked down on the freeway—someone who was methodically aiming and firing with a bolt-action rifle.

In the space of a few minutes, that section of 405 was alive with emergency vehicles, Washington State troopers, Bellevue police detectives, and paramedics who tried to calm the wounded and the terrified. Some motorists, stunned, had simply stopped their cars on the freeway. Some had hit the accelerator and raced past danger.

John Mott was treated and rushed to Overlake Hospital. A young man in his early twenties, he would never again be able to fully extend his left arm, but at least he was alive.

Abe Saltzman was not. There was no rush to remove him from his vehicle, no longer any need to hurry.

Investigators figured the angle of fire and headed up the hill. They didn't know if the man with the rifle was still there or not; he could have had them fixed in his gunsight as they climbed the steep bank. They found the place where he had stood, the grass and weeds stomped almost flat. With a metal detector, they found the brass casings ejected by a .308 bolt-action rifle.

The rifle itself was gone. So was the shooter.

There is a special kind of venom toward society that inspires someone to shoot anonymously and erratically at cars full of strangers. The shooter—male or female?—could have killed mothers, babies, entire families. As it was, those who escaped with only bullet holes in their cars were grateful for their lives.

It could have been so much worse. But that didn't help Abe Saltzman's family, or the dozens of people who called him friend.

The man—and it *was* a man—who had fired the rifle had made it safely away from the brushy area above I-405. He smiled as he found a good hiding place and wrapped the .303 bolt-action rifle in oiled plastic to keep it in good working order. He might need it again.

On June 21, 1973, a little over five weeks later and some twenty miles northeast of the sniper shooting scene, two female camp counselors met a stranger on the trail. The young women, Lia* and Brook*, both twenty-one, were counselors at a religious camp for children near May's Creek Falls in the isolated wilderness in the Snoqualmie National Forest. In keeping with their religious beliefs, both were virgins, something of a rarity in the sexually permissive seventies; they intended to stay chaste until marriage.

On this Thursday afternoon, the counselors had been given some time off and decided to go for a hike along a forest trail. It was the first day of summer and the longest day of the year, which meant, in Washington, that it would be light until ten P.M..

But it was only three when Brook and Lia were startled to see a man who was apparently camping near the trail. He was of medium height, blond, and wore glasses. From all appearances, he must have been in the woods for a long time. They nodded and said "Hi," as they headed up toward the trail head where they had parked their car.

They were even more startled a little later when they saw the same man *ahead* of them on the trail. They couldn't understand how he had managed to get so far ahead. He hadn't passed them; apparently he knew the woods so well that he had taken a shortcut. He seemed harmless enough, though, and made idle conversation as he walked along with them. But some sixth sense made them uneasy. They exchanged glances, each girl letting the other know silently that she was nervous.

When they got to the parking lot, Brook's eagerness to find her car keys was obvious. She rummaged around in her backpack, willing the keys to be there. And then, quietly but firmly, the man said, "Hold it."

Lia and Brook turned around as if they already knew what was going to happen. The man held a revolver in his hand, and he gestured toward a steep bank off the parking lot. "Go down there," he said.

"Don't hurt us," Brook said. "We'll do whatever you want."

"Don't kill us," Lia echoed. "She means it. Tell us what to do."

The stranger ordered them to walk over to a tree. They did as he told them.

"Now take your clothes off," he said. "You can leave your shoes on."

He used Lia's belt, looping it tightly around her neck *and* the tree itself so that she could not move without choking. He told Brook to lie on the ground near the tree.

There was little question now about what he was going to do. They prayed silently that he wouldn't kill them as they watched him take off his shirt and unzip his pants. And then he orally sodomized one of the counselors and raped the other.

They were so far from help that they knew it wouldn't do them any good to scream, and so they used their powers of reasoning. They told him he wasn't a bad person—that he just needed help. Lia offered him a copy of the New Testament, saying, "Jesus can help you more than we ever could."

The rapist backed away, shaking his head, almost as if the Bible frightened him. They were sure he was going to shoot them. Instead, he turned around and disappeared into the woods.

Lia and Brook drove back to camp and immediately called the Snohomish County Sheriff's office. They made excellent witnesses; they could describe the man perfectly. They remembered every one of his tattoos, his T-shirt, the way his blond hair flopped across his forehead. He was back in the woods, but he was going to have to come out at some point. The sheriff's department made sure that every law enforcement officer in the county, every state trooper, and every city patrolman working along Highway 2 had his description.

Mark Ericks, then a deputy marshal in the tiny hamlet of Gold Bar, Washington, in the foothills of the Snoqualmie Mountain Range, was patrolling along Highway 2 when he saw a hitchhiker just west of town.

Ericks felt the hairs stand up on the back of his neck. He *knew* who that hitchhiker was. "You couldn't miss him," he remembered. "He had the T-shirt, the tattoos. He was the guy."

The young deputy marshal whipped his car around and headed back. The blond man with the glasses knew he had been spotted. "He started pulling his gun to shoot me," Ericks recalled. "But I already had my gun on him and I'd made up my mind I was going to shoot."

For seconds that seemed like hours, the two men looked at each other, and then the hitchhiker threw his gun down. It was a .36 caliber Navy percussion pistol, an unusual gun that was a cap and ball replica, but it was fully capable of firing, and it was loaded. The prisoner said he used it only for target practice. A search of his belongings also produced several joints of marijuana.

And his name. Carl Lowell Harp.

Interviewed in the Snohomish County Jail, Harp vehemently denied that he had raped the camp counselors. He remembered meeting two girls at the May's Creek Falls, but said they were mistaken in thinking he had been a threat to them. "I was cleaning my gun at my campsite and it was lying on the ground when they walked by."

Harp said it was the women who had talked to him, asking questions about the area. Yes, he had walked a short ways with them along the trail, talking. If they had been raped, he insisted he wasn't the man who had done it. "I did see a guy farther up the trail that day—he looked a lot like me, you know—height, weight, coloring, even had glasses. *He's* your rapist, not me."

Detectives weren't about to buy that convenient explanation.

What surprised the Snohomish County investigators *and* Bellevue Police and the Washington State Patrol, however, was that Carl Harp had had a very good reason to be camping out in the woods. When the news of his arrest on rape charges hit the media, Harp's ex-wife came forward with shocking information. She led authorities to a .308 bolt-action rifle that belonged to him.

Tests on the weapon, which was perfectly oiled and ready to fire, proved that it was the same gun that had been used by the "Bellevue Sniper."

Carl Lowell Harp aka Troy Asin aka T. Asian aka Carroll Lowell Trimble, who had once been a little boy nobody wanted, was paying the world back—both individually and collectively.

The odd story of two men from such similar dysfunctional backgrounds seemed to be winding down. Both halves of "Troy Asin" were now behind bars.

James Ruzicka was convicted in Oregon on rape charges involving the thirteen-year-old. He received a ten-year sentence. He then went on trial in Seattle in August 1975, on charges of first-degree murder in the deaths of Penny Haddenham and Nancy Kinghammer.

King County Senior Deputy Prosecutors Jon Noll and Ron Clark had a powerful battery of physical and circumstantial evidence to present to the jury in Judge Horton Smith's courtroom. There was the fishing knife, the moldering white draperies which had served as Nancy Kinghammer's shroud, the towels—all taken from Ruzicka's former wife's house—all identified by her in court. And there was devastating testimony from a cellmate of Ruzicka's during his stay in jail.

The witness recalled a conversation with the defendant when Ruzicka bragged of raping and killing two girls. The defendant had told him, he testified, that he liked to "collect" knives. Ruzicka had said that he had hung one of his victims from a tree after he raped her, and that he had lost his knife at that scene. But, according to the witness, Ruzicka had not been concerned about the knife because it had tape on the handle and he knew no fingerprints could be gleaned from tape.

Ruzicka himself did not testify. He sat quietly throughout the trial twisting a gold ring on one finger. He was considerably discomfited by the presence of one of his former victims in the courtroom. Nina Temple, the pretty store clerk whose jaw he had broken when he had tried to strangle her two and a half years before, sat in the gallery section, listening to every word of testimony. Ruzicka's defense counsel cried "Foul" at the girl's presence and asked to have her barred from the courtroom. However, Judge Horton Smith ruled she had the right to stay.

It took the jury only four hours to find James Ruzicka guilty on two counts of first-degree murder.

After his conviction, Ruzicka granted an extensive interview to a Seattle reporter. Chain-smoking, he commented that no one really knew him as a person, that he was actually shy and lonely. He said he had placed ads in underground publications seeking pen pals. He said he was currently corresponding with nineteen women and sixteen men. He readily admitted that he was a sexual psychopath and had difficulty relating to women, yet he hoped one day to marry again and have children. He had met a blind woman, a woman who loved him devotedly, and she was a faithful presence in the courtroom for all his legal proceedings. "She's very nice," he said. "I felt the least I could do, out of respect for her, is learn Braille."

James Ruzicka continued to see himself in a rosy light that had little to do with reality. He said he was positive that even if he were to be released immediately, he would not be dangerous. "I wouldn't rape anyone," he said. "I'd try to get into some kind of treatment program. I want help."

He denied adamantly that he killed either Penny Haddenham or Nancy Kinghammer. He claimed that the thirteen-year-old girl rape victim in Oregon was a willing participant. "There was no knife."

The tragic fact remained that James Ruzicka *had* been granted an opportunity for help—given counseling, understanding, trust, freedom, in the sexual offenders program. And he walked away from it. Fifteen days later, Nancy Kinghammer died a horrible death and her body was cast aside on a junk heap. Twenty-one days later, Penny Haddenham was raped and hung from a tree like an abandoned rag doll.

Their parents successfully sued the state of Washington for allowing James Ruzicka a second chance *and* an unsupervised leave from the sexual offenders program. The Haddenhams and Kinghammers gave a large portion of the proceeds of their suit to the Families and Friends of Victims of Violent Crime and Missing Persons. Families and Friends had helped them survive emotionally when they lost their daughters.

Ruzicka's self-serving version of his life and crimes, which appeared in Seattle papers, omitted a great deal. Chuck Wright, a veteran of the Washington State Department of Corrections and an expert on human sexuality, did the presentence report on Ruzicka. The convicted rapist/killer was more expansive in discussing his activities with Wright than he was with local reporters.

Chuck Wright found James Ruzicka a fascinating study in

denial. Ruzicka listed fourteen former employers on his questionnaire, but said he had never worked for any of them long enough to get a social security number. He said he was "definitely" not a criminal, although he admitted to using many more aliases than "Troy J. Asin."

"I think I'm getting screwed," Ruzicka insisted. "I didn't get a fair trial. I am determined to get out, get a job, and settle down. I want to get married."

James Ruzicka was attempting to portray himself as just an ordinary guy. But he was striving to con the wrong man. Wright knew that Ruzicka had demonstrated a bizarre and precise MO in his sexual attacks. Beyond the use of a knife held against his victims' throats and his ruse about his "wounded brother," he usually removed *one* of the victim's shoes. He had bragged to fellow inmates that he was a necrophile who revisited the bodies of the girls he had killed.

Assuming that Wright's nonjudgmental facade indicated approval, James Ruzicka bragged that he had had "sexual contacts" with at least three hundred different women. He was vehement that he had never had any homosexual encounters beyond his molestation of his younger brother.

As far as other crimes went, Ruzicka admitted a thousand shoplifting episodes, a hundred burglaries—all unsolved.

He said that knives had always been important to him. He had needed to have a knife under his pillow when he was a child—or he couldn't sleep.

For Chuck Wright, who had evaluated countless convicted felons, James Ruzicka was one in a thousand, dangerous beyond reckoning. Wright sought to find some treatment which, while it might not change Ruzicka's mindset, might at least protect future victims.

"I brought up the question of the possibility of his being castrated," Wright recalled. "He appeared to be very angry and stated, 'They can *try*. If they do that, I'll do myself in. I'd rather rot in prison.' I informed him there was a process in which an individual can be *chemically* castrated and that it was reversible. . . . I informed him that we would probably be recommending that he serve two life sentences to run consecutively, and that he be chemically castrated. He seemed quite calm at that time."

On September 30, 1975, Judge Smith ordered Ruzicka to first serve his sentence in Oregon and then to begin serving two *consecutive* life sentences in the killings of Penny Haddenham and Nancy Kinghammer.

"I just do not believe this court should operate a bargain basement for murder—allowing two murders to go for the price of one," Smith commented. He said that when Ruzicka arrived at the Washington State Penitentiary in Walla Walla, he would be placed among the one hundred most dangerous criminals, for whom maximum security was paramount to all other considerations.

Consulting psychologist Dr. John Berberich had found Ruzicka "extremely dangerous and untreatable" and, like Chuck Wright, he thought that castration might be wise.

Chuck Wright had fought hard to have chemical castration considered in James Ruzicka's case, mindful of Ruzicka's history of escape. "Ruzicka is like a lot of cons," Wright recalled. "He always denies everything. I can't emphasize enough that if this man ever gets on the street, he will kill someone. He is very devious and life means nothing to him. He lied to us from the time he walked in the door to the time he left."

At this writing, James Ruzicka is still locked up in the Washington State Penitentiary at Walla Walla. He is now forty-six years old. There was massive publicity at the time of his sentencing in the midseventies. However, other murderers have supplanted his image in the minds of the public and it is important that the memory of his crimes remain fresh. Although it is extremely doubtful that James Ruzicka will walk the streets again until he is an old man, it is not impossible.

It is still questionable whether chemical castration (with the administration of female hormones) can achieve the desired effect; some of the most vicious sex killings in modern history have been accomplished by men who were physically or psychologically impotent. Their anger at their inability to perform only increased their homicidal rage. In several cases, their victims made the fatal mistake of laughing at them.

And chemical castration only works as long as the subject takes the hormones meant to quell sexual violence. One wonders how long a rapist, once free, would choose to continue taking female hormones.

Carl Lowell Harp, the "other" Troy Asin, was convicted on counts ranging from first-degree murder to sodomy/rape to felon in possession of a weapon. The maximum he could have received was five life sentences, one twenty-year and two ten-year sentences. After a number of violent and obscene outbursts—particularly at female parole officers—Harp admitted that he acted "crazy" because he wanted to go to Western State Hospital so he could be examined by experts and proven "a normal person." Instead, Carl Harp went directly to the penitentiary at Walla Walla to begin serving consecutive life sentences. Because, at that time, a "life" sentence in Washington usually meant thirteen years, four months, the "consecutive" stipulation assured he would never be free.

A new statute was enacted after Carl Harp carried out his "sniper" crimes. If a future sniper should act "with utter disregard for human life" as Harp did, he would be tried for first-degree murder.

Carl Harp was not out of the headlines long. In May 1979, he and two other inmates took ten hostages and held them inside a prison office, rigged with two pipe bombs made with plastic explosives. Harp and the other convicts—convicted kidnapers—were armed with knives. Their hostages—including three women—were eight prison counselors, a guard, and a legal aide who worked outside the penitentiary. Harp listed thirty grievances the prisoners had and said the captors would give themselves up if at least three were satisfied. The prison maximum security unit was overcrowded, Harp maintained, and prisoners had no due process for their complaints.

Harp's insurrection was short; the hostages were released at one A.M. on May 10 after they had been held for eleven hours. They were not injured. But Carl Harp was a constant thorn in the side of prison officials. Calling himself an "anarchist," he said, "I am nonviolent. I'm not out to be a hero. I abhor violence. I've been treated like s——. I've been beat, tortured, and maced. I'm not a slave. I'm not an animal and I'm not subhuman."

Of all the men in the world who might have an opportunity to find romance, one would think that Carl Harp, a convicted rapist and sniper, sentenced to life-after-life sentences, locked away in maximum security, might be far down on the list. But that wasn't true. Carl Harp wrote letters constantly, and one went to an "underground" newspaper in Bellingham: *Northwest Passage*. A pretty eighteen-year-old college student had read Harp's letter in 1974 and begun a correspondence with him.

"I wanted to offer friendship and moral support," Susan Black* said later. She had believed what Harp said in his letter—that he had not been given a fair trial.

Susan and Carl began to write to each other often. They exchanged literally hundreds of letters and poems. It was a platonic relationship at first. When Susan got married to someone else, Carl Harp sent one of his drawings as a wedding gift.

Susan's marriage only lasted two years. When she was divorced in 1979, Harp asked her to marry *him*. It wasn't a very romantic proposal, given the location. They were having a "no contact" visit, separated by thick wire mesh. Harp didn't know if he would ever live to be out of prison; he told Susan that he was afraid he might be killed by enemies inside. But she loved him, and she agreed to marry him. He was thirty and she was twenty-three. She had dark sloe eyes, perfect features, and shimmering long black hair. He was the same bland-looking man he had always been; she adored him and believed that he had never hurt anyone.

After the hostage situation in Walla Walla, Carl Harp was transferred to San Quentin prison in California. On September 2, 1980, Susan went to San Quentin to marry him. They lived for the possibility that they might be allowed conjugal visits so that they could consummate their marriage. They wanted to have children.

Susan was happy being married to Carl, and she believed

that he was happy. Still, his drawings were filled with images of death. One was a black-and-white sketch of thirteen men and one woman, all of them hanging from nooses, their hands tied behind them.

In July of 1981, Susan and Carl Harp had their first—and only—conjugal visit. He had been returned to Walla Walla from San Quentin. They were allowed to have some privacy in one of the trailers that the Washington State Penitentiary maintains so that married prisoners can be with their wives.

The two sat in the kitchen and stared at one another. "We almost didn't know how to act after all these years of no contact and no privacy," Susan Harp told *Seattle Times* reporter Erik Lacitis. "(We) sat around and laughed, just acting silly."

And then they made love.

Susan Harp remembers her hours in a trailer behind the walls of the prison in Walla Walla as very romantic. She says Carl wrote to her about his memories of that time. "He was so enthused about the next visit," she said.

"I love you, Wife, in case you didn't know that. . . . Just think, by this time tomorrow if all had worked out, where we would be—sigh." They were to have had a second conjugal visit, but there was a lockdown at the prison and all such visits were cancelled.

"Everything is going to be fine, you watch and see, and our love is going to grow and grow. Think ONLY positive, Susan . . ."

There was never another visit. At 6:42 P.M. on September 5, 1981, when a guard brought Carl Harp's evening meal, he found him with his wrists slashed, slumped on the floor with a television cable cord around his neck. The other end of the cord was tied to a clothes hook on the cell wall.

It took four months for Carl Harp's death certificate to be entered into the Vital Records of Washington. Interestingly, his occupation was given as "self-employed artist." On the line where cause of death was to be specified, the Walla Walla County coroner listed "asphyxiation and strangulation." Under "Accidental?" "Suicide?" "Homicide?" or "Undetermined?" he chose the latter.

Carl Harp had written to his attorneys that a sympathetic

guard had warned him that there was a "contract" out on his life because he was not wanted in the prison. But he had told another attorney that he was "ill with mental exhaustion. I am locked in my cell twenty-three hours a day and when I lie down, I fall into a coma. My whole being is tired."

His widow believed that he had been murdered.

But there was no indication on autopsy that someone had strangled Carl Harp and arranged his cell to make his death look like a suicide. The injuries to his neck were commensurate with death by hanging. The cuts on his arms were not deep enough to cause death. The suicide note was in his handwriting: "I did myself so blame no one for any reason at all." There was, however, a shredded note in the commode in his cell. Although it was pieced together by authorities, its contents were never released to the media.

An enigma he lived, and an enigma Carl Harp died. Detectives and medical examiners know how easy it is to hang oneself, and that it is not necessary for a body to drop from a considerable height. They have seen people sitting under tables who have merely leaned against a rope—and died. Carl Harp could have stood up if he had chosen to do so.

Perhaps he did not choose to stand up and take the cable off the clothes hook. Perhaps the image of Abraham Saltzman in his gunsight came to haunt Harp in his prison cell.

And perhaps he *was* murdered. He had annoyed the prison administration and he wasn't much loved by his fellow prisoners. No one will ever really know *how* Carl Harp died.

It is almost as difficult to choose *which* of two reflections of the mirror image killers was the true leader, the true madman. Was it Carl Harp? Or was it James Ruzicka? When they were separated, they simply went along their own killing and raping paths. And, in the end, could not they both have been considered "madmen"?

Note: Chuck Wright has never forgotten the two "Troy Asins." One is locked away, perhaps forever. The other has been dead for fifteen years. When the unclaimed possessions of Carl Harp were gathered up for disposal, Wright saw a drawing that intrigued him. It is one of the hundreds of sketches Carl Harp did. This sketch (reproduced in the picture section) is entitled "Family Tree, 12/10/74" and signed "Carl Harp *Asin*". (Wright would like to hear critiques of "Family Tree" from mental health professionals, artists, and laymen. There may be subtleties, symbolism, and clues in this drawing that no one has yet detected. Those who have comments are asked to contact Chuck Wright, Washington State Department of Corrections, Suite 100, 8625 Evergreen Way, Everett, Washington, 98208-2620.)

A ROSE FOR
HER GRAVE
and Other True Cases

Ann Rule's Crime Files: Vol. 1

Ann Rule

An acknowledged expert on violent crimes, their causes
and effects, best-selling author Ann Rule now brings us six
more fascinating true cases from her files.

'A Rose for Her Grave' – the principal story of this
collection – vividly re-creates the cautionary tale of Randy
Roth, a misogynistic sociopath from the Pacific
North-West whose rage was directed primarily at women
and children. Addicted to his own greed, Roth exercised a
powerful aura of control over his victims, using his ability
to charm and boyish good-looks to lower their defences. By
the time they saw the reality of the madness in his eyes, it
was usually too late.

This, along with five other chilling cases, bears the stamp
of classic Ann Rule – informed, comprehensive, and eerily
evocative of man's inhumanity to man.

'Fascinating . . . Each page is a gripper . . . Ann Rule is
truly a master crime writer in *A Rose for Her Grave*, a book
that breaks new ground in the true-crime field'
Real Crime Book Digest

<u>YOU BELONG TO ME</u>
<u>and</u> Other True Cases

Ann Rule's Crime Files: Vol. 2

Ann Rule

You Belong to Me is the second gripping volume from
Ann Rule's Crime Files.

The title story focuses on one of Florida's most shocking
criminals – Tim Harris, the poster-perfect 'All-American'
state trooper who hid bizarre and fatal fantasies behind his
badge of authority. This, and the five other cases which
comprise *You Belong to Me*, bears the stamp of classic
Ann Rule which makes her books such extraordinary
page-turners, and once again confirms her status as the
undisputed Queen of True Crime.

'Ann Rule, America's premier true crime writer . . . has
made the exploration of evil people her life's work. She can
dissect the dark heart of a killer with surgical precision.
Nobody does it better'
Edna Buchanan, *Miami Herald*

Other bestselling Warner titles available by mail:

☐ A Rose for Her Grave	Ann Rule	£7.99
☐ You Belong to Me	Ann Rule	£6.99
☐ If You Really Loved Me	Ann Rule	£6.99
☐ Everything She Ever Wanted	Ann Rule	£6.99
☐ The Stranger Beside Me	Ann Rule	£6.99

The prices shown above are correct at time of going to press. However, the publishers reserve the right to increase prices on covers from those previously advertised without prior notice.

WARNER BOOKS

WARNER BOOKS
P.O. Box 121, Kettering, Northants NN14 4ZQ
Tel: 01832 737525, Fax: 01832 733076
Email: aspenhouse@FSBDial.co.uk

POST AND PACKING:
Payments can be made as follows: cheque, postal order (payable to Warner Books) or by credit cards. Do not send cash or currency.

All U.K. Orders   **FREE OF CHARGE**
E.E.C. & Overseas   25% of order value

Name (Block Letters) _____

Address _____

_____

Post/zip code:_____

☐ Please keep me in touch with future Warner publications

☐ I enclose my remittance £_____

☐ I wish to pay by Visa/Access/Mastercard/Eurocard

Card Expiry Date

_____